I'M GONNA TELL GRANDMA!

FAMILY STORIES

Vito "Ted" Pileggi

Coho Publishing ◆ Salem, Oregon

Vito Pileggi – I'm Gonna Tell Grandma!

Second Edition

International Standard Book Number
Trade paperback & e-book: 978-1-7331308-3-7

Design and production by Cohographics, Salem, Oregon
www.cohographics.com

Printed in the U.S.A.

Cover drawing by Tom Pileggi

Also by Vito Pileggi:

Popping The Cork 2019
Once A Dream 2018
My Marines and Me 2016
While Wearing Blue 2015
Easy Company Marines 2008, 2012
Beginnings 2009
I'm Gonna Tell Grandma! 2008

For Grandma

Acknowledgments

Patricia Love, creative writing instructor
Susie Pileggi, editing
Carol Ann Dunlap, editing
Laurel & Hinrich Muller, project management

Table of Contents

Prologue

My mother wanted to write a book about us, her six overly rambunctious offspring. But early on, she was too busy trying to keep us from destroying the universe to write anything. And for one reason or another, she never got to it when she got older either. Had she though, she always said that the title of her work would be *My Six*

Gray Heirs, one "gray heir" for each child. It crossed my mind to use her title for my book. But that would have been a little like stealing from her.

Instead, I chose the title *"I'm Gonna Tell Grandma!"* Those were words that my brothers and sisters screamed at me whenever I did something irritable to them. They still reverberate in my ears, especially the threats that my brother Tom bellowed when I pulled a prank on him. He was my favorite target. But seldom did he or any of my other hapless victims retaliate. Instead, they squawked like a flock of spastic geese, tattling on me to Grandma. So I think the title fits my collection of stories reasonably well.

Grandmother Barnes

The dialogue spoken by the characters in my stories isn't something that I totally remember. But I'm certain it was said much the same as I've written. And I'm sure the events recorded here have also been embellished to some degree. But they are based on things that really happened. They took place during my youth, most of them being the same stories that my mother would have written. Only, she would have put a slightly different slant on them.

There were six of us children, four boys and two girls, I the oldest. And because I was the oldest, it was me who always caught hell when something went awry. Yes poor unfortunate picked on me—the most humble and innocent of the lot. And it never did me any good to deny involvement. By the time I was ten, I'd compiled a notebook of alibis and excuses to fit every occasion. My vocabulary consisted of twelve words, of which six were, *"Who, Me? What did I do?"*

Our grandmother . . . a nice, gentle, peaceful lady when in a coma . . . was tough as rawhide and a strict disciplinarian. Actually, she was a peach. But when she was on the prod, she could break up a union strike with her scalding voice. And whenever one of us did something wrong, she was usually the one who threatened to administer the punishment. And she did so on a few occasions, but not nearly as often as we deserved.

Our family wasn't much different from other families during the times. We lived on a small farm in a tiny run-down house with no indoor plumbing. We were very poor. But we children didn't realize it.

After observing our cramped living conditions, an elderly friend once commented that our family reminded her of a *can of sardines*. Being a curious seven-year-old and never having heard those words used in that context before, I wondered why in the world she would say something like that about us. Sardines were dead fish that smelled bad. And since we weren't dead, I concluded that she thought we stunk. That seemed to explain a lot of things, one being why people referred to us as a bunch of little stinkweeds.

My parents were married in 1931 during the Great Depression, and I'm sure they often worried about the lack of money to run the household. But having none presented no huge complications in our lives. We grew together, played together and sometimes we fought and bickered. But, in the long run, we loved and cared for each other—and still do.

If I had one wish, it would be that every child could have parents and a grandmother as wonderful as mine. They were caring, protective and loving. And we were given the freedom to experience life but, at the same time, were warned to use good judgment and common sense or pay the consequences. No kid could ask for anything more.

My Maternal Beginnings

My maternal grandmother Verna Independence Smith was born in Vernon County in the state of Missouri on the Fourth of July in 1882. She was the seventh of ten children in the family of Mary Jane Hayhurst and William Smith, poor dirt farmers who resided in the Holden area. Instead of naming her after a relative, her parents named her after the county where she was born. And her second name was given her because she was born on Independence Day.

It just so happened that a destructive tornado ripped through the countryside near her parents' home the day that my grandmother was born. Perhaps the twister was to foretell her future. Turmoil swirled about her for most of her life. Even after passing away she created an unintentional stir. Quite by accident, she was interred in another person's burial plot.

When Verna was in her mid-teens, her parents decided to leave Missouri in search of a better life. Leaving two married daughters behind, they moved the remainder of their family across country to the State of Washington. The trek took nearly two years. But Verna didn't finish the trip. She got sidetracked in Montana when she met James Barnes, a cowboy who was extraordinarily tall. He was 6 feet, 8 inches.

James and Verna were married in San Coulee on the 29th of October 1901. She was nineteen and he twenty-six.

Throughout the next dozen years, Verna and James homesteaded a barren ranch north of Billings in the Brusett area. During that time, she gave birth to seven children.

James lacked money to support his large family. So, he frequently left the ranch for months on end to work on other ranches throughout Montana, Wyoming and North Dakota. And Verna was left alone to tend the children.

After being away for nearly a year, he returned home in the dead of winter to find his wife pregnant with her eighth child—a child he knew did not belong to him. James was livid and unsympathetically ran Verna off the ranch. When she asked about her other children, he told her to forget about them and never return. But she swore an oath that she'd see them again some day.

Alone and destitute, she made her way to Fort Dill near Marmarth, North Dakota. There she gave birth to a little girl in an Indian encampment. She named her eighth child Thelma Ethelyn.

The reason for going to Fort Dill was never revealed. Perhaps it was because the father of her child was purported to be an Indian of the Crow and Northern Cheyenne tribes.

Verna returned to Montana with her newborn daughter and settled on the Crow Indian Reservation south of Billings. For the next four years, she somehow managed to eke out a meager existence while living in a tiny floorless shack. But several unsettling incidents occurred that involved her daughter's well being. So, for peace of mind and hoping to provide a safer environment for her tiny child, she moved into Billings.

Problems continued to plague Verna though: a lack of money, loneliness, constant worry about her daughter, and persistent boyfriends, to name a few. So, to protect her child from the realities of a harsh world, she sent her little offspring to live with her grandparents in Anacortes, Washington.

Verna remained in Billings changing her name several times, most likely in an effort to hide from past love affairs. And even though she never remarried, she gave birth to two more girls.

When Thelma was about twelve, her grandmother Mary Jane passed away. She returned home. But Verna was still convinced that she couldn't raise her daughter properly. So, she placed her in a convent in Helena, confident that she'd hit on the right solution. Thelma did well in the convent. But after two years, she yearned to be with her mother again and ran away.

She found her mom in Billings and found a job as well. But in a short time, she'd become disheartened with her surroundings and left Montana to find a new life in Oregon.

Verna, not about to let her young daughter go off by herself, soon followed.

My Paternal Beginnings

Ruby May Tate, my paternal grandmother, was born January 25, 1888 on the Oregon Trail at Pompey's Pillar in Montana. At the time, her French-Creole parents James W. Tate and Etna Jane Tabler were moving their family to the Pacific Northwest.

My paternal grandfather Vito was born to Vito Pileggi and Theresa Amendela in the village of Vallelonga in Calabria, the southernmost province in the toe of Italy. On most documents, in Italy and the United States, his date of birth is recorded as June 22, 1878. But on a few, it varies by as much as ten years. One of five children, two boys and three girls, he migrated to the United States in 1902.

Vito and Ruby first met in the state of Washington when she was 18 or 19 and he ten years older. They fell in love. But there was a problem • she was a married woman and had a child.

Ruby was married to James Hall—a man 26 years her senior. He was seldom home, leaving his young attractive wife unattended. So, Vito seized the opportunity to move in on forbidden territory. And eventually the two lovers ran away to Columbus, Ohio.

Ruby changed her name to Cinderita Tate for one reason or another. Maybe she thought it would be easier to hide from Hall if she used a different name.

Eventually, Vito and Ruby married and had four children, all boys. The eldest, my father, was Elmer Vito. His brothers were Antonio, Vito James, and Jack Joseph.

Returning home from work one day, Vito found that Ruby had gotten into an argument and physically attacked a neighbor lady, believing the woman had become too flirtatious with her husband. Fearing that his wife would be arrested and prosecuted for felonious assault, Vito sold everything the family owned to an old Jewish friend. And sewing hundreds of dollars into the lining of his children's jackets, he moved his family overnight to Portland in Oregon.

How Mom and Dad Met

An ironic set of circumstances was responsible for bringing my parents together. Grandfather Vito was desperate to find someone to help care for Grandmother Ruby. She had been stricken with cancer and, helplessly bedridden, was dying. Their family doctor, William Lockwood, knew that Verna Barnes, my maternal grandmother, was looking for work and asked her to take the job of caring for his patient.

That's how my mother and father met each other. Had one woman not been dying or the other not looking for employment, I wouldn't be here and you wouldn't be reading this story.

CHAPTER 1

1931–1939

Mom and Dad

Pastor Joseph Keating, a Methodist minister, performed the ceremony when my parents were married. Their nuptials took place on April 27, 1931 at the county courthouse in Vancouver, Washington. And both were still in their teens. Not only did Dad take a bride, he also got the bride's mother in the package, my Grandmother Barnes.

Mom and dad were immediately attracted to each other when they first met a few months earlier. He never really had the opportunity to date a girl because he didn't have the time. He went to work at the age of 14 . . . and never attended high school. So Mom was his first and only real girlfriend.

My grandmother lied to school officials when she enrolled my mom in the first grade. She had to be six years old to enter school. So Grandmother informed them that her daughter was born in 1914 instead of 1915.

Thus when Mom and Dad were married, she had just turned 16 and not 17 as recorded.

Dad grew up a protected child and wasn't accustomed to being in the company of the opposite sex. The only women in his early life were his teachers, his mother and his great aunt Eva. Therefore, bossy and aggressive women easily got under his skin. But he was tolerant with them . . . up to a point. And that included Grandma Barnes. She could be as obstinate as a mule and tough as shoe leather if the mood struck her. He didn't have to worry about Mom, though. She wasn't the bossy,

1

controlling type. She was quiet most of the time. But when she did make a demand, he knew he'd better pay attention.

Grandpa taught his sons to treat females with respect and repeatedly warned them, "*You notta strike-a the girls. They break.*"

Dad cared for Mom so much that he would have died before raising a hand to her. And, besides, he knew Mom had ways of getting back at him if he did. And she proved it a few times.

Mother could be sweet and demure one moment and as feisty as a naughty little boy the next. In fact, she was a Tomboy at heart and a bit of a daredevil.

My grandmother told a story about her daughter that was truly unbelievable. But she swore it was true . . . and so did Mom.

Not many months after Mom and Dad were married, they attended a carnival near Portland. Mom was soon drawn to a booth manned by a group of aerialists. They were offering ten dollars to anyone willing to parachute from a plane over the carnival grounds. In 1931, ten dollars was mighty big money . . . and she couldn't pass up the opportunity. Where else could she earn that much money in just a few minutes? With it, she could pay their monthly bills and still have enough to buy her new husband a belated birthday gift.

So, at barely 16 years of age, she went up in a plane and came down in a parachute. She got her ten bucks, Dad got a birthday gift, and a lot of people got a thrill watching my mother's daredevil stunt.

Mom got a kick out of taunting Dad. And, once in awhile, she pulled an underhanded prank on him. And Pa . . . he was never certain how to respond . . . or if he should.

Recounting the first months of their married life, Mother told me that she nearly did her unfortunate husband in on a couple of occasions.

One incident occurred when Pop was sitting on the toilet reading a newspaper. He was completely oblivious to what his bride was about to do to him. With the silence of a slithering snake, she poked the end of a garden hose through the small open window behind him. A moment later, reacting to the sudden shock of cold water hitting him on the back, he darned near demolished the bathroom.

Since she'd played a sneaky trick on him, it was his turn to catch her unaware. He was determined to somehow get even. After cleaning up the mess, he hid in their bedroom closet waiting for her to make an appearance. Mom finally got up nerve to enter the house and cautiously began searching for him, room by room. Having no idea where Dad was hiding or what payback he had planned for her, she warily entered the bedroom, giggling as if she were a little schoolgirl.

He jumped out of the closet in front of her, naked as a jaybird. She let out a scream as if being attacked by an axe murderer and fled from the bedroom. He gave pursuit, following close behind. Passing through the open doorway, she yanked at the door

Mom and her victim

hoping it would close and stop him. She stopped him all right. As it was swinging shut, Dad ran smack into the edge of it with a resounding thud.

Nearly knocked unconscious, he went down in a heap on the floor as if he'd been pole-axed between the eyes. When she heard him crash, she knew doggoned well that she'd done something really hurtful to him. But she didn't realize how bad off he was until an ugly lump formed on his aching forehead.

Mom, feeling deep remorse for what she'd done, was at Dad's mercy. But he simply didn't have the strength, the wits or the heart to retaliate—at least, not at the moment.

Not long after the bathroom incident, Mom played another underhanded trick on my unfortunate father and nailed him again—literally.

Engaged in horseplay in the front yard, she knew that Dad was a real goosey fellow and pinched him on the rump when he wasn't expecting it. Before he could recover from the shock, she'd run around behind the house disappearing from sight. Believing that she'd hidden nearby, he stood pressed against the side of their small home and cautiously peeked around the corner. But Mom had not hidden. To the contrary, she had circled around and had snuck up behind him with a four-foot lath strip in her hand. As he continued to bend over and peer around the corner, Mom, with a big grin on her face, reared back and smacked him across the back end with a mighty *thwack*. My unfortunate pappy, bellowing out in pain, resembled a frog leg leaping from a hot griddle and jumped as if he'd been stung by a swarm of bees.

Mom had done it again—catching her unlucky husband off-guard. She knew that she'd hit him a little too hard and that she had better run. But, too weak from uncontrollable laughter, she was scarcely able to move.

Unwittingly, she did more than just give him a nasty spank on the butt. She failed to notice a small nail protruding from the end of the lath and, when she hit him, she actually nailed it to her poor husband's fanny. Only after he'd wrestled her to the ground did they discover the slat still pinned to him.

Mom felt terrible, unintentionally hitting him too hard and driving a nail into him. But instead of evening the score, Dad forgave his penitent bride and consoled her with kisses, as he'd done before.

Poor Pop! My playful mom darned near did him in more than once, although unintentionally. At least, I think it was unintentional. And for one reason or another, he was never able to get back at her.

Maybe he was just too slow or maybe he knew better than to retaliate. But, most likely, he was just too badly injured and lacked the strength.

The First of Six

Uncertain of her fate, Mom whimpered and squirmed in agony. She'd never experienced pain so intense, so torturous as she did in the final minutes before giving birth to me. Grandmother Barnes and Doctor William Lockwood tried to make her as comfortable as possible, assuring her the ordeal would soon end. But, still, their soothing words and tender guidance did little to erase the misgivings and doubts in her mind.

Dad was concerned about his young wife too. He wanted to be with her. But he'd been instructed by Doctor Lockwood and sternly ordered by Grandmother to stay the hell out of the room.

Nonetheless, unable to control his anxieties, he poked his head through the open doorway. And trying to be a consoling, sympathetic, caring husband, he asked his grimacing wife, *"How you doin', honey?"*

Replying through clenched teeth, Mom painfully screeched, *"You gotta lotta guts askin' me how I'm doing. Oh, dear God! When I get through havin' this kid, Elmer, I'm comin' after you with an axe."*

The first child of two teen-agers, I was born on the 13th day of April 1932 in a tiny white house on Southeast 62nd Street in Portland, Oregon. Dad was only 19 and Mom would turn 17 in two days.

The Stump Ranch

Not many months passed when Mom, Dad and Grandma, decided to move into the country outside Portland hoping to live a better life. They found a couple of acres covered with stumps and brush on

Dad and Mom holding Teddy atop a stump

Mom and six-months-old
Teddy, on the Stump Ranch

Dad's youngest brother
Jack, about nine years old

Prosperity Park Road located southeast of Tualatin. The house wasn't much to look at, not much better than an old ramshackle hut. But, all in all, it was cheap and perfect for what they had in mind.

They named their new place *The Stump Ranch*. Dad bought a few weaner pigs for the meat, a few chickens for the eggs, and a couple of goats for the milk. The goats were also perfect for mowing down brush. But they were cantankerous, stubborn animals and always a problem.

My mom and dad's closest neighbors and good friends were Clarence and Marie Grady. They named their place also—*Starvation Hollow*. They, too, were dirt poor, their lives filled with many difficulties.

To survive, the two families helped each other sharing whatever good fortune they had. The harsh winter and primitive dirt roads made it difficult for them to drive in and out of their places. So Clarence and Dad, working together, constructed wooden-plank driveways to solve the problem.

Nine-year-old Jack, the youngest of my father's siblings, came to live with my parents during the summer of 1933. He was a nice looking kid but was rebellious, particularly so after his mother's death two years earlier. Stubborn, difficult and defiant, he was a big pain in the butt to his father nearly driving the elderly Italian to wit's end. In addition and through no fault of his own, he stuttered.

Grandmother Barnes didn't care for Jack. She couldn't tolerate his disobedience and shiftlessness and often clashed with him. She also believed he could conquer his stammering problem if only he tried.

One morning Granny awakened to find that Jack had gotten himself into quite a pickle. He'd accidentally gotten stuck during the night, his head jammed between two iron bars of his bedstead. He was held tight as if he were a cow in a stanchion. Hoarse from repeatedly calling for help, he begged Grandma to quickly release him. But she, being a little ornery with him, took her sweet time prying the bars apart and threatened to give him a whack across the rump if he didn't stop his squalling.

Later that day, she sent the kid on an errand to move the goats to another grazing area. After a considerable amount of time had elapsed, she realized that he'd been gone much too long. Worried, Grandmother and Mom went searching for him down in a canyon where the goats had been tethered by chains. They found him lying on the ground.

Teddy, two years old, on the Stump Ranch

He was unable to move, a goat chain wrapped tightly around him. Screaming for help for some time, his voice had become hoarse again.

Being mulish, stubborn creatures, goats aren't the easiest critters in the world to control. And Jack immediately had trouble with them. At first he was amused when one of the rambunctious animals began running circles around him. But before he realized what had happened, he found himself bound tight, his arms tied securely to his sides. He was a mess because the goat, now standing over him, had relieved itself.

Within a couple of days, Jack moved back into Portland to live with his dad probably figuring that between the goats, the bed and Grandmother, he was lucky to be alive.

Grandma Barnes holding Teddy

Dad was not one who easily accepted advice from a woman, and in particular from his mother-in-law. Grandma continually warned him that he had better castrate the shoat hogs while they were young or the meat would become too strong to eat. But, being stubborn, he kept putting it off.

My dear pappy had never castrated an animal in his life. But he had his own idea about when and how it should be done. When he figured it was time, he summoned two of his brothers, 17-year-old Tony and 15-year-old Mickey, to come and help him.

The three of them chased down one of the squealing pigs, now a fairly large animal, and rolled it over on its back. Pinning it to the ground, they were ready to do surgery. Tony held a rag and a bottle of liniment to cleanse the wound while Mickey sat on the pig's head holding its rear legs apart. Dad, with a rusty old pocketknife, started to cut. But the pig wouldn't cooperate and, squealing with pain, squirmed around and bit Mickey on the rump. Mickey, suddenly in pain himself, let go of the pig and it escaped . . . but not for long. The poor kid leaped to his feet, the seat of his pants torn away and blood pouring from a nasty bite wound on his bottom.

Grandmother treated and patched Mickey's wound, a wound that was not only painful but also caused him a great deal of embarrassment. The three resumed their disagreeable task. But this time, to better control the pigs, they stuffed them headfirst into a barrel and rolled them over onto their backs.

On October 1, 1933, Mom gave birth to my brother Tom in the decaying shack. She had a difficult time with the delivery. But luckily Doctor William Lockwood was there to help. My grateful parents named their new baby, Thomas William. I don't really know why they chose the name *Thomas* but the middle name *William* was selected in honor of their dedicated doctor.

When Dad paid the kindly physician for his services with a cord of stove wood, the doctor thanked Pop but suggested, *"Please, don't have any more kids for a while, Elmer. I got enough firewood at home now to last me the next ten years."*

Too many problems arose during the two years they lived on the stump ranch: the uncertainty of Dad's job, the expense of driving an old and undependable car, and Mom expecting her third child. These difficulties forced them to move the family back into Portland. They rented a small house near southeast Woodstock Street not far from Grandpa Pileggi's home.

Mom gave birth to my second brother, Richard Lawrence, on August 13, 1935 at home. This time, the delivery was a little easier for her. And this time, to Doctor Lockwood's relief, Dad didn't offer to pay him with a cord of firewood for his services. Instead, he paid him, not many weeks later, with a couple of large Chinook salmon.

The House on Tolman Street

Just after my brother Dick was born, my parents rented a spooky two-story house in southeast Portland. It had been built in the mid 1800s on a large lot on Tolman Street. The first recollection I have of my childhood is when we were living there.

The exterior paint applied years and years earlier had blistered and much of it had peeled away. Two narrow windows in the living room facing the street gave the house an eerie appearance, as if it had two dark squinting eyes. The floors squeaked and sometimes, as if the place were haunted, the interior doors swung shut on their own. The white paint on the picket fence that bordered the front and sides of the yard was in considerably better condition than the paint on the house.

An old decaying shed at the back of the lot leaned to one side, giving the impression that it would soon topple. Had it not been for a dense thicket of blackberry vines covering the back and far end of the rickety structure, it indeed might have fallen. Still, it was dry and large enough to shelter about 200 rabbits in hutches. Dad also stored firewood, garden tools, rabbit food and a lawnmower in it.

Teddy, Dickie (sitting in the pan), and Tommy

Playing in the front yard under two huge walnut trees made it easier for Mom and Grandma to keep an eye on us. As young as Tom and I were, the trees were an attraction, and we wanted to climb them. But that little bit of pleasure was forbidden to us. However, being disobedient little boys, we did anyway. And, a couple of times, we suffered a swat on the rump for doing it. I also walked the top rail of the picket fence, but only a couple of times because I was afraid that if I fell, I'd skewer myself with one of the sharp picket slats.

Grandma planted a garden every year during the few years we lived on Tolman. And she was usually the one who tended it. One type of vegetable that she planted was string beans. And they need something to cling to. So, she used long wooden poles, four poles per hill, tied together at the top and positioned in teepee fashion. When the vines had climbed to the top of the poles, the garden became an ideal place for us to play cowboys and Indians.

Kids need a dog and we had one. Ours was a faithful black and white pooch named Skippy. I can't remember when we got him or when we lost him. I only remember that he was always at our side when we boys romped about the yard.

My youngest brother, a belated Christmas present, was given to us on December 28, 1938. He was born at home. And Doctor Lockwood was on hand just as he'd been when Tom, Dick and I came into this world. I don't know what Dad paid him to deliver Mom's fourth child but it certainly wasn't a load of firewood or fresh fish. Mom and Dad named our newborn brother *Elmer Dee*. Where the name *Dee* came from, I'll never know. But years later a friend asked my brother why his parents gave him the name.

"Well, when I was a little kid in school, my grades weren't very good, so Mom called me Dee."

In those days, students were graded on each subject by a letter. An *"A"* meant excellent; a *"B"* above average; a *"C"* was average; a *"D"* below average and an *"F"* meant failure.

I had to butt in with a better explanation.

"His grades were a lot worse than a 'D' but Mom couldn't call him that."

The Terrible Turk

The billboards posted at the entrance to the downtown arena publicized The Terrible Turk, a professional wrestler, as a growling snarling demon that destroyed opponents with little effort and little care. On Saturday nights, excited, screaming crowds of people came to watch this black-haired menace maul and pound his foes before finishing them off with vicious head butts to the stomach.

But this mean mauler of the ring wasn't as horrible as the posters advertised. He was a pussycat at heart. In fact, he didn't look or act much like a wrestler until he got into the ring. And he wasn't the famous Terrible Turk that wrestled somewhere back east a few years earlier. He was just a good-natured, jovial fellow. And because of his dark hair and neatly trimmed black moustache, he looked more like Charlie Chaplin.

I knew the Terrible Turk very well. He was my Dad.

Pop was not a very large person but he was exceptionally quick and agile and he liked the physical contact. He was a favorite on the wrestling circuit and was willing to wrestle anyone, no matter how large they were. And the few dollars he earned by wrestling helped a great deal to maintain our family during hard times.

Dad had been working the grunt-and-groan circuit for something like four years when he suffered an injury while wrestling a fellow named *Boxcar Nelson*. Nelson suddenly went berserk during the match and, for some reason, tried to break Dad's leg by twisting it around one of the ring corner posts. When other wrestlers realized that Nelson was really bent on harming Dad, they jumped into the ring, restraining him. But they were too late. Dad's knee was damaged, and it swelled like a balloon and remained swollen for weeks.

Pop knew that his leg would never be strong enough to withstand many more matches. But after a lengthy period of inactivity, he decided to wrestle again, at least try one more time. Dad resumed training and, as a gift for my fifth birthday, took me to the gym.

When we entered the building, several huge, fierce-looking men gathered around us. The mere size of these men frightened me. But far from being snarling, growling hulks, they were happy and joking and laughing. A few of them gave Dad friendly but jarring slaps on the back.

Dad introduced me and told them that it was my birthday, that he wanted me to see the inside of the gym and was going to take me to his next wrestling match. One mountainous man, with hair all over his body and hands bigger than dinner plates, bent down and shook my hand with one finger. He looked like a mean giant. But he wasn't. He was a kind person, patting me gently on the head and wishing me a happy birthday. He told me that my father was his most favorite and best friend in the world. Mostly because of his friendliness and compliments, my uneasiness being among these huge men soon faded away.

The gym was an interesting place but it didn't smell very nice. Some of the men lifted weights, some sparred and wrestled in a ring, some skipped rope and some punched bags. And as they did all of these things, they grunted like pigs. I tried to lift one of the weights but it was so heavy that I couldn't budge it, not one inch no matter how hard I tried.

I became fascinated with one fellow who hit, with rapid precision, a bag that Dad called a speed bag. The man offered to let me hit it too, and bet that I couldn't hit it twice in succession. I just couldn't pass up the challenge.

So that I would be eye-level with the bag, he lowered it and then lifted me up onto a wooden apple box tipped up on end. It seemed as if everyone in the gym had stopped to watch me as I wound up like a baseball pitcher and struck the bag, hitting it as hard as I could. I walloped it solidly but, being too close when the bag rebounded, it hit me in the face. The blow knocked me over backwards and I fell into the wooden box, scraping my back.

The sudden jolt in the face and the fall surprised me and when my back began to sting, I screamed bloody murder and began to bawl. Dad pulled me gently out of the box but his consoling didn't stop my crying. Then, the big hairy man, my dad's friend, picked up the box, examined it and pointing to one of the slats said, *"Look, boy! You broke the box. You must be some tough kid, strong like yer old man."*

My sobbing stopped when I saw that the end of the box was indeed cracked. I thought that I must have done it when I fell. I stopped crying and began to grin. The big fellow had figured out a way to take my mind off the pain, and my back no longer seemed to hurt as much.

A few days later, Dad and Mom took me to the arena to watch Dad wrestle his last match. The building was dimly lit, noisy and smoky, filled with yelling people who were watching two wrestlers throw each other about. The rowdiness of the crowd frightened me and, after Dad left for the dressing room, I made a big effort to stay close to my mother. The spectators seemed so crazy at times that I feared Mom and I would be trampled and hurt.

Finally, Dad appeared in the ring and it was his turn to wrestle. His opponent also appeared, and it was Dad's very best friend in the world, the big hairy man. At first, I couldn't comprehend what was happening, that they were going to be opponents. But when it sank in, I began to sob, worrying that my dad would get hurt.

When the bell rang, the crowd erupted, and so did my normally quiet, sedate mother. Dad and the big hairy man lunged at each other and locked arms as their bodies slammed together. They threw each other about, first one on the mat and then the other. They jumped on each other, they pounded on each other, and they grunted and groaned. I cried, the crowd screamed, and my mother went nuts, shouting and ranting and screeching over and over, "*Kill him, Elmer, kill him!*"

Then it happened. Pop went down, flat on his back with the big guy on top of him. Mom leapt to her feet, screaming at the top of her lungs. But it was too late. The referee pounded the mat three times and the match was over. It didn't last long but, to me, it seemed like forever.

Dad's leg was too weak. He'd lost his quickness, his agility, his sharp edge, and his last match.

Dad's big hairy friend helped him to his feet and raised his hand as a gesture of respect. I gradually stopped crying when I realized the match had ended. But I was sad that Dad had not won. Mom, too, felt relief and slumped down in her seat like a head of wilted lettuce, a quiver on her lips, and a little misty in the eyes.

Although it frightened me to death, I'm glad I got to witness my dad's last wrestling match. He didn't have to win to make me feel proud of him. He was my hero and, to me, my dad would always be a winner.

King of the Hill

I loved fairy tales as most kids do. I had a creative and wild imagination. And many times my imagination caused me problems—*mucho problemes.*

One of those instances occurred on a warm sultry afternoon when my mother and grandmother were doing the laundry in galvanized washtubs in the yard. Scrubbing clothing on washboards, wringing it by hand and hanging it to dry on clotheslines was difficult, tedious work . . . and they were bushed. Deciding to take a short rest from their arduous task, they went into the house to have a cup of coffee, and caught me feeding dead flies to my three-year-old brother Tom. I lied and told him they were raisins. He was a glutton; he'd eat anything he thought was food.

After getting my rump tanned, and deservedly so, I went outside to sulk and climbed up into one of the walnut trees, a place I often went to allow my backside to cool. Sitting on one of the massive limbs and feeling sorry for myself, I began to dream about running away, as little boys do when they've been punished.

"Boy, if I ran away, they—meaning my parents and grandmother—they would really be sorry."

My mind soon strayed from running away to tracking down giants to finding gold and diamonds to crossing the desert on a camel and so on. Then it struck me. I could play *King of the Hill.* But, I needed a high, lofty place to play that game. I couldn't play it in the walnut tree because I dared not climb any higher than the bottom limbs. Once I'd climbed almost to the top and got stuck. I had a dickens of a time getting down. And I got a spanking to boot.

Then another idea struck me.

"I'll climb up on the shed roof and I'll make a torch. That's it! I'll make a torch just like that statue has in her hand. Everybody looks at her and they like her. Yes, that's what I'll do. I will be the greatest king in the whole world."

I jumped down from the tree and went into the house, careful not to draw the attention of Mom and Grandmother. They were still sipping coffee and gossiping about Sam the Fish Man who lived a few blocks down the street. I got a wad of toilet paper from the bathroom, some wooden stick matches from a shelf above the old brown wood-burning stove in the living room and, acting as nonchalant and innocent as possible, strolled outside toward the shed. I picked up a stick that was going to be my torch and proceeded to climb the apple tree next to the shed. It was an easy jump from the tree onto the shed roof but, because the shingles were so rotten in places, I had to be careful not to crash through them.

Standing on the roof peak, I wrapped the wad of toilet paper around the end of the stick. Then I scratched a match across the dry cedar shingles. But it wouldn't light. So, I struck it on the head of a nail. And that worked. The match flared and I lit my torch.

The toilet paper flamed high and bright as I held the torch up to the sky. But my dream of being King of the Hill lasted only a fraction of a second. Concerned that I'd burn myself when pieces of the flaming toilet paper began falling from the stick, I dropped it. And suddenly the roof was aflame. The only thing I could think of to extinguish the fire was to get some water, and get it quickly.

Teddy, Dickie, and Tommy

I shinnied down the tree, ran into the house, got a glass from the cupboard and filled it with water. As I was heading out the door, Grandmother yelled after me, asking where I was going with the glass. I answered with an anxious, trembling voice.

"To put out the fire!"

A few seconds passed before my answer took effect on the two women. And when it did, they reacted quickly. In near panic, they practically exploded out the door on a dead run. By the time I got to the tree, the fire had spread considerably, the dried shingles burning like oil-soaked paper. A squirrel couldn't have climbed that tree any quicker than I did. But I had to leave the glass of water on the ground, hoping that Mom or Grandmother would hand it up to me. They yelled and screamed instructions but I had become too frightened to understand anything they said.

Mom went for a garden hose as Grandmother grabbed a dishpan and scooped water from one of the laundry tubs. She handed it up to me. But I wasn't nearly as strong as she and spilled most of the dirty water back into her face. The amount of water left in the dishpan helped a little but it wasn't near enough to put the fire out with one douse.

Mom came running as fast as she could with the garden hose not realizing that she was quickly pulling the hose out to its full length. She was about 30 feet or so from the shed when her feet flew off the ground. Like she was tied to the end of a huge rubber band, she was snapped backwards. She, too, got a good soaking.

I had gotten myself into a horrible predicament and knew that I was doomed . . . my mother and grandmother half drowned and the shed burning down. I just knew when this was over they were going to kill me.

Grandmother continued to hoist half-filled pans of water to me until the fire was finally extinguished. The two women, wilted and drained of all their strength, sat down in the wet grass to catch their breath. They warned me stay put, to stay there on the roof in case the fire rekindled itself. I gladly obliged. I had no desire to climb down and get spanked for what I'd done. Even if the fire came back to life, I figured it was much safer on top of the shed than on the ground with them.

My days of playing King of the Hill were over. But soon I was daydreaming again. This time, I dreamed of becoming a fearless, daring and heroic firefighter, climbing ladders and saving pretty girls.

The Things Adults Say

Listening to adults giving advice and using their logic to solve problems got me into trouble on more than one occasion. One was wetting the bed. Tommy and I slept together and although I had nearly gotten over the problem of bed-wetting he hadn't yet arrived at that milestone in his childhood development.

After several weeks of waking up dry, I found one morning that I'd had an accident during the night. I tried to blame it on my younger brother but Mom and Grandma knew better and would have none of that nonsense. Grandma warned me that she was going to tie a string around that thing if I wet the bed one more time. My young, inquisitive mind began to work.

"Wow! What a great idea. I can do that myself and I'll never pee in the bed again."

I hated waking up and finding myself soaked and I hated catching heck from my mom and grandma. So, that night I got some store string and tied myself up, snug and tight.

About five in the morning, I woke up in pain. I needed to go to the bathroom in the worst way. But I couldn't untie the darned string. I had become so swollen with urine that I could hardly find the knot. Becoming more frenzied by the minute, and quite desperate, I worked frantically, trying to untie it. But it was useless. I even got a butcher knife from the kitchen but, in too much pain, I was too unsteady and feared that I'd cut myself. Finally, I gave in and woke Grandma to help me.

The old woman couldn't believe what I'd done to myself. By the time she found a small pair of scissors, the pressure had become intolerable. I felt as if I were about to burst at the seams.

Granny found it difficult to get any part of the scissors under the string. But she worked feverishly snipping and prying and tugging until the last fibers gave way. The poor woman! She was directly in front of me in the line of fire, and I hosed her down with a stream strong enough to douse a four-alarm blaze.

Another incident occurred about the same time in my youth. Many times, my concerned grandmother told me that I was tongue-tied, that I mumbled and did not enunciate words clearly. She admonished me several times to speak slowly and clearly, hoping I wouldn't emulate my Uncle Jack's stuttering speech. Unfortunately, he stammered terribly, and that irritated Grandma to no end. Time and time again, she told him that his speech would improve if only he placed a couple of pebbles under his tongue and practiced speaking slowly.

Her idea of using pebbles to cure his malady was probably not the most brilliant one she'd ever conceived. But it seemed like a slick solution to me. If she believed pebbles could help Uncle Jack speak clearly, then why wouldn't they help me?

One day while Tommy and I were in the yard playing with our dog Skippy, I decided to begin my own speech therapy and popped a couple of small rocks in my mouth. Tommy, grinning like a little fat-cheeked chipmunk, told me that I talked stupid. But I thought I was doing fine, speaking words very well. I told him that it was he who was the silly one. It was his ears that didn't work well. Then a thought struck me. Maybe he really couldn't hear. Maybe that's why he never paid attention to me when we were playing.

Convinced that my brother had a hearing problem and that I had arrived at a correct diagnosis, I had a good idea how to cure him of his woeful problem. Pebbles! If pebbles could improve my speech, then they ought to improve Tom's hearing.

Grabbing my poor unsuspecting brother, I wrestled him to the ground and stuffed a small stone into one of his ears. Squirming loose, and wanting no part of my treatment for the hard-of-hearing, he ran for the house, squalling as if a bee had stung his chubby little behind.

A few moments later, I sauntered into the house and found Mom and Grandmother feverishly trying to fish the pebble out of my bellowing brother's ear. He told the two women what I'd done to him and carried on as if it was his last day on earth. Grandma asked what on earth possessed me to do such a stupid thing. My mumbled, unintelligent answer peeved her all the more and she gave me an attention-getting swat on top of the head. But instead of hearing a yelp come out of my mouth, Grandma saw three pebbles pop out and spin across the floor. Her eyes widened to the size of washtubs. And for a fleeting second, she most likely thought that she'd knocked my brains loose.

A few nights after the pebble incident, Tommy and I had just crawled into bed when an unexpected, horrific thunderclap boomed through the dark night air like a cannon. In a shivering panic, like two little scared pups, we went scrambling under the covers seeking a place to hide from the angry heavens. Thunderstorms frightened the life out of me, particularly the lightning, and I hid under anything handy, even the bed covers, believing that it couldn't touch me there.

I'd heard stories about people being struck by lightning. Grandma even had a close call one time. She told me when she was a little girl, she had taken refuge under a tree during a thunderstorm and that it was struck by lightning. She wasn't hurt but the force of the thunderbolt knocked her to the ground.

Being alone in the dark also frightened me especially when I was outside and away from the house. But when Tommy was with me, I felt safer, even though he was younger and a bigger chicken. My dad told me that if I didn't stay in bed once I was put there that the boogey-man would get me. Fearing an evil ogre would grab me when I had to go to the bathroom, I wheedled my little brother into looking over the edge of the bed to make certain nothing wicked was lurking about. But in time he wised up to my shenanigans.

The only time Tommy and I didn't share a bed was when I came down with a nasty case of the measles. My face and chest were covered with them. Hoping to prevent Tom from catching them from me, Mom moved him in with our brother Dickie. And she warned him to stay out of my room. But being curious, he peeked in, and with a big grin on his face, told me that I looked funny. Though I didn't feel well, I had enough sass to invite him to come closer. I wanted to rub my measles all over his chubby little cheeks.

Doctor Lockwood told my mom that Tom would likely come down with the measles anyway because he'd been sleeping in the same bed with me right up to the moment that I'd become ill. And it happened just as the wise physician had predicted. Within a few days, we were both down with the measles and in the same bed . . . and I didn't have to rub them on him after all.

The People Around Me

My first day in the first grade at Our Lady of Sorrows Catholic School was a traumatic one for me. Mom had done her best to convince me that I would enjoy going to school. And I believed her. But I began to cry the moment she walked away, leaving me alone with people I didn't know.

Feeling abandoned and uncertain, I huddled with four other children who were also sobbing. We cried for at least an hour. But, our new teacher, Sister Eugratia, had experienced these situations before and gradually convinced us that she was our friend and in safe hands. She survived the day and so did we. By end of the week, I had become comfortable with my new surroundings and my new friends.

Sister Eugratia was a kind and gentle person. But she and the other nuns were far from being pushovers. They were strict disciplinarians. The ladies of the cloth not only knew what each and every child was doing while on the school grounds, they also knew in minute detail what each and every child was doing on the way to and from school. Kids who go to a Catholic School soon learn, and can attest to the fact, that nuns are really the world's most proficient undercover agents. They are like spies and they know absolutely everything.

Not many days into the school year, three or four other boys and I stopped to play in a vacant lot on our way home after school had let out. We climbed a tree, looked into a bird's nest, threw rocks at a tin can, and spent at least a half hour exploring. The next morning, Sister called each of us by name to come to the front of the room. We stood before her as she announced to the rest of the students that we had been disobedient little boys and were going to be punished.

I wondered, *"What did I do?"*

She reminded us that we had been instructed to go straight home from school every day and not stop anywhere to play. Unbelievably, she recounted every single thing that we did during the previous afternoon.

For disobeying her instructions, our punishment was to stand in a corner for 20 minutes, an eternity to a fidgety kid. I was humiliated. I wanted to be thought of as a nice kid. But here I was, caught, tried and sentenced.

After assembling in our classrooms every morning, we went as a group to the church next door to attend mass. It was the first event of the day. The boys in my grade occupied the first pew, and I sat on the end next to the aisle.

Weekday services were short but nonetheless I sometimes fell asleep. One morning I dozed off momentarily. When I awoke, for some reason, I thought the mass had ended. I rose, stepped into the aisle, genuflected and began exiting the church. Like a flock of simple-minded sheep, the rest of the first grade boys followed close behind. Father Fathieu, our parish priest, was quite astonished to see his church emptying prematurely, and ordered us to immediately return to our seats.

Well, I had done it again—albeit unintentionally. But nonetheless I spent more time in the corner. I'd suffered another embarrassment.

I probably wouldn't have felt so ashamed about getting caught had I not had a puppy-love crush on a cute little blonde girl in my class. Her name was Jacqueline Collins. I wanted her to believe that I, a six-year-old Casanova, was a knight in shining armor and not an inattentive, naughty and disobedient little boy. Every chance I got, and trying not to draw attention to myself, I peeked at her, feeling like melted butter.

My Godparents, Nick and Antonia Carlich, lived a few doors from Our Lady of Sorrows School. So I saw them often. They were warmhearted, loveable Austrian immigrants, and an absolute joy to me. My Godmother always had a leaf of parsley tucked under her tongue. She claimed it was healthy for one's digestive system.

Because I was so accustomed to listening to my grandfather, I had no problem understanding my Godparents' cute accented speech. Of the two, Mama Antonia was the one who did most of the talking. Papa Nick usually sat in silence, just nodding his head in agreement

Ted's Godparents, Nick and Antonia Carlich

and interjecting an occasional *"Ja"* into the conversation. When he did speak up, Mama Antonia playfully clapped a hand over his mouth saying, *"Papa! All the time you talking too much."*

My Godmother prepared the best golden fried rabbit in the entire city of Portland. With the rabbit, she served mashed potatoes and gravy and a delicious green dandelion salad seasoned with a mix of vinegar and oil. Whenever I learned that she was going to cook rabbit, I invited myself to their dinner table, certain that I was going to receive a mouth-watering treat.

Most of our friends and many of the people who lived in our neighborhood were immigrants from the old country.

The Cimbollas, a family of full-blooded Italians, lived next door. Sometimes they frightened me because of the way they carried on, and bellowed words that I didn't understand. There were times that I was sure they were going to kill each other when in fact they were just carrying on normal conversations. Italians are a crazy lot and when they communicate, there's a lot of arm waving, jostling and yelling. It's just typical of them, and the Cimbollas were true to form.

Louie, one of the Cimbolla children, was 16 years old. But to us little kids, he was already a big fellow. He loved to drive cars. But his mother cringed whenever he looked at one.

"Louie, you notta see 17, you keepa drivin' thosa cockeyed cars."

Occasionally, my mom and dad gave the Cimbollas a rabbit or fresh vegetables from our garden in exchange for some of Mama Cimbolla's freshly baked pastry or bread. It was almost like everyone was related in some way.

Sherwood was a child about my age. He lived not far from my grandfather's house. Always a pleasant, courteous youngster, he very generously shared his playthings with me when I went to his home to play. The most interesting toys he had were dozens and dozens of tiny toy soldiers that he kept in a shoebox. Some of the metal figures were riflemen, some were machine gunners and some were obviously snipers. We spent hours together, playing war and never once did we argue over who had won.

Sam the Fish Man, who lived down the alley two blocks past Cimbolla's house, always seemed to be a topic of conversation among the women in the neighborhood. I don't think Sam was married. And he seemed to be a well-to-do person, owning his own transport business hauling fish to markets around Portland.

He packed salmon and other kinds of sea fish with crushed ice into wooden boxes and used a branding iron to burn the name of his company into the box lids and ends. Sam quite often had a pile of crushed ice on hand and he seemed not to mind when we took a piece of it. But first, we always gave it the sniff test to make certain it didn't smell or taste fishy. To us curious kids, Sam the Fish Man and his business were very, very interesting.

My grandparents, Vito and Ruby Pileggi, moved to Oregon about 1923 and, within a couple of years, built a house on Southeast 69th Street in Portland. Unfortunately, I never got to know Grandma Ruby. She was the victim of cancer and passed away in 1931, eight months before I was born.

When Grandma Ruby became ill, her Aunt Eva, my great-great aunt, came every day to help Grandpa with the household chores and to ride herd on his four feisty sons: my dad, Tony, Mickey and Jack. And after Grandma Ruby passed away, Aunt Eva continued to help my granddad until she became too feeble herself.

My parents called Aunt Eva, Evvy, and we kids called her Auntie. I can only remember that she was kind and generous, a little heavyset and had dark hair.

Grandpa was born in the province of Calabria in Italy. He was a distinguished and handsome man. Every day, without fail, he wore a necktie and a vest, even when he performed menial chores around the house. Extremely proud to be an American, he refused to speak Italian except when he was conversing with Italian friends or when he was angry and needed to vent his frustrations, using stout language.

It was an easy walk to Grandpa's house, about ten blocks. So we visited him often.

We liked playing in his yard and rummaging around in the junk in his sheds. A large cherry tree that grew across the driveway from his house and a fig tree that grew in the back yard were favorite places for us to climb, but only when Grandpa wasn't around.

Speaking English wasn't easy for Grandpa, but he managed. Some of the words he had the most difficulty with were his own family's names. For instance, he called me *Titty* instead of Teddy and Mom *Ottel* instead of Ethel. Later in life, he referred to one of my sisters-in-law, Eunice, as *Uterus* and bragged about my brother living in an expensive *condom* (condo).

Mrs. Everett, who lived beyond Sam the Fish Man, was either a distant relative of ours or a darned good friend. She was a dear, sweet elderly lady who loved having the neighborhood kids come by to visit.

To my chagrin, she fed her cat one of my favorite foods, tiny cooked bay shrimp. I loved them. To me, they were a delicacy, and I hated to see her cat get any of them. She most likely knew how much I liked eating them myself because occasionally she left an opened can of shrimp on the table while momentarily leaving the room, giving me an opportunity to snitch a few.

Mrs. Everett paid us visits at least once a week just to catch up on the gossip and news of the neighborhood. One cold and blustery morning, she came calling at the back door, chilled to the bone, her dentures clattering and chattering. Grandmother and Mom escorted her into the kitchen, sat her down at the table, and poured a small glass of straight bourbon whiskey for her.

After a couple of hours in casual conversation, all three of them went outside to look for signs of daffodils peeking up through the frosted earth. Minutes later, my little brother Dick, not yet three years old, also ventured outside, and tumbled off the stoop. He'd found Mrs. Everett's nearly empty glass of whiskey on the table and had taken a hefty swig or two of the stomach warming liquid. To the women's dismay, he was tipsy.

Facing The Music

Mom loved music, particularly classical music. And she played the violin. Hoping that I was musically inclined as well, she purchased a quarter-size violin and arranged for me to take lessons from a music teacher in downtown Portland.

The instrument was small compared to the ones adults played. But being three-and-a-half years old, it was huge for me. Stretching my left arm to grasp the neck of the instrument was difficult. Crooking my wrist so that I could form the notes with my fingers made the act even more demanding. And holding it properly for long periods of time was agonizing. But I adapted, worked diligently and learned to play it well.

When I was five-and-a-half years old, I was one of two youngsters—the other a red haired six-year-old girl—to perform in a well-attended, all-violin concert with no less than fifty adult violinists in Portland's impressive Civic Auditorium. We played a selection of beautiful Viennese waltzes, among them *The Blue Danube* and *The Merry Widow*.

An hour and a half prior to the beginning of the concert, Mom and Dad left me backstage with the other instrumentalists. I wasn't comfortable being alone but they assured me that they'd be in the audience, not far away and watching. It made no difference . . . I was still nervous.

The singers were awesomely elegant. The men were dressed in black tuxedos and the ladies in long, colorful flowing gowns. And every one of them seemed to sparkle.

My concert attire was homemade. Mom made it using a soft light-pink satin material that included knee-length pants, a shirt with short sleeves, and a small cape.

While we had been preparing back stage, the auditorium transformed from a huge empty cavern into a blur of color and a sea of faces. Not until we took our places on stage did I fully realize the magnitude of the event. And I was certain the eyes of all 3,000 people in the audience were fixed on me.

The conductor raised his baton and we began to play. And though I'd memorized the music, every note seemed unfamiliar. I began to tremble with fright. And with the turn of each page, my anxiety and nervousness increased. I quivered from the top of my head to the tips of my toes and can only remember my bow bouncing uncontrollably across the strings.

After playing the last piece, we stood and bowed to a roaring ovation. I was spellbound. The applause sounded like continuous thunder. As if quite pleased with me, every one of the performers including the conductor patted me gently on the back and congratulated me as we moved off stage.

To my relief, Mom and Dad, their faces beaming with proud smiles, joined me moments later. Mom told me that she heard every single note that I played and that I had played beautifully. But I couldn't remember playing one single note correctly throughout the entire performance, and knew she was fibbing just to make me feel good.

When I began school in the first grade at Our Lady Of Sorrows Grade School, my visits to the music studio were restricted to once a week. But, to broaden my musical education, Mom arranged for me to take piano lessons from the nuns. Learning to

Teddy, garbed in a pink satin suit with cape, playing his violin

play the piano wasn't any easier than learning to play the violin. It was as demanding and fatiguing. At least I didn't have to hold the thing under my chin.

Six or seven of us children, who took lessons, gave a piano recital in the school for our parents, families and friends. After playing the violin before an assembly of 3,000 people, playing the piano before 50 should have been easy. But it wasn't. I was just as nervous. When it was my turn to play, I walked from behind the piano, bowed to the audience and took a seat on a stool. Only, I didn't quite sit down squarely and fell to the floor. Everyone, with the exception of my instructor and my poor embarrassed mother, thought it funny and laughed.

My career as a piano player never fully got off the ground. We didn't own one. And my lessons ceased when we moved into the country. However my violin practices continued but were restricted to once a week and sometimes only once a month. Then, two years later, I had to give those up too because of a war.

"Miner" Difficulties

Tommy and I were in a happy, carefree mood, and frisky and playful as two puppies because our mother was taking us to see a movie at the Bob White Theater on Foster Road. The movie was *Snow White And The Seven Dwarfs*. It was one that Mom and Dad said was excellent entertainment for everyone, especially children. Well, I didn't care what it was about or that it was excellent for kids to watch or whatever as long as I got to see a cartoon and eat a bag of popcorn. I loved the cartoons. Everyone in the family, including my mom and dad, loved the cartoons. We got a big kick out of them.

Two weeks earlier, Dad had taken us to the movies and, fortunately, two funny cartoons were shown at the time. Mom laughed so hard that she paid little attention to what she was doing and unintentionally stabbed her umbrella down inside the shoe of a man who was sitting next to her. He was obviously irritated and right on the verge of saying something nasty to Mom. But Dad leaned forward and gave him the *Terrible Turk* stare. I guess the guy thought better of it because he moved to another seat.

When Mom told us that Aunt Fliss—she was married to Dad's Uncle Verle—and one of their sons, Bonji, were going with us to see *Snow White And The Seven Dwarfs*, we became even more excited. Bonji was a lot of fun, but he was forever in trouble—much more than me if you can believe that. Even though Mom was pregnant at the time with her fourth child and the theater was about a mile from the house, she and Aunt Fliss planned to walk.

At the moment Aunt Fliss and Bonji arrived, we began acting up and jumping up and down, unable to control ourselves. We were itching to go. Grandmother stayed home to watch over our brother Dick. And as we boys traipsed out of the back door, she cautioned us to behave ourselves and stay close to Mom.

To our consternation, the women walked at a snail's pace and chattered incessantly, exchanging little tidbits of gossip about everybody and everything. Their talking was irritating because it slowed us down. We were antsy boys wanting to get going as fast as we could.

We ate bags of popcorn and enjoyed ourselves just as my parents thought we would. When we left the theater to return home, daylight had faded and it had become foggy. Mom begged us to stay close, and we did for a time.

We loved the seven dwarfs, our minds sparked by their antics. Pretending to be three of them, we marched in single file behind the ladies, whistling and singing songs from the movie. *"Hi ho! Hi ho! It's off to work we go . . ."* It was much fun to pretend.

After a few minutes of frolicking and dodging around the women, we ran ahead. But we went too far. The women, no longer able see us, shouted demands that we remain closer and within their sight. Tom and Bonji obediently waited on the sidewalk for Mom and Fliss to catch up. But not me! Being a brat, I continued to run ahead. Grandma's warning about behaving myself had long faded from my memory. I could hear Mom asking the boys where I'd gone. She was clearly upset and told Fliss that if she weren't so heavy with her baby, she'd chase me down and blister my bottom.

I wanted to scare Tom and Bonji. And when I came to a stack of lumber piled between the sidewalk and the curb, I immediately knew that it was a dandy place for a mischievous boy to hide. When they came abreast of my hiding place, I leaped out growling and snarling, pretending to be a werewolf. To my glee, my sudden appearance startled the bejeebers out of Tom and Bonji . . . and everyone else. I nearly gave my pregnant momma apoplexy.

"If I could catch you, Teddy, I'd spank your damned butt good for you."

Bonji and Tom, trying to help Mom corral me, gave chase. But I easily outran them in the dark.

"Darn that kid, Fliss. He scared me so bad that I thought I was going to have the baby right there on the spot."

Arriving home, Tom and I headed for bed, but only after I got a well deserved, but soon forgotten, scolding for scaring the wits out of Mom. Lying there in the dark, we whispered to each other about how much we enjoyed the movie. We thought it had to be great fun to dig in the ground, discovering hidden riches like the dwarfs did. Then I had a sudden brainstorm, a brilliant idea. Why couldn't we dig for treasures as they did? If we could find some gold, we could buy all the bubble gum and candy bars in the world. My excitement was so overwhelming that I could hardly stand it and blurted out my thoughts to Tom.

"Tomorrow morning, we're gonna dig for gold an' dieminds an' jools and we're gonna be the richest kids in the whole world."

I went to sleep dreaming that soon I would be wealthy, so rich that my pockets would be filled with gold and candy and chewing gum.

About mid-morning the following day, after feeding the rabbits, Dad slowly returned to the house. He looked a bit puzzled when he sauntered into the kitchen where Mom was working.

"Who dug all those holes in the yard, Ethel?"

"Holes? Heck, I don't know Toots. I haven't been outside yet. Prob'ly Skippy did."

But when Tom and I hustled into the kitchen, Pa took one look at us and knew the answer; our faces, hands and clothing were thoroughly smeared with mud.

Mom and Dad and even Grandma had told us many times, swearing that it was true, that pots of gold could be found at the end of rainbows. Being six years old, who was I to doubt my parents when it came to finding buried treasure. I chose to believe every single word they said and, being resourceful little squirts, we made our own rainbows. When the sun made an appearance, Tom sprayed water from a garden hose. And when a rainbow appeared, I began digging.

We dug four or five holes but found no gold, not one shiny nugget. Watching us, our dog Skippy probably wondered why in the heck we had invaded his territory. Prospecting was darned hard work and frustrating too, and it made me hungry for a snack. So we gave it up for a time and ran into the house to wait for lunch.

After gulping down a sandwich, we decided to give it one more try. This time, instead of just digging, we tried panning for gold. Grandma had talked about panning for gold when she was a youngster. But we weren't quite certain how to go about it. So, we filled one of the holes with water and stirred it around with a stick until we had made a good thick pasty gob of mud. Scooping some of the gunk out of the hole with my toy sand shovel, I dumped it onto one of Mom's fine bone china dinner plates. Squatting down beside the hole, we held the plate and just looked at it, hoping to see something brilliant, something glitter. But when we saw nothing interesting, the mud went back into the hole and we added another tin can of water and stirred it again. Then, scooping out another batch, we repeated the process.

Tom and I stared down at the goop and then we saw it—something shiny, as bright as a star. Excitement coursed through my veins as we ran screaming into the house with Mom's plate heaped with mud. When Mother saw that we had one of her china plates and it was covered with mud, she nearly had a conniption fit.

"But Mom, look! We found a real diemind. Just look at it and see."

She picked the shiny thing out of the mud, washed it under the faucet and showed it to us. It was just a piece of broken glass. What a bitter disappointment. She dumped the mud out of her plate and told us to get back outside and fill in the holes, and then clean up.

It was useless. The gold, the wealth, all of it had eluded us. We went back outside and, as we began filling the holes, I suddenly had another thought, albeit a devious one.

Scooping up some mud, I pulled on the back of Tom's waistband and dumped it down the backside of his knee-length pants. His face

Tommy and Teddy playing in the yard with their dog Skippy

screwed up like he was sucking on a persimmon and then he began to bawl and howl as he ran for the house, squirts of mud slithering down his chubby little legs.

Boy! Even on cool, cloudy days, I somehow found ways to get my butt tanned.

Zingers and Stingers

Not only did we have a couple of big walnut trees in our front yard, we also had several mature fruit trees off to one side. And during the few years that we lived on Tolman Street, Mom and Grandma put up jars and jars of apples, cherries, figs and pears. But, to be sure, we boys ate our fill of fresh fruit beforehand. So did a jillion yellow jackets.

During warm weather, it was commonplace for us kids to run barefoot around the yard. And we were continually getting slivers and thorns in our feet. But one hot day, I got more than that.

Venturing under one of the fruit trees in search of a ripe, juicy pear, I was careless not watching where I was stepping. I put my bare foot down on an overripe pear that was crawling with voracious yellow jackets. The result was five stings on the bottom of my left foot.

Squalling like an orphaned calf, I hobbled into the house hoping that Mom and Grandma could make the pain go away. But Granny marched me right back outside and, after extracting some stingers, packed cold mud on my swelling foot. It helped some but I continued to wail and bawl as if I were being tortured to death.

I hated those darned yellow jackets. And so a few days later, I ventured outside with Granny's fly swatter, bent on making those nasty little critters sorry for stinging me. I should have known better but I didn't.

The ground under the tree was littered with rotting fruit and most of it covered with feasting yellow jackets. My target was an overly ripe pear that was just crawling with them. I crept up on it, squatted down, and gave it a flurry of healthy whacks with the fly swatter. But all I succeeded in doing was squish a few of them down into the gooey pulp, and make the rest of them angry. Now, I was in trouble—deep, deep trouble. One of the crazed things flew up and crashed into my forehead. But, fortunately, it didn't sting me. Then more of them came at me. I flailed away with the swatter as they swarmed about me. But there were just too many, and I quickly ran back to the house.

Somehow, I escaped getting stung again. But, as luck would have it, Grandma caught me. She grabbed the fly swatter from my hand, and though it was still dripping with pieces of rotten pear and sticky juice, used it to give me a swat on the rump.

"Are yuh ever gonna learn a lesson, Teddy?"

I guess not because from that day on, yellow jackets and I have been at war.

Say Uncle

If there was a fishing hole within 200 miles of Portland, you could almost bet that two of my father's uncles, Verle Adams and Steve Tabler, had already fished it. They were exceptionally avid fishermen and rugged outdoorsmen.

Verle was a big man with a lantern jaw, tough and strict. But his wife Fliss—her real name was Felicity—was just the opposite. Petite and soft-spoken, she was truly a lady in every sense of the word. They had four children older than Bonji: sons, Clayton, Irvin and Dale and a daughter, Eudelle. And eventually, Fliss would give birth to Gary, their fifth boy, sixth child.

Steve Tabler was my dad's great-uncle and a brother to my great-great-aunt Eva. He was a quick-witted fellow, wiry and shorter than Verle, and a World War I veteran. He and his little redheaded wife, Catherine, had four girls and one son. Although both men were older than my dad, they enjoyed his companionship and often included him in their plans to go fishing.

When I was a very young child, I can remember my dad and uncles leaving the house on cold fall mornings to fish in the Willamette and Columbia Rivers. When they returned home, they nearly always had Chinook salmon that were five-and six-foot-long. Not even Sam the Fish Man had fish as large. To keep them cool and moist until Mom and Grandmother could begin the arduous task of canning them,

Uncle Steve and Aunt Catherine's
children: Betty and Annie in front,
Becky, Margaret, and Eddie in back

they laid them in the bathtub. The fish were so big that their tails protruded above the rim at one end of the tub. Most of the fish was put into pint jars but they always saved enough salmon steaks to have one fabulous meal with sliced tomatoes, corn on the cob and homemade bread.

One Saturday afternoon when I was seven, our family went to Uncle Verle's home for a scrumptious dinner. After feasting on an excellent meal of chicken and dumplings, the men made plans to go fishing at Valsetz, a small remote logging community in the Coast Range. And naturally, their plans included Uncle Steve.

Mom enjoyed fishing too, especially with Dad and had asked him several times if he'd take her. He promised her faithfully that he would but, never finding the time, didn't. Yet, when his uncles wanted to go fishing, he was packed before they could say "*Jack Robinson.*" So, who could blame her for being a little miffed when she learned of his current plans?

In the meantime, while the adults remained in the house visiting, Tom and I went outside with our cousin Bonji to play in a large two-story building that they used to house rabbits, chickens, and store everything else under the sun. The first thing we did was climb up a crawl-ladder through a trap door to the second floor of the building to play and explore. Bonji's older brother Clayton, who was well over 6-feet tall at age 16, had come with us, not to play but to smoke, an act

Irvin, Aunt Fliss, Bonji, Eudelle, and Dale (L to R);
Clayton, the tallest, standing in back

that his mother had absolutely forbidden any of her children to do. It wasn't long before Clayton lit up a cigarette.

We had been playing for just a few minutes when I saw Aunt Fliss. She'd crawled up the ladder and poked her head through the crawl hole. Spotting her also, Clayton turned away. But it was too late. She'd seen the cigarette dangling from his mouth. In a stern voice, her lips pursed tightly in anger, she told him to stay put. After pulling herself up through the crawl hole, she fetched an apple box and placed it in front of him. Then, she climbed atop it and slapped the cigarette from his mouth with the flat of her hand. I had never seen Fliss so angry. And I never knew her to spank any of her children. But Clayton wasn't a child any longer. He was as tall as his dad, so darned big that the swat his mother gave him didn't seem to faze him one bit. And to Clayton's credit, he obediently stood still and never moved a muscle as his mother gave him a stern lecture about disobeying her and about smoking. As for me, I cleared out, beating a hasty retreat down the ladder to avoid the unpleasantness of the incident.

The following weekend, Dad and his two uncles, joking and bantering with each other, departed Portland on their fishing trip. It wasn't long before Uncle Steve broke out a bottle of *hooch* (whiskey) and invited Uncle Verle to join him for a couple of *snorts* (drinks). The two older men informed Dad that since he was their chauffeur, and a kid to boot, he had to remain sober and couldn't have any. That was okay with him. He didn't want to touch his mouth to anything they'd had their lips on, anyway.

By the time the trio neared their destination in the treed hills near Valsetz, the two uncles were feeling little pain.

Uncle Steve needed a rest break in the worst way and begged Dad to stop, and stop immediately unless he wanted a wet back seat. Pop obeyed and pulled to the side of the graveled road. The elderly veteran exited the right side of the car and promptly relieved himself in the roadside ditch.

Uncle Verle, in the 50s

Unbeknownst to any of them, the only house for miles around was right across the road, set back in the trees a couple hundred feet.

Just as Uncle Steve finished his business and was buttoning up, Dad spotted the place. And standing in the large living room window staring at the car and its three occupants were half-a-dozen inquisitive children and two women. Most likely they were curious, probably wondering if someone had come to visit them.

Pa couldn't help himself and pulled forward some 50 or 60 feet leaving his tipsy uncle exposed. Uncle Steve likely wondered what Dad was up to. And when he turned his head, looking back over his shoulder, saw that he had an audience. He knew then that his nephew was pulling an underhanded prank on him.

Hurrying to the car, Steve crawled in the front seat with Dad and barked an order, *"Let's git!"*

As Dad gunned the engine and sped away, his uncle issued a threat. *"If those folks call the cops on me, Elmer, I'm gonna bounce a rock off your conniving skull."*

Dad had pulled a prank on a person that was seldom bested. But he knew that Uncle Steve, even though he was grinning at the time, would sooner or later get even, perhaps ten-fold.

Pranks and good-natured horseplay were the norm on these trips. They were expected, particularly when my dad was about.

Three weeks after taking their trip to Valsetz, the three men planned another fishing trip. Mom was fit to be tied and asked Dad when he was going to keep his promise to take her fishing. He apologized, crossed his heart and vowed to take her next time. It was always *"the next time."*

Certain that he'd renege; she devised a plan to force her husband to keep his word . . . or pay the consequences.

The three men left Portland early in the morning, their destination Breitenbush. It was located seventy miles east of Salem. The drive took them three-plus hours. The last 30 miles of the trip was on rutted dirt roads.

Leaving the car parked near an old abandoned cabin, they descended a steep, forested hillside, following what appeared to be a game trail. Just before reaching the river, Uncle Ed examined the mud at the edge of a creek they had crossed and pointed out some paw prints that he believed were made by a bear. Seldom seen, they knew an abundance of bear and cougar inhabited the area, something that would naturally make a normal person a little uneasy.

Gary Adams, three years old, in 1946

At the river, they decided to separate, Uncle Verle going upstream, Uncle Steve fishing downstream, and Dad staying put. The two uncles made a colossal mistake, though, leaving their lunches in a burlap bag hanging from the branch of a tree near where Dad remained to fish. It wasn't long before Pa became hungry. That wasn't startling; he was always hungry.

Taking his sandwiches from the bag, he unwrapped the first one and found an unpleasant surprise—Mom's wedding band and a note from his peeved wife. She wrote in bold letters that this was the last time he was going fishing without her. She ended the note with two words—*or else*—and the words were underlined several times to make her point. Mom's wedding band punctuated her short message like a hammer.

Pop, mulling over her threat as he ate his lunch, knew that she was darned serious, and that he had better keep his promise. Otherwise he might find himself tossed out of the house on his ear.

He buried her ring deep into his pocket taking care not to lose it, and finished eating the food she had packed for him. But after downing the last morsel, he still felt hungry and began eyeing the burlap bag. There were more sandwiches in the sack, the ones belonging to his uncles.

Now, nothing could curb the old man's appetite if he knew there was food to be had, not a threatening note from Mom, not a worldwide cataclysmic event, not even two angry uncles. Nothing! Not seeing any sign of Steve or Verle, Pa gave in to temptation and before long he'd devoured their grub too, eating six sandwiches in all.

In the few hours that Dad had fished, he'd caught more than enough trout to feed all three of them. He was already in deep trouble with Mom and, now that he'd eaten his uncles' lunches, knew that Verle and Steve would be just a little upset with him too. One could do a lot of things to those two old goats and possibly escape retribution. But one had better keep hands off their grub. He figured he had best scoot up the hill to the cabin and cook up a hot meal for them.

Dad's cooking was certainly not one of his best assets—everything he prepared was fried in a half inch of grease at a temperature hot enough to rival the sun. But, he had to do something before they caught and killed him.

Dumping his catch into the empty burlap bag, Dad packed up his gear and began making his way through the dense woods back to the cabin. He wondered what their reaction would be when they found him and their food gone. When he came to the creek where they had seen the imprint of a bear's paw, he became a little concerned, wondering if the animal was still lurking about.

Just as he was about to jump across the stream, a frightening growl roared from the brush behind. Startled and darned concerned that a bear might pounce on him, Dad dropped the sack of fish and leaped smack into the creek. Frantically, he scrambled about on hands and knees trying to push himself upright. Then he heard sidesplitting laughter. The "*bear*" turned out to be Uncle Steve. Dad, standing in water up to his knees and dripping wet, was a bit miffed and sputtered some obscenities at his uncle for scaring the ever-loving life out of him.

"Serves you right, Toots, for playing tricks on us old men. Boy, if you ain't a stupid lookin' sight standin' there with yer ass all wet."

Still chortling at the comical sight of Dad looking like a dunked donut, Steve jumped the creek and bounded up the hill as sprightly as a white-tailed deer. Dad was relieved that his snarly old uncle didn't throw something at him. He was about to retrieve his sack of fish and equipment when he was again startled by noises. This time it was Uncle Verle emerging from the trees behind him.

"What the hell did ya do with my lunch, Elmer? And why the hell are ya standin' in that there creek?"

Verle knew the answer to his first question. But not waiting for Dad's response to the second, he jumped the creek and, with the same nimbleness as Steve, trotted up the hill out of sight.

By the time Dad joined them at the shack, Steve and Verle were busy cooking up a batch of bacon and potatoes for a tasty meal, a meal that they were determined not to share with their younger relative. To ensure that he wouldn't get any more of their food, they barred the door, locking my poor daddy outside.

Little Soldiers

Tom and I often found ourselves in hot water with our parents and grandmother because we seldom let our four-year-old brother Dick play with us, frequently pushing him away. He was too small, he couldn't run as fast, and he was a pain in the neck, often in our way and spoiling our fun.

One day while we were playing soldiers, we found a fresh molehill in back of the shed and decided to dig up the varmint that made it. But Dick had the shovel and wasn't the least bit interested in digging up moles or sharing the shovel with us. So, like two resourceful, determined little rascals, we simply took the shovel away from him. Right away, he pitched a fit, bawling and screaming at us. But we didn't care. The shovel was ours and, now that we had it, he wasn't going to get it back until we had finished. While one of us attacked the molehill, the other kept our pesky brother from bothering us, sometimes throwing dirt clods at him.

After working for what seemed like an hour, all we had accomplished was digging a hole half way to China. We saw no trace of a darned mole. Nothing! We couldn't even find its tunnel anymore. It was discouraging and much easier playing soldiers than it was trying to dig up some dumb animal. It was a shame, too, that we couldn't use the hole for something. And if we didn't fill it in, Grandma might find out and tan our behinds.

Squatting there, staring into the hole, an idea began to form. And suddenly I had a solution. We could use it to erect a soldiers' tent. And the tent could be our command post. Magnificent idea, I thought.

Fetching a beanpole from the garden, I poked it into the hole and scooped dirt in around it. When the hole was full, I tamped the dirt down. Even though it was a little wobbly, the pole stood upright but leaned just a little to one side. Pulling a bed sheet from the clothesline, I threw it over the pole and we had a tent. It was perfect. We gave the shovel back to Dick. But now, he didn't want it. Tom and I crawled into our command post to play. Dick wanted to play too, and tried to follow. But, being little tyrants, we quickly evicted him, pushing him out, trying to get him to leave us alone and play elsewhere.

We were too much for him and in defiance, our whiny little brother threw dirt on us. Then, he yanked on our makeshift tent, pulling it over. That did it. We weren't about to let him ruin our fun and grabbed him and wrestled him to the ground before he could run away. We stuffed the struggling squirming little squirt under an overturned contractor's wheelbarrow. He was trapped and being too small to lift it, couldn't escape his dark dungeon cell.

We had triumphed, winning our first battle as soldiers, and had conquered our enemy. Our tormentor was now a prisoner of war. Oh, did he ever kick up a fuss, wailing and carrying on something awful. But we paid no attention to him and went back to soldiering, reconstructing our tent.

Like all soldiers, though, we soon faced another foe, a much tougher, mightier and determined adversary. Grandma! She'd come to Dick's rescue and we—two little soldiers with blistered bottoms—suffered our first defeat.

Tommy, Dickie, and Teddy

The Birthmark

One day, when I was seven, my mother caught me in a nearby vacant lot taunting a teenaged black girl who lived in our neighborhood. She was sobbing uncontrollably. Mom, her face flushed with anger, made me stand in front of the girl and apologize. I was so ashamed that I couldn't look her in the eyes; I just stared down at the ground. Mom also apologized to her and then marched me home to give me a scolding and a stern lecture.

"You should be ashamed of yourself, Teddy. How would you feel if someone insulted you the way you insulted that poor girl?"

When I didn't respond, she asked another question.

"So why in God's name did you do that? Can you give me a reason?"

What could I say? I couldn't offer an excuse. I was just being mean.

Mom told me something then that I knew wasn't true. She told me that she, too, was part Negro. I already knew that she was Dutch and maybe part Indian and wondered, *"How many parts could she be?"*

Mom's best childhood friend was a black girl. Her name was Bernice. And because she had dark skin and Mom was thought to be half Indian, they both endured taunting and insulting remarks during their youth. She pointed to a small brown birthmark spot on the back of my hand and remarked, *"You might be part Negro yourself. And remember this . . . don't judge people by their skin. Judge them as individuals and only by their character and their actions."*

As a child, I couldn't grasp the meaning of everything she said. But, as I matured, it became clear. My mother was a good teacher, and it was a lesson that I never forgot.

Another thing about my mother that I never forgot; she could tell some real humdingers and do it with a straight face.

CHAPTER II

1939–1941

Finding Our Country Estate

For some time, Mom and Dad had considered moving back into the country hoping to raise us boys in a safer, more secure environment. The big city with too many people, too many cars and too many social problems influenced their decision. So, late in the summer of 1939, feeling the family was better off financially than ever before, they began searching for a piece of ground not too far out of Portland. But Dad wasn't certain that he'd saved enough money for a down payment on a place with acreage and asked Grandpa if we could move into his house for a few months—rent free.

Granddad had no idea what he was in for. But he agreed. And soon, we'd moved lock, stock and barrel out of the old house on Tolman Street where we'd lived for nearly four years.

In the beginning, Grandpa welcomed the companionship. But having seven people suddenly descend upon him, four of them young children running around his house like wild colts, he soon became distressed and short tempered.

He was exceptionally angry with me one day because I'd cut pictures of wooden soldiers from a magazine and pasted them on his dresser. I didn't know it was made of mahogany and an antique, not that it made any difference to an ignorant seven-year-old like me. In his Italian accent, he complained to Dad, *"Sonamungunya! Titty, he'sa make a mess outa my house."*

Grandpa Pileggi, in the 40s

Grandpa wasn't always upset with me, though. Sometimes he took me with him when he worked. He was a junk man and in the recycling business long before *recycling* became a household word. He collected unwanted household items, like furniture and old clothing, using a horse and a wagon. The wagon was a thing of beauty that attracted adults and kids alike. It was equipped with red sideboards, pillowed seats, and a baby-carriage top that could be folded down during nice weather.

As his horse slowly plodded along through the local neighborhoods, one block after another, he called out to the homeowners in a slow high-pitched voice, *"Junk! Anybody gotta some junk?"*

At first, it was embarrassing. But I soon became accustomed to it and even tried to mimic him a few times. Most of the things he collected, after he'd sorted through them, were sold to two old Jewish friends in Portland.

Grandpa considered Mom a treasure and had the deepest respect for her. But occasionally he did something that just mortified the life out of her. He passed gas—and it was loud. He probably couldn't control himself because of his age. But Mom wouldn't or couldn't accept that as an excuse. And every time he rid himself of some noisy air, he looked about trying to appear bewildered. Glancing from one side of his chair to the other, with a huge grin on his face, he'd say, *"Sonamungunya! Atsa cat! He'sa hide-a sommawhere inna my house."*

He loved to entertain us kids after supper with stories. And, believe me, some of them were real Jim-Dandies—like the one about his horse.

He told us that his horse was magic and that it pooped $100 bills, but only if it pooped exactly at midnight. Naturally, the very night he told us the story, Tom and I bolted out of the house to the horse's stall and, with rakes in hand, waited for the big event. Every time that blasted animal raised its tail, we raked through the stinking steamy mess only to be disappointed at not finding any money. I can imagine Grandpa sitting in his living room chair bursting his sides with laughter knowing what we were doing. Finally after two nights of frustration and sleeping in a smelly stable, we complained that we had found no money.

Grandpa's answer was simple. With his bony finger pointed skyward, he said with a touch of a smile, *"He'sa gotta poopa atta midnight. Only atta midnight!"*

Raking through horse manure was disgusting. And had Grandpa told us that his horse pooped $1,000 bills, we'd made up our minds not to go back out there. Someone else could look.

Dad purchased some interesting grocery items while we stayed with Grandpa. Some of the items were bought at his father's request, such as dried codfish and tripe. The tripe looked weird, like corduroy. But when cooked, it was quite tasty. No one told me that it was part of a cow's stomach, otherwise I might have thought it over and not eaten it. The slender slabs of dried codfish stunk horribly and were hard as iron, hard enough to split wood. It had to be soaked for a full day before anyone could cook it.

Dad brought home two slabs of dried cod one night and laid them on the kitchen counter. As soon as the adults engaged themselves in conversation in the living room, Tommy and I took the opportunity to play with them. Grandpa nearly had a stroke when he caught us having a duel and using his codfish as swords.

"Thosa boys, Tootsie! They crazy kids! They gonna killa each other witta fish."

Dad and Mom located two small farms with houses that they thought they could afford to buy. Both places, each about ten acres in size, were run down but cheap in price. Dad's pay at the time ranged from $16 to $25 a week, and even though the depression period of the thirties was over, money was still tough to come by. Anything affordable on those wages couldn't be much to look at or very comfortable. However, my parents believed they could make either one of the places into a decent home.

At the first opportunity, Dad took the entire family into the country to look at the two properties. The houses were nothing but shacks and neither was equipped with indoor plumbing or wired for electricity.

The first house we looked at sat on a small knoll with a nice view of absolutely nothing. The land around it was barren of trees and shrubbery and looked as uninteresting and bleak as a desert. Nonetheless, we kids ran and romped around the place like wild young colts exploring everything in sight. Unfortunately, during our scampering through the tall dry grass, Tom stumbled across a yellow jacket's nest and suffered a sting.

The second place we visited was in the farming community of Cipole, pronounced *Sigh-Pole*. It was located between Tualatin and Sherwood, some 15 miles southwest of Portland. The house was in worse condition than the first one. But there were some things that we kids liked better. It was near railroad tracks. And forests thick with trees and underbrush nearly surrounded the place. And long ago, a neat old root cellar had been dug at the far west end of the property.

We romped and ran around just like we did at the other place, exploring the outhouse and a couple of old sheds. Soon we discovered lizards. Several dozen of the little critters were clinging to the shingles on the outside of the house and basking in the afternoon sun. We had seen lizards before but not as many at one time. Curiously spellbound, we squatted down on our heels and watched closely, waiting for them to move. What was particularly interesting to me was the way their eyelids closed as they sunned themselves—like a shade being drawn over a window. A few times we conjured up enough nerve to touch one, only to see it scurry off and disappear into a crevice in the shingles.

On the way back to Grandpa's house, we made it known to our parents that we liked the property near Cipole much more than the other place. And they seemed to be in agreement. And so was Grandma; she could hardly wait to buy a few dozen chickens and a milk cow.

My dad was certainly not a farmer, not by a long shot. But he knew that Mom and Grandma could handle the chore of growing crops and tending to livestock until he learned.

We celebrated our good fortune that night, eating a wonderful meal of home-baked bread, spaghetti and Fava beans, all of it prepared by Grandpa.

Christmas had come and gone by the time Dad and Mom closed the deal on the Cipole property. When it was done, we moved everything we owned in just a few days to our new address—Route 4, Box 103A, Sherwood, Oregon. And when the move was completed, Mom enrolled Tom and me in our new school.

Moving and changing schools was exciting. But I had to give up seeing some people I had grown fond of: my Godparents Nick and Antonia Carlich, our parish priest Father Fathieu, my teacher Sister Eugratia, and a cute little blond-haired girl named Jacqueline Collins. I had no problem saying goodbye to the adults because I knew that I would see them again from time to time. But I wasn't as certain about Jacqueline.

Bashful and fidgeting and staring at the ground, I mumbled goodbye to her, furtively touched her hand, and then ran like the dickens for home.

The Cipole Swamp

The soil on our little farm was fine for our needs. But it wasn't the best soil in the area. Acres and acres of rich peat—also referred to as beaver dam or bottomland by the locals—nearly surrounded us. These areas dotted the landscape from Hillsboro to Salem, and perhaps even farther south.

Hundreds of years ago, these areas were a marsh covered with thick vegetation. They were a sanctuary for a multitude of wild animals and birds that thrived in a wet environment. And it was a favorite hunting ground for local tribes of Indians.

When the early settlers moved into the valley, they found the black peat soil exceptionally good for growing row crops. A few acres were all that was needed to make a decent living. So they drained away the excess water with a series of ditches and cleared the land of excess vegetation. Unfortunately, clearing the land drove the wildlife from the valley and destroyed the Indians' hunting grounds.

The farmers around us, many of them Italian, found the black peat soil especially suited for growing onions. And thus they named the community Cipole. It's a word derived from the Italian word *cipolla* (*chip-oh-lah*) meaning onion. The beaver dam flooded during the rainy winter months, prompting the locals to refer to it as *the swamp*. Most years, the water remained two, three and sometimes four weeks and was deep enough for the locals to go boating.

We referred to the beaver dam to the west of us near the small two-room elementary school as the big swamp and the small piece of beaver dam to the south in back of our farm as the little swamp. The families who owned acreage in the big swamp were the Cereghinos, Galbreaths, Fischbuch, Burkes, Johnstons, Dittmans, Youngs and Walgraeves. And those who owned sections of the little swamp were the Coles, Wagers, Walgraeves, Robinsons and Hedges.

Every one of these families owned a bright red barn. But the barns weren't used to shelter livestock or store hay; they were used to store onions until they could be readied for shipping to markets around the States.

The Shack, Our Home

Our small three-room house was horribly crowded even though four of the seven people in our family were children. We lived there—or should I say we survived there—until the late forties when we moved into a new house that we built on an additional ten acres of ground that Dad had purchased a few years earlier. That land lay between Dad's original ten-acre purchase and the railroad tracks and Herman Road to the north. By then our family had grown to nine with the birth of my two sisters.

But for the time being, seven of us were crammed together, like chickens in a birdcage, in a house that was little more than a shack.

To the disappointment of us kids, the dozens of lizards that clung to the shingles during warm weather had long disappeared. And the swallows that had built nests under the eaves were long gone too. We would have to wait until the coming summer to be entertained by their aerial acrobatics.

The house had been built before the turn of the century. And it definitely looked like it. The outside walls were made of shiplap lumber and covered with old graying, hand-split shingles. And the inside was as rustic. It was never finished—no plumbing, no heat and no electricity. Drinking water and water for bathing was pumped from a well just outside the kitchen door. The toilet was an outhouse, as old as our shack, and a good 100 feet from the back door. The nearest source of electrical power was nearly a quarter-mile away to the east. We used kerosene lanterns for light when it was dark. The only heat in the house came from an old wood-burning cook stove in the kitchen. But when the fire died out late in the evening, winter nights became horribly cold. The walls were never finished. Newspapers had been pasted to the shiplap boards and the two-by-four studs to keep the cold air out. At night, as we children lay in our beds, we actually learned how to read by studying the walls.

Our house was situated 30 feet from the eastern boundary of our property and was separated from our neighbor's farm by an old rutted wagon road that served as our driveway. The road was seldom used beyond our house. It extended back to Robinson's old onion barn at the far southeast corner of our acreage and connected to another wagon road that wound westward through the woods.

Our kitchen was at the south end of the house, and the only usable entry was the kitchen door. The other two rooms were both bedrooms and chock full of people at nighttime. Grandmother and we boys slept in the middle one. It was the largest. She had her own bed and Tom, Dick, Dee and I doubled up, sleeping in a bunk bed. The room also served as a living room during times when we had company. When my two sisters were born, they slept in Mom and Dad's bedroom.

A small closet, the only one in the house, was in one corner of my parents' bedroom. And it was stuffed full of the family's best belongings and possessions. Our everyday clothing and personal things were stored in chests of drawers. I stored my clothes and a wooden cigar box full of trinkets in a drawer that I shared with Tommy. Everything else went into wooden fruit boxes that we shoved under our beds.

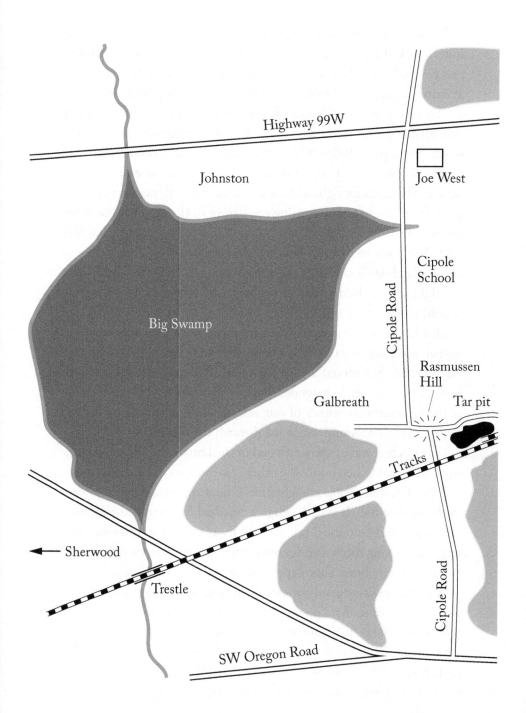

The Cipole Swamp, drawn from memory by the author

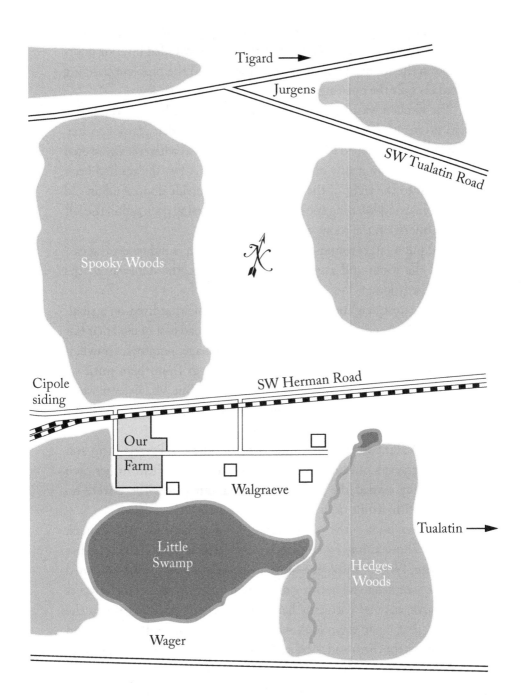

The previous owners used tin can lids to patch the many knotholes in the well-worn shiplap floors. But they never installed interior doors between the rooms. Grandma and Mom solved the problem hanging blankets over the openings thus providing a little privacy.

The kitchen wasn't much to look at either. And because the house had no running water, there was no sink. A wooden plank counter, with flour sacks nailed to the front edge to conceal whatever was stored beneath, took up nearly one side of the room. A few shelves had been built just to the right of the half-windowed outside door. And an old cast-iron, wood-burning cook stove with a warming oven sat on the left side. Otherwise, the room was bare.

Dad put a large, round dining table under the window on the east side of the room and a wooden icebox next to the doorway to the middle bedroom.

Our nearest neighbors were an elderly couple that lived on a small farm a little over a quarter of a mile down the road east of us. Their last name was Everett. They raised chickens, cabbage, potatoes, strawberries and asparagus for a living. We bought eggs from them until we got our own chickens. They were nice people. But Mr. Everett was a bit tight with his money. If an egg was extra large, an egg he called a "*double yolker*", he charged us for two.

Dick Walgraeve and his family lived beyond the Everett farm and Mr. Walgraeve's mother lived across the lane from them in her own home. They owned the acreage bordering our place. There were no houses within a mile of us to the west—it was thick timber.

Whoever owned the place before us must have loved hollyhock flowers. Those things were planted everywhere. Personally, I didn't like them. I didn't think the blossoms were as lovely as some claimed and they seemed to be nothing more than tall dust catchers. The leaves and stalks, covered with tiny hairs, snared every speck of dust in the air, and that made them look musty and dusty to me. But Mom and Grandma kept them and soon added some vibrant color, planting a variety of flowers and shrubs including mom's white tea rose.

We planted a sweet-smelling honeysuckle vine under the kitchen window. It was a gift from Grandma Walgraeve to our Grandmother.

In a few years, it took over one entire side of the shack, nearly concealing the swallow nests built under the eaves. And the Everetts gave us a start from an ancient rhubarb plant that remains in our family to this day.

Pop brought home a block of ice for our wooden icebox once a week during warm weather. It was pretty neat to touch something frozen during a hot summer day. It reminded me of the pile of crushed ice that Sam the Fish Man had in back of his business. Surprisingly, each block of ice lasted three or four days despite the warm temperature.

We children worked hard, played hard, and we were happy growing up in the little shack on our small farm.

Mother asked us boys one day why we liked this place better than the other farm that we'd visited. We were unanimous in our answer, explaining that this place was much, much more interesting. Tommy remarked that the other farm was not to his liking because he had been stung by a yellow jacket. But, I think we liked this place best . . . mostly because of the lizards.

My First Days in Cipole School

Immediately after moving onto our little farm, Tom and I began attending Cipole Grade School, he in the first grade and I in the second.

Cipole School was the heart of our small farming community. There were no stores or service stations, only a sign with the word *Cipole* posted near the railroad track siding. And farther down the road sat our little school. It was far different than Our Lady of Sorrows. It was small—one large room divided into two classrooms by a sliding partition. The classroom to the left of the front entry was referred to as the little room where children in the first four grades were taught. The classroom to the right was the big room for the students in grades five through eight. Even though restrooms, a furnace and a small kitchen were in the basement, there was still ample room for us to play a spirited game of dodge ball.

Two teachers and a janitor made up the staff, and the janitor often served as the cook. Everyone in the community had a hand in running the school. Local farmers cut the grass, maintained the buildings and equipment, and the children took turns taking out the trash and keeping the schoolyard clean. We had no school bus even though some of us lived some distance from the school. Nearly every one of us walked or, if we were lucky enough to own one, rode a bicycle.

Tommy and I were accustomed to walking to school on concrete sidewalks and hearing the constant drone of trucks, busses and cars on the city streets of Portland. Here, except for frogs and crickets and birds, it was quiet. Unless we cut across some of the farm fields, the only route to school was along Herman Road, graveled with stretches of washboard bumps and mud holes.

We were quite curious about the railroad tracks and thought it neat that we could walk part way to school on it. But the tracks were a concern to our mother for obvious reasons. Certainly, my parents realized there were dangers living in the country and particularly near a railroad. But we kids looked upon all of it as one huge adventure.

The walk to school took us only 25 minutes on a nice day. But the walk home often took much longer because we stopped to do a little exploring and playing in the drainage ditch between the road and the tracks. And, when the weather warmed, we ventured down into a tar pit at the foot of Rasmussen's hill near the Cipole railroad spur siding.

Anna Marie McCormick was my teacher. She was a sweet, motherly woman and taught the first four grades. An older man, not much taller than the students, was our principal and he taught grades five through eight. Aunt Cal, as all the kids called her, was our cook and janitor.

Four of us, two girls, another boy and I, made up the second grade class, a class considerably smaller than the one I left at Our Lady of Sorrows in Portland. My three classmates, Ruth Cereghino, Shirley Steyaert and Eddie Wager, were farm children and very intelligent students. The girls' families owned or rented acreage on the Cipole Swamp. Eddie's parents owned a farm within shouting distance of our house on the other side of the small swamp. He was a shy kid when he was around adults and strangers but not so with his classmates. We soon became close friends. He loved to make the girls laugh and giggle by making noises with his mouth that sounded like a Model T Ford climbing a hill. I tried to make the noises too, mimicking Eddie. But I could never do it as well.

The freezing winter weather made our walk to Cipole quite interesting. Water in the roadside ditches and mud puddles froze solid enticing us to walk on them. But before we did, we slammed boulders on the ice to test its strength. When we walked across the fields, our shoes made crunching sounds when they broke through the ice crystals that had formed just beneath the surface of the dirt. Dew formed and froze on old spider webs. But the spiders had long gone. It also snowed, sometimes three to four inches. But despite all the icy-cold weather, we seldom missed a day of school.

I liked Cipole. The lessons were easy for me and Mrs. McCormick told my mother that I was ahead of the rest of my class in skills and competence, capable of doing third and fourth grade work. Well, I remedied that little discrepancy in short order, slowing my mental development down to a crawl. Unfortunately, Tom did too and was held back one year.

I soon became adjusted to my new classmates and the differences in my new school. But I missed the music programs and my teacher, Sister Eugratia. Eventually, the memories of Our Lady of Sorrows School faded from my mind, even the memory of a cute little blonde-haired girl named Jacqueline.

My Friend Eddie

Eddie and I became inseparable playmates and close friends throughout our school years. We made a pact early on to always remain good friends and to help each other when the need arose. Never an aggressive sort, Eddie was a shy kid. He was even shy around my parents and found ways to fade out of sight without making a commotion. And until we graduated from grade school, he wore the same style of clothing every day: plaid shirts, railroad-style bibbed coveralls and ankle-high work shoes.

Eddie was the only boy and the youngest of four children in his family. His sisters were Annette, Frances and Helen. They were lovely girls: slender, talented and very protective of their little brother.

*Eddie, Helen, Frances, and
Annette, around 1937*

Jessie and Frank Wager, around 1937

Mrs. Wager was a sweet, kind and generous lady and like a second mother to me. She was related to the famous pioneer and outdoorsman, Daniel Boone. On the other hand, Eddie's dad, Frank, was a boisterous, gruff, hard-drinking old German who loved to tease us boys. He, too, wore bib style coveralls. Eddie looked like a little replica of his dad when they stood together.

Frank was quite an inventive fellow. One of his contraptions was a scraper used to remove mud from the soles of shoes. It was constructed of dozens of beer and pop bottle caps nailed to a piece of planking. Another interesting invention was a simple fly and moth trap—a sardine can nailed to the wall just below an exposed light bulb at the back entrance to their house. It was filled with used motor oil. Eventually moths, mosquitoes and other winged insects became stuck in the oil while hovering around the bulb. I always thought his bug trap to be much more effective and not nearly as ugly as the honey-colored fly strips that hung from the ceilings in our house.

Their home, nearly as old as ours, was definitely more up-to-date. It had inside plumbing and electricity where ours didn't.

Eddie's family possessed a magnificent upright piano that they claimed had been transported by sailing ship around the horn of South America. The tone was gorgeous and the girls, particularly Annette, played the instrument beautifully. It so captivated me that, had I been allowed, I would have spent hours lounging in their home plinking on it.

Eddie's bedroom was a lofty little place in the attic above the kitchen accessed only by a pull-down ladder. We spent hours and hours there talking about the things that boys do and dreaming about our futures.

Clearing The Land

Covered with trees, brush and stumps, our place wasn't exactly ready to become a farm when we moved in. But Dad planned to take care of that situation in a most interesting way. The brush and poison oak could be removed by hand, digging it out. But Pop figured the quickest and most convenient way to remove the stumps was to blast them using dynamite.

Now, my pop knew absolutely nothing about explosives . . . how to handle them or how to use them. He knew someone who knew someone else who had once used dynamite, and passed his or her knowledge on to him. But that didn't make him a demolitions expert. He'd helped Clarence Grady blow a few stumps at one time too. But that wouldn't necessarily have made him an expert either. Nonetheless he believed that he was the only one to do the job. Not exaggerating one iota, he was flat dangerous with a firecracker, let alone a stick of dynamite.

"What's so darned hard about it? You just crimp a dynamite cap onto a piece of fuse, insert the cap into a stick of dynamite, shove it under a stump, light the fuse and run like hell."

In the spring of 1940, Pop brought home a case of dynamite, caps and fuses and began the dangerous task of blasting the hell out of our farm. One of his first attempts sent chunks of wood, dirt and rocks sailing over our house. It seemed as if the entire world was exploding around us. We children took shelter under our bed believing it was the safest place to be. Even though she said little, deep concern was written all over Mother's face as she fretted and worried about Dad's safety. Grandma was also concerned. But she wasn't one to keep her mouth shut and vocally announced to anyone who would listen that her son-in-law was a mad man, and it would serve him right if he blew his fool head off.

Dad relentlessly blew stumps to smithereens on weekends for several weeks. Pieces of stump and brush lay scattered everywhere. If a person hadn't known better, they would have thought the place had been struck by a swarm of meteorites. It was dotted with craters.

We stayed in the house while Dad worked. And, after becoming accustomed to the place being jolted by an occasional blast, we pretended that we were under siege from some mythical army.

During lulls in Pop's assault on the earth, we helped gather debris into piles for burning and filled in the craters and holes with dirt. Occasionally we found an unexploded stick of dynamite, a worrisome concern for our parents.

Throughout the latter part of the summer, Dad continued to find things to blow up. He surprised everyone and proved that he could do the job. By fall, a considerable amount of ground was available for next year's planting. And there was even enough ground that had been cleared for a small pasture.

But blowing up stumps wasn't the only thing that Dad did during the summer. Wanting to buy a few pigs as soon as possible, he and Grandma set about repairing the fence that surrounded an old pigpen beyond the house near the upper end of our property. Grandma also worked on an old dilapidated shed, turning it into a chicken house. In a few weeks after it was finished, we had chickens.

We boys were awestruck realizing that we were quickly becoming farmers.

Catechism

Two days after completing the second grade, my first year at Cipole School, I unenthusiastically crawled aboard a school bus to attend a catechism class in Wilsonville at St. Cyril's Catholic Church. I thought I was finished with school and could enjoy the next three months playing in the summer sun. But, no! My mother had other ideas and enrolled me in the class. Heck, I didn't want to be stuck in a classroom for another two weeks. I wanted to begin my summer vacation like the rest of the kids, having fun and playing.

Nothing the teachers taught me was new. I had learned all of it when I attended Our Lady of Sorrows in Portland—at least I thought I had. The instructors were nuns and they reminded me of Sister Eugratia. They wore the same style of habit and were nice, kind teachers but strict and precise. And just like the nuns at Our Lady of Sorrows School, they knew every single little thing that we did on the bus coming and going. So, there was no misbehaving or horseplay.

I knew none of the kids in the class. But within hours I'd made some new friends. One of my classmates was a big brute of a kid, much older than me. He wasn't at all like the rest of us.

Daniel Patrick Morrison was huge, awkward, and as strong as an ox but timid and shy. Some said that he had the mind of a five-year-old although he was at least 14. And it was said that he was the product of a brother and sister. I was certain I knew what that meant and knew it wasn't good. The elderly folks who cared for him were his grandparents. He often rode a bicycle that was much too small for his large bulk. It was a weird looking affair because it was equipped not with handlebars but a steering wheel.

Whenever someone asked him his name, his reply was always the same.

"My name is Daniel Patrick Morrison."

Preparing to go home one day, all of us with the exception of Daniel had boarded the bus. The driver, looking in his mirror, failed to notice that Daniel wasn't in his seat. He was still outside, standing beside the bus.

As the driver proceeded to drive away from the church, he heard Daniel cry out. One of the nuns cried out at the same instant, screaming at the driver to stop. He did. He immediately brought the bus to a halt.

One of Daniel's feet had been crushed beneath one of the bus's rear dual tires. But miraculously, the big kid only suffered bruises. Not one bone was broken. When asked if his foot hurt, he replied, *"Naw! Its okay! It just stings a little."*

Had it been me, I would have been screaming my head off. When I got home, Mom asked what I had learned that day. Since I thought I already knew everything the nuns taught us, the only thing I could think of was, *"Don't put your foot under the wheel of the bus when it leaves."*

The Exterminator

Dad's income wasn't much but he was able to save enough money to buy a few hogs and an old smelly nanny goat and her kid before the end of the year. The nanny was great at mowing down brush and grass. But she had to be kept on a chain because we had not yet built a fence.

One of my chores was moving her to different grazing areas throughout the day. This task proved to be an unpleasant one for two reasons. First, she was as stubborn and obstinate as a mule and would not voluntarily move one inch unless I picked up and carried her squirming kid. And second, she and her offspring were always surrounded by a swarm of wretched flies.

Unlike the house in Portland, our old farmhouse in the country had no window screens or a screen-door. The same flies that swarmed around the goats and the pigs also began appearing in the house, swarming around us.

Mom and Dad purchased several honey-colored, fly-catching strips and a few fly swatters to combat those nasty insects. But we couldn't kill enough of them to slow their population growth. It didn't take long before the strips, several of them hanging from the ceiling throughout the house, were thoroughly covered with dead flies trapped by the sticky goop.

No matter how much I tried to avoid those strips, I invariably brushed against one getting a gob of the sticky stuff and some of the dead flies on me.

As much as I hated those ghastly, gooey strips, I disliked the fly swatters even more. But, they were a necessary evil. In nearly every instance, swatting a fly left an ugly mess either on the fly swatter or someplace you'd rather not have a mess, such as the kitchen table or a window. At least the flies that were stuck to the fly strips died intact.

My parents kept the fly swatters handy, placed strategically throughout the house. We all took turns using them. But when Grandmother had a swatter in her hand, we watched her like a hawk, keeping our distance. She wasn't beyond giving us a whack on the backside just for good measure let alone because we'd done something to irritate her. And getting swatted with a fly swatter that was coated with the guts of a jillion flies wasn't at all pleasant.

Figuring there had to be a better way of ridding ourselves of those miserable insects, I began to work on a solution. Soon my juvenile mind had developed a simple but ingenious plan. Lizards!

I'd heard that frogs, lizards and snakes ate bugs, all kinds of bugs including flies. It was too warm for frogs and there weren't many snakes to be had. But we had an abundance of lizards, hundreds and hundreds of the tiny reptiles. They were made-to-order bug exterminators. And they never left a sticky mess. The problem was the lizards were outside of the house and the flies were inside.

My plan was simple . . . Capture 10 to 12 lizards and release them in the house early in the day while the flies were at rest. By the time my parents got out of bed, all the flies would be gone . . . so I thought. And what a *pleasant* surprise it would be for Mom and Dad and my grandmother to find there were no more flies to pester them. And I could take all the credit for conceiving such a magnificent scheme.

So, I set about capturing squirming little lizards. And in no time at all, I'd caught more than enough, over two-dozen of the creatures, and kept them prisoner in a glass gallon jar.

Early in the morning, before anyone else was out of bed, I turned my little fly eradicators loose. I expected them to go right to work. But they scurried away and hid out of sight in dark corners and under things. What a letdown. What a disappointment. I wanted to see them at work.

Later, as the day began to warm, Grandma was up and sipping coffee at the kitchen table. As she was leafing through a Montgomery Ward catalogue, she saw a movement out of the corner of her eye. She leaned over and looked under the table from one side to the other but saw nothing. Shaking her head, she probably believed that it was her imagination and resumed flipping through the pages of the catalogue. Presently, she saw another movement. Something darted across the floor under her chair.

"What in tarnation . . . ?"

Grandmother stood up quickly. She was alarmed and certain that something strange was happening in the kitchen. Then she saw them, lizards scurrying in all directions. Not quite believing her eyes, she summoned my mother.

"My God Ethel! You better come in here, quick! The house is full of lizards. They're all over the damned place."

I suddenly had a feeling of foreboding, a hunch that I might have made a slight miscalculation in my planning, and that Mom and Grandmother weren't going to be happy after all. They were going to be mad at me and I was going to catch it. And I did—right across the butt with one of those dreaded, stinking, ugly fly swatters.

Driving Lessons

When my dad gave me my first driving lesson, it was in our old Plymouth in Walgraeve's stubble field near the house. I was so small that I could barely reach the accelerator, clutch and brake. But, after I got the car moving, I somehow managed to drive it 100 feet or so before stalling the engine. Mom was so impressed that her little boy could drive a vehicle that she decided to try herself. And that was the beginning of many years of torturing cars and killing things—like our apple tree and laurel hedge.

Driving a car that moved gave Mom problems. She could never get straight in her mind which pedal was the brake, which was the clutch, or which was the accelerator. In fact, she lacked the proper coordination to steer, work the clutch, and shift at the same time. Just putting a car in gear gave her grief.

Then there were the hand signals. At the time, there were no mechanical signals on cars; all signals were made manually by sticking the left arm out the driver's side window. But Mom couldn't remember when or how to signal for turns, right or left, or to stop.

Sitting in our car, Dad was testing Mom one day and asked what she must do when she was going to make a right turn. Baffled, frustrated and completely stumped, she could only think of one answer and snapped back.

"Turn the steering wheel, of course."

"For Pete's sake, Ethel! You have to signal with your hand first before you turn the damned steerin' wheel. Alright, now show me how you signal."

Easily annoyed with too many things to do and too much to think about as a driver, Mother often said that riding a horse was a *helluva* lot simpler.

A few times, Dad turned her loose in the family car, in the middle of the pasture or in Walgraeve's stubble field, hoping that she wouldn't crash into the barn or kill a chicken or the dog. Dad was smart. He refused to get into the car with her. Instead, he ran alongside while trying to instruct her. Now, if that wasn't a sight to see—the car lurching and lunging and jumping about like a wounded kangaroo. And Mom hanging onto the steering wheel, sometimes giggling and sometimes looking serious. And Dad running about with his short, stubby little legs churning and scrambling trying to avoid getting run over. They were as amusing to watch as an Abbott and Costello movie.

One morning, Pa wore his dark green bus driver cap adorned with union buttons when he took Mom for a short drive to the mailbox to fetch the mail. It was a distance of a little over a quarter mile. He agreed to let her drive back to the house. What harm could she do? The road from the mailbox to Dick Walgraeve's onion barn was flat and lightly graveled. But beyond the barn to our house, it was deeply rutted. As long as the wheels of the old Plymouth remained in the ruts, she could do little wrong other than stall the engine. Well, it didn't quite work the way he thought.

Before she got to the rutted part of the road, Mom buried the old Plymouth up to the running boards in Walgraeve's cull onion pile. And those onions were really ripe.

Dad backed the car out of the reeking pile and re-positioned it on the rutted road. Then he gave the wheel back to Mom, but only after he did a lot of hollering that included some strong words. She did fine for the first 50 feet. But then she got the old jalopy going much too fast and it began to buck and bounce from one rut to another. Dad could only hang on for dear life as if he were riding a bull in a rodeo, praying that his wife would regain some control. But she didn't. And then it happened.

A 90-degree left turn was required to drive from the road up our driveway to the house. With no clue what to do next, and turned off to Dad's shouted warnings, Mom yanked the steering wheel to the left while driving at the speed of sound and sent the car into a dirt-kicking sideways skid. She managed to make part of the turn, about 45 degrees of it. And that's when she took out the laurel hedge.

A Day At The Beach

As happy as a tree full of larks, we crammed ourselves into Dad's gray 1937 Plymouth Sedan and left home for an exciting fun-filled day at the beach. We always enjoyed the ocean. But the last time we went, Dad got sick and threw up on the ferry, crossing the Columbia River from Astoria to Megler.

Pa wanted to dig clams and do a little fishing. We youngsters just wanted to romp around in the surf and play in the sand. And Mom and Grandmother were just happy, not so much because we were going to the coast, but to get away from the drudgery of housework for a day.

I loved riding in the car but, unfortunately, I often got carsick. Sometimes I vomited, especially when Dad drove on curvy roads. And the roads to the coast weren't the straightest in Oregon. Sitting next to an open window with the wind in my face helped me to cope with motion sickness. When the dog rode with us, it wasn't unusual for both of us to have our heads stuck out the window, the dog slobbering and me gagging.

Mom's stomach was also uneasy that morning but she said it was from morning sickness and not from riding in the car. Well, I didn't know what the heck morning sickness was and I didn't care as long as I didn't catch it.

Of course, we had a flat tire. We always had a flat tire when we went for long drives. And Dad had to stop once to add water to the radiator from a canvas water bag that he carried strapped to the front bumper.

The skies were clear and the weather warm when we left home. But as soon as we crossed over the summit of the Coast Range, it all changed. The weather was cooler, cloudy, and blustery. Nonetheless, our spirits weren't dampened one tiny bit.

Not long after arriving, Dad went to work digging clams. He wasn't at it long before he'd filled a small burlap bag. In the meantime, we kids set about building a fortress in the sand. And Mom and Grandma found a nice sheltered place in the driftwood and sand dunes to build a small fire, making preparations for a picnic. The cold, brisk air made us hungry and, thankfully, Mom and Grandma had packed plenty of grub for us. When it was time to have lunch, we ate like ravenous hounds.

While we were eating, Grandma had a slight but humorous accident. She sneezed and blew her upper denture into the sand. Seeing that thing fly out of her mouth was a hilarious sight. And we couldn't help but giggle and carry on. But Granny didn't think it was as funny as we did and, like a defiant little kid, stuck her tongue out at us. She was always flipping her false teeth at the younger kids, arousing their curiosity and making them laugh. But this was accidental and her denture was dirty, covered with salty sand. Using a bottle of perfectly good orange soda pop, she washed it, popped the gritty thing back in her mouth and was back in business, ready to eat.

After devouring our lunch, we piled back into the car and drove a mile inland on a road bordering the bay, stopping at an old pier. Tom and I went exploring among the rocks on the bank while Dad fished from the end of the dock. The low tide exposed barnacles, starfish and billions of black mussels that had crusted the dock pilings. They gave Tom and me something different and unusual to examine.

A couple of decomposing crab backs, a sand dollar and a few seashells were among some of the souvenirs that we collected to take home. They were neat things for boys to store with their belongings . . . for a week or two.

Dad caught something on his line and yelled at us to quickly bring a net or a gaff hook. We gathered around him peering into the water as he struggled to pull his catch to the surface. His pole was bent double and at first I thought the hook had snagged on the bottom. But then we could see something emerging as he kept tugging and pulling and reeling. Astonished nearly beyond belief, we saw that he'd caught a small octopus. But it wasn't something he wanted to keep. Thank goodness it wasn't hooked; it had merely wrapped its tentacles around his line. Just as he pulled it to the surface, it let loose and, unfolding like an umbrella, glided out of sight back into the dark murky surrounds of the bay.

I don't know what he'd have done had he pulled that thing up onto the dock. But I know I wouldn't have stuck around to find out.

The bag of clams was dripping. And Pa didn't want his floorboards to get soaked with sticky seawater. So, before we left for the long drive home, he tied it to the front bumper, next to the canvas water bag.

In just a few minutes on the road, the smaller kids and Grandma had fallen asleep. My mind was set on eating a big mess of fried clams. But I, too, had become drowsy and soon drifted off into an exhausted sleep, worn out from running in the sand and the cold surf.

Arriving home, Tom and I went to the front of the car to retrieve the clams. But there were none. Dad hadn't secured the sack very well, and the bottom of it dragged on the roadway wearing a hole in it. All of the clams that Pop had worked so hard to dig lay strewn along the highway somewhere between the coast and Sherwood. All we had to show for our day at the beach were a couple of stinking crab backs and several handfuls of sand in our shoes.

Taking The Heat

During summer evenings, and even in the fall when it was still warm, we sat on the old dilapidated wood porch after supper telling stories and visiting with each other. I loved listening to my parents and Grandmother talk about the good old days. Their lives seemed to be filled with adventure and mystery and, sometimes, considerable hardship.

We heard tales about our Grandmother's youth and when she saw the infamous outlaw Frank James. She also related that her family had moved from Missouri to Montana in a Conestoga wagon pulled by a team of oxen. And, unbelievably, she'd eaten rattlesnake meat.

Most of the time, Dad told us fairy tales. But once in awhile, we heard about his many wrestling matches, and about fishing when there weren't many angling regulations.

Mom said very little. But when she did speak, it was concerning her days in school at the convent in Helena and how she learned to dance the ballet and play the violin.

But on Friday nights, warm weather or not, the family sat inside the house around the kitchen table listening to the radio program *I Love A Mystery* featuring Jack Packard, Doc Long, and Reggie York. And we never missed listening to the ever-suspenseful thriller, *The Shadow*. Saturday mornings, it was *Let's Pretend*, a program of fantasy and make-believe that kept us children entertained. I loved to mimic the characters in those programs and my mind wandered easily as I dreamed of adventures in far-off lands.

As the winter months approached, my brothers and I found that the warmest and coziest place in the house was sitting on the floor behind the old cast-iron cook stove in the kitchen. And so, in the evenings, we began to crawl back there. Soon it had become my favorite place to daydream and scheme.

One cool but sunny afternoon, I was camped behind the stove as Mom fried chicken for supper. My mouth watered just thinking about eating one of those golden aromatic pieces of poultry. Sometimes I wished that the world were made of her fried chicken so I could eat my way through to the center of the earth, or even better, clear to China.

Mom put the first of several fry pans of steaming-hot-pieces of chicken on a platter and set it on the warming oven. It was within easy reach and I couldn't resist the temptation. Her fried chicken was the best in seven states and always brought out the thief in me. I not only took one piece, I took the entire platter.

When she was ready to add another batch, she found the platter gone. So was I. Not caring at the moment about the consequences of my act, I made off for the woods to stuff myself with delectable fried chicken. No sooner had I snuck out of the house and was out of sight, I heard Grandmother and Dad calling me to come home right now, with emphasis on the words *right now*. But it was too late. I'd made my bed and now I had to sleep in it. Within minutes, I had devoured every piece, every last morsel of that delicious golden-fried chicken and licked the platter clean.

At first, with my stomach full, I felt quite comfortable and contented. But as darkness began to descend upon the woods, it got cold, shivering cold. I would have stayed put had it been warmer. But unable to stand it any longer I figured it was time to face the music and headed back to the house.

I quietly and ever so slowly opened the door. I was in luck. The house was pitch-black dark. What a relief.

I thought, "*Good, everybody went to bed.*"

I heard a scratching sound against something metallic and suddenly the room lit up as bright as the sun. Grandmother, sitting there in the dark in her rocking chair, was waiting for me and had struck a match. As she lit a kerosene lantern, she said quite sternly, "*Yore dad's gonna skin you alive in the morning, young man. For the life of me, I jist can't understand how a skinny galoot like you can eat so much food. You'd better git yourself to bed right now, Teddy, afore I give it to you myself.*"

I crawled into bed feeling terribly sorry for myself, knowing the worst was yet to come.

"*They're gonna take turns tomorrow killing me.*"

Using an eight-year-old kid's logic, I began to think things out. Normally, I'd have eaten two or three pieces of chicken. So that meant the remaining three or four pieces weren't mine.

"*Three or four pieces . . . Heck, that's not so bad.*"

Hopefully, Dad would see it my way and the punishment wouldn't be so severe. But, in the event he didn't, and gave me a spanking, I was going to be prepared with a magazine stuffed down the back of my pants.

Once when I was reading the comics, I noticed the *Katz-n-Jammer* Kids had stuffed magazines down the back of their pants to prevent their butts from smarting when they got spanked. Those kids were always finding ways to avoid the pain of punishment. And if it worked for them, then why shouldn't it work for me? I finally fell asleep, reasonably convinced that, with a magazine in my pants, I'd be pretty safe.

My brother Tom shook me awake the following morning. With eyebrows raised and a hint of glee in his voice, he whispered a warning, *"Dad's gonna kill you for eatin' up all our chicken last night."*

Why was it that every time I got into trouble, my brothers got a kick out of watching me squirm?

Again, I began to worry about what punishment I would have to suffer. When I dressed, I inserted a magazine down the seat of my pants and mentally prepared myself for a spanking.

But nothing happened. Not one thing. They didn't even look at me. Maybe it was because I stayed out of sight most of the morning or maybe they thought that just believing that I was going to be spanked was enough punishment. I spent half a day with a magazine stuffed in the seat of my pants looking like I hadn't quite made it to the outhouse. For whatever reason, no one said another word about me swiping the chicken. And thank God, my dumb brother Tom kept his dumb mouth shut for a change.

A Special Christmas

When the weather was horribly cold and it was our bedtime, Mom and Grandma heated bricks, river rock and flat irons on the stove and, wrapping them in old sweaters and towels, placed them under the covers at our feet. After the fire had died down in the cook stove, and since there was no other heat source, the house soon became as cold inside as the night air was outside. And that made it difficult to go to sleep. But once asleep, the chilled air didn't seem to bother us as much.

Christmas Night, 1940, was one of those chilly winter nights. But we paid little heed to the cold weather. We boys were quite happy and contented with life as we snuggled down in our beds, curling our feet around the warmed bricks and flat irons.

We'd just had a very nice Christmas. One reason was that our mother had given birth to our first sister in St. Vincent's hospital just a few weeks earlier. Unfortunately, while Mom was away having her baby, all of the males in the house, including Dad, had become ill with influenza. Poor Grandma . . . She took care of us even though she wasn't feeling well herself. But, she managed to get all of us back on our feet in time to welcome our new sister home.

Mom and Dad named their baby daughter Verna Theresa. But we boys nicknamed her Tudie.

Ignorant of the fact that Dad had been laid off from work, we had little money to spend on necessities let alone Christmas. Our small tree was decorated with homemade paper chains, strings of popcorn and stars cut from colored paper instead of the commercially made ornaments. Maybe we should have taken a page from Grandpa's book and decorated our tree like he did . . . using red reflectors from a wrecked truck. Christmas presents weren't plentiful either. But my parents managed to give each one of us something. They gave me a nifty book filled with pictures and exciting stories about pioneers, cowboys and Indians. It was a small book, not very thick. But I figured it might come in handy in the future if I did something wrong that merited a spanking . . . like inserting it in the seat of my pants.

Yes, it was a wonderful Christmas regardless of all the hardships. And the best gift of all was . . . a little sister.

Tossing Tudie

Mom and Grandma heard a shattering of glass in the back bedroom. They were getting up from the kitchen table to investigate when Tom and I zipped through the kitchen running as fast as we could toward the back door. They yelled at us as we rushed by them, *"What did you kids break? What are you boys up to? Where are you going?"*

As we bolted through the door onto the back porch, we shouted a panicked reply, *"We're going to get Tudie."*

There was no response for just a split second. But as we rounded the corner of the house, we could hear them crying out, *"Tudie? What in God's name have you kids done to your sister?"*

Had those two women known what we were doing a few minutes earlier, they would have killed us on the spot.

We were playing with our four-month-old sister, swinging her back and forth by her hands and feet. On the count of three, we tossed her onto the bed. She loved it, smiling and cooing every time she bounced on the soft mattress. But we made a mistake. We didn't toss her far enough and, landing on the edge of the bed, she nearly tumbled to the floor. I cautioned Tom that we had better toss her just a little

Dad holding Tudie, in 1941

bit farther next time. We did, but we put a little too much muscle into it and threw our little sister completely over the bed and through the window into the yard outside. Tudie made no sound when she fell to the ground. But the sound of shattering glass was deafening.

Mother, with apron flying, ran to the bedroom hoping not to find anything wrong while Grandmother rushed outside behind us. Believe me, it was panic time.

We found Tudie lying on the ground beneath the broken window, cut and bleeding and covered with bits of broken glass. A small shard of glass was stuck in the soft spot of her head. And she also suffered a sizeable gash just above the eyebrow. Her crying sounded more like a shocked whimper.

Grandmother's face paled. Tense with concern and nearly in tears, she very carefully brushed glass and debris from our sis and, ever so gently, gathered her up. Then she passed her through the broken window to my trembling Mother. Both of them tried to remain calm but were probably on the verge of hysteria. I know I was; frightened to death and worried that I'd killed my little sister. I felt like running away and hiding somewhere or disappearing from the face of the earth.

There was little doubt that Tudie needed immediate medical attention. But we had no car and we had no telephone to summon help. Mom had little choice but to carry her infant daughter to the doctor's office in Sherwood, a 2½-mile walk down the railroad tracks in freezing cold weather, a trek that would take at least an hour.

Ever so carefully, they removed her outer clothing examining her thoroughly for other wounds before bundling her in warm blankets. Wisely, they didn't touch the one small piece that was still stuck in her head.

Tom and I had no desire to stay home and face Grandmother's wrath. So, when Mom scooped Tudie up in her arms and went out the door, we wisely went with her. Continually apologizing as we walked, we tried to atone for our youthful stupidity, hoping and praying that Tudie would be okay. Mom set a fast, determined pace but said nothing, her face white with anxiety and lips quivering.

Doctor Rucker removed the glass, treated and bandaged little sister's wounds, and with a reassuring smile, told our mother that her daughter would be okay. Mom sort of wilted into the leather chair in the waiting room when she heard the good doctor's welcome report. We were extremely lucky, and thankful, that our little sister hadn't suffered a more serious injury.

Expecting to receive a good tongue-lashing on the way home, we quietly walked behind Mom. But she said little. When we walked in the house, though, it was a different story with Grandma. She said plenty. She gave us a stern lecture that I thought would never end. But she wasn't nearly as tough on us as we'd expected. This was one time that I knew it was more my fault than it was Tommy's because I was older and should have known better.

After supper, I crawled behind the bed and stayed there until well after dark, hiding out of sight more from shame than out of fear of a whipping. I felt terrible about what had happened and gave some thought to running away. But I gave up that notion when it was time for bed. Our parents probably realized how terrible we felt saying little in the way of a reprimand. For the next two or three days, though, Tom and I were indeed very obedient young boys.

Jumping Jack

As a rule, fishing was loads of fun. But there were a few times when it was a little dangerous too.

One day the entire family, including Grandmother and Dad's brother, Jack, went fishing in one of the rivers near Portland. Jack wasn't one of Grandma's favorite people. But she managed to stifle her biting remarks about him during the ride. Parking the car on the shoulder of a graveled road, we walked across a railroad track, crawled through a barbed wire fence and strolled across a large field to the river. Grandmother noticed an abundance of lush dandelions and decided to take Dick and Dee to gather some greens for a salad while the rest of us assembled our gear, baited our hooks and began fishing.

Everyone but Jack was fishing in just a few minutes. Inept at casting, he repeatedly snarled his line. Dad tried to instruct him how to flick the baited hook into the water. But he was never one to listen to instructions of any kind. Untangling the line three or four times after failed attempts, he threw his pole to the ground in frustration and sat down on the ground to sulk.

We had nearly filled a bucket with trout when Jack decided he had to give it one more try. He strung some line out on the ground behind him, picked up his pole, and gave it a sharp snap toward the water. But instead of the baited hook sailing into the river, it skewered him in the right ear lobe. The hook couldn't be backed out; it had penetrated beyond the barb. The only way to remove it was to finish pushing it through and then cut the shank with wire cutters. Jack, squealing like a doomed rat, wanted no part of that solution. But he changed his mind when Grandma suggested that Dad leave the hook in him . . . and use him as bait.

Power and Water

E arly in the summer of 1941, Dad began the arduous task of install-
ing a power line from the nearest electrical source a quarter of a
mile from our house at Dick Walgraeve's onion barn. The project took
several weeks to complete because all of the materials had to be purchased with cash beforehand.

With the aid of a huge tripod, Dad, Dick Walgraeve and two other
men installed several thoroughly creosoted power poles along the
dusty road to our farm. And then, either an electrician or someone in
authority at the power company strung the wires to the house.

After nearly two years since moving in, we had electric lights, one
bare bulb in each room.

Over time, our parents purchased a few electrical appliances: a
toaster, refrigerator and an Easy wringer washing machine. Dad used
the single light socket in the kitchen as the outlet to provide power to
those things. And when everything was plugged in, the area over the
kitchen table took on the appearance of an electrical spider web.

Our water, still pumped by hand, came from a well just outside the
back door. The well, fed by a vein of frigid-cold water, was always full even
though it was only 11 or 12 feet deep. But because there was no lining, Dad
was concerned that the sandy walls would give way, caving in.

Removing the cover over the well, Tom and I went down inside to
shave the walls, widening it a little more, and to dig it a few feet deeper.
As we did, Dad manually lowered three-foot sections of concrete tile
lining using a small tripod set over the opening. It was a slow and dangerous process. But we managed to insert five tiles in all.

The well never ran dry, producing buckets and buckets of exceptionally sweet, cool water even during the driest summer months.

Our old shack wasn't equipped with a bathroom; so we had no bathtub. But we still managed to bathe.

Once a week, Grandma and Mom placed a washtub in the center of
the kitchen floor and filled it with water from pots heated on the cook-
stove. Because pumping, hauling and heating so much at one time was
tedious and time-consuming, all of us youngsters bathed in the same

water. The last one to get into the tub found the water lukewarm at best and a little grimy, causing me to wonder why bathe at all.

Laxative

I got into trouble with my parents and Grandma regularly without even trying. There were a few times that I deserved to be punished. But most of the time I was as innocent as a newborn lamb . . . if you can believe that.

One example was the time that someone mixed a chewable laxative with Grandmother's Chiclets chewing gum. Who knows, she might have done it herself by mistake. The white laxative squares looked much like the chewing gum, even tasted sweet. But she never noticed the difference when she chewed it. But later! Oh, brother did she notice it. It had the prescribed effect on her and then some.

I didn't do the dirty deed but I was the first and the only one that she blamed. Habitually, when she was after one of our hides, she stuttered and stammered as she yelled out our names beginning with the oldest—me—and down the roster until she finally bellowed the name of the one she wanted.

But this time Grandma only spoke one name. Mine! She was absolutely convinced that I was the culprit no matter how much I denied knowing anything about it. Now, certain that I was going to get a good spanking, I gave some thought to hightailing it for the woods. But doing so would really make me look like the guilty party. In most instances, we boys couldn't escape her anyway because she was so darned fleet afoot. Heck, when she was in her sixties, she could easily outrun a cowpoke's quarter horse on open range. But on that particular day, the only running she did was to the outhouse—and she did that frequently.

The following day, Grandma told Dad what she thought I'd done to her and that I deserved a good whipping. Dad agreed and took me behind the shed. As he pulled his belt from his trousers, he asked me to explain myself.

"*How could you have done such a terrible thing to your grandmother?*"

As I prepared myself for a tanning, I looked him squarely in the eye and said, *"Dad, I didn't do anything to Grandma, and I'm tellin' the truth. But I'll take the blame for it and the spanking just to get it over with."*

We talked for a few minutes just as if we were two men settling a dispute. After we finished, he apparently believed that I was truly innocent and commented with just a trace of a smile, *"I wonder who really slipped the laxative to Granny? Well, you'd better make a hell of a lot of noise, Teddy, 'cause your grandma expects you to get a good tanning."*

He slapped the side of the shed three or four times with his belt as I let out with a few faked yelps, loud enough that the Wagers could have heard me from across the swamp. Grandma was satisfied, Dad was satisfied and most certainly I was satisfied.

A half-hour later, Dad and I were in Sherwood enjoying ice cream cones. The ice cream was good but it wasn't nearly as good as the trust, understanding and fatherly love that I got from my dad that day.

Teddy, Tom, Dickie, Dee, and Tudie

Rout 4 d 103 A
Shearwood Ore

January 1, 1941

My Dear Son

I will try and write you
a few lines in ans wer to your most
Welcome letter I received a short time Back
I hope this find you well we have all
Bin down with the flue toots and
Ethel young Bay was offly sick toots was
Sick afant thee weeks. some time he had
to laff of wark if he had of stay
home I dont think would of Bin so
Bad Ethel was in the hospittle and I
had Toots and all 4 Bays sick at once
and I was so well my self so you
see I had my hands full you see
they have a Boby girl Barn Dec - 5 -
she named her fore me and I havent
Bin Very Well all fall last August
I went to the hop field and was there
Just a week when they had to come and
get me I had a Carbunkle on the small

Grandma wrote a three-page letter to Uncle Oliver on January 1, 1941

2

of. my Back it was as Big over as
Saser the Dr took of out 20 are 30
Cars. out Beleve me it was Some Sore
                are you troping any this Winter
I guess he smore to pritty Deepfor
troping thar is it Cold thire gee I
Wish I could Be Where it Snow
are in a While insted of Rain then sine
mare Rain and it shore daying it
shear today all tho it was Clear all
last week But that one week out
of 3 months Oh well he hoft to have
it thae as we dont guan any thing
did your Crops turn out good
last year I thonkt shore you Would
Come out and see us This fall
But I did not see you,
        all three of toots Brather
are in the Amey are 2 is in the
gards the ather one is in the ccc
afout all the Some thin more

3

McKie said that there was some
of the Monttana Boys at Camp.
Mnnig, that the camp he is it right near
Camp Luis in Washington. did you
get to see mam, when you was in
Billings I got a present from her
But she did Rite any when she sent
it But I am going to write her.
did you get your Package ok.
it was very much. But to let you
Know we thought of you when I dont
get knot to Pick hops I dont have
any moning in the fall and Toots
dont woork stedy in the winter time
then he was out so much. right and
ARomd Xmas time it make pretty
Bad all the way Romd Well I will
Clase for this time Ethel will
Write some she is not here
mom. Lat of love and Best
Wishes mother Write Soon over

Howdy Brother:

Just a few lines on the back of Mothers' letter, I guess she told you that I had a baby girl & named it after her, I'm about tired, as my family it getting big enough. any how I have to make up for some of you kids that arnt married. We sent a Christmas card to Jimmie & Myron but I doubt if they ever answer it. I cant figure out whats the matter with them. We didn't have much of a Christmas Good enough tho. Things are kind of tough for us right around Dec & Feb. as Work isnt any to steady. We're trying to buy a second hand tractor I sure hope we make the grade. we sure need one to cultivate with so we'll have a good crop. I hope you have good luck this year with your crops. You aught to get good prices for your crops this year. I'll be running out of paper, so will have to close - write soon & often. your Sis

Mom added page four to her brother

CHAPTER III

1942

World War II

My mom and dad as well as many of their friends didn't pay a great deal of attention to Germany's attack on Poland in 1939. Of course they were concerned about it, but there was always a war raging somewhere in the world. But throughout the months that followed when the mighty German armies invaded other nations, including France, and bombed Britain, the adults around me became edgy and deeply worried. As the hostilities raged on and on in Europe, my parents, my dad in particular, hoped that our nation wouldn't become involved. But it did. When the Japanese attacked Pearl Harbor in December 1941, we found ourselves thrust into the thick of it.

As young as I was, I could sense the urgency and uneasiness in the conversations of adults when they spoke of the attack on our country. Our lives and the lives of every person I knew were suddenly and drastically altered.

Within weeks, one could find long lines of men waiting at military recruiting offices to enlist in a branch of the armed forces. Many were still in high school, some as young as fourteen. And many were too old, some grandparents and some disabled. But regardless of age or circumstance, every single one of them wanted to fight for our country. And women, too, went to work in factories and defense plants to replace the shortage of men. And they, too, began enlisting in the armed forces, flying aircraft, nursing the wounded, and helping wherever they were needed.

These people weren't just patriots, they were heroes willing to go into harm's way.

Patriotism! That was a word that I seldom heard before the war. But after the attack on our nation, I came to know it very well and what it meant. With the suddenness and force of a tidal wave, patriotism, pride and a determination to defeat our enemies swept across the country. Until the war's end, we questioned everything we did to determine if it was necessary and if it was patriotic.

Petroleum, sugar and rubber were soon in short supply. So were many other commodities. These products were sorely needed to prosecute the war. The government found it necessary to control the purchase of these items to prevent waste and hoarding. So, ration stamps were issued to each family. Without them, certain restricted items could not be purchased.

As the war continued, good cuts of pork and beef became a rarity too. Instead of doing without, some people resorted to eating horsemeat. That sounded disgusting to me. But our parents warned us that it might also be necessary for us to buy some even though we raised our own livestock.

Well, we ate tripe, beef tongue, kidney, and lutefisk. But eating horsemeat for some reason just seemed revolting. I think my dad might have brought some home a few times. But I don't remember eating any of it. I guess it wouldn't have been so horrible. After all, I ate apples and occasionally discovered that I'd bitten into a worm. And although I felt like barfing, it didn't kill me.

A certain kind of vegetable oil used in the production of mayonnaise became scarce. So, another type of oil was used in its place. It wasn't good. It went through our digestive systems like water through a sieve. And without warning, it leaked out of us just as fast. We couldn't prevent it. It was embarrassing. Dark greasy spots stained the seats of the boys' pants, and the girls' skirts. But every one of us suffered the same humiliating problem. So we all looked alike.

The students at Cipole School did everything they could to help in the defense of our country. We saved our pennies and nickels to buy war bonds. And we wore hand-me-down clothing until they were nothing more than rags. When the weather was warm, and if they chose, the boys were permitted to attend school barefoot to save wear and tear on shoes. To some, it was somewhat embarrassing. But it was no big deal to my brothers and me. In our family, we were accustomed to going barefooted. And it gave us an excuse to cut across the hay fields and pastures to avoid the graveled roads.

Enemy air raids were always a possibility. Thus, air raid drills were held routinely during school hours. Most of the time we merely ducked under our desks or filed down into the basement. But, on a few occasions, we were dismissed and told to run home as quickly as possible. And we were warned to cover the windows of our homes and businesses at night. Any light that could be seen by enemy bomber pilots could help them find their objectives.

Unwanted or useless items made of rubber or iron was recycled. And everyone collected paper for recycling—all kinds of paper—newspaper, wrapping paper, writing paper and even catalogs.

We also made do with our old car. We had no choice. Detroit stopped making new automobiles, converting their production lines to making military vehicles and weapons instead. Everyone was in the same boat, so to speak. Until the war's end, we saw the same old heaps on the road, day after day, month after month.

Convoys of military vehicles were seen often on the highways. And on occasion, a train pulling dozens of flat cars loaded with Army tanks, trucks and artillery pieces rumbled past our farm.

The Japanese Empire's surprise attack on our nation so enraged the American people that they struck out at anything Asian. Items that bore the words *Made In Japan*, such as dishes, toys, jewelry, clothing, sporting equipment, were summarily destroyed. And no matter what nationality an Asian was . . . Chinese, Filipino, or Indonesian . . . they were in great peril. Unfortunately, many of them were physically attacked and beaten, and a few even killed.

Many Japanese who lived in Oregon were relatively new to the United States and continued to have strong ties to Japan. Some felt they still owed allegiance to their former homeland. When the chips were down, no one trusted that these new immigrants would be loyal

to the United States. Therefore, to remove any doubt about their loyalty to America and to protect them from being harmed by outraged
citizens, all Japanese were moved to guarded internment camps, even
those who had been here for years.

A Japanese man and his family owned a farm not far from ours.
We never could pronounce his Japanese name. But it sounded like
Tomato. Everyone called him Tommy Tomato. He was a sociable chap
and quite friendly with all of his neighbors. Occasionally, he walked
through the woods to our place to visit. Not long after the beginning
of the war with Japan, American soldiers took Tommy and his family
to a temporary internment camp somewhere in California. We never
saw them again.

It was a traumatic time for them, certainly. But it was just as traumatic, and perhaps more so, for all of us who were native to The United
States.

Dad couldn't blow up stumps any more because he couldn't buy
explosives. That was a definite relief to all of us, in particular to my
mother. Dad's nonchalant way of setting off charges had driven Mom
to near insanity more than once.

Saving enough money during the previous summer, he acquired an
old homemade tractor. With the aid of pulleys and cables, he used it to
continue removing stumps and brush. Perhaps it wasn't as exciting for
the old man but it was a heck of a lot safer. But when gasoline rationing
took effect, even that was curtailed.

There was always concern among us that our dad would have to
leave to fight in the war. But the military refused to take him because
he was too old and had too many dependents. So, he took a second job
working swing shift at Oregon Shipyards in Portland.

However, several of our uncles enlisted. Dad's brothers, Tony
and Mickey, went into the U. S. Army. And his brother Jack had already enlisted in the Navy; he joined a few months before the attack
on Hawaii. Mom's brother Mike also enlisted in the Army. And her
brother James, who had already served a hitch in the Marines, went to
work for the Department of the Navy. Uncle Verle's three oldest sons
joined the service too, Clayton and Dale in the Navy and Irvin in the

Army. Dale joined after finishing high school but was still too young and needed his parent's permission. He was just 17. All three boys experienced combat.

When Uncle Tony was stationed at Fort Stevens near Astoria, he was involved in an unfortunate incident. One night, on beach patrol, he challenged a man walking in a prohibited area near military emplacements. When he made no effort to obey Tony's instructions to halt, my uncle fired his rifle, killing him. Upon examination of the man's body, authorities found a suicide note in his pocket.

Prior to the war, it wasn't unusual to see stunt pilots performing aerobatics including tailspins above our farm. Flying had become popular with young adults during the thirties and into the forties.

But after the onset of the war, formations of bombers and fighter planes replaced private aircraft in the skies over Oregon. And once in awhile, we'd see a Naval coastal patrol blimp floating above our farm. Spotting one created a great excitement among us children. And when our chickens saw one, it caused havoc, scattering them in all directions.

The two-engine P-38 Lightning fighter, an extremely fast and agile plane, was easily our favorite aircraft. They drew cheers from us kids whenever one appeared in the skies above us.

Certainly, the war was much more difficult on our parents than it was on us kids. But we still felt the stress of it. They, and us kids too, learned to cope with the tension and the sacrifices. We persisted and we survived.

Sling Arrows and Pea-Pods

It was early in the day and a little cold outside when Dad McGee, an old family friend and distant relative, came to visit Grandmother Barnes. Tom and I squeezed in behind the old wood-burning cook stove to keep warm and listen to the two old-timers reminisce about their pioneering days. We found the stories and tales about their youth captivating.

While they sat at the kitchen table and talked, they munched on saltine crackers and thin slices of canned meat called Spam. Obviously, Dad McGee had suffered through some terribly harsh winters.

His cheeks and lips were a mottled red color, laced with dozens of tiny purple veins, looking very much like the Spam he was eating.

Before Dad McGee's arrival, Tom and I had been playing in a mud puddle with our pea-pod canoes. We made the little canoes by carefully opening the top seams of pea pods and stripping the peas out. Then we placed small toothpick sized sticks crossways in the pods to hold them open giving them the appearance of tiny canoes. They floated beautifully.

Nearly every nickel we children earned, found, or were given, was voluntarily put into war bonds to help with the war effort. We had no money to spend on toys. So we made our own. We were dependent on our own imagination and our inventiveness and sometimes on our parents' knowledge and wisdom. And we weren't afraid to try to do things. Once I dismantled an old alarm clock in hopes of fixing it. But it was beyond repair—maybe not before I had torn it apart but certainly afterwards. Not able to put it back together again, I used some of the parts to make toys.

A *hummer* was a simple plaything and a favorite of the younger children. It's made with a big coat button and a long piece of string looped through the buttonholes and the ends tied. With the button in the middle of the loop, the string is twisted until it's wound tight. Then, pulling on the ends of the looped string, the button spins in one direction and then the other. That makes it hum.

Being just a little mischievous, I once held the spinning button against one of the other kid's head, entangling their hair in the string. As I said, I only did it once because Grandma caught me.

We also carved sling arrows from shingles. The thick end was carved into a point and the thin end shaped like a feathered tail. The mechanism used to launch the arrow was a stick two feet long with a two-foot piece of string tied to one end. A knot tied in the loose end of the string was inserted into a notch carved on the shaft of the arrow. And holding the launching stick in one hand and the tail of the arrow in the other, the launch stick, when whipped, put the arrow in flight. It could be flung 200 to 300 feet with decent accuracy.

After school during the winter months, we entertained ourselves in a number of ways. One was adorning our shirts with pop bottle caps. They gave our shirts the appearance of being covered with voter buttons. All bottle caps at the time contained a thin wafer of cork that ensured the bottle was firmly sealed when capped. With the aid of a table knife, one could carefully peel the cork from inside the cap without breaking it. Placing the bottle cap on the outside of the shirt and inserting the cork back into the cap from inside the shirt, held the bottle cap firmly and made it look like a button.

We also manufactured stilts, scooters, bean shooters, rubber guns and heel cans.

The scooters were made using old roller skate wheels nailed to a two-by-four piece of lumber. The rubber guns were carved out of a board and equipped with a clothespin giving us the ability to shoot large rubber bands. To arm one, we stretched a rubber band from the muzzle to the clothespin that was attached to the pistol butt. Aim, squeeze and the rubber band launched. It was a lot safer than shooting a B-B gun and a lot more fun.

Grandmother passed on many things to us that she had learned early in her life. One handy contrivance that we made was an Indian travois and we actually used it a few times. She told us how to make flutes from sections of green willow branches. But we never succeeded in getting any sounds out of them other than ugly squawks—certainly nothing musical. She also tried to teach us how to throw an axe and a knife at a target. She wasn't just good; she was frighteningly deadly.

A concoction we learned to make was jet-black ink. In addition to acorns, oak trees produce a large fungus-like ball that we simply called *oak balls*. Some of them grow as large as baseballs and the shells, after drying, become quite firm. Using two or three of the fungus balls, we poked a couple of old rusty nails into each one and placed them in a pint jar filled with water. Then, capping the jar, we buried it in a cool dark place. After a month or two, we exhumed the jar and *voilà*, black ink.

The Lower Place

Dad purchased another ten acres of ground and, overnight, our farm doubled in size. The new addition lay adjacent and north of our original ten acres, extending to Herman Road and the railroad tracks. With the exception of two acres of woods in the southwest corner, the land was bare and flat. Immediately, we began referring to it as *the lower place* because it sloped gently away from the house. And we began referring to our original ten acres as *the upper place*.

With this acquisition, we had plenty of ground for growing hay, enough pasture to get a cow, and more garden space. But it also meant more work for all of us.

Dad paid $600 cash for the property, and that amount included the back-taxes owed by the previous owner. When he handed the money to the seller, one hundred dollars of it was in dimes. He'd saved them in a stainless steel bank that one of his friends had made for him.

The small wooded area was a swell place for us kids to play. It was beautiful and so very peaceful and so green. The floor of the woods was covered with patches of thick moss that turned into a paradise in the spring with the blossoming of trilliums and lady slippers. It was easy to run among the trees and shrub-like bushes because much of the underbrush had been removed. Most of the trees were either fir or oak but there was a large-leaf maple tree next to an Elderberry bush and a willow at the southeast corner of the woods. And there was an abundance of dogwood trees and mock orange shrubs too.

One of the fir trees was deformed. It had grown five or six feet straight up and then was bent horizontal to the ground for four or five feet before growing straight up again. How it got that way was a mystery. But it was fun for the little kids to sit on, pretending to be astride a horse. I tried it once and, as luck would have it, got a big gob of sticky pitch on the seat of my britches.

With Grandmother's supervision, we cut posts, dug postholes, strung wire and completely fenced two-thirds of the lower place for a pasture. And the fenced-in area included the woods. We also dug a well, built two more small sheds and another pigpen. At least half of the upper place became available to us to sow oats with a mixture of vetch to feed our livestock.

Over time, our twenty acres turned into a really dandy little farm.

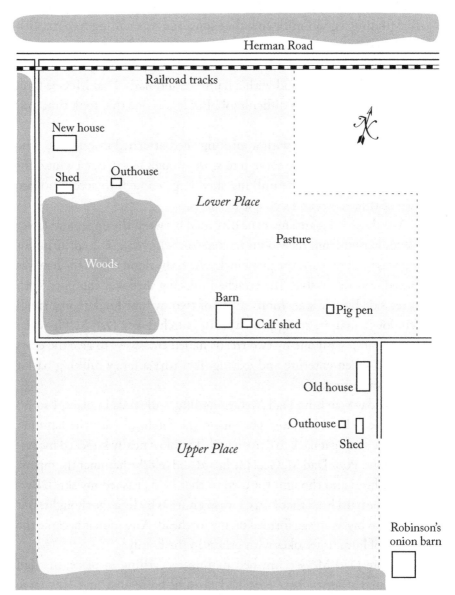

The farm, drawn from memory by the author

Building a Barn

Because of the expense, Dad planned to wait a year or two before buying a cow. But when the war broke out and the price of milk, cream and butter began rising, he quickly changed his mind. But finding a good milk cow that someone was willing to part with wasn't easy.

We needed a barn. And since most of Dad's time was spent working and since he wasn't good with a hammer and nails, Dad McGee took on the task. It wasn't a difficult job. But it was one that took time and ingenuity.

We wanted a barn with a milking shed attached to one side. The barn needed to be large enough to store enough hay to last a winter for three animals. And the milking shed large enough to accommodate two or three cows and a couple of calves.

We chose a flat area near the dirt road between the upper and lower places not far from the woods to construct the barn. The entire building was built on concrete pier blocks. And the floor, where the hay was stored, was removable. The attached milking shed was equipped with three side-by-side stanchions made of two-by-four lumber, one small window, a manure trough and a set of Dutch doors. Dad McGee even built a ramp with one-by-two treads nailed crossways to give the cows traction when entering and exiting. It wasn't a fancy milking parlor but it was functional.

One day watching Dad McGee nailing wall studs in place, I stood too close behind him and got hit on the forehead with the hammer when he swung it back to drive a nail. The blow nearly knocked me unconscious. Poor Dad McGee! He heard and felt the hammer thump me on the head and thought for certain that he'd crushed my skull. But, being the hard head that I was, I wasn't hurt as badly as he thought. But a lump as big as an egg formed on my forehead. And soon it became the object of humorous jokes with others in the family.

Before Dad McGee finished nailing everything in place, my dad purchased a Jersey cow that had already been bred and was large with calf. She was a gentle animal, perhaps because she was older and accustomed to being around humans. It seemed that *Old Jerz* was an appropriate name for her, and it stuck.

Since the barn wasn't finished yet, we housed her in one of the sheds to keep her out of the weather.

Grandma began the chore of teaching me how to milk. At first, I was an eager student wanting to learn something new. But in only a few days the novelty of milking a cow wore off, and it quickly became a drudge. Within a week, I was stuck doing all the milking and doing it twice a day until Old Jerz dried up before delivering her offspring.

The barn was finished just in time for Old Jerz to give birth to her calf. She delivered a female that was a pretty soft brown color. We named her *Taffy*. For several weeks, Taffy nursed Old Jerz, relieving me of milking her. But still I had to make certain that she was milked dry. We called that chore *stripping*.

Jerz didn't give a tremendous amount of milk. But what she did give was thick with rich cream. Dad purchased a wooden churn to make butter and it, too, was a novelty. At first, I found it fun to twist the crank churning the cream and producing butter. But soon that, too, became another boring chore. The one good thing, though, about making butter was the abundant supply of buttermilk it produced. I loved it. But so did the pigs and they, unfortunately, got most of it.

When we asked Dad if he'd buy a mechanical cream separator for us, he blew his cork.

"What the hell's goin' on? I thought movin' to the farm would save us money. But I'm spendin' more now than I ever did. Had to buy more ground, had to build a barn, had to buy a cow, then had to buy hay and a damned butter churn. Where's it stop?"

But, eventually, Pop gave in and bought us a separator. In the meantime, though, we used another method. And it was free. After the milk had cooled and the cream had risen to the surface, we skimmed it off using a big spoon.

Our Dad had a difficult time trying to get the electrical supplies necessary to run power to the barn. So, for a time, we used a kerosene lantern for light when we milked in the evenings. Eventually, when power was available, the milking shed was wired with one light bulb.

The barn became the focal point of our farm, and the place where I spent most of my time doing chores. It wasn't a large barn, just big enough to shelter a few cows and keep a passel of kids working their poor little butts to the bone.

The War Veteran and The Hermit

Clarence Stevens and Joe Miller, two men who lived in the vicinity, led nearly isolated lives. Neither one had a profound impact on my life. But, nonetheless, I still remember them. They were simple, decent, honorable human beings. Too many times we forget to mention folks, like Clarence and Joe, who lived the best way they could with honor and dignity and without harming others.

Clarence Stevens was a disabled war veteran. He experienced combat in Europe during World War I.

In the early 1900s, Clarence and his siblings lived with their parents in a small home not far from the Wager Farm. Just prior to going into the service, he purchased a new Model T Ford. When he left to fight in the war, he parked his car inside the family garage, raising it up on blocks.

Clarence was gone for a couple of years. And when he returned home, he was a different kind of person. He suffered from a severe mental condition termed *shell shock* caused by exposure to intense bombardments of artillery and mortars and raking machine gun fire. He never again acted like a rational, sane human being.

Clarence never drove his car again. In fact, he never took it off the blocks. But he devoted much of his attention to it. Almost daily, one would see Clarence in the garage washing, polishing and dusting his priceless keepsake, keeping it spotlessly clean. As far as I know, he never even started the engine. But, nonetheless, he frequently changed the engine oil, drained water from the radiator, and checked the tires for wear and tear.

We children avoided Clarence because we felt uncomfortable being near him. It wasn't because we were afraid he'd harm us; it was because of his nonsensical actions and rambling speech. One of the odd things that he did was carry an umbrella and wear a black overcoat every time he went outdoors regardless of the temperature and the weather conditions. And he said things like he could hear thunder and see lightening when the skies were clear. I guess we just considered him as being crazy. And that made us feel ill at ease.

Clarence continued to reside in his parents' house after they'd passed away. If one had peeked through the beautiful oval cut-glass window in the front door, they'd have discovered all of the furniture covered with white sheets.

Poor Clarence, his mind muddled and confused, never had a decent chance to experience a full and happy life. Even though he survived the war and lived for a long time, he had sacrificed his mind and his future for his country.

Old Joe Miller lived like a hermit. He was alone and didn't mix much with people. But he enjoyed youngsters dropping in for a chat. He also tolerated adults stopping to chat provided they didn't stay too long. He lived down the road from us in an old shack that was more like a hut than anything else. It was hidden far back in the brush where no one could see it.

His meager little home was constructed of cast-off building materials: discarded shiplap, rough-hewn timbers, and tarpaper. It was so dark inside that I don't believe there were any windows—at least, none clear enough to see through. The place had been built on an old wagon trail that paralleled Herman Road but was well out of sight from passing cars.

At one time, Old Joe had been the janitor at Cipole Grade School. He was rumored to be kin to Chet Fischbuch, a prominent farmer and a member of the Cipole School Board.

A gentle and kindly man who was approaching his eighties, Old Joe had little income to speak of and relied on his own resourcefulness and the goodness of his neighbors. It wasn't that he needed money for food as much as he needed money to buy smoking tobacco for his beat-up pipe. Prince Albert was his favorite tobacco as evidenced by the hundreds of tobacco cans piled near the entrance to his dwelling.

Joe led a fascinating, adventurous life. Hoping to hear about some of the exploits of his youth, we often stopped at his hut on our way home from school. We hung onto every word as he told us frightening, spine-tingling stories of surviving earthquakes, avalanches, blinding blizzards, droughts and devastating floods. When he told a story, time flew by so quickly that oft times we were late getting home to do our chores.

One day, Old Joe was gone and we never saw him again. No one ever told us what had happened to him, whether he died, became ill or moved away to live with someone else. He was just gone. And over time, the old shack, used by passing hobos for temporary shelter, deteriorated and eventually collapsed.

Our old friend Joe was like an old Huckleberry Finn. We missed him and his twinkling eyes and the aroma from his pipe and his tales of adventure. Yes, Joe Miller was a true-to-life legend, a living piece of American pioneer history.

Not The Smartest Kid

I n his younger days, our neighbor, Dick Walgraeve, had been a professional baseball player as evidenced by his gnarled, sausage-sized fingers and large calloused hands. His position was catcher and he played the game before padded mitts were used. Even in his advanced age, he could throw a rock for a distance that seemed like a mile to us youngsters.

A burly man, Mr. Walgraeve was a typical dirt farmer who seldom wore any clothing other than multi-colored checkered-shirts and denim coveralls. He chewed tobacco, ugly foul-smelling stuff, from a plug of Day's Work. It stained the corners of his mouth and sometimes tobacco juice drooled down his chin.

In addition to raising onions in the small swamp in back of us and working his large filbert orchard, he grew several acres of hay and wheat, raised hogs, rabbits and chickens. Most of the farmers used tractors to till their land but he continued to work his farm using two horses, one named Queenie and the other Barney.

Always ready to lend a helping hand, he was a friendly fellow who treated everyone in our family with the deepest respect, especially my dad and mom.

The dead apple tree in our back yard had become an occasional topic of amusing conversation between my parents and Mr. Walgraeve. One morning, Mom stepped outside to get water from the well and was astounded to see a dozen bright red apples hanging from its dead branches. She only needed one guess to know that it was Mr. Walgraeve who was responsible for the tree bearing fruit.

As nice as we kids thought he was, we knew that Mr. Walgraeve had one whale of a problem. He loved to drink alcoholic beverages, beer to be precise, and he drank too much of it too often.

His favorite hangout was a bar in Tualatin called The Spot Tavern. It was a favorite watering hole for several of the local farmers. Getting drunk was perhaps forgivable, but in his case his drinking quite often led to brawling. It wasn't uncommon for his wife, Kate, to ask my father to fetch her husband home. Several times, Dad arrived at The Spot Tavern just in the nick of time to prevent Mr. Walgraeve from becoming involved in a dandy of a donnybrook.

More than once, returning home from grocery shopping in Tualatin, we knew that he'd tied one on the night before because all the mail boxes along Herman Road had been flattened. Driving home in a stupor, he'd run over them with his flatbed farm truck.

One warm day, Mr. Walgraeve was mowing hay near our house when he stopped to get a drink of cold water from our well. But being thirsty for something a little stronger, he asked if my dad kept any liquor. It didn't matter to him if it was beer, wine or whiskey as long as it was alcoholic. And he said he was willing to pay for it.

The wheels began to rotate in my infantile mind. I knew that Dad kept a bottle of whiskey, at least a partially filled one, in his bedroom. As far as I knew, it hadn't been touched in months and months. Never could I remember my dad taking a drink from it. And mistakenly thinking that he had long forgotten about it, I decided to filch it. It was a stupid thing to do. But it seemed like a heck of a good idea at the time, particularly so because Mr. Walgraeve was going to pay me for it.

I couldn't understand how anyone could drink that stuff, though. Once, I secretly took a swig of Dad's whiskey and thought I was going to die. My throat and stomach were suddenly on fire, I couldn't breathe for what seemed like hours and I couldn't see, my eyes blinded by a river of tears. It was the most horrible crap that I'd ever swallowed. And it was certainly much worse than taking a dose of cod liver oil. Heck, drinking whiskey, it's no wonder that Mr. Walgraeve kept running over mailboxes.

The next time he stopped for a drink of water, I produced the bottle of booze and offered to sell it to him for a dollar. That seemed like a lot of money to me. But to my surprise and without asking any questions he gave a dollar bill to me and I forked over the whiskey. I couldn't believe that he'd given me that much money for that awful stuff.

Tickled pink and believing that I'd cut a fat hog, I added the dollar bill to a handful of small change I had saved and put all of it into an old Prince Albert tobacco can for safe keeping. But I worried that one of the other kids would find my treasure. So I decided to hide it in the woods.

I knew of a hole under the base of a maple tree where some varmint had likely lived that seemed like a super spot to hide the can. I stuffed it into the hole followed by several scoops of dirt and a rock to conceal it. Then, I drew a map and wrote directions to where the tobacco can was hidden, all of it written in some kind of kid's code—70 paces southwest from the outhouse to a yew tree, five paces southeast to a large boulder, 18 paces southwest to a fir tree, and 17 paces straight south to the foot of the maple tree. To me, it seemed just like a map that pirates made. But, worried about my treasure, I trudged into the woods every single day for several days thereafter and uncovered it just to ensure that it was safe and to re-count the money.

Then it happened. Dad collared me one day and asked right out of the blue if I knew what had happened to his whiskey. There were no doubts in my mind that he knew that I'd taken it. There was nothing I could do but confess. Pop was angry, blazing mad with me. When I told him I'd gotten a dollar for it, he sternly demanded that I hand it over. He also demanded that I give him the extra change that I had saved, claiming the whiskey was far more expensive than the money I'd collected for it.

Yes, I certainly wasn't smart. My devious little scheme had back-fired and it had cost me dearly. Mr. Walgraeve got the whiskey, my angry dad got all of my money and, in addition to being embarrassed and receiving a good tongue-lashing, all I had left to show for my efforts was the memory of a treasure and an empty Prince Albert tobacco can.

Pitching Onions

Tom and I were two young boys who liked to throw things. One instance was the day we'd gone down the road past Walgraeve's onion barn to fetch the mail. When we were returning home, we took a few moments to test our throwing prowess and accuracy.

A window with eight panes of glass above the large sliding door of Walgraeve's onion barn was a tempting target. There were four panes of glass for Tom and four for me. Using smelly, half-rotten golf-ball-sized onions from the cull pile across the dirt road from the barn, we rifled them like bullets at our target. We knew we were committing a mischievous act. But we never concerned ourselves that there might be consequences.

In a few moments, all the panes of glass had been shattered and onions littered the roadway outside the barn and glass littered the floor inside. It was purely juvenile rationale for us to believe that Mr. Walgraeve would never figure out that it was we who had done the dirty deed. But how could he not know? After all, we were the only two capable boys who lived within a mile of the barn. And we were the only family that lived on the dirt road that ran past it. But, nonetheless, we thought that we would never be blamed.

Twenty-four hours later, Dad found out what we'd done and scorched our ears with a severe scolding. Then we marched down the road to Mr. Walgraeve's onion barn to face him. With our heads bowed in shame, we apologized for our destructiveness and promised never to break another of his windows. After cleaning up the onions and broken glass, we went home to face more punishment . . . rumps blistered red.

Little Crip

We already had a lot of stinking chickens running around loose on the farm, but Grandma just had to purchase more of them, another 200 baby chicks. Most of them would be raised for food. But that also meant that I would be shoveling a lot more chicken manure.

Among the new batch of chicks, I discovered one scrawny, feeble little thing that was crippled. One of its legs was deformed and useless. It could only hop about on one foot.

Unfortunately, the animal world can be cruel and unforgiving. The other chicks viciously picked at the poor thing. And eventually they would have killed it. I couldn't allow that to happen, not even to a chicken. So, I adopted it. And like a mother hen, I chased away any chicken that became too aggressive with my little pet. I liked it and it liked me. And soon a bond formed between us. This was truly the one and only chicken that I ever tolerated.

Hopping about on one leg, it began to follow me. It had the run of the farm where the other chickens had to be penned. I named my little feathered friend *Crip* and it responded to the name when I called. Little *Crip* soon began meeting me near the barn in the afternoons when I returned home from school.

But, one day, my little chicken wasn't there to greet me. I sensed something awful had happened to it. And I was right. It was dead. It had been killed when a set of old bedsprings that had been propped against the apple tree in the back yard toppled over and crushed it. Heartbroken and crying, I took my little chicken into one of the fields and buried it, offering a child's simple prayer, vowing never to forget my faithful little friend.

Crazy Stuff

When having a chat with my grandmother, she couldn't help but interject a few colloquial sayings and euphemisms into the conversation. One of her many expressions was, *"Practice what you preach."*

She had a lot of them, for instance:

"As if you don't know, I oughta skin you alive."
"I'm gonna tan yore britches."
"Jumpin' gee hosiphat."
"You danged rubber necked galoot."
"Yore the spittin' image of . . . ."
"You ain't worth the powder to blow you to hell."
"You ain't worth yer salt."
"Yore a-lyin' thru yore teeth."
"What in tarnation . . . ?"

One amusing saying that she repeated often was, *"If ya gotta go, ya gotta go and if you don't go when ya gotta go, when ya go to go, you'll find you've already gone."*

Grandma claimed that I walked pigeon-toed. And she also claimed that I walked like a knock-kneed camel. I'd seen a live camel at the zoo and pictures of them on packages of cigarettes. They had big humps on their backs but I'd never noticed any that were knock-kneed. But, there was proof that something was wrong with my feet. The heel of my right shoe rolled inward and wore down quicker than the rest of the sole. She believed that walking with my toes splayed outward would prevent the roll and improve my posture. But, being a rambunctious, daydreaming kid, I seldom remembered to practice what she preached. And I'm still walking funny.

"Don't step on a crack or you'll break your momma's back."

We couldn't help but step on a crack when we walked across the shiplap floors of our house. So, that one didn't count. But anything that contained the number 13 meant bad luck, and we avoided walking under ladders too.

One event, though, that I knew would bring me good luck was spotting the first wild trillium lily in bloom. Another was finding four-leaf clovers. And catching a red-winged grasshopper always meant good fortune too.

Grandma had some strange superstitions. I guess we all did. Throwing spilled salt over one's shoulder or taking three steps backward should a black cat cross one's path were silly superstitions in her mind. But she believed that if you slept out on the ground, you should always surround yourself with a rope to keep snakes from crawling too close. And if you suffered a nosebleed, you had to drive a knife into the ground to stop it.

Well, my nose bled easily. Therefore when I had the sniffles, I had to be careful not to blow my nose too vigorously otherwise the bloody flood gates would open. It wasn't unusual for me to suffer from nosebleeds two or three times a month during the summers. So, every time it bled, and hoping that my grandmother was right, I ran out into the backyard and stabbed a knife into the ground. And by golly, they stopped—sooner or later—they stopped just like Granny said they would. By summer's end, though, half of Mom's kitchen knives were stuck in the ground somewhere in the back yard.

Chicken Feet Soup

My resourceful and depression-wise grandmother could make a meal out of weeds, fir cones and apple cores. For one of her homemade meals, she used, of all things, the feet and lower legs of chickens.

When most people butchered their chickens, they discarded the feet. But not my grandmother; she knew that they were the key ingredients to making a thick, tasty soup. It sounds quite disgusting. But believe me it was delicious, especially when it was served with homemade noodles, biscuits or dumplings. And neither Dad nor his children ever turned down a second helping.

The preparation of the soup was simple. She parboiled the chicken feet for a few moments, skinned them and finished stewing them with seasoning and vegetables.

Mom and Grandmother busied themselves one afternoon making homemade noodles and an extra-large batch of chicken feet soup because Grandma's old friend, Dad McGee, was coming for an afternoon visit and dinner. The soup and noodles were one of his favorite dishes. When he knew that chicken feet soup was being prepared, he never turned down an invite to supper. And he never turned down an offer to take an extra helping home.

Sometimes Mom allowed us to help her make the noodles, cutting the flat sheet of dough into thin strips. But we never cut them thin enough to suit her. And on this particular day, when Dad McGee was coming for supper, she refused our offer to help because she wanted them cut perfectly.

We spotted the old fellow's car coming down the road and, letting out a whoop, ran outside to greet him. Although his age caused him to be slow afoot, it certainly did nothing to slow his driving. Like a bucking bronco in a rodeo, his old Model A Ford coupe leaped and jumped and bounced from one rut to another, kicking up a rooster tail of fine, powdery brown dust. As he pulled up to the house, a bag of Bull-Durham smoking tobacco, hanging by its drawstrings from the rear-view mirror, spun and bounced around like a yo-yo.

Most drivers, including my dad, carried bags of Bull-Durham in their cars, most of them hanging from the rear view mirrors. They used them to clean road oils and grease from their windshields during inclement weather. To me, with my imagination always in high gear, they looked like small punching bags bobbing around.

Mom and Grandma served up a very nice dinner. And afterward, we kids gathered around Dad McGee and Grandmother to listen to them tell one story after another about the good old days. I never could figure out why they referred to their past experiences as *the good old days*. Nothing they did was easy and every problem they encountered seemed to be insoluble. And yet, the way they talked and carried on, they believed they had led marvelous lives and had lived during the best of times.

Eagerly, Tom and I presented our model airplanes to Dad McGee for his inspection. Dick proudly displayed his collection of chicken rings, a long string of them. Because we had so many chickens, we slipped colored plastic rings on their legs so that we could easily determine which ones were good laying hens and which were the non-layers. The rings, red, green, yellow and blue, also gave us an indication as to the age of the fowl. When we butchered chickens, Dick was there to salvage the rings to keep for re-use and as souvenirs.

When Dad McGee went home, my parents gave him a jar of homemade jam, a quart of chicken feet soup with noodles, a bag of homemade biscuits and a couple pounds of real butter. Because of the war, real butter was as expensive as gold and he, indeed, was happy to have it. He wasn't very fond of margarine, a substitute for butter that he referred to as *colored lard*. Margarine looked just like white lard and, at the time, a packet of orange powder was included with the sale of each pound so that it could be mixed to give it a yellow color and the appearance of real butter.

Our family wasn't destitute. Still we were nearly as poor as church mice. But, we kids ate well, we were warm, we were loved, and we were happy. We were lucky too. Heck, we didn't know of another kid in the world who dined on homemade noodles, biscuits, real butter and honest-to-goodness chicken feet soup.

The Runaway

Whenever the weather was raining, snowing or sleeting—in other words horrible—I had to wade through ruts and puddles filled with sloppy muck to get to the barn to milk the cow, collect eggs and feed the hogs. To keep my feet dry, I wore knee-high rubber boots.

But, several times during one miserably wet period, I found my boots wet inside as I was pulling them on in the morning. And occasionally, when I turned them upside down, water spilled out. I couldn't figure it out.

"How can water get inside a rubber boot?"

Granny offered an explanation that most likely the boots had tiny holes in them allowing the water to leak in while I was wearing them. Well, she was a wise woman and that seemed to be a plausible explanation. But still it seemed strange to me that my boots were dry when I pulled them off in the evening and wet when I put them on in the morning.

Checking the boots, I found nothing wrong with them, no holes, no cracks, no defects, nothing.

Then, one dreary morning, the mystery was solved. I caught my seven-year-old brother Dick using one of my boots as a urinal. Yes, he was peeing in them. I wanted to kill the little brat on the spot.

Grabbing his arm none too gently, I demanded an explanation why he used my boots as a toilet. Of course, no answer was acceptable. But his excuse was that it was just too cold outside to go to the outhouse. Hoping to inflict a little immediate punishment on him, I squeezed his arm tighter and tighter until he began to squall. Only then did I let go. I would have beaten the tar out of him had I thought I could have gotten away with it without getting into trouble. And had I told my parents what he'd done, I was quite certain that they wouldn't have done a thing to him.

So, determined not to let him escape unscathed, I began to devise a simple but devious plan of my own to get even.

As I was preparing to go to the barn to milk the following morning, the time to repay little brother for his misdeed was at hand. I was certain that no one else was awake but, as luck would have it, I was dead wrong. You can imagine how horribly embarrassing it was when my grandmother caught me peeing into my little brother's shoe. The way she carried on, one would have thought that I had just peed into a blind man's begging cup. Not only did she give me a stinging spank across the rump with a belt, she also gave me a verbal scalding—not just a scolding.

"You ornery little whelp, Teddy! What in tarnation do you think yore doin'? You oughta be ashamed of yerself and you the oldest kid in the family. Are you too blamed lazy to go to the outhouse like the rest of us? I'm gonna tell yore dad what I caught you doin', young man. You oughta have yore miserable hide tanned every day for the next six months."

Why me? Dick had gotten away with it at least a dozen times but not me. I did it once and got caught. The other kids got away with stuff all the time. It just wasn't fair. And no one ever believed my excuses or reasons, either, no matter how legitimate.

One Saturday, I caught my brother Tom playing with one of my model airplanes. Taking it away from him, I found that it had been damaged. He'd probably done it accidentally but, still, he shouldn't have handled it without my permission. His disregard for me and my things infuriated me. He was always messing around with my property.

In angry retaliation, I grabbed a broom and took a swipe at one of his models hanging from the ceiling. And I smashed it to bits.

Recovering from the shock at what I'd done, he became enraged and screamed, "*I'm gonna tell Grandma what you did to my plane, you big brat. You just wait and see. You're gonna get it good.*"

He went running into the kitchen bawling like his world had come to an end.

"*Mom! Grandma! Teddy just broke my airplane with the broom. He just smashed it all to pieces.*"

Well, I got the usual swat on the rear end and a severe rebuking for not being sensitive to other people's property. Yes, that's right—me—not sensitive to other people's property! He did it to me first, the very same thing. And I was the one to catch hell. It did me no good to explain or give a reason. They never listened to my side of the story anyway. No! No one ever did.

Thoroughly convinced that my parents cared little about my feelings and that I was constantly being put upon, I set about conjuring up a scheme to inflict some mental anguish on them, figuring it would bring them to their senses. The best course of action was to make them believe that I had run away and that I would never be seen again. Perhaps that would jolt Mom and Grandma into realizing just how horribly they had misjudged and treated me.

Pouting and filled with self-pity, I scribbled a note, telling them that they needn't ever worry about me again. I was leaving home and running away to some far-off land never, never again to return. Laying the note on my pillow, I left the house, crossed our dirt driveway, and hid in a large, dense thicket of wild blackberries next to Walgraeve's hay field. From there I could watch the house. And from there I hoped to see the concern and anguish on their faces when they finally realized their oldest son was really gone forever.

Several hours passed and, to my disappointment, not one darned thing happened. Absolutely nothing. Oh, occasionally a member of the family ventured outside, but only to go to the outhouse or to fetch water from the well. But not one of them appeared to be worried or disturbed or even looking for me. I fast became disappointed by their apparent lack of concern. Maybe they really didn't care.

With the setting of the sun, I became even more miserable because of the cold and damp weather. And, sitting in that stickery, scratchy thicket of blackberry vines didn't help my disposition much either.

So, until I could devise a better scheme to convince them to listen to my side of the story once in a while, I gave up being a runaway and returned to the house. Besides, it was suppertime . . . and I was getting awfully hungry.

Hops and Strawberries

Like it or not, Tom and I had to work in the berry fields and hop yards with Grandma. She was willing to ride herd on us. And Mom was more than happy to let us go, to get us out of the house and from under foot.

This was my second year going to the fields with Grandma and Tom's first. He couldn't go the previous year because he was too young. But, heck, I was only nine. I remembered that I was in the grip of youthful enthusiasm, eager to earn money and hopeful of being wealthy by the end of summer. But after working just one miserably hot day, I knew that I wouldn't be rich for at least three or four more years. And I knew that Tom was going to suffer the same disappointment.

We picked berries for two weeks in Jess Brown's berry fields in the Silverton Hills. We didn't earn but a small pittance. But the adventures that Tom and I experienced together were exhilarating.

We camped in one of ten worker-cabins that were built near the berry fields. Ours was the first one on the road, perched at the edge of a small creek. Every day, after picking strawberries in the hot sun, Tom and I raced to the cabin, changed into short pants and jumped into the creek's cool water.

Busy making a little dam in the stream one warm evening, we were suddenly startled by the sounds of a loud crash. We whirled around just in time to see a startling sight—our cabin sliding backwards, coming to rest, sitting atilt on the edge of the creek's bank.

When we left to play, Grandmother was preparing to take a bath in the cabin in an old washtub. We could hear her yelling obscenities and threats from the top of her lungs. It was darned evident by the scalding sound of her voice that she wasn't hurt but that someone else was about to be.

"You drunken fools! What in tarnation is wrong with you?"

Tom and I scrambled up the creek bank as fast as we could to see what had happened.

Two men, both of them obviously intoxicated, had crashed their convertible car into the front of our cabin. They didn't appear to be injured but weren't moving, apparently numbed by our grandmother's venomous tirade.

Grandma was standing in the doorway with a wet blanket draped about her, her hair disheveled and covered with soap. She wasn't at all a pretty sight. Seething with anger, she threatened the two fellows with bodily harm if they dared try to run away, her voice blaring loud enough to make a deaf person cringe. No one, not even God, could have saved those two fellows from certain death had she had easy access to an axe.

Jim Muller, a family friend who was also working in the fields with his wife and kids, came quickly with other men to help. He warned the two inebriates to stay in the car otherwise Granny would chase them down and give them a good thrashing with a horsewhip. By the looks on their faces, they knew that he was giving them good advice and did just as he suggested.

After several hours, a deputy sheriff arrived to take charge of the two men. They'd sobered some by then and had become acutely aware of their sorry predicament.

Jim Muller

After restoring the cabin to its pier block foundation, our lives returned to a somewhat normal state, but only after Grandmother's temper had cooled. Even then, anyone with an ounce of sense stayed clear of her.

Tom and I made daggers from dried pieces of oak wood. And we found that they were more durable and the points remained sharper for a longer period of time if we seared the blades in a hot fire.

I had caught an old crawdad and had made a pen in the creek in which to keep it. It had lost most of its dark pigmentation and, with age, had turned a light pink.

One day after picking berries, we were playing at the creek and throwing our homemade knives at a target fixed to the stream bank. Tom, acting a little bit ornery, threw his dagger at my crawdad and, intentional or not, hit and killed it. In disbelief at what he'd done, I became livid and wanted to beat the tar out of him. But he ran lickety-split away from me, knowing that I had no chance of catching him. In my seething anger, I threw my dagger at him. I really didn't intend to hit him, but the dagger found its mark and struck him in the heel. He ran straight for the cabin, screaming at the top of his lungs.

Yes, I was in a heap of trouble again. Grandmother slapped a band-aid on the tiny wound in his foot and then slapped a switch across my backside a couple of times. I know darned well his foot didn't smart near as much as my blistered bottom. That night after he'd gone to sleep, I pinched the daylights out of him and caught hell again. But it was worth it.

One of the downsides we experienced working in the berry fields was the lunch Grandma prepared for us every day. It was Lipton's soup. She must have packed a hundred packages of that stuff in her suitcase. Agreeably, Lipton's is a great soup to eat . . . but only occasionally and not for every doggone lunch.

Grandma allowed Tommy to go to the cabin early every day to heat water for the soup. But she never let me go; claiming that my hands were larger and I could pick berries faster. That was a lot of baloney. She didn't want me going because she was afraid that I'd get into her stash of Chiclets chewing gum.

After ten days in camp, both Tom and I had become infected with boils. Mine was on the outside of my left thigh and Tom's on the back of his neck. Granny told us they were carbuncles because they had multiple core openings. She was certain that we'd become infected when playing in the creek. She worked on us every evening applying salves and bandages to the painful, oozing sores. But they never completely healed, not until we went home. Mine left a nickel-sized scar on my thigh. As for Tom, I don't believe he suffered any scarring whatsoever.

The previous year when Grandma and I were in the hop fields, she suffered from a carbuncle so large and horribly painful that we were forced to go home. That thing didn't heal for a month.

After strawberry season ended, Dad dutifully arrived in the family car, pulling his old two-wheeled trailer to haul us and all of our belongings back home. Tom and I were more than ready to go even though it meant we'd have to do the chores again. And we were more than ready to dig into one of Mom's wonderful suppers. It wasn't as if Granny had starved us; it was just that we wanted something more than soup.

Not many days passed before we were on the road again, this time going to Independence to pick hops and prunes on the Horst Brothers' farm. Conserving fuel, the maximum speed allowed on the open highway during the war was 35 miles an hour. The low speed limit didn't matter, however, because our old Plymouth sedan pulling a loaded trailer couldn't move much faster anyway.

As we rolled down the highway, something happened. One of us pointed, shouting, *"Hey! Look! A wheel's goin' by us!"*

Pop smiled but only momentarily when he realized that it was one of the wheels from our own trailer. Dad slowed our car to a stop as the wheel bounced into the ditch in front of us.

The trailer was packed full of clothing, kitchen utensils, bedding and other supplies to help us survive the next two or three weeks. Pop had been in a good mood before the wheel came off, but when he realized that the tools he needed to reattach the wheel were in the trailer under our clothing and supplies, he became surly and grumpy. We had to unload everything alongside the road. To passersby we probably looked like a family of migrants from Oklahoma. After the wheel was fixed and the trailer reloaded, we resumed our drive down the road. And only then did Dad's jovial mood return, as if nothing had ever happened.

The workers' cabins at the hop yards were just as they'd been in the berry fields—meager, bare, musty, and not particularly clean. All of the cabins were equipped with two sleeping bunks made of rough-hewn plank-timber. And the mattresses were nothing more than huge pillowcases stuffed with straw and not at all comfortable. Each cabin was also numbered. And to my delight, we were assigned the same one that Grandma and I had occupied the year before.

The camp was terribly overcrowded. The number of people was ten times that of the berry fields.

Some of the pickers were migrants traveling from one field to another, from one state to another. Many of them had developed poor sanitation habits and were infected with head lice. Within days of arriving at the camp, nearly everyone, especially the children, had become contaminated with a dose of those minute pests. Grandma had a cure, however, using kerosene lamp fuel and a fine-toothed comb that we called a *cootie comb*. The kerosene stunk and burned our scalps but it very effectively killed the lice.

We itched and squirmed and spent many uneasy nights trying to sleep in our bunks. We weren't really able to determine whether it was lice or bedbugs gnawing on us or if it was just the scratchy straw mattresses that made us feel so uncomfortable.

Every morning, stock trucks hauled us out to the hop yards. We usually began picking at daybreak. And it always seemed like lunchtime would never come.

Because of our ages—Tom eight and I ten—we were probably the youngest pickers in the hop yards. I had my own tiny hop basket that was a quarter the size of a normal hop basket. And we went barefoot, wore coveralls and straw hats. My straw hat had become so frayed and frazzled that it drew everyone's attention.

The previous year, a reporter and photographer from the newspaper in Portland came to the fields to do an article on the hop harvest and the pickers. Before leaving, they took a picture of me wearing my

'RAYED HAT and makeshift basket fail to dampen the spirits of this lad.

Teddy picking hops, from an old newspaper clipping

funny-looking straw hat and putting hops into my little basket. A few days later my picture and an article about me appeared in the newspaper. And suddenly I felt like a movie star, reveling in my sudden popularity.

Hop vines grew up strings, like beans, to a horizontal wire suspended by stout poles about 12 to 15 feet above the ground. If the wires hadn't been so high, they would have looked like clotheslines. To pick the hops that grew on the vines beyond our reach, the wire was fixed so that it could be lowered using a long pole. One only had to yell *wire down* and a man would disengage the wire, lowering it to within our reach.

Grandmother eventually allowed me to yell *wire down* when we needed the wire lowered. At first, I was a little bashful but after a few times I could yell *wire down* as well as anyone else in the field but with a kid's squeaky voice.

By the end of the summer, Tom and I made about eight dollars each. And that included the money we made picking strawberries. It wasn't much by today's standards but it was a tidy little sum for youngsters in those days.

We were so eager to go home that, when Dad came for us, we literally threw our belongings into the trailer not caring whether our things had been properly packed or not.

On the way down the highway, a wheel rolled by us. Yes, it was one of ours. And wouldn't you know it! Those blasted tools were in the bottom of the trailer buried under the blankety-blank load. You can guess what Daddy said.

The year 1942 was the last time we went to the hop yards and berry fields. Gasoline rationing was one reason for not going. And Mom and Dad needed us home to do the chores for another. To be honest, that didn't hurt my feelings one iota.

Spice of Life

Our kitchen was a pleasant room and the focal point of our home. During those times when the weather was nasty and we couldn't sit outside on the back porch, we gathered in the kitchen to relax, converse, and share as a family. With a fire in the old wood-burning cast-iron cook stove, it was as cozy and warm as toast.

We kids did our homework on the kitchen table and even built our model planes and played simple games there. But on weekends, with Dad and us kids hanging around, it was an absolute zoo.

During the summer months when the weather turned insufferably warm and we couldn't sit inside, we tried to cool the place by leaving the unscreened windows and door open for better air circulation. But doing so allowed moths, voracious mosquitoes, pesky flies and an occasional bat unhindered entry.

Mom and Grandmother prepared many delicious meals in that kitchen, especially on Sundays and whenever we had company. The meals were huge because all of us, from the time we could hold a fork and spoon in our hands, were hefty eaters.

Mom's specialty was pan-fried chicken. She couldn't make enough of it to satisfy me. I loved it. Even when I was playing in the woods a quarter mile away, I knew when she was cooking chicken for supper; I could smell the aromas.

Mom and Grandma prepared other scrumptious meals for us too: beef pot-roast with potatoes and gravy, succulent pork roast and, every so often, a huge pot of spaghetti and meatballs. Mom's spaghetti sauce was made with fresh stewed tomatoes, sprigs of fresh basil and a healthy dose of crushed sage leaves. And she made the meatballs with freshly ground sausage and hamburger, spiced with minced onion and chopped cloves of strong-tasting garlic.

The more spices Mom used, the better I liked it. But once in a while, I wished that she'd have used more. One day when I was ten, I got into a bit of trouble when I added my own spice to hers. It seemed like a great idea at the time . . . but it wasn't.

Late in the spring of 1941, Dad took Tom, Dick and me on a fishing trip to the White River near Tygh Valley in Central Oregon. Unlike the green wooded area where we lived, the high dessert was dry and arid. And because it was different, it was exciting and interesting to us kids. But it was also dangerous. Rattlesnakes inhabited the countryside. Walking to the river, I warily scanned every dark crevice, every piece of scrub and sagebrush along the trail looking for anything that slithered on the ground.

The fishing was loads of fun and quite satisfying. So was stuffing ourselves with the lunch that Mom and Grandmother had prepared for us. We kids also did a little exploring and scoured the banks of the river looking for anything interesting to bring home, in particular agates.

Before leaving, I snapped off a branch of sagebrush as a souvenir. Being a stupid kid, I thought that the sage leaves were the same as the spice Mom used in her cooking. Heck, it smelled the same to me. And besides, why was her spice called sage if it didn't come from sagebrush?

It was a Sunday nearly a year later when Mom cooked up a big spaghetti dinner for us with all the trimmings: a green salad, toasted garlic bread and dozens of meatballs in a tomato sauce laced with our own fresh basil. When I overheard Mom mention to Grandma that the basil would have to do because she was out of sage, a light went on in my hollow head. I remembered the branch of sagebrush that I'd brought home some time back. I still had parts of it in a small jar.

"Wow! I can fix that spaghetti real easy."

One would believe that my fly-catching lizard scheme would have cured me of dreaming up something I thought would be helpful. But it didn't. No one noticed as I furtively added a handful of the musty, pungent dried sagebrush leaves to the simmering spaghetti sauce on the stove.

Sitting down to dinner, everyone was eager to dig into some good, flavorful spaghetti, me included. Anxiously, I waited to see if anyone would notice the added spice. And they did. Yes, they certainly did—immediately. In just seconds, their faces screwed up like they'd been sucking on the toes of dirty socks. It tasted just awful, absolutely horrible, and when Dad took his first bite, he winced and gagged as if he had a hair in his mouth.

"What in the world happened to our supper, Ethel?"

All of us began spitting the horrible-tasting stuff into handkerchiefs, cups and any other container we could find. Mom was just as mystified as everyone else—everyone other than me, of course.

Then Tommy pointed at me and said, *"I'll bet Teddy did something to poison us."*

All eyes immediately focused on me and it was my goose that was cooked. What could I say? Had it been the right type of sage, they would have been darned happy. But, because of my stupidity, our supper was ruined. And everyone was put out with me.

We ate pancakes and fried bacon with our salad, not nearly as delectable as spaghetti with meatballs. But it was filling. Actually, though, the spaghetti with my own variety of spice didn't go completely to waste. It made good slop for the hogs.

Not too many months passed when Mom prepared another spaghetti dinner. With the exception of toting wood for the stove, I was banned from the kitchen. I just couldn't understand why they were so concerned; Grandma had found the remnants of my sagebrush and burned it. But, like a good little boy, I stayed clear, not wanting to risk getting into trouble again and missing a good dinner.

Sitting down to eat, Mom dished out healthy servings to each one of us. It was great fare and the taste was excellent, as good as any that I could remember. But Grandmother stopped eating and peering down at her plate, asked Mom, *"What in tarnation is this, Ethel? It's not a meatball. It's too blamed hard!"*

Bewildered, everyone leaned over the table to look at the irregularly shaped, golf-ball sized, pink gob on Grandmother's plate. As she scraped away spaghetti and tomato sauce for a closer examination, I began to get an uneasy feeling as if I were going to be blamed for something I didn't do. But before anyone could accuse me of anything, my six-year-old brother Dick broke the silence.

"It's a piece of salt. I broke a chunk off the cow's salt lick for the pusketti."

For several long seconds, not one of us said a word, just stared at the spaghetti on our plates. In my mind, I visualized Old Jerz slapping her tongue across the salt lick, drooling on it and slobbering on it, slime drizzling from her nose on it. And the moment it all sunk in, I knew that I was going to barf . . . and very soon.

Fortunately, I was closest to the back door and the first one through it. But my daddy was close behind. I made it to the potato patch before throwing up my supper, my lunch and all the meals that I'd eaten during the week. But poor Dad! He barely made it off the back porch before he let loose.

Again, we ate pancakes and fried bacon for supper, and again the pigs feasted on specially seasoned spaghetti. And again, they really enjoyed it.

But the spaghetti capers didn't end there. When Jim and Lela Muller and their kids dropped in unexpectedly to visit one weekend, Mom had little grub in the house in the way of meat, only a few strips of bacon and a couple of pork chops. So, she chopped up what she had, dumped it into a pot with stewed tomatoes, garlic, basil and sage and prepared to feed us a big spaghetti dinner.

In another pot, she boiled the spaghetti. When it had become tender, she stepped out onto the back porch to drain the hot water from it . . . and accidentally dropped the pot. Spaghetti spilled out all over the old porch. Any normal person would have screamed to high heaven and quit right then and there. But not Mother. Undaunted, she scooped it up, threw it back into the pot and, furiously pumping water with one hand, rinsed the dust and grit and farm-yard gunk from the spaghetti with the other.

This was one time that the pigs didn't get our dinner. It was delicious. Every one of us ate heartily. And not one of us noticed the extra *spices*.

Tommy's Experiments

Always thinking up some crazy stunt or experiment, Tom snuck out of the house with Granny's big black umbrella. He was intent on parachuting from the roof. He crawled atop the house with the mistaken belief that he was about to float to earth like the down of a thistle. But, when he jumped, he plummeted like a meteor and crashed among Mom's hollyhocks nearly breaking his fool neck.

Another mystery confronted Granny, trying to figure out how her umbrella got turned inside out.

Not many days passed when the poor woman was awakened from her nap by a noise that sounded like a gunshot. Anxious and worried, Granny hurried outside to find Tom and me standing behind the woodpile, he with a hammer and a screwdriver in his hand. Grandmother asked if we had the .22 caliber rifle and if we'd shot it.

"We don't have the twenty-two, Grandma. It's still in the house and we didn't shoot at anything."

Grandmother returned to the house to find the rifle still in Dad's bedroom where it was supposed to be. She most likely thought that she had only dreamed it was a gunshot and never said another word to us.

But it wasn't any dream. It was my brother Tom performing another one of his experiments. The idiot tried to chisel a .22 caliber bullet in half using the hammer and screwdriver. The blow detonated the cartridge sending the projectile in one direction, the casing in another and Tom and me scurrying behind the woodpile, scared half to death.

Give Mother A "Brake"

Mother was a sweet, loving woman but she killed things—albeit accidentally. Trying to learn how to drive a car, she killed an apple tree, a pig, and our laurel hedge. She put dents in the family car like a western gunslinger carved notches on his six-shooter.

Several times during her life, my mom did her best to master the art of driving a vehicle. But she never quite succeeded. However, she did succeed in scaring the hell out of everyone who lived nearby and managed to rid the neighborhood of a couple of stray cats and a slow-footed 'possum.

Verdi Muller, the daughter of our friends Jim and Lela Muller, had formed a close bond with Mom although she was nine years younger. She had given birth to her second child in April, a girl she named Launa.

Late in the fall, Verdi brought her new baby to visit, staying with us for a week. Tom and I slept on the floor, surrendering our bed to them so little Launa could sleep in something warm and comfortable.

Even though Mom was in her late twenties, she looked as young if not younger than Verdi. And when they were together, they acted like two teen-age kids—especially when they got all gussied up. Both Mom and Verdi smoked. In fact, they used long-stemmed cigarette holders, a bit of a fad at the time. And had they worn evening gowns, they could have posed as attractive models on advertising billboards.

One morning, they braided each other's hair into pigtails, applied makeup and dressed, wearing the latest fashion in women's slacks. Out of cigarettes, they asked Grandma if she would watch the little ones for them while they drove Verdi's car to Jurgens' Park store near Roamers' Rest to buy more, planning to be gone no less than an hour. Grandma agreed but, in one of her snippy moods, she had to make a comment about Mom's appearance.

"You mark my word, Ethel! Yore gonna git yoreself into trouble dressin' up like a couple of dad-burned teenagers. Ya oughta know better'n that."

Mom seldom went to Jurgens' store. But when she did she was always with Dad and a passel of kids. Not recognizing her and believing she was too young to buy tobacco products, Johnny Jurgens wouldn't sell cigarettes to Mom without identification. Irritated by his refusal, her dander roused, Mom commanded, *"Look at me, Johnny. Dammit! Look at me! I'm Elmer Pileggi's wife and I've got five squallin' kids. You've seen me before. You know me, for Pete's sake."*

But Johnny still didn't recognize or believe her and continued shaking his head negatively. Verdi, barely 18 years old, produced her identification and put an end to it, purchasing the cigarettes for Mom. Pretty steamed when they returned to the car, Mom complained that had she looked like a slob instead of being dressed up, she could have purchased the smokes, no questions asked.

Maybe they had agreed beforehand or maybe it was to cool Mom's temper or maybe it was just out of ignorance but, whatever the reason, Verdi allowed Mom to drive the car back to the house, a distance of about three miles. That was a big, big mistake! Mom had no license and she couldn't drive worth a hoot.

Mom began just fine, though—she started the engine. But, as soon as she put the car in motion, bad things began to happen. To return home, she had to drive about 200 feet west from the store on Highway 99W and then make a sharp left turn, nearly a switchback, onto Tualatin Road. When Mom went into the switchback turn, she mistakenly crammed her foot down on the accelerator and lost control. She cut it too soon and drove onto the left shoulder of Tualatin Road, passing an oncoming car. The driver, completely stunned by someone passing him on the wrong side and going in the opposite direction, came to an abrupt dead stop in the middle of the highway. After lurching by the other car, Mom swerved back across the pavement into the right-hand lane and sped away out of sight. She thought the other driver was Grandpa Jurgens and, because of his advanced age, hoped she hadn't caused him to have a stroke. But driving without a driver's license, she wasn't about to go back to find out.

She continued on, driving at speeds no faster than 30 miles an hour on straight stretches, around curves and through stop signs. It didn't matter—she just wanted to get home. Verdi hung on for dear life and not until they arrived at the house was she able to talk coherently.

"Geez, Ethel! Who in the hell taught you how to drive? You scared the holy crap right out of me."

Mother never really ran over a pig. But she did kill the apple tree at the far end of our driveway. Well, she ran into it and I think that's what killed it. During conversations about Mom's driving, we just threw the pig thing in there to irritate the hell out of her.

Grandma's Threat

For days, Tom and I had been acting like two insufferable brats, constantly at war, whining, growling and snarling at each other. On this particular day, however, we went far beyond shouting threats. From the time we got out of bed we jostled, scuffled, shoved and poked each other. Poor Grandmother, exasperated and distraught, finally came to tears. Mom was equally upset, and although she seldom raised a hand to her children, she was right on the verge of walloping the daylights out of us. And had Dad not been working, I know full well that he wouldn't have hesitated and would have busted our butts.

Grandma, had had enough of our feuding and disobedience and informed us that she was leaving home and would never again return. She had threatened to leave home before but she did nothing about it. So none of us believed a word she said, not until she began packing her belongings into an old suitcase. Sudden concern engulfed me, and probably the other boys as well, when we realized that she really meant it. We pleaded with her to change her mind, promising that we would behave. But she'd heard all of this before and, with her jaw set, grabbed her suitcase and went out the door. We begged Mom to intercede, to prevent Grandma from leaving but she only shrugged, saying nothing.

Her leaving home was the last thing in the world that we wanted. So we went after her. When we caught up to her, we tugged at her coat to slow her down. But she persisted and continued to walk down the long driveway past the barn toward the railroad tracks and Herman Road. Her lips pursed tight refusing to speak to us, she continually shook her head negatively as we begged and pleaded with her. By the time we reached the railroad tracks, every one of us including Grandma was bawling. We'd broken her heart and she was breaking ours.

Appearing uncertain about which way to go, she paused, stopping on the tracks. Instantly, we surrounded here, all of us continuing to plead with her to give up the notion to leave. Finally speaking, she agreed to return home but there would have to be some changes. We listened intently as she lectured us about cooperating with each other, minding her, minding Mom and Dad and trying to get along with each other.

"You kids drive me nuts with yore arguin' an fightin' all the time. In my day, young-uns did what they were told, when they were told and we got along jest fine."

We vowed enthusiastically that we would obey her to the letter if she'd just come back home with us.

Ecstatic when she gave in to our pleadings, we hugged the life out of that dear lady to prove that we really loved her. I took the suitcase and the other kids took hold of her hands. Sporting huge smiles and feeling victorious, we escorted her home.

Most likely, Grandma knew that we could never keep all of our promises to her. We tried. And we did well for a time. But being curious, rambunctious, energetic young boys and always into things, it wasn't long before we were raising hob again. Peace and serenity didn't last long but at least Tom and I didn't fight, argue or have words for at least a week. That had to be some sort of record.

Whether Grandmother really intended to run away that night or if she was just trying to teach us a lesson, I never knew. What I do know is that we loved her dearly. But, unfortunately, we seldom expressed it. I also know that, had she left us, we would never have forgiven ourselves.

Cool Fall Mornings

Not many weeks after the start of the new school year, the weather began to get colder. Fall was slowly but surely settling in and the countryside blazed with color. It was a nice, peaceful time of year.

Now that I was in the fifth grade, I was also in the big room at Cipole Grade School. And being in the big room seemed to bring with it more responsibilities. It's similar to being a sophomore in high school as opposed to being a freshman. Going into the big room made me feel as if I'd reached another milestone in my life.

For some reason, the coolness of fall mornings made apples crisper and sweeter. We had a few apple trees but one that grew wild at the edge of the woods produced the tastiest fruit of all. Granted, the apples weren't as large as the ones on the other trees but they were an excellent treat. As long as they lasted, I raided the tree every morning on the way to school, taking a couple with me for a snack.

The onset of cold weather also made it easier for us to spot the lairs of large field spiders. Their webs captured the early morning dew, glistening brightly with rainbow colors in the sun. But the spiders didn't like the dampness and they remained hidden in dry places. Most field spiders were striped, some orange, some red and some yellow. The yellow ones I called tiger spiders. They looked dangerous, with long legs and huge bodies, but I wasn't afraid of them. None of us were. Sometimes we caught a fly or a lethargic grasshopper, feeding it to a spider, marveling how quickly it could overwhelm its prey and wrap it up tight, preserving it for a future meal.

Too Late To Shoot

Another event that came with the fall weather was hunting season. And when I saw a duck swimming in the ditch between the tracks and Herman Road one morning, I figured it was time for Tom and me to do a little hunting of our own. And so the planning began.

Immediately after returning home from school, Tom and I sneaked out of the house with Dad's .22 caliber rifle and the one and only bullet we could find, to hunt ducks in the ponds east of Walgraeve's farm.

We would have taken Dad's shotgun. But it was missing a firing pin. The original pin had broken a few years earlier so, when we had the time, we made our own using a trimmed down eight-penny nail. After shooting the thing three or four times, though, our makeshift firing pin disappeared, probably blown out through the barrel with the B-B shot. In all probability, it was too dangerous to shoot. But we never gave it a second thought.

Our parents had forbidden us to touch Dad's guns. They were adamant about it. But we did anyway. And they'd repeatedly instructed us to inform one of them if we intended to leave the farm and where we were going. But, we didn't always do that either.

We wanted to hunt ducks and had conjured up a plan so that we wouldn't get caught. But like most of the plans we made, it was full of

holes. What would have happened had we shot a duck? How would
we have explained the presence of a dead duck on the kitchen table?
It wasn't the first time that we did something stupid. And it wouldn't
be the last. And to top it all off, we were risking blistered butts just to
shoot one bullet.

It was late in the day when we concealed ourselves in a thicket of
brush at the water's edge to wait for a target to appear. We'd taken
turns hunting with the rifle in the past and this was Tom's turn to
shoot.

A duck soon landed. But I thought it was too far away to risk shooting the one and only bullet we had and cautioned Tom to wait until it
swam closer. Minute after minute ticked by. But the darned thing just
swam back and forth, never coming any closer. Before we realized it,
the sun had set and we could no longer see it. What a disappointment.
We would have to try again another time—if we could survive what
was in store for us when we got home.

As we headed for the house, we knew we were probably in mighty
big trouble. Had Tom taken the shot when we first saw the duck, we
would have been home long ago. Who knows! With luck, he might
have gotten it. But now it was nearly pitch-black dark and we had
missed our supper. And we hadn't yet done our chores. We knew Mom
and Dad would be boiling mad, particularly so if they found out that
we'd taken the rifle. That was another problem we faced: getting the
rifle back into the house before they missed it.

We crept up to the kitchen window and peeked in at our parents,
hoping to determine the extent of their anger before daring to go
inside. We had learned long ago that it was plain dumb to face them
without some sort of excuse to fit their mood.

We could hear them, including Grandma, talking about us. And
they knew we had taken the rifle. And they were more than a little
angry with us.

Dad had been out searching for us with the car, driving back and
forth on nearby country roads. Grandmother had searched the barn
and sheds, and Mom the house. Waving her favorite fly swatter about
as she ranted, Grandma warned Mom and Dad that she was going to

blister our hides when we came home. Brother, we had gotten ourselves into a horrible predicament with no logical way out. It was enough that Dad was mad at us. But Grandma with a switch—that meant certain death. That old gal could cut a switch and use it faster than Billy The Kid could draw a pistol. There was no doubt in our immature minds that we were going to catch it—and catch it thoroughly.

Edgy and a little frightened, we crouched down, hiding among the hollyhocks and shrubs beside the house pondering our plight. We had to conjure up some kind of excuse before facing the music, something that would ease the punishment, a punishment that we were certain to receive.

We were startled and nearly leapt out of our skins when we heard a door slam. It was Dad. He had come outside with a flashlight in his hand and walked right past us going to the barn. We watched the flashlight's beam darting back and forth as he searched for us around the barn and the sheds. A few minutes later, he returned. For some reason, as he was about to pass by our hiding place, he turned the flashlight directly at us. He was seething mad, bellowing, "*Get into the house right now.*"

Into the house we flew, our feet barely touching the old porch. We knew full well that we were in for a well-deserved spanking, maybe more than one. Mom and Grandmother immediately jumped all over us, particularly on me.

"*Why did you sneak off with that damned rifle? You're the oldest Teddy and you know better. We've told you a thousand times that you're not supposed to take that gun anywhere and you did it anyway. We've just been worried sick about you.*"

The only thing I could think of to say in my defense was, "*Tommy! He wanted to go hunting and I had to go with him. It's his fault 'cause he wanted to hunt for ducks and it was his turn to shoot.*"

Now, my dear brother had blamed me dozens of times when he'd gotten into trouble. And it nearly always worked for him. However it never seemed to work as well for me. But I had to try. Taken completely by surprise, Tom could only stammer meek denials. I continued to try to worm my way out of this mess, laying the blame on him. But all I succeeded in doing was make Tommy angrier with me and build a bigger fire under myself.

I kept hearing the same words over and over, *"You're the oldest. You know better than that. You're the oldest. You know better than that"*

It was useless. Dad seldom spanked us but he'd already peeled his belt from his trousers and I knew that he was going to use it. Who could blame him? We had put our parents through a terribly worrisome ordeal and we deserved to be punished. As I bent over to take my licks, I thought to myself, *"Being the oldest is really unfair. I just hope Tommy gets it as much as I do."*

Well, Pop gave us three or four stinging whacks. It hurt but not nearly as much as I thought it would. Nonetheless, we squalled and squirmed as if we were being tortured to death. Our butts smarting and with tears in our eyes, we crawled into bed without any supper. Grandma, following close behind, spoke one last comment before extinguishing the light.

"Well! I hope you two boys learned a good lesson tonight."

I don't know about Tom, but I sure did. I never answered out loud but I thought it.

"Yeah! I should have let Tom shoot that darned duck when we first saw it. Next time, I will."

The Honeysuckle Vine

Mom went into the kitchen to begin cooking breakfast and found Grandma already there. She was sitting quietly at the table sipping a cup of hot coffee and staring out of the kitchen window. Instantly, Mom sensed that something was wrong, that her mother was deeply troubled. When she asked, Grandmother quietly replied with a quiver in her voice, *"I think Grandma Walgraeve died last night."*

Mom was stunned by her announcement and asked how she came to that conclusion.

"When I sat down to have a cup of coffee this morning, Grandma's honeysuckle vine started shakin' and it shook pretty hard. You might

think I'm nuts or somethin', Ethel, but I just know that somethin' musta happened to her."

Grandma was referring to the honeysuckle vine that Grandma Walgraeve had given her when we first moved onto the farm. She'd planted it outside, beneath the kitchen window. Growing considerably since then, it clung to the side of the house and framed the window.

Both grandmothers had suffered through tumultuous times in their younger years. Sharing their experiences, they'd become close friends.

For several weeks, Grandma Walgraeve had been ill. So, our grandma volunteered to stay with her at night. But a few days earlier when she took a turn for the worse, her son and daughter-in-law assumed that responsibility.

Later in the day, Grandma's fears were realized when Dick Walgraeve came by to tell us that his mother had passed away during the night. It was the kind of news that no one wants to hear. And it brought a flood of tears to my grandmother's eyes.

When Mr. Walgraeve left, Grandma revealed to us kids what she'd experienced earlier. Chills ran up and down my spine.

My grandmother was a religious person, reading passages from her Bible every night. She believed in God, in heaven and an after-life. And she was convinced beyond a shadow of a doubt that something spiritual happened that morning—something holy and divine, and that her good friend had come to say goodbye.

Popcorn Christmas

We boys were eagerly looking forward to tromping into the woods with our dad to look for a tree at Christmastime. But since the onset of the war, he seldom had time to do things with us. So all four of us disappointed boys went on our own.

To avoid an argument over which tree to cut, the youngest—brother Dee who was still several days from being four years old—made the selection. Predictably, the tree was a little on the sparse side. But he liked it, so we cut it. We dragged it home and put it up in the middle room.

Decorating it was fun. Nearly all of the ornamentation was simple and homemade. We used tinsel that had been salvaged year after year and made a star out of cardboard and tin foil. We also decorated it with chains of colorful paper loops that we'd made and strings of popcorn that we'd dyed with food coloring.

But the night before we decorated the tree, some of our popcorn vanished. After we'd finished stringing a large batch of it on a thread, we were too tired to color it and left it in a bowl on the kitchen table. Barely able to keep our eyes open, we crawled into bed.

Dad came home about 3:00 A.M., dog-tired and bear-hungry as usual. He sat down at the table and picked up a picture of Mom and Tudie that was taken on Tudie's 2nd birthday. Not paying attention as he examined it, he scooped up a handful of our popcorn on a string and began eating it. Not until he chewed two or three times did he realize that he had something else in his mouth in addition to the popcorn.

In just a few seconds, our father had chomped a good share of our Christmas decorations to pieces. Nevertheless, we used what was left. And our tree appeared quite festive even with a few bite marks here and there.

Little money was available to buy each other gifts, just as it had been during past Christmases. But our parents still managed to give us something. We children made gifts for them: a crude wooden bowl, a bookshelf made from of a piece of shiplap lumber, a stirring spoon made from a piece of an oak tree limb.

We were a poor lot but we were a happy and contented family. And I cannot ever remember a Christmas, or for that matter any holiday, living in that old shack when it didn't feel warm and cozy and comfortable. It was my home and I loved it no matter how old, small, or rundown it appeared.

Mom holding Tudie, 1942

CHAPTER IV

1943

War and Sacrifice

World War II was always on our minds, gnawing at us like a cancer. Not a single day passed that we weren't reminded of it: radio newscasts, newspaper headlines, movie newsreels, billboards and posters, even our mail. It drained us emotionally. Even at my age, I worried that our home would be bombed and often had a sick feeling in the pit of my stomach.

But we knew in our hearts that we would ultimately win and be at peace once again. We also knew that, in the meantime, many of us would endure losses, some of them heartbreaking and tragic.

When a serviceman or woman became a casualty of battle, The War Department notified the next of kin via a telegram. Grandpa received one of those dreaded telegrams. His youngest son, Jack, was reported as missing at sea. His ship had been torpedoed and sunk and he was not listed among the survivors.

Grandpa was devastated. So was my father when he learned about his brother. Watching Dad agonizing over this horrible event was a heart wrenching, sad experience for me. When he was home, he often went outdoors to be alone, to pray and beg God for his brother's safe return. A few times I unintentionally came upon him, sitting on the running board of our old Plymouth sedan in the dark, sobbing uncontrollably. Hearing my dad cry was horrible, like a knife had been thrust through my own heart. I wanted to go to him, to console him and ease his mind, to give him assurance and hope. But how could I, a mere child, simple and helpless?

Several weeks later, Grandpa and Dad received wonderful news. Jack was okay. He was alive and safe. Dad's mood changed from despair to one of euphoria. We all celebrated with a sigh of relief that the nightmare—Dad and Grandpa's nightmare—was over.

Uncle Tony was an Army non-commissioned officer stationed in the South Pacific. When his unit became involved in a fierce firefight with Japanese soldiers, an enemy grenade exploded in his face, temporarily blinding him. But he continued to fire his automatic weapon in the direction of his attackers until reinforcements arrived. He survived, firm in limb and body, to be decorated for heroism.

Uncle Tony in combat gear

Late in the war while still in the Pacific, Tony sent a coin to me as a keepsake, a coin from North Borneo. He also wrote a letter to me, a treasure that I still have in my possession. It was in the form of a photocopy that was called victory mail or V-mail.

At the time, the government strictly censored all letters. They were photo copied and a copy of each missive was retained for security purposes.

Pop helped in the war effort, quite often working at two and sometimes three jobs, 16 hours a day, seven days a week. He drove a truck at the Oregon Shipyards and for the Columbia Distributing Company in Portland. He

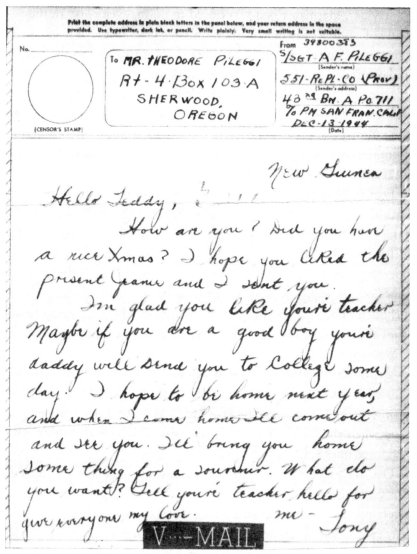

Victory Mail from Uncle Tony

also drove the shipyard worker-bus to and from Tualatin and voluntarily worked as an air raid warden. We saw little of our dad during those difficult times. And when he was home, he was exhausted and slept most of the time.

Several people who lived near us on Herman Road also worked at the shipyards and rode with Dad to Tualatin to conserve gasoline. One wintry day, Herman Road was closed to normal vehicular traffic because of a heavy snowfall. Without missing one minute of work at the shipyards, Pop merely hooked our big clod-busting sled to the tractor and continued picking up his fellow workers.

Late one night, our neighbor Dick Walgraeve came to the house to inform Dad that someone, probably a hobo, was camped next to the railroad tracks near the lower place. Any strangers seen loitering around major bridges, dams and railroads were watched closely by local citizens for fear of sabotage.

Dad and Mr. Walgraeve, wearing their air raid helmets and armed with shotguns, went out into the night looking for the fellow. His campsite was easily spotted. He'd built a huge bonfire next to the railroad tracks. They confronted the vagabond, reminding him that open fires during the hours of darkness were strictly forbidden because of the war. The man claimed to be ignorant of the conflict although newspapers in his possession contained bold, glaring headlines about it. The fire was extinguished. And the tramp voluntarily moved on.

Dad speculated the fellow to be a draft dodger. They were men who refused to serve in the military and took to the road to avoid the authorities. They were considered cowards and traitors and were reviled. And when they were discovered, they risked beatings by those who had loved ones fighting in the war.

One day, when my parents were away, another drifter, ragged, dirty and slovenly dressed, came to the house. He pounded aggressively on the kitchen door. Feeling wary and uneasy, we children gathered behind Grandma as she opened the door to confront him. The fellow was looking for a free handout. But when Grandma offered him food in exchange for doing a few chores, he balked and used foul language. Grandmother, who feared no man on this earth, startled us with her next move and scared the bejeebers out of the guy. She shoved dad's old 12-gauge single barrel shotgun right up under his nose and in an unmistakably stern voice spoke one single word.

"*GIT!*"

The fellow must have been a high hurdles track star at one time because he easily leaped over every fence on the lower place as he sprinted across our pasture, headed for the railroad tracks.

The Pig and The Calf

Dad sold our sow pig and her young litter, sight unseen, to an old Jewish fellow who lived in Portland. Though he made a nice profit from the sale, pa was mystified, wondering what a Jewish person was going to do with a pig. He knew several Jewish People and believed their religion forbade them from touching any part of a hog, let alone consume the meat.

Dad was working when the old fellow, accompanied by two other men, came to the farm to claim his purchase. Their vehicle was an old piece of rusted junk, a 1930s pickup truck with high wooden side racks.

The moment they stepped from their rig, it was obvious, even to us kids, that none of those fellows had experienced handling livestock. With plenty of Grandmother's free advice, but with very little help, they carefully herded the cantankerous old sow and her family of young ones into the back of the pickup.

Noticing that we had three calves, the old Jew asked if he could buy one, making a ridiculously low offer. Grandmother grinning, replied, *"What in the world do you take me for, some kind of stupid idjit? You know those animals are worth a heck of a lot more than that."*

After haggling for 20 minutes, the old Jewish fellow gave in and made a decent offer that Granny accepted.

After capturing one of the calves, they tried putting it in the back of the pickup with the pigs. But the old sow would have no part of the calf being near her brood and nearly destroyed the pickup trying to get at it. They were in a quandary, not certain what to do. They certainly didn't want to return a second time to get the calf, wasting time and money and be subjected to more of Grandmother's chirping. After some discussion among themselves, they arrived at a solution.

We watched in disbelief as they laid the squirming, wide-eyed calf across their laps in the cab of the pickup and drove away. We knew what was bound to happen and were bent double with laughter. A calf that's frightened, and that one certainly was, will soon have a bowel movement, a real gusher.

The Kite

Dad was like a big kid, always dreaming up something crazy. One thing he liked to do was set off fireworks. But the war was on and he couldn't buy any. So, he did the next best thing. He made a kite.

The weather had been blustery for several days. And the one and only day that he had off work during the entire month appeared to be perfect for what he had in mind.

Right off the bat, all of us could see that his kite was going to be an enormous thing. We wondered if any wind in the world could lift it into the sky.

Using a concoction of flour and water to make a paste, each of us helped cut and glue large sheets of newspaper to the framework of his dream kite. Finishing, we tied a strange looking tail to it, a tail made of worn socks. The kite was larger than Dad was tall. And he came up with a wild idea to use his salmon fishing pole and brand new Shakespeare reel to fly it. He figured that he could wind and unwind string much faster with the reel than he could wind and unwind it from a stick. What a novel idea, I thought; just reel in the kite when you tire of flying it.

My brother Tom, being the fleetest runner, had the honor of helping Dad get the monstrosity into the air. It was a heavy and bulky creation but, nonetheless, Tommy managed to hold it upright in the strong wind. When the wind took it, it miraculously soared upward with the ease of an eagle leaving the earth behind. We were amazed. Dad's kite actually took flight.

The silver colored reel hummed as the line sped out—100—200—300 feet. We all watched in quiet awe as the kite gained altitude. But Pop, in his ecstasy, paid no attention to the amount of line left on the reel. When it came to the end, his fishing pole unexpectedly leaped from his hands. His big grin suddenly vanished when he realized his fishing pole and new reel were quickly taking flight. He gave frantic chase, his short stubby legs rotating like pinwheels. But he had no chance to catch it.

As the kite rose higher and higher, sailing over the woods, the pole caught the limb of a fir tree and the line snapped. The last we saw of the kite, it was soaring to the southwest toward Newberg, towing nearly 300 feet of number one fishing line behind.

Tommy could climb a tree like a monkey. He went up and eventually retrieved Dad's pole and reel from its branches. Dad was lucky to get his favorite piece of fishing gear back. And I'm sure that the kite hanging up in the tree was probably the one and only time in Pa's life that he was happy to get a snag.

A Good Defense

Our parents constantly warned us not to talk to anyone about our uncles in the military, or about dad's work in the shipyards. Every little piece of information the enemy obtained could work against our country. And every person that I knew, child and adult alike, worried about sabotage and espionage.

Even though our military was holding its own in the war and gaining strength, rumors still persisted that the Japanese might yet make an amphibious landing on our coast.

Those kinds of remarks were scary to hear. And it made Tom and me put our youthful minds to work.

"Since there's no Army in Oregon, who will defend our family and home if the enemy attacked us?"

The answer was simple. Tom and I would. We considered ourselves old enough to fight—he nine and I almost eleven. We needed a plan, though. And soon, we'd developed one.

It seemed logical to us that our best chance to make a successful stand would be in the woods. We knew every inch of the dense timber and undergrowth and believed this to be greatly to our advantage. The underbrush was so thick in some places that we were able to walk on top of it for several hundred feet and never touch ground. Beneath the underbrush, it was dark as night even during some of the brightest and clearest days.

So, this was where we, two brave tarts, would build our defenses and stand our ground. We'd fight the mighty Japanese army to the death if necessary.

Secretly, we stockpiled rocks—our ammunition—at various locations in the trees and brush to use in hit-and-run attacks. But this, in our estimation, wasn't going to be enough. We needed some sort of fortification, a foxhole or a bunker. It had to be a place where we could observe and fight the enemy, a place where we could make a final stand.

We set about digging a pit in a thick patch of ferns in a brushy part of the woods. After digging the pit, we threw fir boughs over it to make it look like an innocent pile of brush. Being inside was like being inside a cavern. No one could see into our fortification but we could see out. We then strung strands of old barbed wire around the entire thing hoping this would also help keep the enemy at bay. We gathered more ammunition, rocks and green fir cones, and stored them inside. Our plan was to knock the enemy senseless and maybe capture them if they came too close.

One problem: we needed an easy access into our stronghold. To solve this, we dug a ten-foot long tunnel exiting inside the hole with the entrance located among the ferns.

We practiced running into the fern patch, diving down into the tunnel and crawling into our fort. It was great fun to see how fast we could disappear from sight and get to our defensive position. We didn't count on one thing though . . . big green forest slugs finding their way into our tunnel. Crawling over and squishing slimy slugs with our hands and knees was no fun; it was extremely unpleasant. Unable to figure a way to keep them out, we just had to grit our teeth and put up with it.

Our next task was the construction of booby traps: a snare and a camouflaged honey pit. This required a bit of ingenuity and careful planning.

We chose a small dogwood sapling near our fortification and bent it over, anchoring it, so that the top was only a few feet from the ground. Tying one end of a rope to the top of the dogwood, we made a noose at the other end and placed it in the trail. The noose was concealed with fir needles and ferns. If anyone stepped within it, the victim's weight would trigger a release mechanism catching our adversary by the foot.

Next, Tom fetched an old bucket and filled it with a mixture of cow manure and water, making a nice soupy mess. We buried the bucket nearby, camouflaging the open end with a lid made of sticks and leaves. It was perfect. If we couldn't catch the enemy with the bucket of manure, we were sure to catch them in the snare. If the enemy got through that, they then had to contend with the barbed wire and a hailstorm of rocks and hard fir cones. Satisfied that we'd thought of everything, we felt absolutely invincible.

We had often heard the phrase *loose lips sink ships*. So, we kept our work a secret and told no one.

Not many days after we'd finished building the fort, we were playing in the woods when Mother began calling us. I just knew she wanted us to do some kind of chore such as weeding the garden or cleaning the chicken house. Neither of us wanted to do chores and decided to keep quiet and hide. Diving into our tunnel, we crawled into our secret bunker and waited, feeling as snug as bugs in a rug.

We sat quietly peering out through the fir boughs, watching our mother as she neared our hiding place, knowing full well that we had burnt our bridges by not responding to her calls.

Suddenly her foot went flying up into the air. She had stepped squarely into our snare trap. The dogwood tree was too small to completely lift her off the ground but just big enough to hoist her captured leg waist high. Even though Mom was an exceptionally agile person, she was thoroughly trapped and couldn't free herself.

As she hopped about on one foot trying to maintain her balance and, at the same time, trying to keep her dress down, she screamed at us to come help her. She knew full well we were around some place close and that we could hear her calls.

Most of the time Mom was a kind and understanding lady. But she was not someone to be messed with when she was mad. And this was one of those times. We were in trouble and we knew it. We had to make an immediate life and death decision. We could easily crawl away in the ferns and she would never know that we'd been there. But the right thing to do was to free our dear mommy *muy pronto*. Tom grabbed his Boy Scout hatchet and we crawled out through the tunnel.

At first, Mom didn't see us. She was still bouncing around like a pogo stick, one hand holding her dress down and the other arm flailing about trying to keep her balance. When she spotted us emerging from the ferns, she scorched our eardrums like a flamethrower, screaming, *"You kids had better get me the hell out of this damned thing and be quick about it or I'm gonna skin you alive, both of you."*

She bellowed threats just like Grandma and meant every blistering word too. Tom, brave enough to get in close, chopped at the sapling four or five times. And as soon as Mom's weight brought it down, we were off and running, Tom to clean the chicken house and me to work in the garden.

The Bite I'm Glad I Never Got

It was a warm, sunny day when I grabbed my fishing pole and set off for Hedges' woods, dreaming of catching a 12-inch cutthroat trout. I was hoping to get at least one good bite. But, as it turned out, I nearly got one that I didn't want.

Hedges' woods were quiet and serene and as peaceful as paradise. It was an inviting place for youngsters of all ages to play and explore. Wild-eyed trout and gobs and gobs of crawdads inhabited a small creek that meandered through it. Eventually, it flowed into the Tualatin River. The creek wasn't a large stream of water by any means, only a few deep holes here and there. But some were sufficient in size to wade and, perhaps, dogpaddle if the conditions were just right and the weather permitted.

An ancient cedar tree with a hollow trunk, burned out by a forest fire several decades in the past, was a curious attraction. I was forever amazed that it was still standing. And I never failed to crawl into the charcoal-lined cavity letting my mind wander, wondering if Indians and wild animals had taken shelter there at one time or another.

On the way to the woods, out of curiosity, I stopped at Walgraeve's pigpen. Their sow recently had a litter of baby pigs and I wanted to see how many she had.

Little weaner pigs are quick and not easily caught. But I stupidly thought it would be fun to see if I could grab one. I knew how protective mother pigs were of their litters and how vicious they could be. But without giving one thought to what the old sow might do, I crawled into the pen and made a lunge for the nearest one of her offspring. In a discordant chorus of squeals, the little ones scattered, scampering away from me.

Suddenly and unexpectedly, and with the speed of a freight train, the old sow charged. Before I could scramble to safety, with the force of a Roman Army battering ram, the 300-pound animal knocked me down. Flat on my back, she stood over me with her mouth agape, only inches from my face. I was absolutely certain that my throat was about to be ripped to shreds. Helpless and frozen with fear, I let out one horrendous scream. For what seemed like several eternities, the huge sow stood motionless, slobbering offensive drool on me. Then, for some inexplicable reason, she turned away and trotted across the pen to where her brood had gathered.

I leaped out of there with the agility of a frightened gazelle. And for the next 15 minutes, I sat on the ground, weak-kneed, quivering and shivering with fright, unable to stand. I knew that I'd come within a whisker of being viciously bitten and most likely killed.

That was one bite I'm glad I never got.

Life's Lessons

Being farmers, we raised our own livestock for food and had to butcher some ourselves. Processing a pig took more work than any other animal. The first thing that needed to be done after it was slaughtered was remove the animal's hair. Using a stout tripod, we lowered the carcass into a large vat of boiling hot water. After a thorough scalding, we laid it on a flat surface and used scrapers to remove the hairs from the hide, much like plucking feathers from a chicken. Then we set about cleaning out the carcass and carving it into pieces.

Mom and Grandma ground some of the huge chunks into sausage. Most of the sausage was formed into patties and then cooked, rendering out the lard. Dozens of pork chops were cooked in the same way. To preserve the cooked sausage and pork chops, they were stacked in large white crocks and covered with melted lard as it was done in pioneer days. It kept very well throughout the winter and into the next spring.

Dad cured most of the hams, bacon and some of the pork chops using a friend's smokehouse. He stored the smoked meat in our old root cellar. It was always cool, and the meat kept well for a long time. In later years after the root cellar was gone, he stored the hams and bacon in our pump house, which was always cool, or in a rented freezer locker in Tualatin.

When we butchered a hog, we kids could always count on Mom and Grandma making *Cracklings*. They were small pieces of pork hide cooked until very, very crispy, a tasty treat for us.

Many of Grandma's wise sayings or adages stemmed from hard times. One was that, with the exception of the squeal, every part of a pig, including its tail, could be used. What could one do with a pig's tail? She never told me. However, she did tell us that if a pig's bladder was filled with air, it could be used as a ball. So this one summer after Dad had butchered a hog, we retrieved the bladder, filled it with air using a tire pump and made a ball. But Grandma neglected to tell us that it first had to be cleaned and cured. After several days, we rid ourselves of the thing because it got slimy, sticky and smelled like old billy-hell. In no way, can one imagine how horrible that thing stunk.

Planning to have a big dinner one Sunday, Dad killed six chickens and instructed Tommy to bury the heads. But, instead, as if they were hunters' trophies, my brother nailed them here and there to the outside wall of the old shed near the house.

For a fleeting moment, Grandma thought she was seeing things when she stepped out the back door to get a bucket of water. She was certain chickens had poked their heads through knotholes in the shed's walls and were staring at her. After recovering her senses, and realizing that she hadn't lost her mind, she sent Tom scurrying with a swat on the seat of his pants to bury those things as he'd been told.

I wasn't squeamish about shooting a pheasant or a duck for our supper, or even a prowling skunk hanging around our chicken coop. But slaughtering a hog or a calf, or even a chicken, wasn't something I could stomach. If it had to be done, someone else had to do it. I couldn't. And I found ways to disappear until it was over.

One incident that I've never forgotten occurred while I was strolling through the woods with the .22 caliber rifle.

I spotted a little gray lizard lying atop a stump, basking in the sun. It seemed to have no fear of me as I studied it for a few minutes watching its eyelids blink and its sides heave in and out as it breathed. Then, for no good reason, I put the barrel of the rifle near its head and squeezed the trigger. In the next instant, nothing remained of that tiny little reptile. One moment it was a living, breathing, creature and the next, it was nothing more than a memory.

I'd destroyed one of God's creatures for no just reason. The killing of that little lizard bothered me deeply. And from that day on, I hated to see an animal killed, any animal for any reason, and in particular, a little lizard.

That's My Pop

My pop wasn't what I would call a run-of-the-mill type of individual. He was one of a kind, a bit of a nut, albeit a loveable one. He was a people person, full of life and full of fun. He loved visiting and talking with anyone, anyplace, at anytime. And brother could he spread the bull. A good-natured, jolly fellow, he knew how to enjoy life. And did he like to eat. He was a meat and potatoes guy. And when he was, as they say in the military, *chowing down*, one had better stay away from his grub if they valued their life.

All of us kids would say the same thing about Dad, that he was a caring and loveable father, and a wonderful and considerate husband. During the roughest of times, he did his best to improve on our quality of life.

Two or three times a year, if Dad could afford the fuel, he took us on an all-day outing to Sauvie Island on the Columbia River north of Portland. It was a favorite place where we could picnic and build a bonfire to roast hotdogs and marshmallows. And Dad had a favorite place where he could angle for catfish too. And when the weather was particularly warm, we played on the sandy beach and sometimes waded and played in the water where it was safe.

On one of our trips, Pop scared Mom half to death when he swam into deep water with Tom and me clinging to his back. We were hanging on for dear life.

The only access to and from the island was via a small ferry. We kids loved riding it; it was an adventure for us. Crowds of people trickled onto the island during warm sunny summer days, searching for decent places to fish, picnic and swim. But with the setting of the sun, every one seemed to want to leave at the same time. This presented a problem; the ferry could only accommodate about a dozen cars and passengers at any one time. And that meant long lines of vehicles waiting to cross. Sometimes, we waited for up to an hour for our turn.

To make the wait more bearable and less boring for a bunch of weary and fidgety kids, Pop always had a treat for us—a loaf of white bread and a stick of real pepperoni. We could hardly contain ourselves when he began slicing it. We gobbled it down like a pack of ravenous wolves. But because the rascal had the knife, he cut thicker pieces for himself than he did for us. We were jealous and each of us probably had the same thought:

"Someday, I'm gonna have the knife and someday I'm gonna be the one that's gets the biggest piece."

Some of the projects that my dad worked on around the farm often turned into screaming debacles, especially those requiring the use of a hammer, nails, and saw. To put it bluntly, Pa was not a carpenter.

One day, he'd injured himself several times. It seemed as if nothing was going right for him; First off, he busted his knuckles while working on the car. Minutes later, he dropped a sledgehammer on his foot. And a stick flew up and hit him on the cheek when he was splitting firewood. But the straw that broke the camel's back, so to speak, occurred when he was building a small shed down in the pasture near the barn. While driving a nail into a board, he mashed one of his fingers. He'd had enough pain and bad luck to last a lifetime. And in a ranting snit, he tore his project to pieces. Lumber and two-by-fours were scattered everywhere. And that's when he got a splinter in the palm of his hand. The air turned blue with words that were not yet in my vocabulary.

Pa wanted spaghetti for supper one Friday evening. But being Catholic, we weren't supposed to eat meat on Fridays. However, fish was okay. So he solved the problem. He brought home a package of fresh squid. It was certainly different. Mom had no idea how to cook the odd looking stuff. But that was no problem for my dad. He chopped it up with his trusty rusty cleaver, boiled the pieces for what seemed like an eternity, and mixed them into the spaghetti with plenty of tomato sauce, sweet basil and garlic.

It was like rubber. We spent the next two hours chewing and chewing and chewing and chewing until our jaws ached.

Another of Dad's interesting projects was a batch of home brew that he made from scratch. He filled 24 dark-brown bottles with his potent concoction and stored them on the shelves beside the kitchen door. One warm evening, several weeks later, we had just gone to bed when the bottles suddenly began to explode, blowing their tops. The Fourth of July had come early to our house.

Pa was frantic. He found the kitchen a disaster, foam and bubbles oozing from most of his bottles of brew. For some crazy reason, probably out of habit, he slapped his dark green bus driver cap on his head and, in only his boxer shorts and sleeveless T-shirt, carried all of them outside in an old washtub. He hoped the night air would cool the ones that hadn't yet popped and thus preserve some of his precious brew.

Even with the windows and the kitchen door open throughout the night, the house reeked with potent fumes. And to Dad's consternation, we heard a few more bottles blow their caps.

The following morning, the frantic barking of our dogs awakened us. We kids high-tailed it outside to investigate the reason for the racket and to check on Dad's booze. To our amazement, we found half of our chicken population flopping about on the ground. They'd gotten into the old man's suicide sauce and, drinking it, had become crocked to the gills.

Fortunately, or unfortunately, Dad was only able to salvage a half dozen bottles of his bubbling beverage. But there was still enough to make someone tipsy.

High Octane Ethel

Mother was an intelligent woman. And being smart as a whip, she could solve the most difficult crossword puzzles in mere moments. Most people who knew her called her Ethel. Dad's brothers called her Babe and Grandpa called her *Ottel*. Dad shortened it calling her *Ott*. Sometimes we children called her *The Beetle* . . . but not to her face if we wanted to live to a ripe old age.

She was a sweet woman who could be described as quiet, reserved and unassuming. But there were a few times that our dear little mommy did something really harebrained, something stupid and way out of character.

One evening as Tom and I were leaving the house to milk the cows and do the evening chores, we noticed a half dozen bottles of Dad's infamous homemade brew sitting on the kitchen table. They were all that was left of his concoction, most of it blowing up several weeks before. Mom and Dad, sitting on the back porch soaking up the warmth of a peaceful summer evening, were talking about drinking a few of them. Being inquisitive boys, Tom and I stopped momentarily to listen to their conversation and overheard Dad warning Mother, "*If you drink any of that stuff, Ott, you'll get sick as a dog.*"

Surprisingly, with a smirk on her face and the sound of a dare in her voice, Mom's reply was defiant and challenging.

"*You're just afraid that I can drink more of it than you can, Toots.*"

Grandmother, not one to remain quiet, piped in,

"*You're gonna talk yourself into something here, Ethel, that you can't get out of.*"

"*Oh, don't you worry about me, Ma. He's the one that's doin' all the yakkin'.*"

Dad continued trying to discourage her.

"*I'm just tryin' to tell you, Ethel, that you'll get sick. You know you can't drink that stuff. It's kinda strong and it'll knock you on your butt.*"

Mom, quite out of character, continued to brag, that she could drink as much or more of the beer than any man and not suffer any ill effects. You could almost see the hair rise on the back of the old man's neck. We knew that he wasn't about to let her off the hook now, not since she had practically thrown a challenge in his face.

"Okay, Ethel! But, when you get sick and start throwin' up, you're on your own."

Tom and I were amused and really doubted Mom's seriousness. But because we had to take care of our chores, we couldn't stick around to find out if she'd actually follow through with her dare.

We seldom witnessed either one of our parents consume liquor of any kind. In fact, Dad seldom ever drank wine even though he was raised Italian. So their conversation about drinking the beer was a surprise to us.

An hour later, after finishing everything we had to do at the barn, we returned to the house to run the milk through the cream separator. When we walked into the kitchen, Mom and Dad were sitting at the table. At least Dad was sitting; Mom was kind of draped over it, slouched down in her chair, her head lying on the table and her arms dangling at her sides. Five bottles, a few of them empty, were sitting on the floor. They had consumed some of Dad's brew.

He was reading a newspaper and appeared to have suffered no ill effects. But Mom on the other hand—well, she was a complete mess and was stewed out of her mind. The poor woman had no chance. Dad's homemade inebriant could flatten an elephant.

"Where's Grandma?"

"She couldn't stand to look at your mother and went to bed."

Mom had pulled some crazy stunts but never before had we seen her like this. She talked and acted ridiculous. Tom and I were in shock, dismayed by her condition but, at the same time, I thought she was funny. Just looking at her was like watching a cartoon.

With a hint of a grin on his face, Dad rose from his chair and asked us to help carry our dear mummified mommy outside. We were as concerned as he was that she might become sick to her stomach. But we boys couldn't help but giggle.

She was so limp that picking her up was like picking up spaghetti with a spoon. It was almost like she was made of jell-o and had no bones. Tom and I each took hold of a foot and Dad lifted her by the arms and we packed her outside onto the back porch. We tried sitting her in a chair. But she kept sliding out of it. So we took hold of her again and, like a sack of grain, packed her through the house and dumped her sorry carcass onto her bed.

The next day, Mom only left her bedroom a few times to run to the outhouse. It's certain that she couldn't have felt any worse than she looked. And Grandma never said a word, just shook her head in disgust. That evening, acting as if nothing had happened, Mom emerged from her room to eat supper.

Dad knew better than to razz her about the events of the previous evening. And, so, he cautioned us not to tease her too much. We knew better too; she had a mean left jab. But, just to make certain that she was aware that we'd seen her at her worst, each one of us including Dad pinned a Lucky Lager Beer button to our shirts.

It's The Law

Uncle Jack returned home to Oregon at the height of the war. He'd been discharged from the U. S. Navy because of mental instability albeit under honorable conditions. It was a time in the war when men were most needed. So, he must have been one huge problem to his commanders for them to dismiss him.

Jack had brought a surprise home with him. He'd married a cute red-haired belle from North Carolina. His bride's name was Catherine. They moved in with Grandpa, planning to stay but a few days. But after a month, my uncle showed no signs of looking for work. So Catherine, wanting a place of her own, put pressure on her husband to find employment. Amazingly, he did. Being a person who thrived on attention, he applied for work with the Portland Police Bureau. And quite surprisingly, he was hired.

When my parents and my grandma heard about Jack's new job, they were dumbfounded. And Grandma couldn't keep her opinion to herself. Dismayed, she very vociferously exclaimed, *"Good God almighty! What kind of a stupid fool hired him? He's nuthin' but a dadburned good-fer-nuthin' lay-about."*

Mom voiced some concerns too. But Dad didn't want to hear those kinds of remarks about his brother, even though he probably agreed with them.

At the time, police departments were desperate to hire able-bodied men. Very few that were qualified were available. And why the city authorities thought Jack was qualified was a mystery to most everyone who knew him. He had many faults. He was incompetent, unreliable and thoughtless to name just a few. On top of that, the city overlooked some crucial facts. Jack stuttered and had a difficult time communicating; he had run-ins with the local authorities before; and he'd been discharged from the Navy because of mental problems. Those were definite concerns. And had the city fathers dug into Jack's military background, they'd have discovered that he'd spent more time in the brig than out during his 20-some months of service.

Jack's military records reveal nothing about him being in combat either, or on a ship that sunk at sea. Why Grandpa and Dad had been notified that he was missing in action is a mystery. In all likelihood, he was in a military brig, his personnel record punctuated with numerous entries of absences from duty.

Jack could be a likeable person though: charming, handsome, strong as an ox and gregarious. He was a slick talker; he could sell refrigerators to Eskimos. Meeting him for the first time, people often overlooked his stuttering problem because of his other qualities. When in conversation, he loved using words that were seldom heard or spoken, believing that no one else knew their meaning. The interesting thing was that he didn't know their meaning either. And even the least educated and naïve soon discovered that he was nothing more than a slick-talking blowhard.

Just a few days after being hired by the police bureau, Jack appeared on our farm. To our stunned surprise, he was in his police uniform and riding a three-wheeled police motorcycle. Wanting to show off and brag to his relatives, Jack left his assigned beat, some 20 miles away, without authorization.

He impressed us all right. We children were agog, having never before been near a police officer or a police vehicle. We examined his badge, uniform, gun and handcuffs with a child's curiosity. And then he offered to take each of us for a ride. And in the worst way, we wanted to go. But that worried Mom.

Chortling and stammering and always full of himself, he said, *"Aw, don't be so p-p-p-p-paregoric, Babe. The k-k-k-k-kids will b-b-b-b-b-be okay."*

We put the pressure on Ma until she finally gave in. But she made Jack swear to God that he wouldn't go too far or drive too fast.

Taking one of us at a time in the trike's box, he drove Herman Road to Tualatin and back with emergency lights blazing and siren wailing. He loved the attention we gave him and, although he'd only been in uniform a few days, bragged non-stop about his exploits as a policeman.

His commanders weren't stupid. They soon found out what he'd done. And not long after his unauthorized visit to our farm, they fired him for incompetence and disobedience to orders.

He was unemployed again and looking for another job. And his marriage of less than three months was already in trouble.

The Threshing Machine

Dick Walgraeve planted wheat in the field next to our house. And when it was ready to harvest, he used a piece of farming equipment called a binder. As the binder cut the wheat, it automatically gathered the stalks into small bundles (sheaves) and bound them with string. Then, to ensure that the bundles remained dry, he stood them on end against each other. To us kids, they resembled teepees.

Threshing was the next step in the process. The piece of equipment to do the threshing was, of course, called a threshing machine. It was a monstrous thing and looked like a giant mechanical praying mantis. And when it was in operation, it shook the ground, made chugging, crushing noises and belched dust and straw into the air.

Mister Walgraeve didn't own a threshing machine; they were too expensive for the amount of work he had. So he hired a crew of men who owned one to do the job.

It was late on a Friday afternoon, several days after Mr. Walgraeve had cut his wheat, when some men brought the threshing machine down Herman Road and pulled it into Walgraeve's field, parking it not far from our house. The next morning, Mister Walgraeve, a few friends and the threshing crew arrived early to begin the dirty, tiring task of threshing wheat.

All of us kids were looking forward to watching the awesome looking machine in action. But Grandma wasn't—not for one second. She'd just washed her underwear and hung it out to dry and didn't want the threshing crew gawking at it.

"Why in God's name did they have to show up today?"

Mom assured her that they wouldn't see a thing because bed sheets hanging on the outer line concealed her things from view.

That seemed to satisfy Granny. But neither woman was aware that Dad had given the threshing crew permission to use our outhouse when the need arose and to help themselves to the water from our well.

The crew shut down the thresher about 10:00 A. M. and took a break. And they relaxed, sprawled out under the apple tree in our back yard . . . next to the clothesline. A couple of the fellows immediately made a beeline to the privy located at the other end of the clothesline. They couldn't help but see every stitch of Grandma's unmentionables.

Poor Grandma was mortified. As soon as the crew went back to work, she ripped her undies from the line and hauled them inside the house. She made no bones about it; she wanted to kill Daddy. And she was a bit miffed with her daughter, as well.

"Darn you, Ethel! I should have known better. Now every danged galoot in the territory knows what I wear."

Later in the day, Tom and I were in the back yard when we noticed Dick and Dee racing across the stubble field chasing after a sizeable dust devil. It had swirled over the thresher and its crew, spiraling tubs and tubs of dust and straw upward a good 300 feet into the air. As the mini-twister neared Walgraeve's onion barn, we spotted another cloud of dust. It was from a car bouncing toward us on our dirt road.

Grandma saw it too and moaned, *"Oh Lordy! Not that danged rough-necked pea-brain!"*

A short, stocky, older Italian fellow by the name of Bill Veedee was driving the car. He owned a small grocery store in the Multnomah area of Southwest Portland. He was one of Dad's delivery customers,

Dee, five years old

and an old friend. An avowed bachelor, Bill lived alone in a small room above his grocery store. He was feeling lonely and, on the spur of the moment, decided to visit us.

All of us boys got a big kick out of Bill. He was funny, jolly and a character. He loved horseplay and on occasion playfully grabbed one of us in a headlock to give us a billy-rub on the top of the head. But Grandma didn't like him. She considered him too mouthy, too crude, too rough and too rowdy with us boys.

Bill and our dad often bantered with each other. And sometimes feeling frisky, Bill challenged Dad to wrestle with him. But he had no chance with Pop. Bill was too old, too fat and too slow. Besides, Pop had been a professional wrestler and knew all the moves. But when Bill persisted, outside they'd go to do their jousting.

They grunted and snorted like two old bulls. Usually their scuffling ended with Dad flipping Bill unceremoniously on the seat of his pants into one of Mom's flowerbeds. And once, he threw Bill headfirst into the laurel hedge. The poor guy suffered several small puncture wounds in his scalp, and they had to hurt like the dickens. But losing a little blood never stopped him from being the rough and tumble sort.

The women busied themselves in the house preparing dinner while all of the males sat outside, visiting and watching the threshing machine operation. It wasn't long before Bill began to horse around with us boys, trying to grab one of us. Tom and I circled him like a couple of chicken hawks, darting about trying to see how close we could get to him without getting caught. It was a big game.

"Hey, you boys! I got beeg knife. I catch you, I cut off your ears and sell to Gypsies."

Bill's attention was on Tom and me because we were the aggressive, taunting ones. But my feisty eight-year-old brother Dick wanted to get in on the action too and snuck up behind Bill, snatching his white Panama straw hat from his head. With the hat in hand, Dick ran out into the stubble field toward the threshing machine. Bill didn't waste any time before giving chase, afraid that Dick would soil his prized possession. Dick was never the fleetest kid in the

Tudie, three years old

family and soon Bill, as fat as he was, had closed in on him. Dick, realizing that he was about to be nabbed, gave Bill's hat a flick, sending it sailing away like a Frisbee. To Bill's horror and to our utter amazement, the hat soared right into the threshing machine's hopper. Immediately, it was mashed, mauled and torn to shreds.

Dick continued to run, hiding in the woods for the remainder of the day. Only after Bill had gone home did he return to the house.

Dad was angry with his number-three son. But Bill wasn't. He knew he hadn't done it intentionally. And the incident never once dampened Bill's friendship for Dad.

The next time the elderly Italian came to visit, he was wearing that same silly grin and another white Panama hat. Dick warily kept his distance not certain what Bill might do to him . . . but not Tom and me. We had fun jostling with him and enjoyed his rowdiness and rough and tumble ways.

One day, stirring the pot just a little, Pa posed a question of Grandma concerning Bill, *"Don'tcha think he's a real sweet guy, Ma?"*

She winced at the question and grumbled, *"Oh, hell yes! He's sweet all right! Jest about as sweet as a box of California lemons. Wormy ones at that if there is sich a thing."*

Grandma Leaves Home

Although Grandma frequently talked about finding a job to earn money, we never on this earth believed that she would leave home. She had few skills. But one day she told us that she'd obtained employment with Oregon Poultry in Portland. With the war going on, the company needed workers. And the job was something she was capable of doing.

Renting a room within walking distance of the plant, she was gone within a few days.

But Grandma wasn't out of our lives, not by a long shot. She came home often, mostly on weekends, most of the time to relax and visit with Mom. But sometimes she came home to take care of some big chore, like canning peaches or putting up hay. She either rode home with Dad or took the bus to Tualatin and walked home on the railroad tracks. And, of course, within minutes of walking through the door, she had us toeing the line again like good little boys.

Grandma's new home was a single-room apartment on the second floor of a second-rate hotel on Grand Avenue on Portland's east side. Even for those times, it was Spartan by most standards. It contained nothing more than a small two-burner gas stove, kitchen sink and a small refrigerator. The bathroom, not much larger than our outhouse, took up one corner of the room and was barely adequate for a single person. The light-colored ceilings were higher than normal and had become yellowed and dirty from years of neglect.

Dad moved all of grandmother's belongings including her bed, bedding, clothing, table, chairs, and kitchen utensils in one trailer-load. As we packed furniture up the stairs to her room, Grandmother and Mom transformed the tiny place into a comfortable living area. It was late at night when we finished putting things away. And being tired and ready for bed, we left Grandmother alone in her new dwelling.

It wasn't until the next day that I began to miss her. But I didn't miss her bossing me around or bellowing at me when I slipped up on a chore. The house seemed a little too empty and a little too quiet. Other than working in the hop yards, she was never gone, always around watching us and helping Mom.

We did our best to obey Mom and help her with chores. But it didn't take long for us to slip back into our old slipshod, lazy ways.

Dad stopped by Grandma's room to re-supply her with eggs, butter and milk from the farm during times that she wasn't able to come home. Occasionally one or two of us stayed with her over a weekend, a treat for us because it was an adventurous change from our humdrum farming routine. It was a treat for her too because she had someone to comb and brush her silky-white hair. Grandmother's hair, when not worn in a tight bun atop her head, hung well below her waist. And combing it reminded me of the horsehair used in violin bows only because it was long, soft and snowy white.

As far as I was concerned, Grandma's job at Oregon Poultry was not a pleasant one. I would never have done it had I been old enough. The place reeked of foul odors. And the chickens were killed in a disgusting way even though it was probably more humane than us shooting one with an arrow or our .22 caliber rifle.

Live chickens, taken from crates, were hung upside down by their feet on a long moving conveyor line. And each one was slaughtered by a single stroke of a knife. The automated conveyor moved the dead birds through the plant from one station to another. First, they were dipped into a large vat filled with scalding hot paraffin. Next, they went into a cooler. When they emerged from the cooling area, pickers peeled the paraffin from the chickens removing their feathers. That was my grandmother's job; she stripped paraffin and feathers from chickens. Eventually they were conveyed into an area where they were gutted, cleaned and packaged.

Grandmother said many times that working at the plant was much easier on her than watching after us. It was much easier on us too. But, in time, the wet concrete floors took a toll on her legs. But she appeared to be happy and relaxed. Mom worried about her safety, though.

One night while visiting Grandma, she voiced her concern.

"Ya know, Ma, this certainly isn't the safest part of town to live in. There's a lot of bums and strange lookin' creeps hanging out around here at night. Aren't you ever afraid to go out?"

Grandmother meant to be serious, replied, *"Are you kiddin', Ethel? It's got to be a heck of a lot safer living here than stayin' at home with those damned hellion boys of yores."*

Grasshoppers

We children caught and collected more insects than most entomologists. It wasn't unusual to see one of us running across a hay field or pasture with a jar in hand chasing down a grasshopper. Grasshoppers aren't the easiest critters to catch. The best way that I found to latch onto one was to creep up on it from behind. Even at that, they most often escaped.

Grasshoppers are much the same in appearance with the exception of the color of their wings. The most common have pale green or nearly white wings. And those were the easiest to catch. On the other hand, red winged grasshoppers were the least common and the most prized. But bright green-winged grasshoppers were the most difficult to catch of all of them. They seemed to be more wary than the other kinds when on the ground. And when they flew, they dipped, dove, zigged and zagged like ping-pong balls bouncing off a wall. They also made a raspy, harsh grating noise when in flight. Another prized variety was the black-winged grasshopper. They were the giants of the grasshopper family. And yet, as big as they were, they were the most difficult to spot when resting on bare ground. Their body color blended well with the dry soil.

So, when we talked about catching a grasshopper, we referred to it as a *"pale-winger," "green-winger," "red-winger,"* or a *"black-winger."* And when we caught them, the darned things spit a dark fluid on our fingers that we called tobacco juice.

Mom probably got sick and tired of us bringing bugs into the house, especially grasshoppers. Other insects like June bugs, click beetles and glow worms didn't move about very fast if they happened to escape. But when a grasshopper was on the loose in the kitchen, it often led to chaos. And do you know what Tom did? He ate their drumstick-shaped hind legs. Other than my brother, what person in his or her right mind would want to eat any part of a bug, and in particular one that spit tobacco?

The Swimming Hole

Every kid should experience the thrill of paddling around in a swimming hole. We had one. Well, kind of. It didn't belong to us but we claimed it as ours. It was in the creek that meandered through Hedges' woods and past Dick Walgraeve's farm. That's where we first learned to swim, or should I say dogpaddle.

The creek was dotted with several natural pools but they were small and not very deep. They were perfect, though, for little kids to play and wade. As we grew older, we outgrew them. So, one summer, we decided to make a swimming hole large enough that we could actually swim.

Selecting a nice wide pool back in the woods, we set about constructing a dam using boulders, sticks and chunks of sod. The nicest thing about the spot we picked was the bottom wasn't muddy like most of them. Well, our weird little weir didn't look anything like a Dutch dike but it worked. And after a few days, we'd trapped a sizeable reservoir of water with it. It was barely waist deep but still it was deeper than it had been and a good deal deeper than any of the others in the creek. And it was large enough that we could swim five or six strokes and not kick a bunch of rocks before reaching the other end. Not only was it lots of fun, it was private and it was free.

Nothing on this earth had been explored more thoroughly than that stream of water. Except for a few places downstream from Walgraeve's, we knew every inch of it. Never once giving thought to the water being impure, we drank from the creek where it rippled over a thick carpet of tiny red roots that grew from nearby bushes. It was the only place that the water was clear. And to us, clear meant clean.

In addition to trout and crawdads, it teemed with interesting little critters: water bugs, periwinkles, water skippers and caddis worms, to name a few. The skippers were elusive little rascals, bounding across the surface of the water like aquatic ballet dancers. Caddis worms were plentiful too but hard to spot because they lived with the periwinkles on the creek bottom in shells made of hundreds of tiny pebbles.

And there were plenty of trout to catch if we weren't interested in swimming. When we fished, we nearly always brought home one or two but seldom any more than that. We had specific places to fish and we used a specific tactic for catching them.

First, using a worm as bait, we caught a mud dauber—a small trash fish we also called a mud head. Skinning the dauber, we used it as bait to catch a crawdad. Then, we took the tail from the crawdad, peeled it and used that for bait to catch the trout. For us boys, it was, indeed, all very scientific.

Growing Pains

Accidents happened to us boys all the time. We were forever getting hurt, sometimes because of our stupidity and sometimes because of inattention and sometimes because of recklessness.

Tom and I made a baseball bat out of a dried limb from an oak tree and wrapped the handle with electrical tape for a better grip. But the tape didn't work as well as we'd hoped.

While playing a game of work-up in Walgraeve's stubble field near the house, Tom inadvertently lost his grip on the bat when he took a hefty swing at one of my pitches. The bat flew at me like a spear and before I could duck, it struck me on the forehead smack between the eyes. It was as if I'd been hit with a hammer. I wasn't knocked completely unconscious but everything turned black as night. Momentarily without sight, I staggered and reeled but somehow remained upright, refusing to go down. It took some time for me to regain my senses. And for hours, I suffered a smashing, throbbing headache. I can assure you that, even though Tom was not yet ten, he was still able to swing a bat with some force.

A week later on the railroad tracks near home, Tom launched a rock at a telephone pole using a bean-shooter. And, being a good shot, he would have hit the pole had I not been standing in front of it. Unfortunately for me, the rock hit me just above the left ear and knocked me to the ground. And although I suffered a nasty cut in my scalp, the impact didn't knock me unconscious. But it hurt like the dickens and blood gushed from the wound. And within minutes, it turned into a huge swollen, gory lump.

I'd bet Tom a nickel that he couldn't hit the pole twice in succession. But getting my head busted open to prevent him from winning the bet certainly wasn't my intention. Now I had double the pain and two lumps on my head. But the biggest pain of all was that he never paid off.

Encounters With Bobby

Dick Walgraeve's oldest son, Dickie, was a favorite playmate of ours. He was a super decent kid and Tom and I got along well with him. But not his younger brother Bobby; he was an ornery unpredictable brat. On several occasions, with no provocation or warning, the little sneak attacked us with rocks. And he viciously bit us too, even our youngest brother Dee. We learned quickly not to trust him and not to play with him.

Once, when I was riding my bike down the road to get the mail, he shot me in the back with a BB gun. I tried to catch him but he had too much of a head start and beat a hasty retreat into his house. Another time, he unlatched the door to our squirrel cage and released a couple dozen of our prized captives. We gave chase again, but again he escaped into his house. He knew that if we caught him, he get a well-deserved thumping.

One day, Dickie, Tom and I were playing a game of marbles in his family's back yard. Totally absorbed in our game, we were unaware that Bobby was lurking nearby. He crept up behind us and suddenly, without any warning, struck Tom on the head with a stick of stove wood.

Dickie immediately pursued his younger brother, tackled him and gave him a good drubbing. Bobby's screams got his mother's attention. And she flew from the house catching Dickie pounding on his brother. Not satisfied with her oldest son's reason for smacking his brother, she gave him a swat and informed him that Tom was old enough to fight his own battles.

Not a half hour later, Bobby was at it again, flinging rocks and sticks at us. Again Dickie chased him down and, again, gave him a well-deserved pounding. And again, Dickie's mother descended on him like a barn owl on a field mouse, demanding to know why he'd struck his younger brother.

For once, Dickie thought he had the perfect answer.

"I'm old enough to fight my own battles."

His quick-witted response did him no good though, and she swatted him again.

Tom and I had had enough of Bobby for the day and, gathering up our marbles, went home where it was safe.

Poor Dickie! We felt sorry for him. His life had to be a nightmare to be saddled with a brother like that.

One day, while fishing in the creek not far from the Walgraeve house, I was surprised when Bobby approached me with a proposition. He offered to give a dollar to me for two things: a trout that I'd just caught and a promise not to hit him anymore. I told him that if he'd stopped stealing our things and attacking us for no good reason, I wouldn't have a reason to smack him. He promised that he'd leave us alone. But I knew better than that. He couldn't be trusted to keep his word about anything. And he certainly couldn't be trusted not to attack us when we weren't looking. I agreed to sell the trout to him but nothing more. The little sneak handed the dollar bill to me, took the fish and ran for home.

Getting a buck for one fish made me happy, elated in fact. It wasn't often that I had the experience of holding a dollar bill in my hand. Examining it closely, it took a few seconds for me to realize that the bill I was holding wasn't really a dollar bill but a $100 bill. My eyes nearly popped out of my head. I'm not certain that I'd ever before seen a $100 bill, let alone hold one, and it took me a few minutes to get over the shock.

I was awestruck. I wondered where in the world Bobby had gotten that kind of money. No doubt he'd stolen it. And later on, I found out that I was correct in my assumption. He'd taken it from his aunt's purse. But for the moment I wasn't at all certain what I should do. The temptation to keep it weighed heavy on my mind. But I knew that wouldn't be right. Besides, how in the world could I, an 11-year-old kid, ever explain to my mom and dad or anyone else how I'd gotten a $100 bill? Returning the money to Bobby's parents was the logical and correct thing to do and, hopefully, they would retrieve my fish for me.

I rapped on the back door of Bobby's house. When his mother opened it, I sensed that she was miffed about something. She said nothing, only stared at me. Quite nervously, I explained what Bobby had done; that he'd given me money for a fish, money that I thought was a dollar bill. I held the $100 bill up so she could see it. Her eyes widened. Not saying anything, not even a word of thanks, she snatched it from my hand and slammed the door shut.

Once again, that little devil had victimized me. Regardless if his parents punished him or not, I knew with absolute certainty that I would, that I'd give him a most hellacious thumping and get a fair-sized piece of his rotten hide—at least $100 worth.

Who's Chicken?

Except for Little Crip, I hated chickens. As far as I was concerned they were the most repulsive creatures God ever created. The only way I liked them was after they'd been fried to a crispy golden brown.

Almost immediately after moving onto the farm, our dear granny began buying the dumb creatures, at least 200 chicks every spring. And we children were the ones who had to care for them. We were miserable. Cleaning a chicken house of ghastly gassy chicken manure is absolutely the worst chore on this earth. And it often nauseated me. And those louse-bound feathered creatures running loose had no concern whatsoever about where they deposited their droppings.

Well, Tom and I had ways of reducing the chicken population . . . chicken cookouts, secretly done in the woods. There were so many chickens running around that we were able to get away with this dirty little deed a half dozen times a year without our parents finding out. They never seemed to miss a chicken or two. And we figured the fewer chickens we had on the farm, the less chicken manure we had to shovel.

We made plans with a couple of our friends to have a cookout in the woods in back of our place at a prearranged time on a Saturday when Mom and Dad were shopping in Sherwood. But our scheming suffered a serious setback. Friday night, Granny came home, staying the weekend. That night while lying in bed, Tom and I talked it over. We were going to shoot the chicken with the .22 caliber rifle but she was certain to hear the shot. So, we decided to dispatch it with an arrow.

It was autumn and Saturday morning was beautiful, warm and comfortable. Right on schedule, Mom and Dad left the house, driving to Sherwood, to go shopping. Grandmother stirred around for a time and finally settled down at the kitchen table listening to her favorite singer, Kate Smith—she was famous for singing God Bless America and other patriotic songs. Soon, Granny dozed off. Our luck was holding and the time seemed perfect for making our move.

Tom had plenty of practice with the bow, having picked off pesky poultry for our past cookouts. It was his chore to kill the things and mine to clean and cook them.

When it came to chicken cookouts, Tom and I worked together like a well-oiled machine.

We thought it best to shoot the chicken from inside the house, through a knothole in the wall behind our bed. We had discovered the knothole long ago and used it as a peephole to spy on the world outside. If for some reason Grandma woke from her nap, we reasoned that we weren't as likely to get caught if we were inside the house when he made the shot.

Peeking through the hole, Tom spotted a big Rhode Island Red digging and scratching in the dirt just a few feet away. It was an easy shot for him. But the last time he shot a chicken with an arrow, he hit it in the head and we had a dickens of a time trying to catch it. It ran around in circles and, after flopping wildly about on the ground for a time, flew onto the shed roof before dying.

Not taking any chances that this one might run off with an arrow sticking in it, Tom tied one end of a string to it and gave the other end to me to hold. Poking the arrow through the knothole, he took careful aim and let fly. The string went *zzzzzziiiip* as the arrow sped through the knothole. Tom's aim was perfect and the arrow found its mark. As Tom scurried outside to finish killing it, I held tight to the string, feeling like I'd caught a salmon with a thread.

Grandma hadn't stirred and was still snoozing when we made a mad dash, sprinting for the woods, I with a butcher knife and skillet in my hands and Tom with the dead chicken.

Sketch by Tom Pileggi

Tommy Pickens, Eddie Wager and Dickie Walgraeve were waiting for us and had already started a fire. I quickly dry-picked the feathers from the chicken, singed it over the fire and cleaned and cut it into pieces. In 15 minutes, I was cooking.

The others gathered close around the fire in a tight circle, conversing with each other about kid stuff and watched me cook. Looking up occasionally to acknowledge comments, it gradually sunk into my skull that another kid had joined us. He was holding a plate and fork in his hands. But this chap was no ordinary kid. It was my dad. My heart jumped and my mouth dropped open as wide as a barn door. The other kids, when they realized that my pop was standing there among them, stopped their conversations in mid sentence and stood motionless like dumb stumps, staring at the fire. Not one of us heard him coming and no one noticed him when he squeezed into our little crowd.

Pop, his face lit up like a neon sign with a broad grin, finally broke the silence.

"If you kids give me the biggest piece, I won't tell."

What a relief. We were thrilled that's all he had to say and gladly obliged allowing him to take the choicest piece.

Years later, after Dad had passed away, my brother and I were reminiscing about our youthful escapades. Reflecting on our chicken cookouts, and Dad catching us that day, we finally realized something that we'd never considered before. Since he was the head of our household, to whom would he have told had we denied him the choicest piece of chicken?

The sneaky old rascal had put one over on us again.

"Next Time, you'll mind Grandma." Sketch by Tom Pileggi

CHAPTER V

1944

Bohlens

J ohn and Frances Bohlen were my parents' closest friends during the 40s and 50s. Dad had become acquainted with them while working in the shipyards. And although they were 10 years older than my mom and dad, the two couples had quite a lot in common.

They lived in a large older home on a few acres of ground on the banks of the Tualatin River between Tualatin and Roamers' Rest Park and only a few miles from our place. They'd turned part of their ground into a thriving nursery. And they did very well with it.

John was tall in stature and a handsome man. His hair clung to his head like a shock of loose hay. But he'd become a little stooped in middle age because of a painfully nagging back problem.

Frances was the key-man, or woman, in this marriage. From early on, my dad referred to her as *Fanny*. Because of her Spanish and French ancestry and dark mysterious complexion, she could easily have passed for a gypsy fortuneteller. She dressed the part too, adorning herself with oodles of flashy jewelry and long flowing housedresses. She was a striking, exotic and sophisticated woman. But she could be a little stuffy at times. And she

Frances Bohlen, some years later

certainly was no prude. She could easily hold her ground in the tough language department if it ever became necessary.

John and Frances had several children, all of them older than we. Their daughter Mary Jo, whom I believe was the youngest, was at least four years older than I.

The Bohlens' home was tastefully decorated with furniture that appeared to be beautiful antiques and family heirlooms. It was an impressive display. But to me, the most fascinating feature of their home was the huge fireplace in the living room. The face of it covered a sizeable section of one wall, reaching from floor to ceiling. It was made with large porous stones, like pumice. And unbelievably, patches of

John Bohlen

thick, lush, dark green moss grew on it. John and Frances assured us that it was really moss, and to maintain its health, they sprayed water on it daily.

Two or three Siamese cats, with hypnotic green eyes, had the run of their home. They certainly didn't like my company. Many times, and for no reason at all, when I looked at them, they arched their backs and hissed at me. They disliked me and I disliked them. And had I not been afraid of drawing attention to myself, I'd have hissed back.

But, most interestingly, the Bohlens owned several peacocks. The huge birds were not caged and had free run of their property. Over the years, they grew wild, multiplied and inhabited the treed banks on both sides of the river.

Roosting high in the trees at night, the peacocks made excellent sentinels. They emitted horrific frightening ear-piercing screams when anyone or anything approached the Bohlen house.

*John and Frances' house, after the house underwent
a facelift (note the peacock in front)*

Folks who didn't know about the peacocks swore that banshees from
hell were about to pounce upon them when they heard their shrieks.
And if, for some reason, the screeching peacocks couldn't frighten off
a prowler, Frances' gypsy-like stare could.

A Little Stinky

We kids were playing *hide and go seek* in the high grass that grew
around the old no-longer-used pigpen at the edge of the woods
when I saw something move not ten inches from my face. I peeked on
the other side of a board that had been nailed to the bottom of the
pigpen fence and saw a tiny ball of black fur with white stripes. It was
a baby skunk.

My unbelieving yet inquisitive brothers came running lickety-split from their hiding-places when I yelled that I'd found a real live skunk. Even though we were curious about the tiny creature, we kept our distance, not wanting to get squirted. And, at the same time, we kept a watchful eye out for its mother.

We weren't very keen on skunks hanging around our place because they harassed our chickens looking for food. And occasionally, they squirted our dogs when they became too curious. And so, after observing the little animal cuddled up against the board for a few minutes, we decided it was best to kill it.

Dick ran to the house to fetch our single-shot .22 caliber rifle. But it took him a few minutes to convince Mom that we were really going to shoot a skunk before she allowed him to take it. To make certain that we wouldn't shoot anything else, she gave him one bullet.

I loaded the rifle, took careful aim at the middle of the furry ball and fired. It flinched the instant I shot giving me reason to believe that I'd killed it. It lay motionless appearing dead. But it wasn't. After a few seconds, we were surprised when it stirred and casually ambled along the fence a few feet farther before hunkering down again. Not only was it not dead, I didn't even wound it. How I missed, I'll never know. And though I took some ribbing about my marksmanship, I felt somewhat relieved that it was unharmed.

We continued to watch it for some time before one of the younger kids suggested that we ought to keep it. We already had a menagerie of squirrels, chipmunks and mice. So why not add a skunk? What a fabulous idea. But, how does one cage a skunk and could it be tamed? Those were problems we would have to ponder. It looked harmless and, even though it seemed to be aware of our presence, it hadn't tried to squirt us. And, there was no noticeable odor. So we conjured up a plan of action.

Dick and Dee ran back to the house, made a quick report to Mom, and returned with a cardboard box and a saucer of warm milk. We were very cautious not to do anything to upset it, whispering to each other and not making any sudden moves. When we put the saucer in front of it, it backed away momentarily and then, sniffing the air, moved to the saucer and began to drink. We knew right then and there that we were going to triumph. Using the milk, we lured it into the open end of the box and carted it home.

Mom came outside as we gently laid the box down on the back porch.

"Well, I'll be . . . ! It really is a skunk."

To say that we were just a little curious about it would have been a colossal understatement. We were fascinated, so captivated that we couldn't take our eyes off the little creature. It acted quite content, curled up in one corner of the box, its stomach bulging, filled with warm fresh milk. Mom was just as mesmerized by our furry prize as we were. Throughout the day, we did little but hover around it, admiring the newest addition to our horde of animals. A few times it seemed to become a little frightened but never once did it let loose a stream at us.

"Just wait'll Dad and Grandma see what we've caught."

Naming our newest pet *Little Stinky*, we began to touch it, letting it smell our fingers and gradually become accustomed to us. By day's end we were petting it as if it were a dog or cat. We just naturally referred to Little Stinky as a male even though we were never quite certain of the little animal's sex. And no one had nerve enough to look under its tail to find out.

Naturally, when it got dark, all of us wanted to bring it inside the house. But Mom had some serious reservations about doing that.

"Suppose'n it squirts somebody? Then the whole house is gonna stink to high heaven and it won't be a fit place for any of us. And what's your dad gonna say when he comes home from work tonight and finds he's got a live skunk loose in the house?"

We were always bringing something into the house: snakes, turtles, grasshoppers, lizards, moles. Maybe Dad wouldn't mind a skunk. We continued begging Mom until we prevailed. We put our newest pet behind the stove, and to ensure the tiny varmint stayed put, placed a lid over the box, held in place with a shoe.

The next morning, Tom, Dick and I were up first. We'd already toted Little Stinky from behind the stove to the center of the kitchen floor, and were feeding it a bowl of fresh warm milk when Dad and

Mom got up. Mom had told him that we'd caught the little critter so he wasn't at all surprised. In fact, he was just as curious about our new pet as we had been.

When Dad told Grandma about Little Stinky, she was just as amazed as he. The next day, everyone at Oregon Poultry heard the news of her grandkids capturing and taming a real live skunk.

All of the other animals gave Little Stinky a wide berth. Puddles, our dog, wanted no part of it in the beginning. But, eventually, she learned to live with our little skunk as another part of the family.

Within a few days, we were playing with it like any of our other pets. It followed us around like a little puppy. And we took turns carrying it in our arms. And not once did it ever act like it was going to squirt us. We trusted Little Stinky and it trusted us. The little thing had the run of the house and, with the exception of Puddles, was the grandest pet we ever possessed.

Feeding it for the first few days was by trial and error. We learned that it loved raw hamburger. But its most favorite food by far was grasshoppers.

While it was still quite small, we chased and captured grasshoppers, dozens of them, putting them in a wide-mouth gallon jar. Then we stuffed our little pet inside the jar, capped it, and watched as it tried to catch its supper. It went wild and so did the jar, spinning and rolling crazily around on the ground. Stinky caught every one of them and when we removed him from the jar, its stomach was bulging.

When we turned Stinky on its back and tickled its stomach, it squealed like a little pig. When we teased it, it sometimes reared up on its back legs and slammed its front paws to the ground. One of its warnings to let us know that it had had enough of our horseplay was to raise its tail straight up and flick its rear end toward us. No one had to tell us what that meant.

Dad told everybody at the shipyards about the skunk too. But few believed him until John and Frances Bohlen backed up his story.

Pop returned home from work about 2:00 a. m. every morning. And when he crawled into bed, he nearly always found Little Stinky curled up under the covers at Mom's feet, keeping warm. It didn't mind sleeping with Pop. But Pop wasn't about to sleep with a skunk. And so the little varmint was evicted, kicked out of bed onto the floor. But Little Stinky was persistent. And by the time Dad had fallen asleep, it was back under the covers, curled up in a warm furry ball like a little kitten.

When it wasn't sleeping with Mom, it curled up in a box behind the stove. And if our furry little friend failed to show up when it was time to retire for the night, and that was seldom, it got locked out and was on its own to find a bed.

One night, Little Stinky hadn't shown up when we went to bed. So Mom closed the door and retired for the night. Quite a commotion erupted in the chicken house some time later. We boys got up to investigate and found our little squirt huddled under the chickens trying to keep warm. Stinky didn't mind the new sleeping arrangements . . . but the chickens sure did.

A Rotten Idea

The afternoon was unusually warm and made me lethargic and sleepy. Not much could have stirred me. But when I made a fantastic discovery, my scheming brain went into overdrive.

Grandmother told us kids that a bee was most likely going back to its nest if we observed it flying in a straight line. Well, I saw a couple of them fly into the willow not far down the road from the barn. And they flew in a straight line. Despite the hot weather, I was curious and went looking.

I found a volley-ball-size paper nest in the tree's branches a mere six feet above the ground. But the occupants weren't bees; they were black hornets. And black hornets are mean critters that will sting a person without much provocation.

As I was backing out from under the willow, I spotted something else . . . three chicken eggs in a nest partially hidden by leaves and twigs. They were directly under the hornets' nest. And without question, I knew the eggs were very, very rotten. And immediately, I knew what fate would befall them. In no more than three seconds, I'd conjured up a plan to stink up my brother Tom's life.

I wanted to do two things: retrieve the eggs and destroy the hornets' nest and its occupants.

The best way to destroy a hornets' nest is burn it. But if I burned it before I retrieved the eggs, I'd probably destroy them too. Obviously, I had to retrieve them first before burning the nest and do it without getting stung. Thinking about it for a few minutes, I hit upon a solution.

I found a long pole and tacked a wire loop to the end it. I crept under the willow as far as I dared and was able to extract two of the eggs without stirring up any trouble. My contraption worked fine. But the third egg was stubborn and, no matter how persistent I was, I couldn't rescue it.

Two eggs would certainly be enough to fulfill my devious scheme. And if the third one survived, it would be a bonus.

Ditching the two eggs in a safe place, I began the task of eliminating the hornets. Tying an oily rag to the end of the long pole, I set it aflame and shoved the fiery end of it under the nest. But it didn't catch fire as I'd hoped. But the dry grass and twigs beneath it did when part of my burning torch fell to the ground. Immediately, like a black tornado, a swarm of angry hornets swirled upward from a concealed exit at the back of their nest. Well, I discarded my torch and hightailed it out of there as fast as I could and ran up the road toward the barn.

When I turned to see if any hornets were following, I saw a frightening sight. In my panicked haste to escape, I'd thrown the torch into the hay field. And the dry hay was on fire. So was the dry tinder beneath the willow. It seemed as if the entire world was ablaze. What a predicament!

Grabbing two burlap bags, I raced back down the road and began beating at the flames. Mom saw smoke and flames from the house. She grabbed a spade and hurriedly joined me. And shortly after, Tom came to help too. Eventually, we succeeded in extinguishing the blaze but not until a large patch of our hay had burned.

I managed to get rid of those pests but, in doing so, I destroyed the last rotten egg and burned up a good share of our hay. I was lucky; it could have been far worse. Had the fire reached the woods, it could easily have gotten out of control. And, in the hot weather we were experiencing, that would have been disastrous.

Mom agreed that destroying the hornets was a good idea. But I should have waited until dark when they weren't as active. My carelessness had cost us dearly. And I knew Dad wasn't going to be nearly as understanding as Mom. And to make matters worse, Grandma showed up, walking home from Tualatin with a couple of shopping bags filled with dirty laundry. When she found out what I'd done, she shook her head in disbelief and muttered something like, *"Every blamed time I come home I find out you've done somethin' dumb."*

Why was it that everything I planned turned out so rotten—kind of like an old egg? Well, perhaps not everything. I had conceived one plan that I was certain could be executed successfully. And I was about to find out the following morning.

Hiding among the corn stalks in the garden with the two rotten eggs in my hand, I waited for my little brother to appear. He was right on schedule heading for the old outhouse. After he entered and closed the door, I waited until I was certain that he'd comfortably seated himself before I took careful aim and flung the eggs in rapid succession at the back of the privy. My aim was perfect and the eggs made a sound like *kersplat* when they struck.

This wasn't the first time that I'd thrown something at the outhouse when it was occupied. And it wasn't the first time that Tom had been my target. Without question, he knew who was picking on him but thought that I'd thrown a couple of dirt clods. Within seconds the horrible stench of those rotten eggs closed in on him. And he began bellowing threats of killing me. I was beside myself knowing that I'd stunk up my little brother's day.

Then I saw my grandmother hurrying toward the poop palace. She, too, needed to use it. But I knew that once she got a whiff of what I'd done, my very existence would be in jeopardy. And just when my scheme seemed to be working so well.

Tom suddenly burst out of the door. He nearly bowled Granny over but didn't stop. She watched his mad dash for the house and then, unaware about what she was to encounter, entered the putrid potty.

Ready to retreat to the safety of tall timber, I heard her cry out with a gasp.

"My Lord, Tommy, what in the world did you do in here?"

Alas, Grandma believed that Tommy was responsible for making the place stink. Fantastic! Absolutely fantastic! Perhaps I'd achieved some success after all.

My Very Own Dreamland

On cloudless, warm, sultry days, I often hiked deep into the woods to a large log that lay suspended across a small moss-covered gully. There, the ground was covered with lush foliage, wet ferns and dainty elegant wildflowers like the honeysuckle, lady-slipper, wild violet, lambs tongue and trillium. And drooping skeins of moss made the thick underbrush and trees appear as if they were sporting long unkempt beards.

Scurrying little animals, the beating wings of flitting birds, and the occasional echoing rat-a-tat-tat of a woodpecker were the only noticeable sounds. Otherwise, the air was still. It was an idyllic place for a kid to dream.

My favorite perch was out on the end of the log, lying on my back. It was there that I experienced interludes of pure bliss and peaceful moments, gazing up through dusty rays of sunshine into the foliage above me. The peace that I felt was soothing and inhaling the exotic aromas of our Mother Earth intoxicating.

My mind always wandered and I never failed to fall into a sleepy trance, daydreaming about all sorts of things.

Sometimes I transformed myself into a great magician, dreaming that I could appear and disappear at the wink of an eye. And sometimes I dreamed about rescuing a beautiful, blond-haired maiden from certain disaster. And sometimes I dreamt of eating tubs and tubs of Mom's golden fried chicken.

If I were quiet and moved little, I could hear squirrels and chipmunks scrambling up and down the backside of trees trunks, eventually peeking around them, curious about the big thing that had invaded their forest home. I could even hear lizards scratching the bark on the underside of the log where I was lying. Tiny birds darted through the trees from bough to bough, and some even clung to their rough trunk bark.

One leaf that hung on the end of a dogwood tree branch fluttered in the motionless air, as if some invisible hand fanned it back and forth.

There were things that I never saw and knew were there . . . like the red fox, the coyote, the rubber boa, and the elusive deer. But I had no fear of them, not any of the creatures that lived in the forest.

Not far into the woods, a gigantic old-growth Douglas fir stood, towering above all other trees like a majestic sentinel guarding its realm. We children simply called it *The Big Tree*. We sometimes visited the old tree, admiring its longevity and its size, paying it respect as we would an elderly person. Seven of us, with outstretched arms, hugging its massive trunk, could not reach around it. It was precious to us, like an old friend.

The forest seemed like a paradise . . . a magical paradise, replete with imaginary spirits and little wild creatures and, yes—one very dreamy young boy.

Stirring Up Sherwood

We talked Mom and Dad into taking us to Sherwood with them one Saturday morning hoping that they would buy each of us an ice cream cone. For the fun of it, we took "Little Stinky" with us. Had we known the hubbub a tiny skunk would create, we might have had second thoughts and left it home.

Intending to stop for just a moment while Mom and Dad went shopping, we stepped inside Walt Bowen's appliance store to show our pet to him. Walter, an old and dear friend, had heard about Little Stinky and was absolutely enchanted by it. After holding it for a few minutes, he asked if he could take it down the street to show some other people. That was okay with us. But we were a little concerned about Stinky being in another person's care and tagged along.

Walter, a quiet, dignified, respected businessman and a pillar of the community, had something up his sleeve. With a huge grin spreading his chubby cheeks and with the little skunk cuddled in his arms, he nonchalantly strolled into Monty Brickell's barbershop.

Very innocently, he asked, "*Did any of you guys leave this here kitten in the street outside?*"

Monty, the barber, stood transfixed, staring at the little striped animal . . . but not his three customers. The fellow in the chair with lather on his face led a frenetic stampede out the door onto the sidewalk. Had someone yelled that the place was afire, they couldn't have evacuated it any quicker.

Walter was beside himself rolling with laughter that intensified when the fellow with lather on his face shouted at him, calling him a dumb old coot that should be strung up to a tree.

Retrieving our little pet, we walked back up the street with Walter. His chuckling was nearly uncontrollable at times.

Just as we'd crossed the street, an attractive red-haired woman driving a shiny bright convertible, a lady whom Walter knew, pulled

Strolling with "Little Stinky," sketch by Tom Pileggi

up to the four-way stop where we stood. His face nearly frozen into a permanent grin, he whispered, *"Lemme have it again."*

Taking our little pet in his arms, he stepped off the curb, opened the passenger side door of the woman's car and slid in beside her. The woman, all smiles, began conversing with him paying scant attention to the animal he was holding. She most likely thought it to be a small kitten. A few seconds elapsed when, upon closer examination, she realized that her friend wasn't cuddling a kitten but a real live skunk. She was so startled that she alarmed all of Sherwood with an ear-piercing, high-pitched shriek. She bolted from her car and, with skirt flying, ran like a galloping gazelle in high heels to the opposite curb before stopping to blister Walter with a few unmistakably strong, threatening words. She demanded that he get that thing out of her car immediately before it did something to ruin her upholstery.

Of course, Walter laughed his head off. He was having fun. And he didn't want to give Little Stinky back to us. He wanted to create more havoc.

And so for the next hour, he toted our little skunk about town, causing one heck of a stir.

Sherwood was a small community, not many shops and businesses, but he managed to empty every single one of them in short order. People just weren't at all comfortable with a live skunk in their place of business. But Little Stinky didn't mind the commotion, not one iota. In fact, it seemed to enjoy all the attention—and so did Walter.

The Case of The Cuddly Kitten

Mother walked into the kitchen holding a cute little month-old kitten in her hand. When she went to fetch a bucket of well water, she found it curled up, sleeping on the back porch. We had cats but none the color of the kitten and none that we knew were going to have a litter. We had no idea where it had come from.

Quite naturally, when we cuddled and petted it, we wanted to keep the cute little thing. But Mom knew that Dad would put his foot down and order us to get rid of it. It was senseless to argue. So, later in the morning, we reluctantly toted it across the swamp and down the Sherwood-Tualatin Road to Irene Orr's house, giving it to her.

The next morning, Mom walked into the kitchen and, to our surprise, she had another kitten in her arms. We children thought it was the same one because it looked identical to the kitten she'd found the day before. It was a female, the same approximate age and the same color. But Mom thought differently, quite certain that it was a different one. We had heard of dogs finding their way back home but it seemed preposterous to Mom that a kitten could do that. We kids were dreamers, though, and it didn't seem so unbelievable to us.

We already had too many cats so we knew that Dad wouldn't let us keep it. Besides, it was a female and that meant more kittens in the future.

When Dad saw it, he shook his head negatively even before we had a chance to ask. But he had a solution of how to dispose of the tiny animal. He knew that Frances Bohlen adored cats. But her husband John wasn't as keen on them. If she wanted it though, he would have no say, whatsoever in the matter.

So, since Dad and Mom were going to their nursery to buy a couple of fruit trees, Pa took the kitten with them.

Before John could object, Dad handed the kitten to Frances and, just as he knew, she fell in love with the tiny furry creature, refusing to give it back.

Realizing that his so-called good friend had just pulled a fast one on him, John made a prediction.

"You just wait, Elmer. One day you might just discover a mangy Nubian goat lounging on his doorstep."

When Mom and Dad returned home, he made a proclamation.

"If it's the same kitten and if it finds its way back here again, I'll eat my hat."

He was confident that they'd seen the last of it. But the next morning, Mother came in from the back porch with . . . another kitten. And it was the very same color, sex and approximate age as the others. This was number three.

Mom, grinning from ear to ear, smugly prodded Dad, *"Well, Toots! You'd better get ready to eat your hat. The cat's back!"*

Mom and Dad were certain now that a litter of kittens was around somewhere, perhaps under the porch, the house, or under the barn. But we kids hadn't seen a stray cat around. And surely if the mother cat had gone under our house, we would have seen it emerging at one time or another. And if there were a litter under there, we would have heard the little ones. We had a dilemma, a mystery on our hands.

A rap at the back door interrupted our discussion about what we should do with the kitten. It was our neighbor, Dick Walgraeve. Entering the house, he was grinning from ear to ear. He, too, was holding a small kitten. And it was absolutely identical to the one that Mom was cuddling in her hands.

The mystery was solved. It was one of his cats that had had a litter, a litter of five kittens. And having too many cats himself, he wanted to get rid of them. But he had no heart to kill the tiny creatures. So, he decided to give them away to us. He knew full well that we kids wouldn't think of destroying them but instead would find homes for them. He was right on target.

Now Dad was the one who had been victimized. Taking a page out of John Bohlen's book, he informed his good friend that he might find a stray animal on his doorstep someday—a mangy Nubian goat.

Our Own Daniel Boone

Grandmother had taught us how to make box-traps to catch animals without injuring them—animals like squirrels and chipmunks and rabbits. It wasn't hard catching them but keeping them caught was another matter. Most of them escaped within a few hours.

Since I had been about nine years old, we had been capturing squirrels using a drop-lid box trap and pieces of apple as bait. At one time, we had caged nearly two dozen of them in an old rabbit hutch and although they probably didn't care to be in there, they thrived on a diet of fruit, nuts and grain. But, invariably, they escaped one way or another back into the wild.

About half the time when we set out to trap something, it was one of us who got trapped. For instance, an adult squirrel that we'd caught gave us all kinds of trouble. We managed to dump it from the trap into a burlap bag. Then, after resetting the trap, we took it home and tried to release it into the rabbit hutch. But, no matter what we did, we couldn't get the darned thing out of the bag. We even turned the bag upside down and vigorously shook it. But the squirrel continued to hold on for dear life.

Pa became amused by our plight and took the sack from us saying, *"You kids just don't know nuthin'. Just reach in there and grab the danged thing by its tail and pull it out."*

Our Pa believed himself to be the greatest outdoorsman of all time, a modern-day Daniel Boone.

Reaching into the sack, he grabbed the squirrel by the tail and pulled it from the bag. In a flash, the furry little varmint turned on him, crawled up its own tail and sunk its sharp, chisel-shaped teeth into the old man's forefinger. In pain and bellowing like a wounded bull moose, he vigorously shook his hand, trying to rid himself of the squirrel. But it doggedly held on for several excruciating seconds before letting go. Then, being free, it ran up the road. And for the next three or four hours, it sat atop a stump not far from the house and chirped as if it were defiantly mocking Dad and celebrating its victory over man.

The bite wound on Pa's finger looked horrible. And by the time he went to work at the shipyard that evening, it had become a reddened, swollen, throbbing mess. When his boss saw it, he feared that it had already become infected and ordered Dad to have it treated immediately by the shipyard's medical staff. His buddies, being curious, crowded around him wanting to know what had happened. Well, Pop was pretty well known for telling a good story. And when he told them that a squirrel had bitten his finger, they were quite amused but few really believed that's what truly happened.

Not long after the finger episode, Dad was clearing some brush when a blackberry vine whipped across his face. A thorn made a clean slice across the end of his droopy, bulbous nose and laid it wide open. The wound should have been sutured but Dad relied on Mom's medical skills. Bandaging his snoot was like wrapping a plump hot dog that had ruptured.

Again confronted by some of his shipyard work mates, they quizzed him, wanting to know what had happened. Pop kind of figured that telling the truth would be too mundane. So he made up a whopper of a story. And before the night was over, everyone in the shipyards had heard of Dad's heroic hand-to-hand fight with a black bear and the unaimed shot that had dispatched it.

My pop could really lay it on thick. He was just a city slicker and most certainly hadn't the skills of a Daniel Boone when it came to the outdoors. He probably never saw a bear in the wild let alone shoot at one. And it would be a safe bet to say that he was far more of an expert when it came to shooting the bull.

The Accidental Arrow

The bows and arrows that Tom and I made were deadly. And knowing how lethal they were, we took extreme care when we used them. But even then, we weren't careful enough.

We made the bows from straight, pliable limbs of the hazelnut bush and the arrows from the straight limbs of the mock orange shrub. Our arrowheads were 16-penny nails, hammered until flat. After filing barbs on the pointed tips, we inserted and tied the heads to the arrows. And feathers from a chicken's wing worked perfectly for the tails.

One day, Tom and I took our bows and arrows with us when we visited our friend, Dickie Walgraeve. We found him in his dad's stock barn doing chores and invited him to join us, shooting arrows at a target. But before he could, he had to finish doing his work. So Tom and I waited outside.

Being impatient and without giving much thought to what I was doing, I carelessly launched one of my arrows at the barn door. Instead of the arrow striking the door, as I had intended, it quite by accident went through the only knothole in it and into the barn. Seconds later, the door creaked open and out staggered Dickie, wide-eyed and stunned, with my arrow buried to the bone in his cheek. It was an unbelievably horrifying sight.

With the barbs filed into the tip of the arrow, it wasn't easy extracting it. But we managed to do so without obtaining any medical assistance. Fortunately, Dickie suffered nothing more than a small puncture wound and a sore jaw. It healed in a few days.

Although it was unintentional and accidental, no one could have felt any worse than I did for the stupid thing that I'd done to my friend. We were grateful that the arrow hadn't hit him in the eye or throat. I shuddered thinking about what could have happened.

Columbia Distributing

During the summer months of the war years when Dad had a day off at the shipyards, he sometimes took one of us youngsters to work with him at his other job. And when he asked me to go, I was in the car before he could get his pants on. Fortunately for us kids, in those days, parents were not restricted by a lot of rules and regulations preventing them from taking their children with them to work.

Going anyplace with Pop, especially to work, always proved to be educational in addition to being downright fun.

When the war began, Dad was employed as a truck driver, salesman and warehouseman for Columbia Distributing Company in Portland. The company sold and distributed beer and carbonated beverages throughout the city and surrounding communities. The beer, in kegs and bottles, was shipped in from other states but most of the soda pop, in various flavors, was bottled on site. The pie-shaped building, where all the work was done, was referred to as the plant, and had been constructed on a similarly-shaped lot on the east side of Portland.

The Starvaggi family owned Columbia Distributing Company and, as I recall, three brothers, Jack, Joe and Johnny, ran the business. Jack was a well-dressed, nice-looking young man with a Victor Mature profile and seemed to be the overall boss. Joe, an expressive sort, and Johnny, the youngest in his late teens, did most of the day-to-day manual work.

My dad, for his stature, was an amazingly strong man. He could pick up several cases of bottled pop at one time and easily hoisted full kegs of beer onto his shoulders. Not only were the kegs heavy, they were bulky and round with not many places to get a good grip. After maturing into a husky teenager and playing football, I attempted to lift a few kegs but I could never successfully hoist them any higher than my waist.

Another driver who worked for Columbia Distributing was a crude talking bull of a man named Johnny Barber. Johnny and Dad were great friends and they amused everyone with their good-natured kidding and bantering. I loved to hear Johnny speak because he had a hoarse, tenor-pitched voice that boomed with occasional expletives when something went wrong—like the morning he dropped a fully loaded case of soda pop on his foot. I heard words that I had never heard before and hoped that I'd never hear again.

Before I was old enough to be of any help, as long as I was careful, I had free run of the plant. My mind went wild with wonder: the stacks and stacks of soda pop in so many flavors, the varied odors and sweet aromas, the tinkling of bottles, the hissing of steam, ringing bells, and the noise of machinery; everything was an attraction to a young, imaginative and inquisitive mind.

The bottling machinery consisted of a conveyor belt, a dispensing machine and a capper. They were probably the only automated

Columbia Distributing, around 1935

equipment in the building. The conveyor moved a never-ending line of empty bottles into the dispensing machine. It was an apparatus equipped with several hoses, and filled the bottles with pop. The conveyor continued carrying the bottles, each one filled to the same exact level, to a second machine. It clapped caps onto them. One of the brothers, Joe or Johnny, removed the capped bottles from the conveyor, three in each hand. And after giving them a vigorous shake, inserted them into wooden boxes.

One day as Joe was removing the bottles from the conveyor and shaking them, he noticed something floating in one. On closer examination, he discovered that it was the end joint of one of his own fingers. He had grabbed the bottles too soon and, just as the capping machine clapped a cap on the bottle, it snipped off a fingertip. At first, he felt only a twinge. But a few hours later, it was a different story. His hand wrapped in a bulky bandage, the twinge turned into throbbing, excruciating pain.

Not long after World War II began, Joe enlisted in the Army. At a going-away-party, he was asked how he was going to shoot a rifle with a short finger. Jokingly, he replied that he would have to shoot a short rifle.

Someone else asked him what he would do if he came face to face with a Japanese soldier in the jungle.

He thought for a moment and then said, "*I will politely bow to the guy and say, 'you go your way and I'll go mine.' Then when the little son-of-a-bitch returns my bow, I'll run like my tail's on fire.*"

Early one Saturday, Dad had to go to the plant to load his truck with some of the company's product for an early delivery the following Monday. Tom and I went with him. We were too small to help and since no one else was around, we were free to explore the cavernous interior of the building. Ogling the mountains of soda pop crates, we had high hopes that sooner or later Dad would give each of us a bottle of pop.

We found a hand truck and began wheeling each other among the stacks of bottle crates. We became too careless and reckless . . . and then it happened. With Tom aboard the hand truck and me pushing him much too fast, I accidentally slammed it into a stack of crated empty bottles. The stack toppled over, making a horrible crash and strew broken glass across the concrete floor. My unfortunate brother suffered a nasty gash on his leg that needed bandaging and, poor me; I suffered a nasty blistering on my butt. And what seemed to be an even worse punishment, I got no soda pop.

Rationing and shortages of certain products and materials also affected the breweries. The Starvaggi Brothers began distributing a brew called *Chrystal Beer* that I believe was bottled in the state of Washington. The beer was certainly not of high quality but it satisfied the wants of the thirsty tavern dwellers in the Northwest. Dad said it tasted like water but looked like pee.

Every Saturday morning, he delivered 200 cases of Chrystal Beer to the Gateway Tavern just across the bridge west of Newberg, a dry town with no taverns within its city limits. That one delivery took Pop several hours to complete. Near the war's end, I was able to accompany him a few times to make the Gateway Tavern delivery. With my help, we most often finished about noontime—just in time for lunch.

Pop loved steaks and no matter where Dad was in the State of Oregon, you could just bet that he knew the location of the best restaurants especially the ones that served terrific rib steaks—like the restaurant in Newberg.

Even though the work was difficult and tiring, I didn't mind helping my dad. I got to share some valuable personal time with him and, to me, just being with Pop was rewarding. Rewarding—like in a steak—medium rare.

Tommy Gets Skunked

The evening was warm and the inside of the house stifling hot. So we sat on the back porch gazing at the sky, watching for shooting stars. The only one of the family not there was Tommy; he'd gone to the barn to milk his cow.

Returning a short time later with his pail full of milk, he came upon a skunk near the house and thought it was our Little Stinky. To his astonishment, when he reached down to pick it up, he got a good dose of skunk juice.

We heard him bellow and, almost immediately, he rounded the corner of the house on a dead-run, splashing milk all over. He smelled really, really bad. Stammering and sputtering, he was able to blurt out, *"Stinky just squirted me!"*

But Stinky didn't squirt him. At that very moment, our little pet was lounging contentedly in Mom's lap getting its little tummy rubbed.

One of us toted Tom's pants off on the end of a pitchfork for a solemn burial deep in the woods. Mom opened a couple of jars of stewed tomatoes and rubbed the juice on his ornery hide believing it would eliminate the smell. Well, it didn't. And no matter how much of it she applied or how often he washed, the stink still clung to him. He also splashed aftershave lotion on himself. But that, too, did little good. Actually, the mix of skunk stink and sweetness was just as nauseating.

As expected, no one wanted him in the house. And I sure-as-the-dickens didn't because we shared a bed at night. So, for the next three or four nights, he slept in the barn. The poor kid really didn't smell quite right for a long, long time.

As Little Stinky matured, we noticed more skunks appearing on the farm. Then the little *squirt* began to disappear for a few days at a time. And eventually it left us for good, probably eloping with another skunk.

We loved that little animal and we missed it very much . . . but not its playmates. And even though it was just a Little Stinky, it was a wonderful pet.

Exploring the Creek Downstream

Tom, Dick and I had never bothered to explore Hedges' creek downstream from Walgraeve's farm to any degree; the brush seemed to be too thick along its banks. But one warm, sunny morning, with my fishing pole in hand and my mouth watering for fried trout, I went looking. Soon, I found myself hung up in blackberry vines and on the thorns of small scrubby Hawthorne trees. But being persistent and ever so careful, I inched my way through the brambles to the creek's bank. Sunlight filtered through the dense thicket of briars and limbs to reveal beautiful deep pools of still, black water where trout just had to be hiding.

Working my way along the bank a little farther downstream, I came to a place that appeared free of snags where I was less likely to lose a hook. The only obstacles that I could see were a few limbs dangling in the water and a floating piece of shiplap lumber. Crouching down and surveying my surroundings, I again focused my attention on the board floating in the water, and saw something that chilled me to the bone. Atop it laid the strangest, most hideous and repulsive creature I'd ever seen in my young life. It had the body of a snake about 18 inches long, a huge, green head with bulging eyes and two small legs. I wondered if it sensed my presence as I stared at it in disbelief.

Gradually it became clear to me, as I studied it, that what I was looking at was a snake swallowing a live frog.

Immediately I was enraged believing that no living thing should die like that—eaten alive by a slithering snake.

I hated snakes with a passion. And instantly, I was determined to save the frog. The best way to free it, I figured, was to kill the snake with a stick, then flick it and its prey out of the water. I could then extract the frog. With this plan in mind and a stout stick in one hand, I moved closer ever so slowly. With my free hand, I grasped a limb that hung over the water and leaned out as far as I could. As I raised the stick to strike the snake, the darned limb broke, and I fell into the water atop my target and its victim.

Being in the murky water with a reptile wasn't exactly a pleasant situation and it took me just an instant to pull my feet out of the muddy creek bottom and scramble up onto dry land. When I looked back, the snake and its lunch were nowhere in sight. At that instant, an unpleasant thought raced through my mind.

"What if that thing is in one of my pockets or has slipped down inside my shirt?"

With the speed of Superman, I disrobed on the spot, nearly ripping my clothing off, hoping not to discover anything unpleasant. And, quite relieved, I didn't.

Plowing my way out of the thicket, I made a vow never again to return unless I was armed with a knife or an axe and accompanied by two or three hunting dogs lest I encounter another snake munching on some poor creature. The place gave me the willies. And so I decided to fish in places where I felt more comfortable.

Making my way back upstream, I found a place where I thought I could easily leap across to the other bank. When I jumped, I landed on a board with a nail in it. The nail punched through my tennis shoe and penetrated deep into my foot. I had a terrible time trying to extract it. In severe pain, I had to stand upright holding the board to the ground with my good foot while pulling my injured foot upward.

About a mile from home and my foot throbbing, I slowly hobbled for the next half hour to the house.

While I related the events of the morning to Mom about the frog and the snake and jumping onto the nail, she doctored my foot, cleaning the wound with peroxide and swabbing it with Mercurochrome. My mother could work miracles with tape, gauze and a little Mercurochrome. She had a lot of practice.

Instead of eating golden pan-fried trout for lunch, as I'd planned, all I got was a bowl of hot oatmeal with raisins. Well, it wasn't the tastiest fare in the world but it was a sight better than what that stupid snake had to eat.

Tobacco Temptations

One misty day, I heard Eddie Wager calling me with his high-pitched shriek, a signal that we used when one of us wanted to talk to the other. After doing my chores, I high-tailed it across the swamp and met my school chum in his dad's barn. He had a surprise for me. He'd swiped one of his dad's cigars and wanted to share it. Eddie didn't want to take any chances getting caught and figured the best place to smoke the thing was in the swamp.

Mom had caught Tom, Eddie and me red-handed, smoking cigarettes in the outhouse a few days earlier. Puffing away like steam engines, we had lit up two of the things when she startled us, yelling loud and clear from the house, *"You kids put out those damned cigarettes and do it right now."*

Her sharp command so frightened Eddie that, without the slightest hesitation, he bolted out of the door and ran for home like a skittish deer.

How did she know we were in the outhouse and what we were doing? What gave us away was the cigarette smoke. It poured out of the knotholes like smoke rising from the stacks of a Pittsburgh steel mill. She was mad as a wet hen but remained calm. And instead of giving us a whack on the behinds, she sat us down, blew some cigarette smoke into a white cloth, and showed us the results; a yellow nicotine stain that she said would remain forever in our lungs if we smoked. It was a good lesson and she was a good teacher.

By the time Eddie and I had found a good place in the swamp to smoke the cigar, it began to drizzle rain. Eddie cut it in half and we lit up. With cigars in our mouths, we felt like big shots, like two Chicago politicians. But it didn't take long before the world began to spin like a merry-go-round and my stomach boil like a butter churn. Sitting in the mud, I started to wretch, trying to throw up whatever I had eaten during the past month. I just wanted to die. I found myself wishing it would pour down rain, flooding the swamp and drown me, putting me out of my misery. Disoriented, dizzy and his eyes watering, Eddie staggered off for home looking as rotten as I felt. I really didn't want to see him again, not for a long time for fear that he might have another one of his bright ideas.

Managing to stumble home myself, I reeled like a drunk. I lurched into our outhouse and spent another half hour with my head stuck down inside that stinking hole.

My parents smoked cigarettes. But cigarettes were expensive and difficult to come by because of the war. Dad solved part of their problem, though, when he purchased a manually operated hand-held cigarette-rolling machine, a can of tobacco and a pack of cigarette papers. The cigarette-rolling machine was no toy. But to us children it was an intriguing contraption. We curiously watched our parents every night as they took a little time to roll a supply of cigarettes for the following day. Even though we boys were forbidden to touch the machine, we wanted to roll a cigarette ourselves.

A couple of times when the adults weren't around, Tommy and I were able to get to the machine, but not the can of tobacco. They hid it well and in places we dared not look. Grandma told us more than once that, when she was a youngster, she used her dad's pipe to smoke dried corn silk. So, we took a page out of her book and made cigarettes using dried corn silk.

We lit and smoked them. But they tasted horrible and the smoke burned my tongue like acid.

Then one day I surprised Tom. I offered him a cigarette that I'd made using real tobacco stripped from several cigarette butts. And he eagerly took the thing and lit up. But he should have known better than to trust me. I'd added another ingredient . . . sun-dried cow dung. It was the same color as the tobacco and even smelled disgusting.

I didn't think he'd notice anything unusual right away. But he did. A couple of puffs were all it took. He spit and barfed and turned on me, his face purple with rage, and screeched, *"You dirty rat, Teddy! I'm gonna kill you. I'm gonna tell Grandma what you did."*

I nailed him good, the best prank I'd pulled on him in ages. And his threat to tattle on me didn't worry me in the least. I knew he wouldn't tell Grandma . . . or Mom . . . or anyone else for that matter. He couldn't. Had he, he'd have had to admit that he was smoking. And that confession would have landed him in bigger trouble than me.

Poor Tom . . . I almost felt sorry for him . . . but not quite.

The Medicine Women

Most families equipped their homes with a medicine cabinet and some with a medicine chest. But we—we had to be different. We had a medicine trunk. Mom stored most of the family's medical provisions in an old trunk beside her bed. And she constantly retrieved supplies from it to patch our cuts, scratches and scrapes. I think Mom had enough bandages, tape and disinfectant in there to operate her own clinic.

While handling a couple of weathered two-by-four studs, one of them slipped and slid across my arm, driving a sizeable splinter deep into the underside of my wrist at the base of my palm. I felt as if I'd been stabbed. Writhing in pain I somehow removed a piece of wood from the nasty, bleeding gouge.

Several days passed. But instead of healing, the wound became an oozing mess. Obviously infected, it was red, swollen and hot to the touch.

Mom doctored it several times applying salves and Mercurochrome, but none of it did any good. It only worsened.

Examining the wound, Grandma suggested that I try squeezing it to force the infection out. I didn't like the idea but I did it anyway. To my surprise, a large splinter ¾ of an inch long and the diameter of a wooden match stick popped to the surface. Immediately I felt relief, and in just a few days my wrist was on the mend. It healed nicely.

But as soon as one of us recovered from an accident, another got hurt.

Tom and I wanted to play ball in the pasture. But as luck would have it, Grandma came home for a couple of days. Not in the house ten minutes, she put us to work and informed us that, come morning, we were going to cut wood for the winter.

The moment we finished breakfast the following day, we gathered up axes, saws, wedges and sledgehammers, and marched off to the woods as if we were in a prison gang. She had chosen two large fir trees to fall, trees that grew not far from the old root cellar where we had already cleared brush.

Because we were so agile, it was much easier for Tom and me to trim the limbs from the trees once they were on the ground than it was for Grandma. But we weren't careful doing our work and left several chisel-shaped knots protruding from the trunks.

After completely trimming both trees, Tom hopped atop one of the logs, walking quickly to the other end to help Grandmother pile brush. For a 10-year-old kid, he was nimble footed as a goat. But, nonetheless, he slipped and fell, gouging a large piece of flesh from one of his legs on one of the sharp knots. The wound gushed blood like a fire hydrant. Immediately feeling weak, he slumped to the ground. Grandmother tore through the brush like a bulldozer to get to him, and pulling a bandana from around her neck, quickly wrapped it around his leg to stem the bleeding. I ran to the house like my tail was afire to alert Mom and to get something more suitable to use as a bandage.

Tom was in excruciating pain, so severe that it made him sick to his stomach and unable to stand. We had to get him home quickly. He was too heavy to carry but I knew the perfect solution for transporting him—our own homemade Indian travois. It was made for this sort of emergency. And it worked perfectly.

Since Dad was working and we had no telephone to call for help, it was up to the women to do the doctoring. Very expertly, they cleansed, disinfected and bandaged the worrisome looking mess. And in just a few days, Tom was as good as new. Other than a large concave scar, his leg healed without any complications. Like Indian medicine women, Mom and Grandma had again done an excellent job.

Not many weeks later, another one of us suffered a freakish accident. Tom and I went to the barn to milk and do the evening chores, unaware that our younger brother Dick was already there. He'd fallen asleep atop the bales of hay stacked in the hayloft. Using a hooked pitchfork, Tom swung it, driving the tines into the top-most bale to pull it from the stack to feed the cows. Dick had awakened at that very moment, and crawling to the edge of the stack, had put his hand on the bale that Tom was after. One of the pitchfork tines went completely through Dick's hand, pinning him momentarily to the bale. Extracting the tine from his hand wasn't easy and, as we did, some of the flesh seemed to turn inside out.

The wound turned an ugly, purplish color and bled little, giving Mom some concern about infection. She went to work again, dabbing antiseptic solution on his hand and wrapping it with sterile gauze. To Dick's credit, he cried very little during the entire ordeal. But it must have hurt like the dickens. He, too, healed quickly and, luckily, suffered no ill affects.

Mom was whipping through a crossword puzzle after supper one night when Dad mentioned the nasty accidents that Tom, Dick and I had suffered and how lucky we were that our wounds healed so nicely without any problems. Mom was quick to let Dad know that it wasn't just luck that did the trick but her expert medical skills.

The Seventh Grade

M oving up to the seventh grade and into the third row of desks was another milestone in my youth. In addition to proving that I was a little smarter, it also meant that I was one of the oldest and largest boys in school. The fourth row of desks next to the windows were reserved for the eighth graders and hopefully, if I played my cards right, I would find myself in that row next year.

Tom had also reached a milestone. He'd moved up to the fifth grade and was in the big room with me. His desk was in the first row nearest the door.

On Monday, the Second of October, Mrs. Martin, our teacher discovered that Tom's birthday was the day before. He had turned eleven. She beckoned him to the front of the room and surprised him, announcing to the other students that he had just celebrated a birthday. But that wasn't the only surprise that she'd planned for him. She also intended to give him a traditional swat on the seat of the pants. When she grabbed him by the arm, her quick move startled him. He jerked away and accidentally upset a bottle of black ink, splashing some of it on her lovely print dress. Instead of Tom being the surprised one, it was our teacher.

Mrs. Martin seldom missed teaching a day of school. When she did, it meant that she was really sick and home in bed or someone else in the family was quite ill. Even when the swamp flooded, covering the road with water, she arrived at school on time . . . thanks to Chet Fischbuch. He lived just beyond the flood area and always came to the rescue, voluntarily ferrying the teachers and students to school in his rowboat. That had to be a big adventure for those kids. I envied them; they had all the luck.

There'd been talk for some time about raising the height of the roadbed to prevent it from being affected by the high water. But the war put a temporary halt to the plan. Eventually, though, it was fixed, but not until long after I'd graduated

A wood-burning furnace in the basement of the school kept us toasty warm during cold weather. Local farmers donated the firewood. They cut it from their own timber and even hauled it to the school. But it was up to the janitor, cook or one of the teachers to keep the fire going throughout the day.

Each of the two classrooms was heated through large wooden grills built into the floor. When the weather turned cold, the girls often stood over them to get warm. And when they did, the rising heat caused their dresses to billow out like parachutes. It never happened . . . but you can guess what we boys hoped would occur.

In the worst way, I wanted to play a musical instrument. But the school was too small to offer a music program. Yet, at most of the school's functions, we provided entertainment of a sort. We had what some people called a rhythm band. But a more fitting name would have been *chaos*.

The participants, students in the upper four grades, used drums, tambourines, cymbals, clapper sticks, triangles and bells as their instruments. In fact, we used just about anything that we could find to beat, bang, or smack with a stick to make a noise. And that's what it was too, a noise, a loud one. Mashing cans at the local dump made a better sound.

Whoever participates in a rhythm band should have some natural rhythm in his or her soul. But unfortunately most of the kids in our school had none. The din was horrible. And whenever a parent or teacher was accompanying us on the piano, we easily drowned him or her out. Some students couldn't participate . . . and some students wouldn't participate. Therefore, they were the poor souls who were forced to listen to the rest of us. And that danged near killed them. They grimaced, rolled their eyes, clapped hands over their ears, and squirmed as if they were being vaccinated.

The school was normally quiet during study time but it was pure pandemonium when the recess bell rang. The students in the two classrooms were separated for study and, quite naturally, they were separated during recess. The little ones played tag in the basement or rode the merry-go-round in back of the school. We, in the big room, played

Annie, Annie over, dodge ball, basketball or softball, depending on the weather.

When the weather was stormy, we played basketball and dodge ball in a large open structure, a building that we called a play shed. It had been erected in back of the school.

Playing basketball was difficult because the shed's floor was not conducive to dribbling the ball. It was dirt, uneven and covered with a layer of coarse sawdust. And the baskets were nailed flush to the end walls. It was little wonder why none of us ever became a basketball star in high school.

Nearly everyone in the upper four grades, boys and girls, participated on the school's softball team. None of us had any equipment, gloves and so forth. But the school owned a couple of old beat-up bats and a soft ball, a thing that was bound up with tape to keep it from unraveling. It wasn't as round as it should have been and sometimes, when it had been hit solidly, it flattened out, sailing through the air like a squished grapefruit.

Saint Paul's Lutheran School and Rex Hill Elementary School also fielded softball teams, providing competition for us.

I wondered about those Lutheran kids. Never having been around people who professed to be Lutheran, I wondered what they looked like. Maybe I expected to see someone with horns or claws or bulging eyes. But when they came to play, they were all nice looking youngsters, neatly dressed, clean, quiet and obedient. From their appearance and demeanor, I was falsely impressed believing we would kick the tar out of them. But, instead, it was we who got stomped into the ground. Well, I reasoned, we were Swamp Rats and accustomed to throwing dirt clods and rocks, not perfectly round softballs.

In a game with Rex Hill Elementary School, not one soul who witnessed the contest ever realized that I made the greatest catch ever in Cipole School's fabled sports history. At the time, I was wearing a pair of loose-fitting pants held up with a leather belt that I'd found in my granddad's junk pile. The belt was unusual in that it was equipped with a half dozen well-worn snaps instead of a buckle.

I was playing in right field when, mid-way through the game, a batter hit a high fly ball in my direction. I gave chase and, as I reached up to catch the ball, all the snaps on my belt popped loose at the same time. Immediately, my britches headed south. Somehow I managed to catch them with one hand before they reached my knees. At the same instant, I miraculously caught the fly ball with my other hand, preventing our opponents from scoring a run.

I was never known for my quick-thinking or super dexterity but, nevertheless, I am living proof that it's possible to catch two *flies* at the same time.

Cousin Gaylen

M y cousin Gaylen was lonely and unhappy as a youth. He grew up without a father in his life. When he was less than a year old, his mother Freda (pronounced Fray-duh) divorced his dad, my Uncle Mickey. She would not allow him to visit his son except on special occasions. Until my uncle joined the Army in 1942, he was given permission to see his son two times.

Uncle Mickey fought the war in New Guinea and the Philippines. When he returned home after four long years in the South Pacific, he met with the same hostility from his son's mother as before. Sadly, not until Gaylen had become a teenager and went on his own did he have any kind of relationship with his father.

When Gaylen was a little kid, he was cute with light curly hair and a wonderfully shy smile, the spitting image of his father. And he was a well-behaved youngster too. But I

Uncle Mickey (left) with Army Buddy

felt sorry for him because he lived a life of near total isolation with his mother. He seemed to have little fun and true happiness eluded him in his youth.

Aunt Freda was an overly protective mother and seldom permitted her son to play in the dirt, as did most boys. Nearly every day she dressed him in short pants, shiny shoes and a white ruffled shirt. The kid looked like Little Lord Fauntleroy.

A strict person, she was difficult with people. But she remained close to our family. All through the war, my parents did their best to maintain contact with her, occasionally visiting her home in east Portland. And Aunt Freda brought Gaylen to our farm for a few visits.

Even though he was much younger than me, we became quite close to each other, as close as brothers.

All of us piled into the car one mid-December morning and called on Aunt Freda and Gaylen, taking them Christmas gifts. After visiting for several hours, she prepared dinner for us, things like canned beans, hot dogs, store-bought bread and margarine, certainly nothing like Mom prepared at home. After we'd finished eating, I tried to thank Freda for the meal. But not having a glib tongue, the words didn't come out of my mouth as I'd intended.

"Thanks Aunt Freda. Mom's a good cook too. She baked some pies for us so when we go home we'll have somethin' good to eat."

Although she had a smile on her face, I could easily tell that she wasn't very pleased. And my poor flabbergasted mom wanted to hide her face. What could I do? I wanted to kill myself. But that would have been the easy way out. I figured the only way I could make up for my bumbling remark was with the Christmas gift I had for her.

With no money to buy presents, I made my gifts, using my new jack knife. I made a miniature wooden Ferris wheel for Gaylen. The wheel rotated and had seven seats that swung freely. Using a nail, I made a crank so the wheel could be turned manually. Aunt Freda's gift, I admit, was a little strange. But it was one of a kind. It was a flower-pot made from a soup bone. After carving out the bony lacework in the marrow cavity, I painted it. Then I filled the cavity with dirt and planted a flower in it. I thought it looked pretty nice. But Freda didn't seem impressed by my creativity. After looking at it for some moments, she commented that she'd never before received a soup bone as a present for Christmas or, for that matter, on any other occasion.

Our relationship had suffered another setback.

Gaylen, two years old, and his mother, Freda

Chapter VI

1945

A Historic Year

Nineteen Forty-Five was an unforgettable year in many ways. Some were good and some were bad.

When the year began, World War II was still raging. And all of us, adults and children alike, were constantly under its repressive thumb. We did things to take our minds off the fighting but it was always in the back of our minds. And though our armed forces were forcing our enemies to give up ground, I worried that I might have to leave home to fight in it some day. After all, I was growing older—soon to be 13—and large in stature.

No sooner had we become accustomed to a new year than memorable events began to occur rapidly in machine-gun fashion. Among them, the death of Franklin Delano Roosevelt, the 32nd president of the United States. He died on the 12th day of April, one day before my 13th birthday. When I heard the news on the radio, I felt as if my world had come to an end and cried. We all did. It was a terribly sad day that I'll never forget.

Less than a month later, Germany surrendered and the war in Europe came to an end. That was a fantastic day, a day of celebration. We couldn't get enough of the revelry. The radios blared with reports of victory and the papers printed the news in bold headlines. For days, the theater in Sherwood re-ran the newsreels of the wild ticker-tape parades on the streets of New York.

Then in June, our mother gave birth to Charla Marie, Mom and Dad's second daughter, increasing the size of our family to nine. And all of us were still crammed into our little three-room shack.

Because the weather in August was so warm, we kids went barefoot more than usual. But the dry weather also brought on another forest fire in the Tillamook area of the Coast Range. For days, thick, suffocating smoke rolled down into the Willamette Valley far from the burn area.

Another event occurred in August that was earthshaking. The United States Armed Forces dropped atomic bombs on two Japanese cities: Hiroshima and Nagasaki. The news reports about the enormity of the blasts were frightening and awed each and every one of us. How could a bomb make a blast that large and create so much destruction? But those two bombs brought the Japanese Empire to its knees and within days it surrendered, bringing an end to World War II.

Peace returned to our country and relief returned to our family. And more celebrations, most of them spontaneous and raucous, erupted across the country.

Late in the fall, our four-year-old sister Tudie became seriously ill with a sickness diagnosed as Infantile Paralysis or Polio. But, after several worrisome, nerve-wracking months, she returned home from the hospital as good as new.

Driving toward the house, returning home from a movie one night, we noticed the kitchen lit up like a neon sign. We never locked the door and speculated that perhaps a hobo had gone inside and was raiding the pantry.

Someone was there all right . . . but it wasn't a hobo. To our delight, and to Mom's outright joy, it was her brother Mike. A hero in our eyes, he'd just come home from the war in Europe. And he had indeed raided the icebox. When we walked in, he was sitting at the kitchen table slurping down a glass of whole milk and relishing a slice of homemade bread smothered with fresh butter and Grandma's strawberry jam. It was simple fare to us but a banquet to him.

Before the year had come to an end, Detroit was again making new cars and trucks, war-time defense plants and shipyards had shut down and the work force was flooded by thousands of unemployed servicemen and women. The *G. I. Joes* and the *Rosie the Riveters* were out of work.

Embarrassing Moments

I'd arrived at a time in my life when I was easily embarrassed. One instance occurred when our friends Frances and John Bohlen were visiting. I happened to walk into the living room just as my mother and Frances were conversing about me. My timing was not good. Mom took me by the arm and commented, "*See how pretty his hair is, Frances? It makes him look so cute.*"

No boy my age wants to hear his mother refer to him as being cute, and in particular to someone outside the family, let alone to someone in the family. I would soon become a teen-ager and, if anything, I wanted to be thought of as handsome.

Another embarrassment was the mention of sex or anything that inferred it while conversing with anyone, especially a female, regardless of age or relationship. I lived on a farm. I knew enough.

When Old Jerz came into heat, I had to tow her over to Chet Fischbuch's place to have her bred to his bull. Dad worked a lot of hours, every day of the week. So he had no time. It was up to me. Since I was only 12 at the time, I wasn't keen asking Chet if we could use his bull for a job. But at least he was a male and understood. Had the owner of the bull been a woman though, I wouldn't have done it.

That wasn't the worst of it though, not by a long shot. When I learned that my mother was going to have another baby, I was mortified. I was so humiliated that I didn't want to show my face in public. I was actually ashamed of my parents. I kept thinking that everyone in the world was going to know what my mom and dad had been doing. They were too darned old to be fooling around. My dad was 33 years old and Mom was 31. In my mind, they were ancient.

I cringed just thinking about what the consequences would be when my seventh-grade classmates found out. Would they taunt me? Would they make fun of my mom and dad?

Eventually they did find out. So did the entire community of Cipole. It wasn't possible to keep something like that a secret very long, especially when Mom's tummy began to swell. And whenever someone asked or commented about her pregnancy, I blushed and squirmed. I just couldn't help it. But thank the good Lord; no one ever made a crude remark.

One night, I asked Mom when the baby was due. I wanted her to hurry up and get it over with.

"About the time your school year ends. So you'd better inform your teacher that I might need you at home when I make the delivery."

Her answer made me cringe. I didn't want to reveal my mother's pregnancy to anyone, let alone my teacher. She might ask a few embarrassing questions like, *"Are your mom and dad planning more children in the future?"*

Making Things

Tom and I built several toy airplanes, he far more than I. Some were homemade and others were from model airplane kits that cost anywhere from a dime to a quarter. The ones that we made from scratch were usually carved from old dried shingles, glued together with homemade paste, and covered with tissue paper. Several of these crude model aircraft hung from the ceiling of our house for months on end.

One of the kit aircraft that Tom built was a replica of a German Stuka dive-bomber. He did a magnificent job assembling it and, being proud of his work, took it to school for everyone to see. The teacher was so impressed that she hung it above one of the windows in the classroom.

One day, without thinking, she raised the window, and accidentally crushed Tom's beautiful handiwork. His Stuka took a dive for the last time.

Tom made a boat too. But it wasn't just a toy; it was huge, large enough to accommodate a couple of grown-ups. It was built using *borrowed* lumber from Robinson's onion barn. One had to really concentrate before one could visualize his creation as a boat. When it was fully assembled, he had to contend with big cracks in the hull. It wasn't easy getting a tight fit using rough-hewn one-by-twelve planks. But he had a solution, as he did for most problems. He caulked the cracks using tar, gobs and gobs of it, salvaged from the tar pit at the Cipole siding.

A crew of six kids helped Tom tug the thing down to the little swamp after it had flooded. Working in muck, sometimes up to their knees, they slid it into the water. But his boat was too heavy. It became hopelessly mired in mud. They tried and tried to move it, using pry-poles, ropes, and so on. But they just didn't have the proper resources or the strength. So, it was abandoned.

Tommy's boat was still there long after the water had subsided and the ground had dried. And it was smack in the middle of Dick Wal-graeve's onion field.

When it came time for Mr. Walgraeve to plant onions, he couldn't move the thing; it was too heavy and waterlogged. He called a couple of his friends and they tried prying it loose. But they couldn't budge it either. So, he finally towed it out of there using his horses. It sat un-claimed on the edge of the swamp . . . and was still there year later when Tom and I left home.

We kids wanted a new bicycle. But we had no money to buy one. And our parents certainly couldn't afford the expense. We owned a bike but it was so beat up that it wasn't worth repairing. And a bicycle was the one thing that Tom couldn't create.

So, we searched our minds trying to figure a way to earn some quick cash so we could buy a bike. After pondering on it for some time, we thought we'd come up with a fantastic solution . . . peddling dairy-men's bag balm and packages of flower and vegetable seeds from door-to-door.

We talked Mom and Grandma into ordering a batch of each item for us. And that's when things began to unravel.

First, we had to pay for each item in advance. And the payments were non-refundable. Second, we lived out in the country where homes were far, far apart. Third, those who lived in the country were mostly farmers and had their own inexpensive sources for these same products. Fourth, those who weren't farmers had little need for our product. And fifth, we were too dumb and shy when we approached people.

But, we tried. For days and days, we walked and walked, miles and miles, on graveled roads, through fields, on tree-lined paths, after school and on weekends, in the rain, in the snow, trying to find someone willing to buy the darned stuff. We sold, maybe, two or three of each product earning a few pennies, but certainly not enough to buy a bicycle. And we had ordered enough bag balm to equip a dairy farm and enough seed to plant a section the size of South Dakota.

We gave up. And guess who inherited the rest of our product? It was Mom and Dad, of course.

The Smelt Run

It seemed that every time Dad picked up a newspaper, he read something that irritated him. On this particular morning, it was the price of grocery items.

"Did you read this, Ethel? Hamburger's gone up another two cents a pound. It's the damned war that's done it."

Granted, grocery prices always seemed to be on the rise. But fortunately we raised nearly all of our own food. Furthermore, we knew of something good to eat that was nearly free . . . if we worked for it. Fish! And one of those fish was smelt. Every one in our family enjoyed smelt . . . a platter of Mom's pan-fried smelt to be precise.

Every year in the early spring, smelt runs occurred in the Sandy River east of Portland. But the runs didn't last long, only a few days. So, we had to get at it quickly if we wanted some.

From the moment the run started until it ended, one could find hordes and hordes of people, with nets in hand, along the banks of the river attempting to catch enough of the tiny fish for a meal or two.

One cool and misty day, Dad took the entire family including Grandpa Pileggi to dip for smelt in the Sandy near the town of Troutdale. We left home early hoping to beat the crowd. But by the time we arrived, the banks of the river were already crawling with thousands of people. Grandpa had never before witnessed a smelt run and was astonished at the huge numbers of people and the beehive-like activity at the river's edge.

People were lined up elbow to elbow on both banks. Nearly every one of them was working the waters with some kind of dip net. A few fishermen used expensive, commercially made nets. But most of them had modified small inexpensive trout nets, taping or wiring long wooden poles to them. A few so-called nets were ingeniously fabricated out of window screen, cloth netting or some sieve-like material. One fellow, wading where the water was shallow, had fashioned a peach basket into something nearly as good as a net. He bored several small holes in the bottom to let the water pass through. And maybe he didn't catch as many fish each time as the others with their commercially made nets. But, still, he caught enough to satisfy him and he didn't spend a lot of money doing it.

One fisherman's net was so full of squirming smelt that the 15-foot wooden pole handle snapped. Without a second's hesitation, the fellow jumped into the swirling, frigid waters to retrieve his expensive net. Grandpa, watching the entire scene from the road above the river, thought the fellow had lost his mind. Over the roar of the river, we could hear his excited Italian voice, *"Sonamungunya! He'sa craze. He'sa go swim."*

We caught a lot of smelt, several buckets of the small, silvery fish, enough to feed our family for a couple of days. And when we returned home, each of us had a hand in cleaning and cooking our catch. After snipping the heads off with a pair of scissors and stripping the innards and eggs, the fish were thoroughly washed and dusted with flour, salt and pepper. Mom pan-fried them to a scrumptious, mouth-watering golden brown. With homemade bread layered with dollops of butter, Tom, Dad and I could down 24 smelt each, at one sitting. It was a feast we thoroughly enjoyed and figured was fit for royalty.

Kibitzing

You would never find one of us kids hanging around the house when Mom was washing dishes, ironing clothes or cleaning. But just let her sit down at the kitchen table and deal out a game of solitaire and you could bet that one of us would soon show up to do a little kibitzing. Every one of us was a know-it-all kibitzer when it came to cards.

Mom hated it when we watched her because she knew one of us would invariably ask, *"Why doncha play this card on that one?"*

Mom was good and quick with caustic comebacks.

"Why don't you mind your own damned business?" or *"Why don't you go outside and play in a mud puddle or something?"* or *"Have you done all of your chores?"* or *"Go play with the dog. It's lonely. I'm not!"*

One Sunday afternoon, Mom took a break from her kitchen duties, dealt out a game of solitaire on the kitchen table, and was in the midst of playing when Dad walked in. Leaning over her shoulder, he butted in asking, *"Why doncha play that card on that one?"*

Mom was in a petulant mood having just chased a couple of her innocent offspring out of the house. Her jaw set like granite and staring at the opposite wall, she responded in a firm and stern voice.

"You know, Toots, if I was lost in the middle of the Sahara Desert and dyin' of starvation and thirst, not one damned soul, including you, would ever find me. But, just let me deal out one lousy hand of solitaire and every Tom, Dick and Harry in the country would suddenly show up to tell me how to play the damned game. Now, get the hell away from me and bug somebody else for a change. Go outside and play with one of your idiot kids!"

The Steyaerts

When I came home from school, I walked through the kitchen, on my way to the middle room to put some things away. Mom was sitting at the table playing a game of solitaire and didn't bother to look up but asked,

"How'd school go today?"

"Okay, I guess. Chuck Burck threw pepper juice in my eye and darned near blinded me. And I found a neat agate on the railroad tracks this morning. But I can't find it now. I guess I lost it."

As I passed behind her, I spotted a crude drawing posted on our small cork-backed bulletin board hanging on the wall. It was an indecent caricature of Shirley Steyaert, one of my classmates, with her name printed beneath it. It was shocking. I was confused and totally humiliated that this horrid sketch had been tacked up in our house. Staring at it for just a moment, I turned to Mom to ask for an explanation. But before I could open my mouth, she said, *"Well?"*

She wasn't making a statement but asking a question.

Confused, I was unsure what she wanted me to say,

"Well, what?"

"Did you draw that?"

It was horrible to think that my own mom or anyone else could believe that I'd drawn something so vulgar, so offensive. But that didn't bother me nearly as much as someone believing that I couldn't draw a picture more artistically. I was proud to be the best artist in school and this drawing was done poorly, absolutely horribly, not to mention the indecency of it.

"Heck no, I didn't draw that. And I don't know who did either. But it sure as heck wasn't me. If I drew it, it would be a heck of a lot better than this."

Mom ripped the drawing from the wall and threw it in the stove apparently satisfied for the moment that I was telling the truth. Where she found it or how she came by it, I never found out. But I think one of the teachers must have given it to her believing I was responsible. Nothing more was ever said, not from Mom or the teachers.

I liked Shirley. She was a nice girl and I would never have depicted her like that.

Once, when we were still in the little room, our teacher scolded Shirley for something that she denied doing. I was certain that she was innocent. She never told an untruth and was the most honest kid in our school. Nonetheless, the

Shirley Steyaert

teacher was convinced that she was guilty and put her in the cloak-room to sit alone for an hour as punishment. When the hour was up, the teacher opened the door to allow Shirley to return to her desk. But she was gone. Not about to be punished for something she hadn't done, she'd climbed out a window and went home.

Agnes Steyaert, Shirley's sister, was six or seven years older than me. She had flaming red hair. And she had a temper to match, something that I found out the hard way.

Enjoying a beautiful warm day, several of us, including Agnes, took a leisurely stroll through Hedges' woods. My brother Dee had some-what of a problem and, needing to relieve himself, scooted into the brush out of sight. Finished, he summoned me and asked that I fetch him a handful of leaves. Seizing the opportunity to do a little mischief, ever so carefully, I picked three stinging nettle leaves. And he took them. They didn't sting his hands but they certainly stung something else. I admit it was a rotten thing to do to my little brother and I de-served a good kick in the rump. And that's exactly what happened.

When Agnes heard Dee squall and found out what I'd done, she became furious, so angered by my insensitivity to my little brother that she hauled off and slugged me in the shoulder. The blow knocked me ass-end over teakettle right into Hedges' creek.

All of those Steyaert girls could hit like Joe Louis. With ten kids in the family, the girls probably learned to slug it out in self-defense. They were just as strong as their brothers.

Mrs. Steyaert was probably the smallest person in the Steyaert family. A little on the portly side, she was bent over from years and years of hard work. One of her sons, Francis, was stooped as well. But part of his problem was the result of a hernia. The family was so poor that they couldn't afford the operation needed to correct his problem. And so he put up with the pain for years and years.

Poor or not, tough times or not, every one of them was quick with a smile and eager to share what little they had.

I liked Mrs. Steyaert. She was a nice person, witty, kind and gener-ous. One evening, six or seven of us Cipole Swamp Rats had a party in the Steyaert home playing games and feasting on homemade ice cream

and cake. Mother Steyaert had as much fun as we had. We were playing *musical chairs* when she asked, with a twinkle in her eye, if we ever
played pony express. When I asked her how the game was played, she
giggled and, coyly covering her mouth, whispered, *"Well, it's a lot like
playin' post office cept'n there's a whole lot more horsin' around."*

Yes indeed! I liked that woman.

A New Sister

When Dad brought Grandma home to stay with us for the weekend, Mom told them that she was certain she was going to
deliver her child within the next two days. She was correct in her as-
sessment. Later in the evening, Mom began experiencing serious labor
pains. She packed a few things and Dad took her to the hospital. And
Grandma stayed home with us kids. I'd never seen my grandmother so agitated, a bundle of nerves, worrying every minute about her
daughter.

Though it was long past our bedtime, most of us where still up when
Dad returned. The news was wonderful . . . another girl and Mom was
doing quite well.

Our youngest sister was named Charla Marie. She was born on Saturday, June 9, in St. Vincent's Hospital near Beaverton. And since she
was born on a weekend, I didn't have to explain to my teacher that I
had to stay home because Mom was having another kid. Thank the
good Lord for that.

Charla—pronounced Shar-lah—was Mom and Dad's sixth child
and the ninth member of our family, including Grandma. The first
four of us, all boys, were born at home. And then came our two spoiled
sisters, both born in the luxury of a hospital.

The following evening, Grandma went with Dad to the hospital
to visit Mom and to see her new granddaughter. It was up to me to
fix supper for the rest of the family. Before the other kids could begin
bellyaching that they were hungry, I began cooking a special meal for
them, fried potatoes smothered with homemade gravy. Frying three
or four finely sliced potatoes, a few minced garlic cloves, and half an

onion diced into small pieces in a glob of butter was the easy part. Making the gravy was another matter.

Now, I had watched my mom and grandmother make gravy many times. It was simple, so I thought. They put several spoons of white flour into a small bowl of milk and stirred it until it was smooth. And then they dumped the mixture into a pan of hot bacon grease or, in this case, a large gob of melted butter. And when it thickened, they added a little more milk to make it creamy. Simple!

So began Chef Teddy's first attempt at making gravy. Stirring my mix into the hot pan, it appeared much too thick and pasty. So, I added milk. But before I allowed it time to thicken and believing it was too thin, I added more flour. Then it was too thick again. So I added more milk. Trying to get the mix just right, I repeated the process again and again until the pan was full to the brim. In just minutes, I had created a huge blob of thick, bubbling, sticky stuff. Had I a larger pan to transfer it to, I'd have kept working at it. But since I couldn't do much more, I sprinkled salt and pepper on it and served it hot.

When Dad and Granny came home, instead of asking about Mom and our new baby sister, my tattletale siblings squawked about their supper and the huge sloppy-looking pancake that I'd made. They were nothing but a bunch of ingrates.

When Dad brought Mom home, the moment she stepped through the door, we kids crowded around her to see our new sister. We were all smiles with the exception of little brother Dee. He was disappointed and whined, *"Aw, Ma! She ain't new, not like Dad said she was, She's all wrinkled."*

The Old West

The day was comfortably warm when I plopped down to read a book in the doorway of one of the sheds near the barn. It was a paperback Western written by the famous author, Zane Grey. I found it among an assortment of old books in a box that Grandpa had given me. Any story about the Wild West fascinated me. They made me dream.

Being barefoot, I buried my toes in the warm dust and got comfortable. Settling back against the shed's door jam, I opened my book and began to read.

Soon I'd become engrossed in a tale about a cowboy who was romancing a beautiful young girl. She swore that she loved him. One day, as he held her close, he discovered her true feelings. He could feel her heart beating against his chest. It was not beating with the excitement of a lover but that of a devious scheming woman.

The plot thickened becoming more exciting and complex with the turn of each page. And then it happened. Something brought me out of my trance, something grating and harsh. It was my grandma's bellowing voice.

"Teddy! Where in blazes are you? You got some weedin' to do in the garden. Teddy! You hear me?"

Mulling over the thought of working was irritating and ground on me, and in particular when I had just gotten comfortable. I hated weeding. It never seemed to do much good because the darned things grew back quicker than ever. And the garden was so blasted large. Never in her life had my grandmother planted a small one. Instead of four tomato plants or even fourteen, she'd plant 40, bearing enough tomatoes to feed the population of Tibet. Corn, beans, potatoes, carrots, it didn't matter . . . she'd plant them by the acre instead of by the row. We always had a garden of at least 37 acres, a strange phenomenon too since we only owned twenty.

I complained out loud to no one but myself, *"Blast it, anyway! Why can't she get one of the other kids to help instead of always bothering me? And it's always when I'm comfortable and relaxed."*

In frustration, I shouted back, *"I'm coming, doggone it!"*

Wearing a big broad brimmed straw hat, as large as a sombrero, and a pair of men's coveralls, Granny was waiting for me in the garden with a couple of hoes ready to put me to work.

"It's about time you showed up. Where in tarnation were you, anyhow?"

Still annoyed, my voice probably sounded terse when I answered.

"I was down by the barn readin' a Western."

Scarcely speaking a word to each other, we hacked and chopped at the weeds.

My mind kept wandering back to some of the Westerns that I'd been reading and the romantic exciting lives cowboys lived.

Then it dawned on me; Grandma had lived on ranches and had been around Indians and cowboys all her life. She was raised in the Old West. She even lived on an Indian reservation.

These thoughts stirred my imagination, prompting me to ask a few questions.

"Have you ever worn a cowboy hat, Grandma?"

"What in blazes are yuh runnin' on about now? No, I didn't. I wore a cowgirl hat."

"Didja ever have a boyfriend who was a cowboy?"

"Quit yammerin' and git back to work."

But she answered my question . . . and a few more. In fact, she told me of several adventures she'd experienced that I'd never heard before.

I wondered if she was attractive, beautiful, small, gentle and petite when she was a teenaged girl. It wasn't easy picturing her that way because she was in her sixties and heavy set with gray hair. But Uncle Oliver said that Grandma was once a gorgeous woman and that his sister Mary was the spitting image of their mother. If Grandma looked anything like Aunt Mary, then she had to have been a knockout.

Aunt Mary, Grandmother's fourth child

As we worked side by side, I began to visualize Granny as being a dainty little 16-year-old cowgirl living in the Wild West. And I could just see in my mind a gaggle of moonstruck young men pursuing her. Never before had I thought of her as being anything more than an old lady from Montana. But she could have easily been a real true-to-life heroine of the Wild and Wooly West. In fact, I would have wagered that, had Zane Gray known her, he'd have featured her in one of his novels. Too bad he didn't. He'd have had a best seller.

Thinking to myself, *"Well, who knows? Maybe, one of these days, I'll write a story about her myself."*

Dad's Fabulous Finds

Throughout the war, and particularly as the war was winding down, we could bank on Pop occasionally bringing home something odd, something unique and weird.

One interesting item was a small box of Mexican jumping beans. As curious young children, we marveled, wondering how in the world a bean could leap and hop about. Two days later, they'd disappeared. We bigger kids figured that they'd skipped out of the house. But not so! Little sister had added them to a bag of dried pinto beans stored in the kitchen cupboard. As kids, we thought it would be easy sorting them out.

"Just wait until they jump and then grab 'em."

Among some of the other things he brought home were a hunting dog, a real lively adult skunk, canvas hammocks, army cots, a flare-gun and a large, heavy army tent.

The skunk didn't stay long, five or six weeks maybe, before it ran off. It was just as well because it wasn't nearly as friendly and sweet as our Little Stinky. Perhaps it left because it had been fixed.

The hunting dog was a beautiful full-grown tan colored male pointer. And it soon became Dad's favorite pet. He bragged about it, he brushed it and he pampered it until Mother, in disgust, was ready to throw both of them out of the house.

One Saturday afternoon, Dad, armed with his old break-action, single-barrel shotgun, took his favorite pet outside to determine if it would retrieve. He set up a target in the field in back of the shed and, with the dog at his side, proceeded to blow the hell out of a small wooden crate. Dad's fabulous pointer turned and bolted for the house as if it's tail had been dipped in turpentine. It bounded onto the back porch and sprang into the air with a mighty leap, crashing through the glass window in the back door. Mom, sitting at the kitchen table folding clothes and sipping coffee, was nearly bowled over as the dog blew past her. Like a runaway torpedo, it headed toward the other end of the house. Instantly the kitchen had been transformed into a garbage dump of broken glass, spilled coffee and scattered linen. For a fleeting moment, my dismayed mother thought that her crazy husband had taken a shot at the fleeing canine.

Mom and Dad found the terrified animal, quivering and whimpering, under their bed. At first, they tried to coax it out. But it wouldn't budge. Then, they tried to get a grip on it to drag it out. But the pooch dug its paws into the floor, crying out as if in pain. Dad became so exasperated that he dismantled the bed to get at the poor shaken thing. Lifting it into his arms, he carried his champion hunter into the kitchen where it curled up behind the stove and stayed put, watching our every move. Dad's mighty hunting hound didn't want any part of the great outdoors, and was never anything more than an oversized loveable lap dog.

In my opinion, the worst item that he ever brought home was a set of hand-operated hair trimmers. The cutting heads sliced back and forth when the handles were manually squeezed and released. The old goat figured to save some money by cutting hair—our hair. Whoever owned the trimmers before our dad got them must have used them to cut steel wool because several of the cutting teeth were missing, they were dull as a board, and some of the chrome plating had peeled away. In other words—they were junk.

Come Saturday morning, Pop took my youngest brother Dee outside, sat him down on a chopping block in the back yard by the old dilapidated shed, and proceeded to deprive the poor kid of his lovely curly tresses. Poor Dee! He was soon squalling, squirming and squealing. He pleaded with Dad to stop but the old man kept chopping and shearing and yanking hair off his head. I even thought I could see a little blood and skin.

Tom, Dick and I wanted no part of this haircutting business and tried to escape. But, in a vice-like grip, Pa caught his next victim, little brother Dick. He, too, squirmed and wriggled like a can of worms . . . but to no avail. As Dad dragged him toward the bloody chopping block, our brother begged, promising to do anything if he could only forgo the haircut. But, Pa didn't give in to his son's frantic pleadings and unsympathetically began to destroy a perfectly good head of hair.

As if our tails were on fire, Tom and I lit out for the woods, running as fast as we could. Our destination and our safe haven from this Mad Barber of Fleet Street was a big red fir tree at the edge of the woods near Robinson's onion barn. We figured to climb it to the very top, if necessary, to save our scalps. Having climbed it many times in the past, we had driven spikes into its trunk, using them as a ladder to get up to the lower branches.

Tom was behind me when we began our sprint to freedom but, by the time we reached the tree, he was ahead of me by a good 30 feet. We went up that thing like two squirrels up a telephone pole, certain that Dad wasn't likely to climb after us. We shinnied up so high that, where we finally perched, the diameter of the tree-trunk wasn't much larger than one's thumb. And from there, we could see the house.

Swaying back and forth in the wind, we clung there like two curious chipmunks watching Dad skin our unfortunate brother's head. When he finished, he stood back to admire his work. Unbelievably, he thought that his barbering was improving. A few patches of hair still remained on Dick's head but he wasn't any better off than poor Dee.

Then it was our turn. Looking about, he called us to come and get our haircuts. Not being stupid, we stayed put and kept our mouths shut. But Dee squealed on us and told Dad where we'd gone, that we had run to the woods and had climbed up a tree.

Pa came after us—with his antique, break-action, single-barrel shotgun cradled in his arms. Standing at the foot of the tree, he ordered us to come down. Otherwise he was going to shoot. Daredevil Tom, who was above me, yelled back, *"Go ahead and shoot. Ted 'n' me are stayin' up here."*

At first, I chuckled at Tom's bold challenge. But then I realized that I was below him and would be the first to get a load of buckshot. But we weren't worried that he'd pull the trigger feeling pretty certain that he was just bluffing. Still, there was just a teensy bit of doubt in our minds. Nonetheless, we were steadfast in our refusal and wouldn't give in. Dad did though. He had other things to do and finally gave up, returning to the house.

We stayed in the tree, perched on limbs like two wary 'possum, until we were certain it was safe to come down.

When night came, we opted to sleep in the barn rather than go near the house, fearing the old man would be waiting in ambush. The next day, we visited our neighbor Frank Wager and, explaining our predicament, asked him if he would give us a job so we could earn enough money to get a haircut. Frank, nearly in hysterical laughter but feeling sorry for us, put us to work weeding his turnip patch. Several hours later and 50 cents richer, we walked to Sherwood, got a haircut, and had enough change left over to buy a chocolate soda at Frank Gardinier's corner drug store.

Brother Dee was forced to wear a stocking cap for several weeks to keep the sun from burning his bald noggin. And Dick stayed clear of Dad for some time, not trusting that he wouldn't do something else to him. Tom and I—well, we just waited, curious about what crazy thing that our dad would bring home next.

A Close Call

Dad had adapted an ancient horse-drawn disk to pull behind our tractor. It consisted of two opposing sections, each section equipped with four or five 16-inch blades. It worked but it wasn't the best setup in the world. And when he was on the tractor, he couldn't always keep an eye on its operation.

Every so often a rock got stuck between the two innermost opposing blades, jamming both sections. So, I tagged along behind the disk and kicked them loose, eliminating the need for Pa to stop.

Dad was disking a large piece of ground one day, preparing it for corn and hay. And, as usual, I was tagging along behind when a rock jammed the disk. I gave it a kick. It went flying. But my shoe got stuck. In the blink of an eye, I was pulled into the rotating disk, my right leg caught between two blades. Somehow, I grabbed the framework, keeping my hands off the blades' sharp edges, and prevented the disk from dragging me under. Everyone in the family screamed to high heaven at the same time. Pop was off the tractor the instant it stopped.

That disk was one heavy piece of machinery. But, with his adrenalin running at an all-time high, Pa lifted one section of it by himself. And Tom and Dick worked quickly, untangling me from the blades. Other than a slightly sprained ankle and the loss of a little skin, I was scarcely hurt. But the incident scared the life out of me and everyone else in the family.

We boys stayed away from the disk from then on. But there were plenty of other things around that could cause us harm and, sooner or later, we found every one of them.

The Back Porch

Our back porch was our parlor and entertainment center. When the weather permitted, it was a place where we could relax and spend time in conversation with each other. It really wasn't much of a porch as far as porches go: no fancy railings around it or roof over it, no filigreed arches to adorn it or multi-colored lanterns to light it. It was just an old rickety, rotting, dilapidated deck. The rough-hewn lumber used in its construction was weathered and worn smooth from years and years of use. The boards were nailed to a few four-by-four beams that were perched atop river rocks and old fireplace bricks.

On warm summer nights, after the chores had been done, we often gathered on the back porch for a few hours, waiting for the inside of our crowded little three-room house to cool down. Sitting together in the dark, we sang tunes and lullabies and told spooky stories about ghosts, ghouls and monsters. And as we watched brilliant sunsets slowly evolve into star-studded nights, we made our plans for the future and solved family problems. Some of our chores were done right there on the porch too. Mom rocked our little sisters to sleep and folded clothes and knitted and darned socks. And we boys churned cream into butter, shelled peas, snapped beans and shucked corn for canning.

There was no room in the house to do our laundry. So our wringer washer sat outside on one corner of the porch next to the house, near the well. Tom and I thought we had a good idea once and tried to shell green peas, feeding them through the washing machine wringer. Some of the peas squirted out of the pods. But most of them got mashed into baby food. So much for our inventiveness . . . that little stunt did nothing more than turn the wringers green and get our butts tanned.

And it was on the back porch that we listened in tense silence to radio broadcasts reporting news of the war, worried and concerned about the fate of our uncles and friends in the service. It was also there that we heard the welcome news of the surrender of Germany and, later in 1945, the surrender of the Japanese Empire, ending World War II.

One hot July night, we had all gathered on the porch after dark to watch the heavens for shooting stars. While making wishful plans for the future, we were suddenly startled by a large insect as it buzzed past us and crashed into the side of the house. It was a huge copper- and brown-colored beetle, a mammoth creature nearly three inches in length. Equipped with mandibles as large as small fingernail clippers, it could easily clip small twigs and straws in half. Even though it appeared docile, we took no chances getting nipped when we handled it. None of us had ever before seen a flying insect as big, not even Grandmother who claimed to have seen nearly every thing worth seeing on this earth. Because it was July, we named the creature *The July Beetle*.

We seldom spent a night without hearing hundreds of crickets performing nature's music, entertaining us with a never-ending chorus of chirps. Flying termite ants, swarms of them, streamed from the dead stumps and logs in the woods. And bats! Dozens of them filled the evening skies at dusk with their aerial acrobatics, darting, diving, hunting for their food: moths, flies and beetles—all kinds of night insects.

A bat fluttered by our heads and through the open kitchen door right into our house one night. My three brothers and I were immediately after it and, using a small bulletin board, knocked it out of the air. We put it in a jar, keeping it for a few days before setting it free.

I held my two baby sisters, Tudie and Charla, for the first time while sitting on the back porch. Burping Charla after she'd had her milk, she lost her lunch on me. That's when I found out how awful babies stink.

One afternoon, we found Dee lying on his stomach peering down one of the many knotholes in the porch looking for a nickel that he'd dropped. Tom suggested he try fishing for it using a long stick with a gob of tar on the end of it. Being a little lazy, Dee had no hankering to walk down the railroad tracks to the tar pit. So he went into the house and crawled under the kitchen table looking for gum. There was plenty of it stuck under there. He had a choice of several brands: Wrigley's Spearmint, Peppermint, Chiclets, Black Jack, Juicy Fruit, and two kinds of bubble gum. Dee, chewing wad after wad of used gum to soften it, dabbed it on the end of a stick and went fishing. But, alas! Poor Dee spent an entire afternoon peering down that dumb knothole but never recovered his nickel. The old porch claimed it just as it had claimed other small trinkets and baubles over the years.

It was small payment, however, for the wealth of happiness we had experienced, sitting there evening after evening, summer after summer, growing together as a family.

Yes, that old porch wasn't much to look at, no fancy railings or roof over it. But, nonetheless, it was a place where lasting memories were made.

Running The Rails

Dusty and bumpy Herman Road bordering our farm also paralleled the railroad tracks for a three-mile stretch. Many times we pedaled our bikes down the road, racing like the wind beside a freight train, at the astounding speed of 17 miles an hour. We got a big kick out of being acknowledged by the engineers when they shouted greetings, waved at us, or blew the train's whistle. The tracks connected communities west of Tualatin with the communities east into Portland. Until the onset of World War II, a trolley carried passengers every day from Sherwood to Portland, sharing the rails with the freights.

My brothers and I often visited with the men who worked in the section gangs on the tracks. The gang foreman, who spoke with a strong

Italian accent, was a small but stout fellow whom we called Shorty. When he had the time, he entertained us with many stories about railroading and the free life of hobos. With Mom's permission, he sometimes gave us rides on his little section car, a small rail-track vehicle. Because of the sound made by its engine, we called it a *putt-putter*. Once when I got to ride with him, a one-way distance of just over two miles, we made a round-trip to Tualatin to fetch some tools.

An old railroad station once stood at the Cipole siding. But it had been demolished in the early thirties. Only the foundation and a few scraps of old rotting lumber remained. The five-foot deep foundation was forever full of trapped rainwater, even during the hottest summer months. It was inhabited by cattails, lily pads and a horde of frogs and orange-colored salamanders.

Dense blackberry vines surrounded a deep depression behind the old station. And at the bottom of the depression lay the pit where Tom gathered gobs of tar to caulk the cracks in his boats. The pit was the size of a small house. No one knew the depth of the tar or how it happened to be there. It should have been avoided but it was something that we, as young curious children, needed to explore.

During the summer, the tar softened in the hot sun and sometimes trapped small wild animals and birds that lived in the surrounding blackberry thickets and brush. Whenever we found one stuck in the tar, we did our best to free it. Freeing a bird was not a problem but freeing a squirrel, now that was a little bit tricky because they bite. Nearly always successful, we felt good that we had saved one of God's creatures from a horribly slow death.

We, too, got stuck a few times and had to leave a shoe behind—but only temporarily. Shoes were far too expensive to let sink out of sight in a pit of tar.

After the rail station had closed, the local farmers continued to use the siding to ship tons of sacked onions in freight cars to the large market centers. The freight cars were like a magnet and not one of us could resist climbing atop them. Walking from one end to the other, we pretended to be hobos. I sometimes wondered from where the cars had come and to where they would be going next.

Being curious and probably a bit mischievous, a lever on the side of boxcars was an attraction to us. Pulling on them sometimes released a whoosh of air. Most likely, it was air pressure that ensured the boxcar's brakes were locked. Admittedly, it was a dumb thing to do. But it never seemed to affect the cars; they always stayed put and never moved.

There's something about walking along a railroad track on a warm day that makes a kid feel carefree. We searched the roadbed for agates, walked balancing ourselves on the rails and practiced jumping across the nearly five-foot span from one rail to the other without falling. We placed pennies and tokens on the rails so the train would flatten them. And trying to hear an approaching freight train that had not yet come into sight, like Indians listening for the iron horse, we dared to put our ears against the rails.

New Neighbors

We had heard for some time that Dick Walgraeve intended to sell his farm. But, still, when it happened, it came as a surprise to us. His son, Dickie, told us that they were moving to a house on Herman Road nearer to Tualatin.

When the new owner, Herman Aschwanden, and his family took possession of the place, they moved into Grandma Walgraeve's old house, using the smaller one to store baled hay. They had two or three children, the youngest a girl about two years of age named Anna. She and Charla eventually became close playmates.

About the same time that the Walgraeves were moving, a family of three moved onto the old Everett farm. Their last name was Reichel. Her first name was Ann and his Leo. They had a young boy by the name of Bernard. But everyone called him Butchie. He was also about two years older than Charla.

We became acquainted with the Reichels almost immediately, selling eggs, milk and butter to them. Leo was not a farmer but a concrete worker. His wife, Ann, a short, stumpy red-haired woman and a stay-at-home mom, was feisty as the dickens and could easily embarrass a crew of loggers with her salty language.

But, as far as the Aschwanden family was concerned, we had no convenient opportunity to become acquainted with them right away. And not being aggressive sorts, we were hesitant to march up to someone whom we'd never met and strike up a conversation.

With the weather warming, we yearned to go swimming in Hedges' creek. But the only easy route to the creek was the road through Aschwanden's farm. We worried that he wouldn't allow us to use it. But eventually we got up nerve and one day approached Mr. Aschwanden at the onion barn. He wasn't as large in stature as Dick Walgraeve. But I was amazed by the size of the man's chest. He was built like a tank.

Friendly but a no-nonsense person, he gave us permission to use the road but asked that we stay out of his barn and off his farm machinery. That was all there was to it. What a relief it was to us that the ice had been broken, so to speak.

Mr. Aschwanden turned out to be a decent fellow and not the ogre we were afraid he'd be.

Catching Critters

My brothers and I were always capturing a wild animal of some kind: squirrels, chipmunks, mice, and moles for instance. But mostly, it was mice. And we caught those little rascals with our hands and not with a trap. But catching a mouse without getting our fingers nipped was a challenge and proved a little tricky. Sometimes they caught us.

Tom and I finished our chores early one morning and set out to catch a few field mice while following Dad as he plowed. Turning the ground often uncovered a variety of small rodents, and sometimes chased up a few rabbits too.

In just a short time, I'd caught more than a dozen of the critters, had been bitten a couple of times, and also found a pocket of snake eggs. Carrying the mice in a gallon jar and the snake eggs in a can, we went to the house to show Mom. For some strange reason, she didn't want the mice or the snake eggs in the house. Heck, we wondered, what was the big deal? The house was full of mice anyway, so what could a few more hurt? But the snake eggs, I admit, were a different matter.

Before long, though, the snake eggs had rotted and all of the mice had escaped back into the fields.

One morning we found a hawk with a badly broken wing. We threw a sack over its head to keep it quiet and took the creature to the house to show Mom. Grandma was there too and told us the kind of hawk it was. As we were examining it, the hawk unexpectedly grabbed one of Dick's fingers with its super strong talons. Dick was immediately in horrible pain and tears flowed down his cheeks. Frantically, we tried to pry the talons apart. But the bird hung on tight. Grandmother quickly solved the problem. She whacked the bird's head off with a cleaver, thus relieving it and Dick of their agony.

A few days after Tom's birthday, he trapped a China pheasant rooster under a wooden box using an ear of dried corn as bait. His biggest problem wasn't so much catching the bird but getting it from beneath the box. Like many large birds, mature pheasant roosters grow sharp spurs on the backs of their legs. They use them to fight rival roosters and predators, as Tom soon found out.

Carefully lifting the box just a little, he slid his hand underneath trying to catch hold of the pheasant's feet. But, instead of Tom catching the pheasant, the pheasant caught Tom, digging its spurs into the back of his hand. When Tom felt piercing pain, he jerked his hand away, upsetting the box. The feisty rooster, now free, skedaddled, taking flight into the wild blue yonder.

All types of wild creatures, including muskrats, lived in the drainage creek that meandered through the swamp in back of our house. At the time, there was a market for muskrat hides. And although I took no pleasure in killing an animal, I needed money for school clothes and decided to go into the trapping business. With a borrowed trap and youthful enthusiasm, I just knew I was going to catch hundreds and hundreds of muskrats and make myself a big bundle of money. But, the first thing I caught wasn't a muskrat. It was me. During one of my first attempts at setting the trap, the thing snapped shut and caught one of my fingers. It hurt like blazes and caused a nasty blood blister to form. But, after a few more close calls, I finally mastered the technique and was ready to do some trapping.

I set my trap in an animal runway near the edge of the creek. To prevent the trap from being dragged away, I attached its anchor chain to a stick that I'd driven into the ground.

Checking the trap the following morning, I knew I'd caught something. I couldn't see what it was because it had dragged the trap below the surface of the water. I began to pull the chain to retrieve my catch when, suddenly, the water seemed to explode. My catch was a weasel. And it climbed up the chain at me with the fury of a wolverine. It happened so quickly that it nearly caught my hand in its teeth.

Not able to get near the trap, I had to use a stick to hold the weasel at bay and a piece of planking to press on the trap's release lever to free the animal.

I tried trapping for several days but never successfully caught a muskrat, not a single one of the elusive things. So I gave up the business. It was probably for the best because the only thing I caught was one very angry weasel . . . and a stupid kid.

Cream Soda

Soon after the end of the war, Oregon Shipyards shut down. And hundreds and hundreds of men and women found themselves unemployed. But Dad wasn't without a job. He'd been working at a second job, even though it was part time, for Columbia Distributing, driving a truck on his days off. Since equipment and products needed for bottling soda pop were no longer restricted, the business picked up quickly and Dad's once-full-time job was restored.

We kids were more than a little curious when Dad came home one Saturday afternoon, driving a brand new red International delivery truck. His bosses had purchased three of the vehicles and asked our dad if he would store them on the farm for the time being.

He parked it in the pasture near one of the sheds and called to us boys to come and help him. Our eyes nearly bugged out of our heads when he opened the truck's rear doors; it was loaded with one hundred cases of soda pop. His bosses had asked him to temporarily store them for the company as well.

Dad put us to work, packing the wooden crates of pop from the truck to the shed where he stacked them one atop the other. Every flavor of soda pop on earth was there on our farm right under our noses, a tantalizing target for young, thirsty thieves. We were in heaven, in a dream. But Pa knew what we were thinking. And when we finished our chore, he locked the door with a padlock large enough to secure the gates of Fort Knox. But we were conniving young scamps determined to get at that pop. And nothing as trivial as a prison padlock was going to stop us.

Within two days, we had crawled all over that shed like a colony of ants on a ripe peach looking for a way in. And finally we found it—a flaw in construction. A board in the back of the shed was loose, not much but just enough. With a little coaxing and the use of a crow bar, we loosened the board a little more, giving us just enough space to reach into the shed to get at the pop. Wedged as tightly as the bottles were in the stack, it wasn't easy pulling them out. But we managed. Recapping the bottles after drinking the contents, we forced them back into the wooden boxes before pushing the loose board back into place.

In just a week, we had swigged down all of the pop within easy reach. Desperate to guzzle more of the forbidden liquid, we pried two or three more of the shiplap boards apart so that one of us could squeeze inside. And once inside, we were really in the chips.

Tom and I stood outside as our younger brother Dick, being the smallest, squeezed in to hand pop out to us. At first, it mattered not what kind we got as long as we got something. But then we began to ask for specific flavors, as if we were ordering a soft drink at the malt shop.

When Dad was home, he occasionally opened the door to the shed to make certain everything was okay. But the cases of pop that were stacked directly in the doorway concealed what was going on in the rear of the shed. He had absolutely no clue that he was losing close to a case of soda pop every day. By summer's end, we had consumed three quarters of the stock. A few of the cases stacked in the front of the shed were still full. But nearly every one behind was empty or nearly empty.

Dad drove a company truck home again, this time to take the pop back to the plant. He yelled for us to come and help load it. But we knew what was coming and scattered like BB shot fired from a smooth-bore cannon. I lit out for tall timber, figuring the woods were going to be my home for the rest of my life or until he cooled down.

Well, when the old man found out what had happened to the pop, he went off like a volcano. Had I been in the next county, I could have felt the earth tremor. Of course, when he asked the other kids who had instigated the theft, all fingers pointed toward the woods where I'd fled. For several days, I hid in the brush and only went home when he was gone.

Eventually, Pa cooled down . . . some . . . but only to a slow boil. He salvaged about half a dozen cases that had not been touched and re-locked the shed door, leaving dozens of partially full cases for us to plow through.

By the end of fall, nearly all of the remaining pop was gone. Occasionally searching through the empty cases, we discovered a full bottle that had been missed during a previous search. But, before long, there just wasn't another full bottle of pop to be found.

Rummaging through the empty cases one day, I picked up an empty cream soda pop bottle. A devious thought crossed my mind. Tom had swiped the last bottle of pop that I'd found. And I wanted to get back at him. The time was at hand.

The color of cream soda pop looked like pee. So, I peed in the bottle and replaced the cap. And the color was nearly perfect. After the bottle had cooled, I yelled to Tom and told him that I'd found a full bottle of cream soda pop. The stupid jerk couldn't believe it and came running just like I knew he would. I held it up for him to see. Without stopping, he grabbed it from my hand, continuing to run in the direction of the woods. I'm sure he thought that he'd pulled another fast one on me and knew that I couldn't catch him. But, he was mistaken. He was already caught . . . but didn't know it.

In a few moments, I heard a gurgling shriek echoing from the trees. *"Arrhhhgh! You dirty rat! I'm gonna kill you, Teddy."*

Well, he damned near did. He chased me for at least an hour before I gave up, so exhausted that I couldn't run another stride. And then he pounded the bejeebers out of me.

One would think that Tom was too smart to fall for the same stunt twice. But I knew my curious brother. He'd come running at the speed of light if he believed that I'd found . . . a bottle of beer.

The Electric Fence

During my youth, I suffered quite a number of jolting electrical surprises. And they often left me feeling a little odd and out of sorts.

The worst shock I ever got was when I was working for Mr. Everett. I grabbed a light socket to steady it so I could unscrew a burned-our bulb. I guess one of the wires was bare because I suffered a horrific shock. It nearly knocked me down. And for the remainder of the day, I felt as if my chest were about to burst.

But the electric fence was the most common source for getting unwanted zaps. And being a family of pranksters, we used it to play a few underhanded tricks on one another.

When we bought Old Jerz, we enclosed our pasture with a large-mesh, heavy-gauge wire fence stapled to wooden posts. It was stout enough for one animal but when we added more, they began to knock it down. So, we added two strands of barbed wire tacked above the existing fencing. It helped but still they found ways of getting through it.

After chasing after those critters countless times, Dad decided to add an electrified wire to the existing fence. Even with the war coming to an end, it was still difficult getting supplies. But he managed. He bought a roll of smooth wire, a bucket of insulators and a fencer. The fencer was an electrical timing mechanism that sent small jolts of low-voltage electricity through the wire at intervals of about five seconds.

We nailed insulators to the inside of the existing fence posts and strung one strand of wire, surrounding the pasture. We even wired the pigpen. But the wire in the pigpen was lower, only eight to ten inches from the ground to dissuade them from rooting under it.

In the meantime, Dad hired an electrician to hook the fencer to the electrical wiring in the barn.

Our one strand electrified wire was quite effective . . . and the cows and horses and the pigs soon learned to avoid it. So did we.

Chet Fischbuch's horses kept knocking his field fence down too. And tracking livestock all over the countryside wasn't the kind of exercise he enjoyed. So, like us, he installed a one-strand electrified fence. But the electrical charge was too weak and his horses continued to escape. Unlike us, he hooked the fence to a 110-volt outlet. It did the job but killed one of his mares.

Pigs stunk and were an awful nuisance. They were stupid too and just about on a par with chickens.

One weekend, I set about conducting an experiment on animal behavior. I wanted to see how the pigs reacted to an electrical shock. Had Grandma been around to see what I was doing, she'd have kicked my butt all over the county.

I dropped one end of a short strand of wire into the metal feeding trough and the other end over the electric fence. Then I poured a mix of sour milk, mash, and table scraps from a bucket into the trough. I'd forgotten that electricity travels upstream as well as it does downstream. With half a bucket dumped, I suddenly got zapped. I suppose it served me right for being as stupid as a pig.

As expected, those gluttons came running and drove their snouts into the trough. Immediately a jolt of electricity stung them. Emitting short grunts of surprise, they quickly backed away looking at their meal in bewilderment. But being pigs, one of them immediately dove right back into the trough. And the others quickly followed, bulling their way in only to be shocked and driven back again. They didn't like what was happening. But they weren't about to let their brothers and sisters devour all the food and kept plunging their snouts into the soup only to get zapped over and over. As pigs usually do, they persisted eating until nothing was left.

The only gate at the 20-foot-entry to the pasture was just one strand of electrified wire. A wooden handle attached to one end of it made it easy for us to latch and unlatch it by hand without experiencing a shock. It was quite safe . . . unless the handle was wet.

One stormy day, Dad needed to drive the tractor into the pasture. He yelled at me to open the gate. As I reached to grasp the handle, I noticed he was grinning. I should have known the old coot had something up his sleeve. The wooden handle was soaking wet and I got a jarring jolt of electricity. I must have lit up like a neon sign. I know I leaped ten feet in the air. Pop went nuts, his belly bouncing with gleeful laughter. He'd pulled a good one on his oldest son. So be it, I thought! The gauntlet had been thrown.

Not many days later, Pa turned the power off to the fence and busied himself at the far end of the pasture, replacing a couple of insulators. I quietly walked up behind him and gave him the royal goose. Emitting a surprised yelp, the old rascal went straight in the air with his feet kicking and arms flailing. And I went straight for the barn as fast as I could run. I hadn't taken more than ten strides when a pail of insulators whizzed past my head. Six inches to the right and the old man would have had one less dependent to claim on his income tax form.

Well, I got him . . . but I wasn't satisfied. Mom was in the barn, had seen what I'd done to Dad, and had gotten quite a kick out of his reaction. Although she was smiling, she still admonished me, but mildly.

"You should be ashamed of yourself Teddy."

"You ain't seen nuthin' yet, Ma! Watch him."

He was busy again attaching an electric wire to an insulator when I threw the switch, turning on the current. He really straightened up, just about as straight as the center stripe on a Nevada desert highway.

Like a wisp of smoke, I disappeared. As expected, Pa came hunting for me. But I stayed out of sight. Thankful that the weather had turned warm, I was forced to spend the night in my favorite hideout, deep in the woods.

Working In The Swamp

Nearly every youngster who attended Cipole's small two-room elementary school had worked in the swamp at one time or another. We were known as *swamp rats*. Most of us began working on the local farms in our early teens, weeding onions, pulling carrots, or picking beans. If we were lucky, we were paid a quarter an hour.

Not long after we'd moved onto the farm, Mr. and Mrs. Everett hired Tom and me to pick strawberries and clean their chicken house. I was eight and Tom was six. Mr. Everett claimed that we ate far more berries than we picked and that we should have paid him. Then I helped Gerda Cereghino pick up onions one day when I was eleven. She gave me 30 cents for my work. That was a huge sum of money for me. But truthfully, I don't think she needed any help; she just wanted someone to talk to.

Our first real job working in the swamp for any length of time came one day when Clarkie Johnston paid us a visit. He asked Tom and me if we would like to weed onions for his dad. We jumped at the chance, figuring we were going to get rich. But, Mr. Johnston, tight with his money, would only pay us a dollar a day, and he only needed our help for about ten days. Still, earning nine or ten dollars seemed like a lot of money to us.

We soon discovered that pulling weeds in the onion fields was pure torture as well as boring. Looking over the rows, they appeared endless, blending into a sea of green at the far end. No matter how hopeless it looked, three or four of us could weed several acres in a week if we worked at it diligently.

On our hands and knees, we crawled hour after hour in the hot sun weeding three rows of onions at one time. Some of the old-timers weeded five rows at one time.

The black peat dirt actually bleached white and reflected heat back into our faces. It helped to wear a straw hat to protect our heads but it didn't prevent our cheeks and necks from sunburn.

We tried to make the work interesting by telling stories and tall tales to each other. If one of us was working too fast, the others peppered the speeding violator in the rump with dirt clods . . . but only when Mr. Johnston, a strict, no nonsense person, was elsewhere.

Lunchtime never came fast enough. When it did, we made a beeline for the nearest tree where we could relax in the shade. Never lacking for vegetables, we ate raw carrots, cucumbers and immature onions with our sandwiches.

During the two weeks that Tom and I worked for Mr. Johnston, Mom got a lot of rest and relaxation. We were just too darned worn out to be feisty and troublesome to her.

A few weeks after working for Clarkie's dad, we got a job picking beans for the Galbreath family. Picking beans was easier, not as back-breaking, and it was much cooler. But we didn't get rich picking beans either, only working two or three days a week for a couple of weeks.

Working on the farms, we endured long hours, grueling work, sunburns, inhaling dust, blisters, calluses and little pay. It was for the birds and it was obvious to me that farming wasn't going to be my lifelong occupation.

Polio Strikes Our Family

Late in the fall, my four-year-old-sister Tudie became critically ill. The doctors informed my mom and dad that she had been stricken with the disease Infantile Paralysis, commonly referred to as Polio, and that her lungs, throat and voice had been affected and her breathing impaired. She was immediately hospitalized in Portland's Doernbecher Hospital.

A terrifying, fretful fear engulfed me, as I'm sure it did the others in the family. I was certain that my little sister was going to die or become permanently paralyzed and possibly confined forever to an iron lung. Not only did those same agonizing concerns occur to my parents, they also worried that another one of us might catch the dreadful disease, in particular our newborn sister, Charla.

At first, we had hopes that Tudie would return home within a few weeks. But it wasn't to be. She missed being with us at Thanksgiving, her fifth birthday, and at Christmas. Mom and Dad spent every possible moment they could with her. But the remainder of the family was never allowed to go near the hospital.

Thankfully, her illness was only a mild case and she recovered completely, suffering no noticeable after affects. Within days of returning home, her illness was all but forgotten and our lives returned to normal. And hers did too.

CHAPTER VII

1946

The Eraser

Nearing the end of our eighth-grade year in Cipole School, one would believe that Eddie and I had developed a certain amount of intelligence and common sense. But we hadn't. We were still a pair of fun-loving empty-headed imbeciles.

One cloudy day our teacher, Mrs. Martin, assigned the two of us the task of cleaning chalkboard erasers. We hated that chore. We'd done it before many times. And every time we finished, we were covered with chalk dust from head to foot. It got in our ears, under our shirts, everywhere. It was miserable. The only reason we never balked at performing the task was because it got us outside and out of the classroom for 15 or 20 minutes.

Eddie, being rather inventive like his dad, got one of his bright ideas, the kind that often got us into trouble. Using teenage logic, he figured that he could knock the dust out of them much quicker by throwing them against some sort of hard object.

"I got it! You throw yours in the air, Teddy, and I'll hit it with mine. That way, we can clean both of 'em at the same time. And we won't get chalk dust all over us."

Well now, that sounded darned clever to me. And so I lofted an eraser skyward. And Eddie let fly. But his eraser missed. And it sailed and sailed and sailed until it came to rest atop the schoolhouse roof. We were panic stricken. We could never in a million years retrieve it from there.

Eddie Wager

Losing an eraser shouldn't have been any big deal. But back in those days, teachers weren't nearly as forgiving when a student did something dumb. Based on past experience, we were certain that this little bit of stupidity would surely get us into trouble. After all, there were only eight erasers in the entire school. And those teachers were bound to notice that one of them was missing. And if they didn't, sooner or later, they were bound to see an eraser perched on the school roof. And besides that, some mouthy girl would probably spot it and tell on us.

We had to have a plan. We needed to do something so stunning that it would put us in the best favor possible with our teachers. And we had to do it before they discovered what we'd done. The answer seemed simple—a bouquet of flowers. All women loved fragrant flowers and a beautiful bouquet of them should do the trick.

We decided it was best that we go to school together the following morning. So Eddie walked across the swamp, meeting me at my house. I had picked a huge bouquet of mock orange blossoms and tied the stems together with wire and string. The luscious, white flowers smelled glorious, and this bouquet was certain to make points for us.

The school was only a mile from home and I usually walked. But Eddie and I opted to ride my old Montgomery Ward bicycle. With the exception of a clicking sound the pedal made when it hit the pant-leg guard, the old bike was still usable . . . but barely.

I was accustomed to carrying the little kids on it but they rode sideways on the framework. Eddie was too big to sit there and, instead, had to sit facing forward on the handlebars while holding the bouquet.

Immediately, I found the bike a challenge to steer because of the extra weight on the front wheel. Herman Road being graveled made it even more difficult. But, as long as I kept the bike out of the loose gravel, I was certain that I could manage okay.

The only real obstacle that presented a problem, I figured, was Rasmussen's hill. But, surprisingly, peddling over it was not nearly as difficult as I'd expected. It was going down the other side that became a problem.

Topping the crest, I began coasting. But with Eddie's added weight I picked up speed more rapidly than I'd anticipated. Approaching the bottom of the hill where the road made a sharp 90-degree, right hand curve, I discovered too late that I couldn't slow the bike to safely negotiate the turn. As we entered into the curve, Eddie shouted warnings to be careful. But I swung too wide and got into the deep gravel on the far shoulder of the road, sliding out of control. The bike fishtailed a few feet and then we crashed, tumbling end over end into the drainage ditch bordering the road.

Hitting with a thud, I landed in the bottom of the four-foot-deep channel with the bike. But Eddie flew off the handlebars and splattered spread-eagled on the far side of the ditch. He looked like a giant bug that had just hit the windshield of a Mack truck. Luckily, neither of us was injured, just shaken and dazed, and the bike was only slightly damaged. We were fortunate we hadn't spilled in the gravel.

Eddie peeled himself off the ground and began shouting curses at me. He was angry as a nest of disturbed hornets. Before I could completely regain my senses and catch my breath, he gathered up my beautiful bouquet of flowers and used it to whip the dickens out of me. And as he flailed away, he continued shouting volumes of obscenities. I was absolutely stunned by his outrage.

After whacking me several times, he threw the remnants of my once lovely bouquet at my feet and shouted in an angry voice, *"I'm takin' your dumb bike and I'm goin' home."*

My mind muddled, I wondered why he was returning home. Then I saw the reason. The seat of his pants was missing. A piece of striped cloth the size of a dinner plate hung from the bolt that secured the bike's handle bar to the steering rod.

He hopped on my bike and pedaled off, leaving me sitting in the ditch amongst flower petals, leaves and stems, the remnants of a once beautiful bouquet. We were in trouble; I had nothing to offer our teacher.

As it turned out, our endeavor to score some much-needed points with our teacher was for nothing. The eraser was never missed, and no one ever reported seeing it on the roof.

By end of day, Eddie had forgiven me for ripping the seat out of his pants and I was no longer upset with him for defoliating my beautiful bouquet.

The eraser remained on the roof for years. And every time I passed by the old school, and saw it perched up there, I was reminded of my once beautiful bouquet of mock orange blossoms. And I was also reminded of a childhood friendship with a great kid named Eddie.

Teddy's eighth grade report card

SCHOLARSHIP PROGRESS

S—Satisfactory.   U—Unsatisfactory.   I—Improvement.

A rating of (S) indicates satisfactory work. (U) indicates unsatisfactory work. (I) indicates improvement being noted.

	1	2	3	4	Ave
ARITHMETIC — Rating	S+	S+	S	S	S
1—Fundamentals	S+		S	S+	S+
2—Reasoning	S+		S	S	S
ELEMENTARY SCIENCE —	S	S	S	S	S
HEALTH —	S	S+	S+	S+	S
LANGUAGE — Rating	S	S	S	S	S
1—Oral Expression	S+		S	S+	S+
2—Written Work	S		S	S	S
PENMANSHIP — Rating	S	S	S	S	S
1—In drill work	S		S	S	S
2—Good writing on all papers	S		S	S	S
READING — Rating	S	S	S	S	S
1—Comprehension	S+	S+	S+	S+	S+
2—Oral Reading	S	S	S	S	S
SOCIAL STUDIES —	S+	S+	S+	S+	S+
SPELLING — Rating	S+	S	S	S	S
1—Assigned lessons	S+			S	S
2—Written work	S+	S+	S	S	S
ARTS & CRAFTS —					
HOMEMAKING —					
MUSIC —					
PHONICS —					
PHYSICAL EDUCATION —					

PERSONALITY PROGRESS

Only those traits which characterize the child quite noticeably, one way or the other, are marked. A minus (—) means that improvement is desirable. A plus (+) means a point of special excellence.

	1	2	3	4
I WORK HABITS				
Makes good use of time				
Follows directions			+	
Makes original contributions				
Is neat and accurate				
II SOCIAL HABITS				
Plays and works well with others		+	+	+
Is careful of school and personal property	+	+	+	
Has self control	+	+	+	
Is dependable		+	+	+
Is courteous		+	+	+
Accepts criticism well				
Displays leadership				
III HEALTH HABITS				
Has good health habits	+	+	+	
Has good posture	+	+	+	
Is careful of personal appearance	+	+	+	

Conference with parent desired in regard to work

1st quarter	2nd quarter	3rd quarter	4th quarter
☐	☐	☐	☐

The Big Flop

Two or three times a year, the older boys assembled a prefabricated stage in Cipole School's big room for Christmas plays, skits, and graduation ceremonies. It was made of pre-cut two-by-twelve planks. When assembled, the only exit off stage was down three steps into the cloakroom. A curtain made of green burlap, hanging on a draw-wire and opened and closed by hand, was meant to conceal any activity on the stage between scenes. But it was so porous that it hid nothing. And the stage floor squeaked when stepped on and was dotted with knotholes. If one of the boys couldn't be found, it was almost certain that he was under the stage looking up through the knotholes at the girls.

When the sliding partition separating the little and big rooms was opened to form one large room, the school took on a carnival-like atmosphere for a few days.

"Me, an actor on stage? I think not."

But I was. Mrs. Martin talked me into performing a role in one of our school plays, a role that proved to be a gigantic flop.

The play was about two cruel giants who were twins. Since my classmate Joe West was gone and I was the largest boy in school at the time, I played both roles in sequential scenes. My worry about being in the play was forgetting lines. But Mrs. Martin assured me that I only needed to snarl and growl once in a while. Well, I could handle that. I could snarl with the best of them.

Mrs. Martin thought it necessary that I look taller than I was—more like a real giant. To attain the necessary height, I strapped two eight-inch high blocks of wood to my shoes, using pieces of leather from an old belt to hold them in place. It was clumsy and difficult to walk. But I managed to do it even though the stage flooring was uneven.

Erwin Galbreath, the hero in the play, but a person who was just naturally a clown, was to slay both giants with a sword. Then, the giants—me—were to stagger off stage and die making a loud crashing sound as if dropping dead.

During the performance, everything went well—at least for a while. Fortunately, I only had to take four or five steps during each of the two scenes. And my extended legs worked well, considering.

To kill the first giant, Erwin thrust a sword between my arm and side pretending to run me through. I turned, trying to act mortally wounded, and staggered off stage. Just as I was about to descend the steps down into the cloakroom, a tricky maneuver on my blocks of wood, Erwin gave me an unexpected shove from behind to help me along. The shove wasn't in the script and took me by surprise. With the blocks of wood strapped to my feet, I wasn't nimble enough to keep my balance and fell, tumbling onto the floor of the cloakroom with a loud crash. To my consternation, one of the leather straps broke loose.

I was in a terrible fix because I was supposed to go back on stage as the second giant seeking to avenge his twin brother's death. I had little time, no material and no tools to replace the broken strap. Working frantically, I managed to hook the shredded strap to a nail head and, prayed that it would hold tight.

Cipole Grade School's student body, 1945–1946

Teachers: Mrs Bander, Mrs Martin

Back row: Gordon Burke, Eddie Wager, Betty Copperud, Shirley Steyaert, Ted Pileggi, John Forrest, Joe West

Fourth row: Irma Cereghino, Elaine Peterson, Ruth Cereghino, Erwin Galbreath, David Cereghino, Leonard Peterson

Third row: Carolyn Young, Bernice Cereghino, Joan Steyaert, Chuck Burke, Jim Forrest, Tom Pileggi

Second row: Unidentified girl, John Forrest's sister, Aurilla Cummerow, Dennis Dimbat, Clark Johnston, Dick Pileggi

Front row: Lacey Modrill, Ken Cereghino, Erna Mae Peterson, Barbara Iles, Carl Steyaert, Judy Beagen, Richie Burke, Dee Pileggi

Ever so carefully, I got to my feet and climbed the three steps to the stage. But just as I stepped into view of the audience, the strap broke loose and the block tumbled down the steps into the cloakroom. Now, one of my legs was shorter than the other—by eight inches. And instead of shedding the other block, I continued with one short leg and a gigantic limp. I must have looked like I was walking with one foot in a gutter and the other on a sidewalk.

The look on Erwin's face when he turned to confront me was one of stunned confusion. For the first five minutes, nothing that he said was in the script. And about half the time I had no idea how to respond. With no clue about where he was going with his ad-lib stammered jabbering, I could only look out at the audience part of the time and shrug my shoulders as if I were deranged, and then growl menacingly. The audience of families and friends were laughing so hard that they could no longer hear the dialogue on stage anyway. So it really didn't matter.

After a brief confrontation, and me standing on one block doing a balancing act, Erwin skewered me with his sword, as he did with the first giant. As I turned to stagger off the stage, the straps on the remaining block also broke loose, and I fell to my hands and knees. I struggled off stage dragging the block behind me, trying my best to look as if I was dying—and I was.

The play was supposed to be humorous. But it was more than that. It turned into a roaring sidesplitting comedy. My blocks of wood were a gigantic flop . . . but the play turned out to be a colossal success.

Grandma Comes Home

Welcome news! Very welcome news! After nearly three years, Grandma quit her job at Oregon poultry and came home. Even though we knew that she'd lay down the law the moment she walked through the door, we were happy youngsters and grateful to have her back.

When the day finally came to fetch her, Dad made absolutely certain that the tires on the trailer were in good shape. He didn't want a wheel falling off in the middle of Portland with the trailer chock full of her belongings as it had done so often when we went to the hop yards and berry fields.

When we arrived at her tiny apartment, Grandma was ready, her smile lighting up her face like a Christmas tree. She had already packed most of her things into cardboard boxes. In less than an hour, we'd loaded everything into the trailer and headed for home, singing and happy as a tree filled with larks. The family was complete again.

That night, sitting at the dinner table, the main topic of Mom, Dad and Grandma's conversation wasn't so much about her returning home but about building a new house near the railroad tracks on the lower

Grandma Barnes, 65 years old

place. Grandmother had saved a sizeable amount of her earnings for its construction. Quite curious, I listened intently, hoping to learn if I'd be getting my own bedroom. It would be super not sharing a bed with Tom . . . and his long toenails.

An uncertainty existed about that time, though, that we youngsters hadn't known about. Pop's current employment had become tenuous.

Until Dad could be certain of a steady income, construction of a new house was put on hold. And it wasn't mentioned again, not for a long time.

In the meantime, all of us boys had plenty of work. Our Grandma saw to that.

The Main Event

Nineteen forty-six was a year of major changes in our country. Since we were no longer at war, tens of thousands of soldiers were returning home and Detroit was making cars again. And my dad was no longer working three jobs; he was only working one and home on weekends. Our lives were rapidly returning to normal. And my voice had changed. I was no longer a squeaky tenor but a deep bass. But what hadn't changed were my shiftless ways; I was still a lazy kid.

Two events that took place in June that I looked forward to were my graduation from the eighth grade and the world heavyweight boxing championship between Billy Conn and Joe Louis.

Two or three days before the big fight, Grandma and Dad had given me strict orders to weed the garden. It was my turn again, and the weeds were taking over. But being lazy, I put it off, thinking up one lame excuse after another.

On the day of the championship fight, I still hadn't taken care of my chore. And Grandma was on the warpath.

When we youngsters were obedient, our grandmother was as sweet as a bushel basket of fragrant flowers. But, on this particular day because I hadn't obeyed her, she was no daisy. She gave me one final warning.

"Git it done today young man or else . . ."

"Okay, Grandma, I will . . . I promise."

I tromped out to the garden feeling dejected and sorry for myself. The moment I looked at all those weeds, I felt as if I'd been sentenced to ten years of hard labor. Right then and there, I made a really stupid decision and headed for the barn figuring that I'd do the weeding sometime later. For the remainder of the afternoon, Tom and I played ball and talked about the heavyweight championship fight due to begin in a couple of hours.

Of all the famous boxers, Joe Louis was my favorite fighter and Archie Moore and tough Tony Galento were right there with him. I liked Tony Galento because he was a character, a zany character, and an unconventional fighter. Archie Moore was a little zany himself. But he was a tremendously skilled pugilist. And Joe Louis, as far as I was concerned, was a classy individual who had no equal in the ring.

Minutes before the fight was to be aired, Grandmother discovered that her oldest grandson hadn't done one blessed thing to complete his assigned task. Tom and I had finished with the milking and were preparing to run the milk through the cream separator when all hell broke loose. I felt as if I'd walked into a nest of nasty fire ants.

"What in God's name did I tell you to do earlier today, young man? And you didn't do it."

Her ranting burned my ears like scalding water. Slapping a fly swatter on the table, she pointed at the door and bellowed, *"Now, you git yer lazy butt out there right now and weed that garden afore it gits too dark, or I'm gonna tan yer good-fer-nuthin hide."*

I was doomed . . . doomed to miss the fight.

Feeling horribly sorry for myself, I tromped out to the garden and began chopping hell out of weeds. As I was tearing up the soil, I began wishing that I had a radio. If Dad hadn't removed the one in the barn, I could have snuck down there to listen to the fight.

Then a thought struck me—the car was equipped with one. And it worked without a key. I could listen to the fight on it if I was sneaky and careful enough. And I reasoned that if the bout ended in an early knockout, I could still hoe weeds for a while. But if it got too dark, I'd just have to take my lumps.

Dad had warned us kids over and over not to use the radio when the car's motor wasn't running. But, in my simple mind, I considered this an emergency.

Crawling furtively into the car and lying on the front seat keeping out of sight, I switched the radio on and turned the volume down low. The fight hadn't begun yet; the ringside announcer was still talking. I hadn't missed any of the action.

Finally, the fight began. And just as I'd hoped, Louis was the winner. But when it was over, it had grown pitch-black dark. I was lucky though. No one had ventured outside. And not one soul looked up when I sauntered into the house. They probably thought that I'd been out in the garden all along taking care of business. And I doubt that anyone even missed me.

The following morning, I was determined to fulfill my promise the second Tom and I had finished our chores. But as we were leaving to do the milking, Dad announced that he was taking us to Sherwood the moment we returned.

I wanted to go . . . but what about the garden? I was really pushing my luck, but it just had to wait a little longer.

An hour later, the entire family, with the exception of Grandmother, climbed into the car, crammed in like a bunch of nuts in a can. We were happy as larks, anticipating a fun time in Sherwood. But it wasn't to be, at least not for me.

The car wouldn't start. It just growled once and then did nothing. The battery was dead, flat as a pancake. And I knew why. So did the old man. He should have been a detective. In just a few seconds, he figured it out. I hadn't switched the radio off. And he remembered that when I entered the house, I never asked one soul who had won the fight.

"I'll bet if I go out to that garden, Teddy, it'll still be full of weeds."

Everyone was mad at me. Mom and the little kids went back into the house to wait as my grinning brothers, Tom and Dick, and I heaved, pushed and shoved that old crate down the road. When we got up enough speed, Pa popped the clutch and the car's engine chugged to life. He drove it back to the house and parked, letting it run for a spell to allow the battery time to recharge. And he didn't mince words when he told me that I could forget about going to Sherwood.

"You'd better get your tail out there right now before Grandma catches you."

But, it was too late. She was already in the garden. I knew I'd better find someplace to hide. So I skedaddled into the outhouse. While in there, peering out a knothole at Grandma, the others piled back into the car and drove off to Sherwood to have fun. With both hands on her hips, Granny watched our car disappear down the road in a cloud of dust. She probably believed that I'd gone with them.

The moment she returned to the house, I dashed into the garden and hoed weeds with the fury of a tornado tearing up Kansas.

Nearly three hours passed before I finished the job. During that time, I worked out a plan to confront Grandma, hoping that she would have some compassion for me.

Sitting at the kitchen table, she was browsing through a Montgomery Ward catalog when I walked in. My unexpected appearance startled her. She was even more startled when I handed a hazelnut switch to her. She didn't take it but after studying it for a few seconds, looked up and asked,

"What's this for?"

"In case you wanna whip me for not weedin' the garden when you told me to."

She waved it aside. I was pretty pleased with myself. Offering the switch to her was an absolute stroke of genius. She appeared really stumped and almost speechless—but not quite. Looking sternly at me, she asked,

"Is the garden weeded now?"

"Yes'm!"

"Did you do a good job?"

"Yes'm!"

She sat there, staring at me over the top of her glasses for the longest time probably trying to figure out what next to say, what next to do with her disobedient grandson.

"You overgrown whelp, Teddy! Why don't you ever do what yore asked to do the first time instead of puttin' it off? Yore gonna be the death of me yet. I oughta tan yore britches good for you jest to teach you a lesson."

Feeling quite relieved, I sat down at the table across from her, and being as polite as possible, asked what she was doing. Answering, she said that she was searching through the catalog for corsets. She needed a new one because the little kids had pulled all the whalebone stays from the old one again, and wearing it was like being wrapped in a horse blanket.

Grandmother led a tough, isolated life, always sacrificing, always giving. She never had many personal possessions and browsing through a catalog was entertainment to her.

Soon, we were chatting about everything under the sun, as if we were two old friends having a visit. Her face had grown softer with a pleasant smile and occasionally her eyes twinkled when she talked about some enjoyable event that had occurred earlier in her life. I began to see a completely different person, not the hard and unyielding woman that she pretended to be. She was a big bluff... most of the time... and down deep, she was a loving, caring, beautiful person.

During those few hours that we spent together, I think I matured in many ways and began to realize why she pushed us kids to be obedient. She wanted us to become responsible, dependable and thoughtful youngsters. And never once did she mention my shiftless ways. Deep within me, I found a new respect for my grandmother and without any doubt, I loved her and knew that she loved me and I was proud to be her grandson.

When the family returned home, Tommy, with a big stupid grin on his face, bragged about how much fun they'd had in Sherwood. I should have been jealous but I wasn't. Not at all! And I'll bet anything that it was I who was the happiest.

The Menagerie

Kids and their pets naturally go together. And our farm flourished with both. The first pet that I can remember was Skippy, our dog.

I also remember when we got our dog Puddles. Dad brought her home when she was just a tiny puppy. He said that she was a miniature German shepherd. We couldn't help but fall in love with her. She was one rambunctious little animal and smart as a whip. And because she piddled on the floor during her first few days in our care, we gave her the name Puddles. In no time at all, she became our constant companion.

In addition to our domestic pets and farm animals, we had captured, at one time or another, every varmint imaginable: squirrels, chipmunks, field mice, moles, weasels, shrews, a skunk, lizards, June bugs, spiders and snakes. We seldom kept them in captivity for any length of time because most escaped or were released but, unfortunately, a few also died. Only our skunk, Stinky, was domesticated and became an outstanding pet.

We had several pigs, a couple dozen geese, two goats, two horses and three cows.

My cow, *Old Jerz*, was the mother of Tom's cow, *Taffy*. Both were from Jersey stock and both gave an abundance of cream that we churned into butter. Dick's cow, *Betsy*, was a Guernsey and provided us with a huge supply of milk that we sold to a local creamery.

Taffy had a nasty temper, the temperament of a bull, and she wasn't the easiest cow in the herd to control. She tolerated none of the other animals in the pasture, not even her mother. But Puddles was one animal she couldn't bully. If the feisty little dog got too close or bothered her in any way, Taffy tried to drive her away by hooking her with a horn. But the pesky little pooch merely dodged away barking at the ill-tempered cow, further angering her.

One of our horses was a quarter horse that we named Beauty. She was as fast as a bolt of lightning. And sometimes, like a few females I've known, she was hard to control. Mounting Beauty was a life-threatening adventure. At the moment she felt the least bit of pressure on the stirrup, she broke into a sprint. Many times, I found myself half mounted, hanging onto the saddle horn for dear life and desperately trying to throw my other leg over her back to get seated. All too often I lost my grip and crashed to the ground skinning some hide off my carcass.

One day while riding Beauty, I suddenly found myself astride a bucking bronco. Tom had frightened her, jumping from behind a stack of straw as I was riding past. My little horsey suddenly went berserk and bounced, heaved and bucked across the pasture. Unable to hold on, I vacated the saddle *muy pronto* busting my rump when I hit the ground. And Tom, he vacated his hiding place just as quickly running for the house to save his worthless hide.

Queenie, our other horse, was a huge beast. She was a draft horse that had been used to drag logs out of the woods. Dad bought her when he found that she was going to be retired and possibly sold for dog food. She was as gentle as a lamb and all six of us children could ride on her massive back at the same time.

Dad decided to use Queenie to cultivate a patch of cane berries instead of using his tractor, hoping to save 20 cents in fuel. He harnessed the old girl to a small garden cultivator and gave her a whack on the rump.

Now Queenie was accustomed to pulling thousands of pounds of logs and this little harrow thing only weighed 30 pounds, if that much. Probably expecting to be pulling a log, she bellied down almost to the ground and, with a steam-engine snort, drove forward with all her might. Before you could blink an eye, she'd pulled the cultivator and Dad, like they were a piece of string, through the cane berries and through the potato patch and into the cornfield. All we could see were clouds of dust and Dad's heels and all we could hear were his frantic cries, *"Whoa! Dammit, Queenie, whoa! Stop! Dammit, Queenie, stop!"*

She finally came to a halt, but only after she had torn up half the garden. It would have been a heck of a lot cheaper had Dad purchased gas for the tractor instead of being a skinflint trying to save a few pennies. So Queenie was re-retired.

In the fall of 1945, Dad brought home a couple of surplus army cots. Tom, Dick and I loved sleeping out under the stars on warm nights. And the cots were ideal for that purpose. So, one sultry night, we set them up in the pasture between the barn and the woods and settled down to enjoy ourselves. While lying there in the dark, scaring each other with spooky stories, we thought we heard the bleating of a sheep in the nearby woods. Being just a little curious, we wondered if it really was a sheep or some other animal. We had no sheep and knew of no one living nearby who had any.

Dick offered that perhaps it was a wolf that we heard. But Tom countered, saying, *"Naw, wolves can't make a sound like that. It's got to be a sheep."*

My brothers wanted to catch it and put it in the barn. After all, with so many animals on the farm, who would ever notice a sheep?

Nearly hugging each other, we crept into the woods listening for an occasional bleat and tried our darnedest to catch a glimpse of the thing in the dark. But staying just far enough ahead of us so that we couldn't catch up, it led us around in circles among the trees for several minutes until we completely lost it. Disappointed that we had never caught sight of our prey, we gave up our quest, deciding to track it down in the morning.

Just as we were exiting the woods, a huge figure jumped from behind a tree into our path, growling menacingly, scaring the pee out of us. The beastly figure was our prankster father. We should have known that it was he who was the sheep in wolf's clothing—or vice-versa.

Dad returned with us to our cots and sat on the edge of one, joining us for a time. Settling down for the night, we resumed telling our stories. Dad told a few too, and they were real Jim-Dandies. Eventually, we fell into a deep, happy, and contented sleep, comforted knowing that our father was there, watching over us, his little menagerie.

The Price of Being the Oldest

During the past winter, torrential rains and high water had caused considerable damage to our swimming hole in Hedges' woods. The homemade dam that blocked the water had all but washed downstream.

When the weather turned warm, Tom and I decided one day that it was time to repair it so we could go swimming. But Dee and Tudie wanted to go with us. Heck, I didn't want them tagging along because they would just be a nuisance. Mom refused permission but the two little ones kept up a steady din, whining and carrying on, until she finally gave in to them.

Mom wasn't as concerned about Tom or me going to the woods because we were old enough to care for ourselves. But Tudie and Dee were a different matter. She worried they might fall into the creek.

Another thing that concerned Mom was Tudie's health. Not many months had passed since her bout with polio. She was still frail.

I knew what was coming. Mom wanted me to keep watch over them and to keep them out of the water.

"Ah shoot, Ma! I can't have no fun watchin' little kids. We wanna work on our dam. And what about Tom? Why can't he watch them too? Why do I always have to be the one?"

Dee, the frog catcher

My whining did no good and I had no choice. Reluctantly, I agreed to keep watch over them and off we went, trudging down to the swamp and along the irrigation ditches for at least three-quarters of a mile to Hedges' woods.

On the way, Dee spotted a large bullfrog near the edge of the ditch and, with the stealth of a cat, crept up and caught it. It was a beautiful, powerful specimen and as large as any bullfrog I'd ever seen. Immediately, Tudie began to whine, wanting to hold it. But Dee told her that she couldn't, concerned that she would let it go. But she kept it up until our softhearted brother gave in to her. She took hold of the frog. But it was just too big for little sister. With one kick of its massive hind legs, it leaped from her arms right back into the irrigation ditch, disappearing under the water among the sedges and swamp grass.

Poor Dee! His face went blank. He couldn't believe what had just happened and was dismayed that Tudie had let his bullfrog escape. For several seconds, he stared dejectedly at his little sister, his lower lip puckered and quivering as if he were on the verge of bawling. Had it been one of us boys, he would have whaled away at us in an instant. But since it was Tudie, a girl, and his little sister, all he dared do was moan and groan and fling his arms about in despair.

Tom and I were quite pleased to find that some of our dam was still intact. Wasting no time at all, we slipped out of our shoes, rolled up our pant legs and waded into the cold water to go to work. Right off the bat, the little kids began bugging us, wanting to get into the creek too. I knew darned well that they were going to be a pain in the neck before we left home. How could I work on the dam and watch them too? So, disregarding what Mom had asked of me, and my promise, I told them to scram.

"Ya can't get in the water. Mom don't want you to get wet. So go away. Go play in the hollow tree or sumthin but stay outa the water."

In only a few moments, they'd wandered off and out of sight. Dee began searching and exploring the banks of the creek and Tudie picking dandelions in the lush meadows. Busy working on the dam, I soon forgot about them. Our project was more important than being attentive to my little brother and sister.

And then it happened. We heard splashing and a lot of commotion downstream. I knew that one of them had gone into the creek and was in real trouble. There weren't many deep holes and none large enough to swim more than a few strokes. But, unfortunately, poor Dee found the deepest one and fell in. He had been under water for several seconds thrashing about before we fished him out. Conscious but blue in the face and choking, he had inhaled and swallowed a lot of water. Believing we knew all there was to know about first aid for drowning victims, I got down on all fours and Tom slung our little brother across my back, face down. He gurgled, drooled, sputtered and moaned. He was okay, just wet and shivering with fright.

We were all upset and just as frightened as Dee. And when he said he wanted to go home, not one of us objected. Over Tudie's whiny protests, we took her brown overcoat and, after wrapping it around Dee to keep him warm, retraced our steps back to the house.

Being the oldest was for the birds. All I could do was hope that Mom wouldn't notice that Dee looked like a drowned rat. But, as soon as we walked through the door, my sweet, sensitive little sister, her eyes as big as milk pails, blared loudly, *"Momma! Dee Dee! He fell in the water and he almost drown-ded to death."*

You know, it's darned tough being the oldest sibling and having all that responsibility on one's shoulders. But it becomes even more difficult when your little sister's a big blabbermouth.

The Biggest Kid of All

My father loved fireworks. And since the war had ended, the sale of fireworks was no longer restricted. The antsy old goat was just like a big kid. He could barely wait for the arrival of the Fourth of July so he could begin blowing up the planet.

The year 1946 was the best. It was the first time since the war that we could get fireworks. And it was time for a big celebration. And Pa went all out . . . and then some. He must have visited every fireworks stand between Portland and Sherwood and purchased a gunnysack filled with fireworks of every description: huge firecrackers, rockets, Roman candles. You name it . . . he had it. He'd bought enough stuff to blow our little farm to kingdom come.

Pop wouldn't allow us kids to fire off the big stuff. He claimed it was too dangerous. In fact, he wouldn't allow us to fire off some of the small stuff either. We were lucky if we got to light a sparkler or ignite a tiny ladyfinger firecracker.

Pa planned to fire the rockets out over the swamp. So, he built a trough-like chute to direct their flight. It was made of four-foot-lengths of shiplap boards propped up at a 75-degree angle on two sticks that he'd stuck in the dirt.

We were surprised. Preceding the big show, he allowed us to set off some small stuff—a few strings of firecrackers and a few Roman candles as the little kids waved wands of sparklers about.

When it was good and dark, he fired off two or three small rockets using his homemade contraption. It worked perfectly. Then, with a huge grin on his face, he dug out this gigantic thing that looked like a torpedo. It had to be the king of all rockets. It was red and it looked dangerous. Even though Pop was in control and we were confident that he could handle it, we were still a little fearful and stood back some distance. Our hearts began to race as we anticipated the spectacular sight that this pyrotechnic monster was going to create when it shot high into the night sky.

Dad laid it in the trough, lit the fuse and backed away. Just before it ignited, the sticks holding the chute gave way and the entire setup collapsed. The rocket blew. And in just a split second, it left our back yard, ricocheting off the ground and slashing a path through Aschwanden's hayfield. After one big bump off the ground, it somersaulted, gained a little altitude and disappeared out of sight into the swamp. It was indeed spectacular, but not in the way we had hoped or the way Dad had intended.

Fortunately, the rocket didn't start any fires or do damage other than mow down a narrow swath of hay. Understandably, Pop was disappointed. But most of all, he was mad at himself because his trough took a flop and ruined his fun and ours too. The biggest kid of all, my dad, did a lot of things well. But a carpenter, he wasn't.

Barnyard Antics

Most barns in the county were painted red. But not ours! Oh no, we just had to be different. Dad wasn't about to pay good money for red barn paint when he could get surplus paint, regardless of the color, for little or nothing. The color didn't matter to him as long as the barn was painted.

He brought home this paint, cans and cans of it, that was the most hideous bluish-gray color imaginable and not really fit to cover any kind of building. We'd heard of the color battleship gray. Well, we called this paint *destroyer blue*. There was enough of it to paint the walls of the Grand Canyon.

For several days, Tom, Dick and I did our very best, slapping and swabbing and dabbing the thick gooey stuff on the barn. The paint wasn't runny, but it kind of sagged and hung here and there as though it were old, wrinkled skin. After thoroughly covering the barn, we stood back to survey our work. It looked just awful, as if someone had dumped a huge dead whale in the middle of our pasture.

"Just wait 'til Grandma sees this."

Our cows, too, appeared intimidated and confused, probably wondering what in the world happened to their home. Until they got used to it, we did a lot of pushing and prodding to get them into their stanchions so we could do the milking.

After several years of growing our own hay, Dad began buying it in bales because he needed more acreage for pasture. Not cutting and raking as much hay as in previous years was just fine with us boys. Putting up loose hay was, and still is, miserable, hot, tiring, dirty work that has to be done quickly while the weather holds.

Back a few years when Dad was working long hours at the shipyards, Dick Walgraeve helped Tom, Dick and me store hay for the winter. Mr. Walgraeve pitched hay into the loft as Tom and I pulled it back into the inner recesses. Dick, not as strong as we were, had the task of sprinkling rock salt and tromping on the hay to pack it down. Mr. Walgraeve could pitch as much hay as ten normal men and was so strong that he easily overwhelmed Tom and me. He finally stopped when he heard our panicked cries that we had buried our brother Dick. The loft was suffocating and the air so hot and thick with dust that, when we found him, he was listless and nearly unconscious.

Stacking baled hay in the barn was also difficult, but not so much as putting up loose hay. Always seeking a way to have fun, we intentionally left small passageways among the bales when we stacked them. After the barn had been filled, we played the game *Hide and Go Seek*, crawling and burrowing through tons of baled hay as if we were a family of mice. It wasn't uncommon for two of us to be scooting along on our hands and knees in the same pitch-black passageway and suddenly meet head on, cracking heads together. One could walk into the barn, look at that mountain of baled hay and not have the slightest idea that it was crawling with a horde of kids.

Two or three weeks every year, after the old hay was gone and before a new batch was stacked in the barn, we removed the flooring to allow air to circulate throughout the structure. Removing the floor exposed the floor joists, the dry dusty ground beneath, and everything else including a beat-up toboggan, used lumber, a broken wheelbarrow and a set of rusty bedsprings.

It wasn't easy but we played cross-out ball inside the floorless barn with only two or three boys on each team. We used a tennis ball instead of a real baseball, and we used the supporting concrete pier blocks as bases. The ball couldn't travel far when hit; it just bounced and ricocheted off the walls much like a ping-pong ball. And that made it difficult to catch. It was a wild game. Running the base-path was like running an obstacle course. The batter had to jump over bedsprings, floor joists and whatever else lay in the way.

One day, Tom walloped the ball and took off leaping over things and touching pier blocks on the way around the barn. Knowing the cross-out play at home base was going to be close, he slid into it head-first. But instead of touching the pier block with his hands, he hit it with the top of his head. The collision opened a sizeable gash in his scalp and blood poured out of him like a flash flood. Dee ran to the house to warn Mother what had happened as Dick and I hauled Tom across the pasture in a wheelbarrow.

Mom and Grandma quickly removed the blood-matted hair from his wound, staunched the flow of blood, and covered the laceration with a bandage. They did quite well with medical emergencies. By necessity, they'd become skilled medical practitioners.

During warm summer nights, most of us gathered at the barn to do the milking, feed the livestock, and play. Milking was done by hand and, for the most part, it wasn't a terribly difficult chore, just boring. Sitting on small stools, two of them homemade with scrap lumber, we held the buckets firm, squeezing them between our knees to leave our hands free. While milking, we played music on a small portable Arvin radio and sang songs. The cows seemed to like it. The neighbors seemed to enjoy it too, often commenting about the pleasant laughter, music and merriment echoing across our pasture.

Our cats loved fresh warm milk. And, like clockwork, they appeared in the barn at milking time. We never fed them from a bowl because they were very adept at catching squirts of milk in their mouths, even climbing the walls to get at it. The dogs, on the other hand, weren't at all fond of receiving a treat that way and beat a hasty retreat whenever a spurt of milk came shooting their way.

Cows constantly switch their tails to prevent flies from pestering them. It's in their nature. Sometimes, but not often enough, we tied their tails down to keep from being swatted. When we didn't, we chanced getting slapped across the nape of the neck with a wet tail coated with manure. For the fun of it, and for practice, our sisters braided the cows' tails. Maybe it was fun for the girls but it wasn't always fun for us. Getting belted by a cow's braided tail was like being slugged with a club.

Sometimes the cows weren't in a good mood for one reason or another: bothersome flies, tender udders, and so on. And when cows aren't content, bad things happen. Many times, I got stepped on or kicked. And being kicked resulted in losing a bucket of milk as well as being dumped on one's butt on the barn floor. Nonetheless, we seldom bothered to use hobbles. Instead, we buried our foreheads in their flanks. That didn't stop the cows from kicking but it gave us a split-second warning that a kick was coming.

While milking one evening, I spotted Tommy coming across the pasture, walking toward the barn. An unburned pile of scrap boards nearer the barn also drew my attention when I saw a movement. It was a rat. Rats certainly weren't uncommon on farms. But it was a unique experience for me because I'd never seen one before. It must have sensed Tommy approaching and scampered in my direction toward the barn.

Without a second's hesitation, I leaped to my feet nearly dumping the milk and bolted out the door toward the rat. I was bent on killing it. Rats were bad news and I didn't want it making a home under our barn. But I had no time to grab a club or a pitchfork to use as a weapon. My only option was to kick it. If it escaped, never again could I enjoy sleeping in the hayloft knowing that I had to share the premises with a dirty, loathsome, disease-infested rodent.

The rat suddenly veered its direction and ran straight at me. Its apparent aggressiveness caused a chill to run down my spine. As if I were a football player kicking off in a ball game, I hit the animal square in the head with the toe of my boot and, instantly killing it, sent its carcass sailing. Tom was near enough that, for just a split-second, he believed it really was a football. Had I been playing in a real game, I could have made a forty-yard field goal—easily.

The Victim

Most folks probably don't know that cows love eating raw onions. Ours did, and we knew it. Just as Dick Walgraeve had done, Herman Aschwanden discarded his cull onions into a sizeable pile outside the onion barn, eventually using them as fertilizer. They were a tantalizing, mouth-watering attraction to our animals.

A few years back, long before we had an electric fence, our cows escaped every so often. And whenever they did, we usually found them up the road stuffing themselves with cull onions.

The effect that onions have on a cow stays with the animal at least three days. The milk smells and tastes absolutely awful. We couldn't drink it. But the pigs had no problem. Cleaning the barn, however, was a different matter. I had a terribly queasy stomach. And I couldn't tolerate the rank and offensive odor of the manure. It made me throw up.

But it didn't bother brother Tom. The guy was immune to stink. He could wade barefoot though manure and it wouldn't bother him.

It was my week to clean the barn when the cows had an onion-gorging picnic. I knew that cleaning the barn would upset my stomach. So I tried to get my brother to swap with me. My proposal was that he work two weeks in succession and I'd work three, adding an extra week as payment for his trouble. But, he wanted more; he wanted me to milk his cow too. I balked. But he wouldn't give in. And, so, I accepted. I had no choice. But, one way or another, he was going to pay a price for taking advantage of my unfortunate problem.

So, the scheming began. And before ten seconds had expired, I knew exactly what I was going to do to him . . . douse him with a bucket of cold water.

One morning a few months later, I set my plan in motion, knowing that my brother would be along any moment to take care of a few chores.

I filled my milk pail with freezing cold water and, tying one end of a short length of rope to the bail and the other end to a rafter, balanced it atop the nearly closed barn door. If it worked correctly, he'd get a good soaking when he pushed the door open.

Barely able to control my mirth and chuckling to myself, I hid atop the baled hay and waited.

At least 20 minutes passed when I saw fingers reach inside, grasp the door and push it open. In that brief instant before my trap was sprung, I was horrified not to see Tom, but my dad.

My poor father became my victim. But instead of the water pouring on him, the bucket slipped off the top of the door, swung down, and smacked Pop on the side of the head with the force of a battering ram. The impact sent him sprawling backwards on the seat of his pants down the ramp. His rear made a thrump-a-bump sound as it bounced over the ramp treads.

A dreadful feeling swept over me. I might have killed my dad.

Scrambling down from the hay, I prayed that I'd find him still alive. He was. He wasn't hurt, only stunned a little. But he was a mess, his clothing soaked and coated with a layer of smelly cow manure.

"What the hell happened?"

Mentally groaning, I wondered how I was going to get out of this predicament. As Pop was getting up, I saw a way of laying the blame on my brother and grabbed the swinging bucket. I muttered, *"I wondered what Tom did with my milk pail."*

Well—one look at Dad and I knew he wasn't buying it. So, I made a wise and prudent decision to save my conniving hide and run for tall timber.

Poison Oak and Hazelnuts

My brothers and I wanted to play, not work. And when Grandma told us she wanted us to clear some brush, we dug in our heels.

A half-acre of hazelnut brush, Scotch broom, and poison oak remained to be cleared from the far end of the upper place. And Granny figured the best time to remove it was while the ground was still wet. For two days, we kept putting her off, giving her all kinds of lame excuses. When she finally had her fill of our shiftless ways, she gave us an ultimatum.

"I kin go down there and cut a switch from one of those bushes and give yore worthless backsides a good blisterin' or you can come with me now and help me while you can still sit. Now, what's it gonna be?"

I was as tall as Dad and nearly old enough to go to war. And she still treated me like a little kid. But, what choice did I have? There was a benefit to pulling the brush, though. It eliminated one of Granny's sources for switches.

We gathered up our well-used brush-hook axes, shovels and dirt picks and unenthusiastically followed her down the road to the patch of brush. And soon, we were whacking away at it.

Tom inherited the chore of removing most of the poison oak and stacking it for burning. Poison oak didn't bother him. Not one tiny bit! If anything, he thrived on it like a billy goat. He could wade through it, rub it over himself and even eat the darned stuff without it ever causing him trouble. But, on the other hand, I had a horrible, sometimes agonizing time with it, itching something terrible. I even had to avoid the smoke when we burned it. Long sleeve shirts and gloves helped some but, still, I often became infected with a bad case of the itches.

Hazelnut bushes were difficult to dig out by hand. They had huge root systems and taproots as strong as steel cables that grew deep into the earth. We found it easiest to pull them out using Dad's old home-made tractor, but only after we had dug around the root systems first.

One hazelnut bush gave us a problem. The root system was one of the largest we'd ever encountered.

Just as I'd done with others, I wrapped one end of a steel cable around the base of the bush and attached the other end to the tractor. I drove forward to take up the slack in the cable and, when it was taut, poured the gas to the old crate. But all I succeeded in doing was dig ditches with the massive rear tires. The bush didn't budge. So, I backed the tractor up a few feet and got a short running start, hoping to jerk it out of the ground. But still, the bush held tight.

Grandmother suggested I get a longer run at it. So, I backed all the way up the bush, put the tractor in a higher-speed forward gear, and gunned the engine. The tractor leaped forward. At the instant the cable stretched out to its full length, I heard a loud bang. The tractor left mother earth for an instant, and then slammed to the ground.

Clutching the steering wheel in a vise-like grip, I sat there bewildered because I was now staring nearly straight up into the sky instead of looking at the woods directly in front of me. When I came to my senses and looked back, I found that I'd jerked the entire rear-end assembly from beneath the tractor. Gears, wheels, axle, bearings, drive shaft and other things lay strewn out behind me.

Grandmother just about went nuts.

"Oh, Lordy! Yore dad's gonna have a conniption fit when he sees what you've done to his tractor, Teddy. He's gonna skin you alive."

Why did bad things always happen to me? And I couldn't believe what she was saying; she was laying all the blame on me. For Pete's sake, she sounded just like one of the kids.

I dreaded thinking about what Dad would do when he saw this mess. Trying to eliminate any trace of skid marks, I filled in the ruts.

Just as I'd expected, Pop was mad as a wet hen. But, fortunately, he was angrier with the tractor than he was with me. He knew we were pulling brush. But never did he think the tractor would fall apart doing that chore. He figured a defective part was to blame and never found out what I'd done. And lucky for me, Grandma kept her mouth shut.

We cleared brush as best as we could for the next two or three days. But finally we had to give it up until Dad fixed the tractor.

Unfortunately, I wished that we'd have stopped working sooner because I'd caught a horrible case of poison oak between my toes. It was a mystery to me why my feet had been infected. But infected they were and they itched like crazy.

I smeared lotion on my tootsies and sometimes went barefoot for a couple of days. But the itching wouldn't clear up. It just about drove me crazy and I couldn't resist scratching, an act that made it spread and become more agonizing.

Then, I found out the reason I couldn't cure my problem. Someone had placed a leaf of poison oak in the toe of each of my socks.

I had no problem guessing who the culprit was. Tommy, boy! And, as soon as I quit scratching, I worked out another of my infamous plans to inflict a little misery on my brother.

Roamers' Rest Park

Tom and I were tired of working at home when we could do the same thing for someone else and get paid for it. Besides, we could use some money. So we asked several of the farmers if they needed help in the onion fields. The only one who did was Clarkie Johnston's dad. He needed help for about a month. But we were reluctant to work for him because he wouldn't pay any more than a dollar a day . . . the same as he did the year before. But, a dollar a day was better than nothing, so we accepted his offer.

Mr. Johnston paid us every night in quarters. But, if he thought we hadn't worked hard enough, he docked us 50 cents apiece. He did that a couple of times. And we didn't dare argue with him if we wanted to continue earning a few cents.

Pulling weeds under an ungodly hot sun six days a week wasn't at all pleasant, especially if we only got 50 cents a day. We wished many times that we could go swimming at Roamers' Rest Park.

One day, I told Tom that I had a plan. And I was certain that it was foolproof.

"Why not go swimming every other day? We'll simply tell Mr. Johnston that we're needed at home. He won't know the difference. And Mom will think we're working. And since we don't have a phone, how can they check up on us?"

Before I got the last words out of my mouth, he was ready. And so we put our plan into action immediately.

The next day after work we told Mr. Johnston that we'd have to skip a few days of work now and then because we had work to do at home. He didn't like the idea and told us so. But, after mildly objecting he told us to come whenever we could. And so we began skipping work every other day to go swimming.

The owners of Roamers' Rest Park had built a large wooden platform in the river that was securely anchored to the riverbank and accessed by a ramp. It was often referred to as a float. The structure contained two reasonably large swim tanks, one for small children and the other for adults.

The tanks were constructed of wooden slats spaced an inch apart to allow water to easily flow through. No chlorinated water was used in those days and most probably the pools were considered state-of-the-art.

Admission to the park was a quarter. But we didn't want to spend our meager earnings and snuck in.

One day early on, the manager, a woman, caught us as we tried to enter without paying. Our hearts sank as we begged and pleaded with her, *"Please don't tell our parents on us. We just wanted to learn how to swim."*

She sternly admonished us. I'd never been scolded by a stranger before and it was unsettling. I was worried that we were in more trouble than I could have imagined.

But quite unexpectedly, the tone of her voice changed and she offered us a job. We were dumbstruck, nearly speechless. She needed three or four young boys to pick up trash, maintain the park's equipment and help the lifeguard watch the swimmers. If we accepted, we'd be allowed free entry every day and hamburgers afterwards.

What kid could turn down an offer like that? Tom and I gleefully jumped at it. We reported to the lifeguard on the swimming platform, a woman named *Chips*. Thus began several weeks of juggling work at Johnston's, eating hamburgers, swimming and having fun. And neither Mr. Johnston nor our mother ever found out.

Chips was about 25 years old and always wore sunglasses, a navy cap with the brim pulled down, white shorts, and a sloppy sweatshirt. She taught us the various swimming strokes, how to tread water, how to speed dive and, if a person were having trouble in the water, how to pull them to safety. We also learned how to right an overturned canoe, shake the water out of it and crawl back in.

A friend, Tommy Pickens, and another kid from Tualatin joined us. We ranged in ages from 12 to 15 years. And each of us eventually received a small lifesaving patch that we proudly sewed to our swim trunks.

Sticking my toes between the slats in the bottom of the tanks was a daring challenge. Crawdads lurking beneath might latch onto one of them. Occasionally one found its way into the tanks causing pandemonium among the girls. Afraid of being pinched, they screamed and vacated the tanks in a hurry. But, to us boys, it was no big deal. We weren't afraid of crawdads. Proving our heroism to the young ladies, we jumped in, caught the little critters and tossed them into the river.

Several days after our job with Mr. Johnston ended, we talked Mom into going to Roamers' Rest with us. It was a hot day and we were dying to get into the water.

Mom had no idea that we knew how to swim. She was a little apprehensive about her little boys being near deep water. Not a good swimmer herself, she nervously warned us not to go near the side of the float next to the river.

We changed into our swimsuits and waited for our unsuspecting mother to appear. As soon as she was close, Tom and I made a dash to the river and dove out into the stream. Mom was horrified. About to jump in after us, she quickly realized that we could swim and swim very well and were in no real danger. Although she was pleased that we could navigate in the water, she was a bit miffed at us for playing a trick on her. Playing it smart, we stayed in the river treading water for a time to allow her to cool her heels in one of the tanks.

Tom was easily a much better swimmer than I. He had read about people attempting to swim the English Channel and probably thought that he might be up to swimming long distances himself.

One day before the gates to the park opened to the public, Tom began testing his endurance; swimming back and forth in the river past the float with me following close behind in a small rowboat. He had been in the water for over an hour before he decided he'd had enough. He was exhausted and gasping for air when he crawled into the boat.

That convinced me, then and there, that swimming for pleasure was my only goal.

My First Date, Sort of

I was quite surprised when I discovered two teen-age kids had moved in with our neighbors, the Reichel family. I discovered that they were Leo's children, a daughter and a son from a previous marriage. The boy, David, was about Tom's age and the girl, Gaynell, was a few months older than I. And surprisingly, she was as tall as I, and quite lovely. One only need look at her dark complexion, black hair, and dark eyes to know that she was part Native American Indian.

One warm day not many weeks after the two youngsters came to live with their dad and stepmother, I got up the courage to ask Gaynell if she'd walk to Roamers' Rest Park with me. Her answer was yes. I was surprised and very pleased, indeed. She was the first girl that I'd ever invited to go anyplace with me.

Of course, we didn't go by ourselves. My brother Dee, sister Tudie, and Gaynell's half-brother Butchie tagged along close behind. The trio of snoopy brats kept a close eye on us and giggled every time Gaynell and I spoke or my hand brushed against hers.

The kids wanted to play in the swimming tanks. But Gaynell didn't want to get wet and hadn't brought a swimsuit. That was fine and dandy with me; I didn't want to swim either. I wanted to be alone with her. And what better way to make that happen than a romantic canoe ride.

When I asked if she'd like to go for a ride in one, she smiled and cooed, "*Of Course!*"

Oh, brother! Her expression, her smile, her voice convinced me—a 14-year-old-Casanova—that my masculine charm had won her heart. I couldn't get that canoe into the river fast enough. I couldn't wait to embark on an odyssey into the world of romance.

I assumed that Gaynell had ridden in a canoe before. But she hadn't. I also assumed that she knew how to swim. But she didn't. Yet, she never said a word about doing neither.

I held the two-man-craft steady against the float as Gaynell got in. Then I climbed in and began paddling upstream away from the prying eyes of our siblings.

Ten minutes later, gliding silently past a family of ducks, we approached a small private dock, tucked away under some overhanging trees. It was a beautiful place to stop, to enjoy the coolness and beauty of the river and to sit and talk and hopefully, if I got up enough nerve, to hold her hand.

Before I could tell her not to reach out for the dock, she did. As she caught hold of it with her hands, the canoe slipped away, sliding from beneath her. In an instant, Gaynell lay stretched out in the water, her toes hooked to the edge of the canoe and her hands firmly grasping the edge of the dock. Most of her body, other than her head, hands and feet, was under water. How she was able to scream so blasted loud from that position was beyond me. But scream she did. And it was so piercing that it echoed clearly up and down the river.

Unintentionally, she'd given me a huge problem and put herself in some danger, a horribly difficult predicament for both of us. I managed to reach her feet without overturning our unstable craft. And ever so gently, I reeled her in like a fishing line, pulling her into the canoe and the canoe safely to the dock.

My romantic moment had been completely destroyed. Wet and shivering with fright, Gaynell wanted to return to the park. Frustrated and dejected, I took my time paddling.

A crowd of people including the kids gathered around us as we docked, asking what I'd done to her. Everyone on the river heard that horrible shriek and naturally they could see that she was soaked to the skin. For fear of embarrassing her, I said little and she, too, refused to speak.

Gaynell's clothing dried as we walked back home. We stopped a few times, standing close to each other. But I was too chicken to hold her hand or to give her a hug. After all, I couldn't do much with those snoopy kids watching our every move.

At supper the brats, my sister and brother, taunted me saying over and over, *"Teddy's got a girl friend. Teddy's got a girl friend."*

I pretended to be upset with the kids for teasing me, for telling everyone in the house about Gaynell's scream, and that she was soaking wet when we returned to the park. Mom and Dad looked on for a time with amusement. But finally Dad asked me what we had done, what we talked about, where we had gone. Curiosity was killing him.

"Oh! We didn't do anything. We just talked. That's all!"

The answer contained no juicy little tidbits and it certainly didn't satisfy anyone. Again, he tried to pry some information out of me but after each question, I just shrugged and smiled and said little or nothing. Pa just didn't understand. Great lovers never tell.

I suppose Gaynell could be considered my very first date. Unfortunately, though, that was the first and only time we went anyplace together.

Goodbye, Miss Chips

It was a beautiful, sultry autumn day when Tommy and I arrived at Roamers' Rest, joining Tommy Pickens and the other kid to clean the walkways around the pools and prepare the canoes and boats for winter storage.

Just as we finished doing some repair work at the edge of the floats, Chips gave my brother Tom an unexpected shove into the river. She wanted to play. And we thought we were up to the challenge. The rest of us attacked. But we attacked singly and with no plan. Chips flipped each one of us into the river as easily as someone flipping a coin in the air. We went at her over and over but never once did she get wet.

Crawling out of the water numerous times, we eventually gave up, knowing that we were beaten and would never succeed in dunking her. None of us could believe how strong, how agile, and quick she was, and that two of us probably couldn't handle her. As we lay on the float in the warm sun, we kidded and giggled and laughed with Chips just as we would have with any close buddy. In our book, she was one of the guys.

The following day was our last day at Roamers' Rest Park. Our summer was at an end and school soon beginning. The four of us had gathered on the float waiting for Chips when a beautiful young woman strolled down the ramp toward us. She was wearing a flowing pink dress with lacy trim, a broad-brimmed sun hat, high heels and makeup. She was indeed a sophisticated vision of beauty. We stood close together like a quivering mass of Jell-o, staring in awe at this gorgeous creature as she walked toward us with all the grace of a princess. Then she called us by name.

In total disbelief, Tommy Pickens gasped, *"Holy cow! It's Chips!"*

Unbelievably, it was her ... our Chips. We were numb—numb and speechless. None of us had ever before seen her without her navy cap, sloppy sweat shirt and sunglasses. As she walked up to us, her golden hair shimmering and flowing about her shoulders, we caught the scent of her perfume. And suddenly, four young teen-age boys had fallen in love with their swimming instructor.

Tommy Pickens abruptly shoved me aside and standing in front of Chips, pleaded, *"Will ya throw me in the river again, Chips? I'll let ya, if you wanna."*

Chips married not long after and we never saw her again. Too bad! I was a very disappointed, moon-struck youngster.

Being envious of her new husband, I smugly thought to myself, *"Well, I'll betcha he'll never have as much fun with her as I did."*

I was such an idiot.

The Turnip Patch

Eddie and I were about to enter Sherwood high school as freshmen and needed money to buy new clothes. Our checkered shirts, bibbed coveralls, and lace-up boots, the clothes we wore while attending Cipole, were fine for farming but not at all appropriate for wearing to high school. Most of the young men, including the freshmen, wore bleached-white corduroy trousers, a nice shirt, and dress shoes, somewhat expensive but mature in appearance. If we wanted to fit in, and impress the young ladies, we needed to change our wardrobe.

So, I conjured up a sure-fire plan to earn a few dollars. And I was certain that I'd conceived a good one too. Turnips! We'd plant a patch of turnips and sell them to the produce markets, certain that we'd make a bundle of money.

Why turnips? Well, for one thing, several local farmers raised them year after year. So I figured they must be making money or they wouldn't plant them. Second, they were easy to take care of and, third, turnips were healthy for people.

When I was in the sixth grade, one of our Health and Physical Education assignments was to report what we'd eaten Friday mornings for breakfast. Most kids drank orange juice to get Vitamin C, an important element in our diets. Since Dad didn't earn enough money to buy oranges, I raided Wager's turnip patch. Turnips are also rich in vitamin C. And I liked them with a sprinkle of salt. Eating a couple, I could truthfully make an honest report.

But one day our teacher, doubting that I ate turnips for breakfast, questioned me about it. I was surprised when Eddie readily backed up my story.

"Oh, he's eatin' 'em alright. He's stole at least ten bushels from us just this year."

We asked Eddie's father if he'd let us use an acre of his swamp ground to raise a crop if we paid him ten percent of our earnings. He did, giving us a patch of ground at the edge of the swamp near the woods not far from our house. Frank plowed and prepared it for us too. And soon Eddie and I were planting row after row of turnip seed with the anticipation of earning a small fortune.

After a few weeks our turnips had sprouted and were growing nicely. But so were the weeds.

We met early one Saturday morning after doing our chores, forgoing our favorite Saturday morning radio programs to begin caring for our crop. Barefoot and shirtless, wearing only bibbed-coveralls, we hoed and pulled weeds throughout most of the morning. And we'd nearly finished the patch when something struck me on the leg.

On the ground by my foot lay a fir cone. It didn't take a genius to figure out that someone had thrown it at me. And *that* someone was very likely my brother, Tom. He had to be the guilty party. And he had to be hiding nearby in the woods.

We warily watched the brush and trees as we continued to work. When he lofted more fir cones and a clod of dirt at us, we pinpointed his hiding place. Not only was Tom there, so was my youngest brother Dee acting as his ammo carrier.

Weeding turnips in the heat of the day wasn't the most enjoyable way for me to spend a Saturday. And it was even worse when someone was pestering and teasing me. Their harassment had gone far enough and we figured it was time for us to have a little fun of our own. So, we set about to exact a little revenge upon the two bushwhackers.

Scheming and plotting to get even—now that was something right up my alley. And it took only seconds for me to conjure up a plan of action.

Working our way close to where they were hiding, we pulled a surprise counter attack and charged at them, flinging our own barrage of dirt clods. They ran off into the woods.

We knew this wouldn't be the end to it, though. They'd eventually return to annoy us again. And when they did, they were in for some surprises. Booby-traps! Two booby traps: one made of manure similar to the one Tom and I made during World War II to catch the Japanese Army had they invaded our farm and the other a bombardment trap.

The big fir tree at the edge of the woods near Robinson's barn seemed the best place to rig them. This was the same tree Tom and I had climbed to escape Pa and his toothless hair clippers. And the spikes were still in the trunk to help me climb. Eddie dug a shallow hole at the base of the tree as I went off to fetch some supplies. I returned shortly with a bucket of cow manure, some string, and a burlap bag stuffed full of tin cans and a few dirt clods.

My plan was to rig the bombardment trap up in the tree, and when they were under it, shower them with cans and dirt clods. Getting the bulky bag of cans up the tree proved to be a challenge. But I managed by temporarily hooking the sack to the spikes and limbs until I had climbed about 30 feet.

Balancing the bag on one of the higher limbs, I tied the bottom ears of it to the limb with some string. Then I tied one end of a long string to the top of the sack, looped it over a fragile twig to keep the sack upright, and dropped the other end to the ground. We scrawled a sign that simply read *"Don't pull this"* and tied it to the bottom end of the string, hanging it a few feet above the hole that Eddie had dug. Placing the bucket of soupy manure in the hole, we made a lid for it of sticks, fir needles and leaves. Very neatly camouflaged, we hoped one of them would step in it.

We went back to work smugly confident that two things were certain to happen. First, the two mischief-makers would eventually return to pester us and, second, they would become deserving victims of our traps.

Sure enough, not a half hour passed when they crept back to the edge of the woods to watch us and plan more harassment. Knowing full well that we might have concocted some payback for them, they cautiously surveyed the area and eventually spotted the sign. Poor Dee couldn't resist the temptation. Creeping under the tree, he reached for the string and stepped into the honey pit trap. Until we heard him cry out in disgust, we had no idea they were there.

Being a little smarter, but not smart enough, Tom prodded the ground around the tree. Satisfied that he wouldn't step into something unpleasant, he reached out and, peering up the tree, pulled the string. He became victim number two. The small twig snapped and the bag pivoted, releasing dozens of tin cans and dirt clods. They fanned out as they fell through the lower limbs, showering the two mischief-makers before they could make an escape. We couldn't see them. But when we heard the racket and their bellowed threats to get even with us, we knew our booby traps had worked to perfection. Laughing and giggling, we finished our work, giddy and delighted with our successes.

Turnip prices were not at all good that year. We barely made enough money to buy our corduroy trousers and dress shoes. Working on our farming project wasn't as rewarding as we'd hoped. But it kept us busy and out of trouble. Well, maybe it didn't keep us entirely out of trouble . . . but it did keep us busy.

Freshmen Hurdles

Eddie and I were two innocent and naïve kids. A better description of us might have been *dumb as stumps*. We knew absolutely nothing about what we were getting into or going to face when we entered high school. So, Eddie and I made another pact with each other. We were always making a pact for one reason or another. But this one seemed to be the most important of all.

If one of us got into a fight and was losing, the other would come to his rescue. But if the one in the fight were successfully defending himself, the other would stay out of it.

We soon discovered that we had a bully in our class, a tough kid whose first and last names were the same, Charles Charles. He was tough, tough enough to fight a wolf for a deer carcass and mean enough to eat it raw. Every day, from the moment he entered school in the morning until he went home at night, he created problems and caused disturbances.

A few days after beginning school, Eddie had an encounter with Charles during the lunch break. The bully began shoving my best friend around and calling him farmer boy. Eddie, quite out of character, had had enough of it and decided it was time to fight back. But he didn't stand a chance. I heard a scuffling in the hallway and saw Charles sitting on top of my unfortunate buddy, giving him a pasting.

Eddie, spotting me, yelled pleadingly, *"Remember our pact! Remember our pact!"*

Oh, I remembered the pact all right. I never remembered anything in such detail in all my life. But not wanting to get the tar beat out of me too, I yelled back, *"You're doing just fine, Eddie. Keep it up. You're doing just fine."*

That night after school, we met down in the swamp as usual. I was really hoping that he'd forgotten that I hadn't kept my part of the bargain. He hadn't. And he quickly demonstrated his displeasure. After a few nasty curse words, he slugged the soup out of me and then punctuated his disgust, kicking me in the shins.

Three of our new classmates, all from Tualatin, gave the school's secretary some concern when they enrolled. She wasn't at all certain they were truthful when they gave her their names. They were the same as the ones that belonged to two popular movie actors and a pilgrim. But the names John Smith, John Garfield and Clarke Gabel were really theirs. In fact, John Smith's middle name was Teegarten. Who would want to fake that?

Instead of one teacher instructing us on all subjects, as was the case at Cipole, we had a teacher for each subject. And instead of remaining in one room throughout the day, we moved from one room to another. One of our teachers and the coach for all boys' athletics, Cliff Wyncoop, gave our class a nickname. He called us *"The Prune Shakers."*

Nearly every morning that winter, I woke feeling nauseated. I couldn't figure out what was ailing me. But my mother told me one day that she believed it was morning sickness. I didn't know what morning sickness was; I thought it was just something a person caught, like a cold. I remembered that Mom had complained of having it some time back, but not since Charla was born.

While conversing with a group of my classmates, I related that I hadn't been feeling well and told them of my mother's diagnosis. They said nothing, only walked away with their hands clamped over their mouths.

On the bus after school en route home, I told another classmate, Marion Andrews, about my queasy stomach and again what Mom had told me. Marion was my buddy and quickly set me straight.

Talk about being humiliated. I'll bet I turned every shade of pink, purple, red and crimson known to man. In the worst way, I wanted to get even with my prankster mommy. But I couldn't—at least, not at the moment. But, sooner or later, I would.

New Jobs For Dad

After the Oregon Shipyards closed down and Dad went back to working full time for Columbia Distributing Company, he had no reason to worry about the security of his job. But within six months, his employer began struggling to stay in business. And he found himself working part time again. He had to find another job and quickly. But there weren't many available.

Dad's brother Mickey worked for a new taxi service in Portland and told him that the company needed experienced drivers. He didn't particularly care for that kind of work but applied anyway. And he was hired.

The salary was minimal. But working part time during the day for Columbia Distributing and driving a cab full time at night provided him with enough income to make ends meet. However, the long hours took a toll on him. And so did the worrying.

Dad looked the part of an experienced cabbie when he wore his dark green bus driver cap. He knew people and he knew the streets of Portland inside and out.

But driving a cab wasn't easy. It could be dangerous. Cab drivers were sometimes beaten and robbed and even shot or stabbed. The most dangerous time was during the wee hours of the morning when the seedy side of life was most active. And those were the hours that Dad often worked. He never knew when dispatched to pick up a fare if it was going to be a load of rowdy drunks, a prostitute, a pimp looking for an easy mark, or a criminal wanting to rob him. He was quite capable of defending himself in a physical confrontation, and on a few occasions he had to. But, in the event he couldn't, he carried a billy club under the front seat.

Fortunately, however, most of his fares were common, ordinary people. And some tipped well.

Dad's brother, my Uncle Tony opened a pizza parlor in Portland. We had never before heard the word *pizza* nor had we ever eaten any. It was new to us. And we liked it. We thought our uncle was a celebrity because he advertised his pizzas and home delivery in *Tony's white jeep* on the radio in the evenings. Later on, Tony opened a nightclub and, possessing a dreamy Bing Crosby type voice, performed his own musical entertainment.

In the meantime, my uncle Jack, who'd been unemployed for eons, also went to work driving for the same cab company as Dad and Uncle Mickey. But he didn't last very long before he was fired for being incompetent.

Uncle Mickey eventually quit the cab business and went into business for himself, purchasing the Lucky Tavern on the east side of town. He was a natural for that kind of work.

Dad, never one to sit idle, found another job more to his liking. It was full time for Albert's Distributing Company, one of his former employer's competitors, delivering soda pop and beer. But after working there a short time, he came to the conclusion that they, too, would soon go out of business.

Frustration was setting in but Pa wouldn't give up and kept searching the job market.

We children were never aware of the worries and the uncertainties that Dad was experiencing. Times were tough. But my parents never once let on. And Dad never gave up and kept his nose to the grindstone.

CHAPTER VIII

1947

Meridian Hill

When we awoke one winter morning, we were elated to find that snow had fallen throughout the night and had covered the earth with inches and inches of frosty white fluff. We loved the snow and, bent on having some wintry fun, knew how to take advantage of it. The snow-covered road on Meridian Hill beyond Tualatin beckoned us.

From beneath the barn, Tom and I retrieved an old scarred, and seldom-used toboggan that was large enough to accommodate three or four kids. In a carefree mood, we trudged down Herman Road pulling it through Tualatin and a mile beyond to the hill. We were eager to experience the thrilling half-mile slide down the slope from the crest where Dorothy Hinderman lived to the curve at the bottom.

By the time we arrived, several kids from Tualatin and the nearby farms were already there with their skis and sleds. And some also had ice skates and were skating on a frozen pond near the curve in the road at the bottom. The hill was steep and, when covered with snow, difficult for cars to traverse unless equipped with chains. And even then most of them couldn't make it. We virtually had it to ourselves.

We knew Dorothy Hinderman. She attended Sherwood High School as well. But she was a couple of grades ahead of me.

We invited her to ride with us on the toboggan. Her added weight made it slide faster and farther. But, she also provided us with another benefit. In addition to being a very lovely young lassie, she was also very well developed—if you know what I mean. We figured that, if we crashed, we needed something soft to land on—if you know what I mean. And crash we did, nearly every time, sometimes accidental and sometimes intentional—if you know what I mean.

Dorothy was a good sport. But after nearly three hours of Tom and me rolling atop her, she'd had enough and, to our disappointment, went home to thaw out. Strangely, Tom and I were already defrosted— if you know what I mean.

A few of our friends had brought skis with them. Some of the skis were so warped that they resembled slats from a barrel. I wasn't certain that I wanted to strap those things on my shoes after watching others fall. Most of them tumbled end over end, piling up in awkward positions in a snow bank. Finally I got up enough nerve to try. But in the event that I lost control and needed to make a quick escape, I didn't secure my shoes to the skis; merely stepped onto them.

On my first attempt I managed to ski a dozen feet before taking a flop. And after repeated attempts, I did no better. Since my skiing skills didn't appear to improve one iota after several tries, I gave up any thought of being a cross-country Olympian.

I fared no better at skating either. If someone had figured a way to comfortably and gracefully skate on ones ankles, I could easily have become an expert.

It was nearly dark before Tom and I returned home, happy but cold and tired, and missing lunch, very, very hungry. Within a few days, all the snow had melted away and the seldom-used toboggan went back under the barn to wait for another snowy winter.

Spit and Polish

When I was a kid, my grandmother often cleaned my ears with a handkerchief moistened with spit. It was truly gross. Mom sometimes used this method too. But most of the time, it was my dear grandma who nabbed me. I wasn't the only one to get it either. My brothers suffered this degradation too. Nothing in this world can cause a kid to rebel against a parent quicker than having a gob of saliva poked into his or her ear, or slathered across the back of one's neck. It was a mortifying experience, and particularly so when it was done in public. Granny never intended to embarrass me. I knew that. She only tried to make me look presentable. Still, having my face and ears cleansed with spit was doggone ugly and downright disgusting. I swore that if I ever had a child, I'd never, ever do that to the kid.

Even at home when a washcloth and warm water were handy, Grandma sometimes cleaned my face and ears using the spit-on-a-handkerchief method. I was never convinced that it was more sanitary and a better cleanser than good old-fashioned warm water. And who in the world would ever have gotten close enough to inspect my ears, anyway?

Many times, trying to escape her wet forefinger, she snatched me by the ear and dragged me to a window just to see if there was a little dirt in there. By the time I was ten, she'd grabbed and stretched my ears so often that I began to look like an old and weary, sad-eyed, floppy-eared, basset hound.

She was never gentle when she scoured my ears either. Her finger-nails, and I'm not exaggerating this one iota, were like miniature spade shovels, hard as sheet metal and as sharp as a switchblade knife. More than once she drove her hanky-covered forefinger deep into the side of my head, twisting, probing and drilling as if she was digging a post-hole with an auger. I suffered from nosebleeds, and I suffered from ear-bleeds too. The inside of my ears never really had a chance to heal, not until I left home to join the service.

Dad, on the other hand, was never as concerned about his boys' cleanliness as he was about his little darling princess-like-daughters. They had to look as cute, pure and clean as Snow White if they were to accompany him anyplace.

Pop was actually much gentler cleaning the girls' ears than Grand-mother was with the boys. But the handkerchief he used wasn't exactly clean and sanitary. He carried the same putrid rag in his hip pocket for months on end. And not only did he use it to wipe his nose, he used it to clean the oil from the car's dipstick, wipe dust from his shoes, polish restaurant silverware, and probably wiped the toilet seats in service sta-tion restrooms.

Mount Etna erupted more often than the old man changed handkerchiefs. More than likely, he left more filthy stuff in the girls' ears than he removed. At least he didn't scrub, grind and dig until their ears were raw like Granny did.

Had we any brains, we'd have worn earmuffs.

The Holiday Ham

Pa was a big, spoiled, overgrown kid in striped coveralls. When he hung around the kitchen, he was like a chicken hawk circling over a farm, waiting for a chance to snitch some food. Grandma, always on the alert to someone pilfering the pantry, kept a wary eye on all of the males, including our dad. And she wasn't at all bashful about whacking one of us on the hand with a wooden spoon if she thought we were about to get into something. So what chance did any of us kids have to scrounge a snack when the old man was there?

Dad loved having fun and he loved the holidays. We all did, for that matter. But they meant more to him because he could be home with his family.

Easter, The Fourth of July, Thanksgiving and Christmas—those were his favorite holidays. They meant relaxation, having fun and enjoying life. But the primary reason that he liked them was the food. Pa considered himself a connoisseur of good grub. And his eyes gleamed with anticipation at the mere mention of pies, baked bread, roast turkey and ham. And Mom and Granny did a fantastic job, whipping up those kinds of vittles.

Easter and Christmas were big food days for us but Thanksgiving was THE day to chow down. And, brother, did we ever. After stuffing ourselves until we were absolutely sick, there was a rush for the softest chairs, the winners soon falling asleep. By early evening, everyone was sleeping. The place looked like a morgue, bodies lying everywhere, even under the dinner table.

Traditionally, the parishioners of St. Francis Church in Sherwood held an egg hunt after Easter Sunday Mass for their tiny toddlers. The ladies provided dozens of beautifully decorated hard-boiled eggs, many of them works-of-art, for the event.

The scenario was the same every year; the older kids hid the eggs outside in the lawn, shrubbery and flowerbeds around the church. And then the little kids, many carrying Easter egg baskets, filed outside onto the sidewalk to begin the hunt.

Dad went with Dee and Tudie joining the other youngsters on the sidewalk. Mom, standing off to one side, wondered what her husband was up to; he was like a big kid. While the children waited for the signal to begin, Pa surveyed the landscape, spotting eggs and recording their location on a mental map.

The instant the signal was given, the kids scattered about the church grounds like a covey of quail. And Dad was right in the middle of them. He'd scooped up Charla, his nearly two-year-old daughter, and joined the hunt.

Presently he spotted an egg and put little sis on the ground so she could grab it. But another youngster went for it at the same time. He didn't get it though; Pa bumped him away with his stomach.

Mom was so embarrassed that she couldn't watch any longer and went to the parking lot and got into the car. I guess she wanted to avoid anyone who knew that she was married to the big ham.

Gaylen's Fun

When Aunt Freda brought our cousin Gaylen out to the farm for a visit one afternoon, I could hardly believe the way he was dressed. Nearly eight years old, his mother still made him wear short pants and fancy shirts. Of course I was tickled pink to see him. But he looked like the kid in the *Blue Boy* painting.

When I greeted her, I sensed her coolness toward me and guessed that she was probably still miffed because I'd given Gaylen a pocketknife for Christmas. Or maybe it was the homemade soup-bone flowerpot that I'd given her as a gift one time. So I vowed to keep a low profile and hoped that just this once I could get through the day without upsetting her.

We invited Gaylen to accompany us to the barn when we did our evening chores. Since our cousin hadn't been around many farm animals, Tom, Dick and I set out to educate him, filling his head with

Gaylen James, age 11

all kinds of stories. Gaylen absorbed every word we told him about Queenie, our big workhorse. He wanted to sit astride her—that is until he saw the huge beast. He was fascinated. But her enormous size concerned him. He was afraid that she'd step on him if he fell off. After a little coaxing, though, he gave it a try.

Shinnying up a small tree near the barn, Gaylen perched on a limb so he could drop onto Queenie's massive back. When we led her beneath the limb, he dropped but failed to grab her mane. And sure enough, he tumbled off onto the ground with a thud. The horse didn't budge an inch but stood patiently. Gaylen, now undaunted and determined, went up the tree and dropped onto her again. But, as he'd done before, he toppled off into the dirt. A third attempt was successful, and he stayed put.

Grinning from ear to ear, as if he'd just conquered the world, Gaylen proudly sat atop Queenie, looking much like a pea sitting on top of a bowling ball. We led the old mare around the pasture until he'd had enough and slid off once and for all. He was pleased. But his nice clothing had become thoroughly soiled with dirt. And he reeked like a stable.

As we prepared to milk, we informed Gaylen, swearing it was true that, depending on the day of the week, the cows gave chocolate milk, sour milk, pasteurized milk and buttermilk. And when it snowed, they gave milk shakes. We also told him that milking a cow was a lot like pumping water out of a well. With our instructions, he took hold of a cow's tail and began pumping it up and down as one of us began the milking routine, sending steady squirts of milk into the bottom of the pail, making it ring like a musical instrument. Occasionally, we sent a stream of milk toward our cats and, when Gaylen stopped pumping, we sent a few toward him. The cats loved it. But not Gaylen.

It was nearly dark by the time we finished our chores and returned to the house. On the way, Tom spotted a freshly built molehill and promptly jumped on it packing it into the earth. Moles were nuisances and we never passed up the chance to discourage them from burrowing in our pasture and garden. As Tom was flattening that one, Gaylen spotted what he thought was another and, mimicking Tom, jumped on it with both feet. We were too late to warn him that the hill was an old cow pie.

When we walked into the house and Aunt Freda saw her little prince, she nearly had a conniption fit. His clothing was as filthy and wrinkled as an old saddle blanket. And he was scratched and bruised and stunk to high heaven. But, from the huge grin on his face, it was apparent that he had enjoyed himself.

My cousin was a tired little boy and a happy kid. But Aunt Freda wasn't happy; she was one upset mother. And she couldn't conceal her irritation with me either.

I'd done it again. And just as Gaylen had, I'd stepped in it too.

Fish Tales

The Tualatin River was in no way a pure, sanitary stream. Sewers from many of the homes emptied directly into it. And it was never a fast moving river either. In fact, during a few hot summers when there was little or no rain, the stream appeared to flow backward. But, still, we ate the fish that we caught from it.

Occasionally, we hooked a trout but mostly we caught blue gill and crappie (pronounced *craw-pee*). And we were always assured of catching an enormous number of crawfish.

My brother Dick told me one day that he and Clarkie Johnston had found a small boat in the river. It was adrift and appeared to have been abandoned long ago. And he believed it would be ideal to use when we went fishing.

I asked him if he thought it was safe.

"You'll see! It's a little bit old and rotten in a few places but I think it's okay. Good enough for us."

With a boat, we could get into the more remote areas of the river where most anglers couldn't to fish.

So, lugging our fishing gear, we walked to the river one morning, eager to catch a few fish. But when I saw the boat, I knew my little brother was nuts. No wonder the thing had been abandoned. It was a floating coffin, half-rotten and half-full of water. It even had clumps of grass growing in it. Against my better judgment, however, we bailed the water out and, ever so carefully, climbed into the spongy thing and set sail.

Dick rowed upstream for some distance to a place where the river cut through a densely wooded area. The sunny sky above was barely visible through the overhanging trees. We spotted a couple of decaying pilings sticking out of the water beneath a dense umbrella of branches. I assumed that they'd been part of a dock at one time. It seemed a good place to moor the boat, and a likely place to catch fish.

As Dick eased in close, I nimbly crawled to the bow with one end of a rope, preparing to tie our craft to a piling to hold us fast. I had made two or three loops around it when an ear-piercing scream from the trees directly above our heads frightened us out of our skins.

It was a cougar, lying on a large overhanging branch not more than 20 feet above us.

Stricken stone cold with fear, neither one of us could move for a few terrifying seconds. But a healthy shot of adrenalin quickly thawed the frozen blood in our veins. We sprang into frenzied action, knowing that we had better high tail it out of there and be quick about it. Dick frantically whipped at the water with the oars as I tried desperately to unwrap the loops of rope. But, my finger was caught, pinched between the taut rope and the piling. Jerking at it with my free hand, we broke loose. I nearly tumbled into the water as our waterlogged skiff literally shot, stern-first, out into the middle of the stream.

Dick's rowing churned the water so vigorously that our crummy little barge must have resembled a miniature sternwheeler at full throttle. With all the stress that was put on it, it was a marvel that the old boat didn't disintegrate.

Not until we reached a populated area did we steer the boat anywhere near the bank. And never again did I fish in that part of the river. But Dick did. That gave me another reason to believe that my little brother was just a bit touched in the head. He was probably safe from any meat-eaters that might have attacked him, though. Anything biting him risked getting stomach ulcers.

My Madcap Mother – Part One

When Dad began buying baled hay, the amount of ground needed for growing our own oats and vetch was reduced to about three acres. And, although there wasn't as much hay to cut and store, it was still a big pain in the you-know-what.

Tom, Dick and I had just finished loading the trailer with the last shock of hay, preparing to take it to the barn, when Mom intercepted us. Surprisingly, she wanted to drive the tractor. Dick was behind the wheel and appeared a little stumped by her demand, knowing from experience what kind of driver she was. And he wasn't the only one who was bewildered. We knew right off that this could suddenly turn disastrous. But we dared not argue with her if we wanted supper. So, Dick relinquished his seat behind the wheel and Mom climbed aboard. And just as we figured, bad things began to happen.

In the lower gears, our old tractor was as slow as the seven-year itch, and wouldn't start out fast even by popping the clutch. But somehow our dear mommy managed to make that thing leap and jerk and jump over and over like a jackrabbit trying to escape the jaws of a starving fox. It was a miracle that the trailer and hitch assembly didn't disintegrate. Laughing and giggling, Mom just hung on, as if she were riding a bronco in a rodeo.

By the time she reached the barn, not one single straw of our load remained on the trailer. Our hay was scattered all over hell's half acre. Only minutes before, we figured we had it made in the shade and soon we'd be finished with haying for the summer. But Mother . . . our dear madcap mother . . . quickly changed all of that.

Thankfully, she seldom yearned to drive the tractor or the family car. But when she did, she always seemed to find things to bang into or run over. When she crawled behind the wheel, the safest place to be was up a tree or, better yet, in another county. We once told an acquaintance that she had run over our pig. But that really wasn't true. She would have, though, had she not run into the apple tree first.

We thought we'd found the perfect solution, the perfect motorized vehicle for Mom to drive and yet not be in harm's way ourselves. It was the bumper car amusement ride at Oaks Park in Portland. Those vehicles were made for ramming into each other, a kind of destruction derby without destroying anything. A waist-high barricade surrounded the ride area, preventing the small, two-passenger electric cars from hitting anything other than each other and the barricade itself.

We loved to ride them so much that it nearly took an act of congress to extract us boys from the cars once a ride had ended. Out maneuvering and banging into each other was the name of the game. But the one person we really wanted to slam into was Dad, a feat we seldom accomplished because he was tricky and much more skilled.

One warm afternoon, we went to Oaks Park and made a beeline straight for the bumper car ride. Mom, Dad, Tom and I each took a car. They were identical with the exception of the color. So, Tom and I paid particular attention to the color of the car that our dad had picked. It was bright red, a beautiful color and a beautiful target. A half-dozen people, all strangers to us, also hopped into cars. They provided a little more competition and excitement. But unfortunately for them, they were soon to encounter my maniacal mother.

The ride manager rang a bell to signal the ride was about to begin and flipped on the juice. Dad bumped Mom's car and she immediately had trouble. She couldn't get her car to move in the right direction and caused a huge traffic jam. No one could move. The ride manager, sauntering onto the floor, dislodged Mom's car and got things moving again—for at least two seconds. Mom's lack of driving skills and being bumped again caused another jam. Again, the ride manager entered onto the floor, crawled over a few unmanned units, reached her car, spun the steering wheel and shoved her car aside, clearing the jam. One circuit around the track and it was jam time again—for the third time.

The ride manager, pretty well vexed by this time, told Mom that she had to do two things at once to make everything work: steer and step on the accelerator. And if she did just one thing without doing the other, she'd do nothing but cause trouble. His admonishments only miffed her, causing her to complain that it wasn't her fault because people kept hitting her with their cars and getting in her way. It was obvious she'd have done much, much better riding a horse.

To everyone's relief, Mom began to catch on and did well, circling the floor a few times until one of us rammed her again, sending her car crashing into a half-dozen unmanned cars parked in a corner. The first words bellowed out of her mouth weren't very nice, and then she added a mild threat, *"You just wait 'til I get you home tonight."*

She scarcely got her car straightened out when Dad, grinning like a mischievous school kid, banged into her again. Mom was weary from being picked on and knocked around. Riled, she was determined to pay him back.

Regaining control of her car, she hunched over the steering wheel, her teeth tightly clenched, and went after her spouse. Spotting a bright red bumper car stopped on the backstretch, she zeroed in and rammed into it from behind, sending the car careening into the barricade.

With her hands raised in victory, she yelled, *"Take that you big dumb dope."*

Mom was in for a humiliating shock. She'd picked the right color of car to bang into but not the right person. She'd demolished an innocent, hapless stranger. The fellow probably asked himself, *"Why is this crazy, ranting woman picking on me?"*

My Madcap Mother – Part Two

One Saturday night, Frances and John Bohlen, took my parents to dinner at the Tai Ping Restaurant on Barbur Boulevard near Tigard. Mom wore an attractive dress and makeup and looked absolutely alluring. At 33 years of age and having given birth to six children, she was still a dish.

After dinner, the two fellows wanted to stop for a cold beer at the tavern next to Roamers' Rest Park. It was quite out of character for Mom or Frances to go to a tavern to drink beer, and they didn't want to stay long.

When they went in, the two ladies took a booth so they could trade little tidbits of gossip in private while their spouses sat at the bar to visit with patrons and friends.

After some time had passed, Mom and Frances had grown weary and called to their husbands to tell them they were ready to leave. Unfortunately for Mom, she failed to notice that her spouse had moved to the other end of the bar and another fellow had taken his seat.

When neither of the guys answered, Mom got up and moseyed up behind the one that she thought was Pa. She put an elbow on each of his shoulders and her chin atop his head and seductively pressed her body against his. And then she whispered, *"Let's go honey."*

The guy didn't move, not a muscle. But, Dad did. He was standing right behind Mom and spoke up.

For a fleeting second, she was confused. Dad's voice . . . something was wrong . . . it was behind her. When my mortified mother realized that she was draped over a stranger and not her husband, she straightened up as if she'd been jolted with a cattle prod. And then she reared back and slapped the poor unfortunate sap on the back of the head as if laying all the blame on him for her mistake.

It turned out that Mom's unfortunate victim was Chet Fischbuch. Dad knew him well but Mom didn't. She'd only met him face-to-face perhaps three times during the eight years we lived on the farm. And, yet, each one of those times, she managed to do something inadvertently to embarrass the life out of him.

Chet was a shy, timid man and not one who would make a pass at another man's wife, and certainly not a woman who was the mother of six children. Knowing Dad's reputation for being a tough hombre, he probably figured he was about to be pulverized by a jealous husband.

Pa wasn't angry with Chet, though. To the contrary . . . He'd seen what his flush-faced wacky wife had done. And smiling broadly, in a round about way, he apologized to Chet.

"I'm sorry Chet. When she's had a beer or two, she gets kinda goofy."

Goofy, yes! But my madcap mother didn't need a beer to get that way. It just came to her naturally.

Building a New Home

The topic of building a new house surfaced again. Grandma wanted to begin construction immediately. And all of us kids were quite happy when the folks agreed. Dad and Granny seldom collaborated on anything. But this was something both of them wanted.

The site for the new house was on the lower place near Herman road and the railroad tracks. Another house had been built on the same location many years earlier. But, except for a few fruit-bearing apple trees and a shallow well, there was no evidence that it ever existed.

A couple of weeks after bringing electrical power onto the site and taking care of all the paper work, the first nails were driven.

Our new home was meant to be a one-story structure. But strangely, I never once saw a floor plan. The large attic was roomy enough to accommodate three beds and still have some privacy. The main floor consisted of a living-dining room, a kitchen, two bedrooms, utility room, a stairwell and a bathroom. The house was heated with a cast-iron wood-burning stove situated in the living room.

Grandma, Tom, Dick and I did most of the work. Dad couldn't help because he had to work. That was probably for the best anyway. A carpenter, he wasn't. But occasionally we received help from friends and carpenters when we had something tricky to work on. And we also got plenty of advice, some good and some bad. We made plenty of mistakes, some rather costly.

Leo Reichel helped us with the forms for the foundation. And soon, concrete was poured and construction began. We were supposed to rap on the sides of the foundation forms to make the concrete settle as it was being poured. But we neglected to do that simple little chore. And when the shiplap forms were peeled away a few days later, dozens and dozens of air pockets, pits and gaps, some large enough to hold a baseball, were exposed. The foundation appeared as if it had been pockmarked by gunfire. But it was good enough for us.

Our house slowly took shape, stud-by-stud and board-by-board. And when it was time to do the roof, Tom and I were the only ones capable of climbing up there. But, with Grandma coaching from the ground, we did an adequate job.

When it came time to wire the house for electricity, Grandma hired a young man named Sonny. He was related to someone that she met while working at the poultry plant. He was not a licensed electrician but claimed to know all there was to know about wiring a house. Before stringing one wire, Grandma made the huge and costly mistake of paying him in full.

After several weeks of unnecessary delays, and with the job only partially finished, Sonny absconded. He couldn't be found anywhere. Grandma was so angry that had she gotten her hands on him, she'd have strung him up by the heels from one of our oak trees using some of the wire he wasted.

She hired another electrician, one who was experienced and licensed. He cringed and rolled his eyes when he examined Sonny's work. And when he informed Grandma that it was substandard and dangerous, she nearly ground her false teeth into powder.

The new man re-wired the house and did a good job. But unfortunately, he was only able to salvage part of the material that had already been installed.

We learned the hard way that it didn't pay to hire someone's relative, or anyone else for that matter, without a guarantee that they were qualified.

About that time, all of the money that Grandma and Dad had saved to build the house had been spent.

The stairs to the attic had yet to be built. The only access to the bedchambers upstairs was a crawl ladder built in the back part of the house. A shower, toilet and washbasin had been installed in the bathroom but because hot water wasn't available and a septic tank had yet to be installed, they weren't usable. We still had to depend on the outhouse. A hot water tank hadn't been purchased or installed either. So, we continued to heat water on the stove to wash dishes, take baths and do the laundry. Dishwater and, later, gray water from the washing machine were drained into a small sump in the back yard.

But we had electric lights and receptacles in every room. And Mom had a sink, an electric range and a refrigerator in the kitchen.

Even unfinished, the house was a sight better to live in than the old shack and we moved in. Grandma was elated; she had her own bedroom and closet. We boys were happy too; we slept upstairs at one end of the attic. So did Mom and Dad; their bedroom was at the other end. And the girls' bedroom was the smaller of the two downstairs.

Many months passed before the back porch was finished. Eventually, Dad purchased and attempted to install an electric hot water tank. But, when he flipped the electricity on, the resultant fire nearly burnt the place down. Eventually, the tank was installed correctly. And for the first time in years, Mom had hot water to wash dishes and do laundry. It took a couple more years before the septic tank was installed and the stairs had been constructed. By then, I'd left home.

Route 4, Box 196 was the address of our new home. It was considerably larger than the old decaying shack. But it wasn't a pretty thing, not by any stretch of the imagination. It was adequate, though, and that's what counted.

Saving Man's Best Friend

From early morning until past noon, we heard the forlorn howl of a dog coming from the forested area on the other side of Herman Road. The woods were dense, dark and eerie and no family, other than ours, lived near it giving us cause to wonder why a dog was in there.

When we were younger, the neighbors told us stories that those woods were haunted, dotted with sumps of quicksand, and inhabited by evil beings. Like any child who feared the unknown, we seldom ventured any farther than the brushy fringes. Someone, a family most likely, had lived in the woods years and years before. But all trace of them and their home had long disappeared.

As the day wore on, the howling became less frequent and fainter. We knew that some poor creature was in trouble. So Tom, Dick and I, unable to stand it any longer, decided to have a look. But first we armed ourselves with a butcher knife and some rocks just in case we ran into something or someone unpleasant.

We searched the thick underbrush for some time until a faint whimpering sound led us to a long-abandoned well. It was almost completely concealed by a thick growth of ground-hugging blackberry vines. Peering into the black hole, we could see a dog clinging to some sticks and rotted boards with its forepaws. Most of the unlucky creature's body was submerged in frigid water. It was quite apparent the poor thing was barely hanging onto life, its strength quickly ebbing. We immediately sprang into action knowing that it had no chance to survive if it weren't soon rescued.

Ted, Tom, and Charla with our dogs, at the lower place facing north toward the tracks

Tom and Dick ran back to the barn to fetch some rope and an old blanket as I put more limbs down into the well to give it more things to crawl upon. Within minutes, they returned. Dick and I held the rope tight as Tom, being more heroic and athletic, slid down to the dog and wrapped an arm around the wretched thing. With the animal securely in his grasp, we pulled and tugged until we'd hoisted them up to safety. The dog, exhausted and quivering, was a sorry sight and so weak that it couldn't stand. After wrapping it in the blanket, we carried it home

We nursed the poor creature back to health, adding it to our menagerie of animals. We felt proud of ourselves, knowing that we had saved a life even that of a poor hapless dog.

A few years earlier, we'd rescued another dog. It had been imprisoned, locked inside a boxcar that had been parked at the Cipole siding. That dog had nearly starved to death and looked like a skeleton when we found it. It, too, was so weak that it couldn't walk and had to be carried home. Naming the dog *Bones*, it became another close companion until its death some years later.

Scotty's Feed Store

The word went out. Meet at Scotty's Feed Store in Tualatin at 11:00 a.m. on Saturday for a ball game. Since we had no telephone, the only communication with our friends was by word-of-mouth. And whenever the words "*ball game*" were mentioned, we could be assured that several of our friends would be there.

Tualatin was a quiet, peaceful little town of, I suppose, 200 residents. The only exciting events that ever took place there were a few late-night fistfights at the local tavern. The main travel route through town, the Lower Boone's Ferry Road from Portland, formed the north and west boundaries of Tualatin making a 90-degree turn to the south at the town's primary intersection.

Some of the establishments along the road were Johnny Bauer's Chevron Station, The Spot Tavern, Scotty's Feed Store, The Brick Store at the intersection, Mae's tiny restaurant boasting the best hamburgers and milkshakes in town, Chet and Goldie's Mercantile Store and Frank Hanegan's Mobil Station.

We played ball in a vacant field on the south side of town where someone had built a backstop. We had no bases. So, we used old feed sacks scrounged from Scotty's.

Tom and I walked the railroad tracks to Tualatin and eventually made our way to the Feed Store to wait for the others.

Scotty, the owner of the feed store, was a true Scotsman with a true-to-life Scottish accent. It was rumored that his daughter was married to a famous wrestler who went by the name of *Gorgeous George*. None of us really knew whether it was true of not. But Scotty swore an oath that it was. Of course, he swore oaths to many things being true, some that we knew to be preposterous tales.

Tommy Pickens, Bill Werth, Jesse Cagle, Dickie Walgraeve, Melvin Remillard, Alan Hanegan, John Teegarten Smith, Gene Gehring and Tom and I had gathered on the loading dock and engaged Scotty in conversation while waiting for a few more of our friends to arrive. Our attention was suddenly drawn to a big fancy red convertible automobile that had pulled up to the stop sign. The top had been lowered allowing us to see a bag of golf clubs in the back seat. The driver was a smartly dressed middle-aged man. And we knew he was going to the Tualatin Country Club. When he saw us resting atop the loading dock sitting on feed sacks, he yelled at us in a haughty, smug voice, *"Hey you guys! How long has this town been dead?"*

We were proud of our little community and his insulting question offended us. But as kids, we were too timid to offer any smart-alecky retorts. But not Scotty! No Sir! Without a second's hesitation, he blurted out a comeback in his Scottish brogue.

"Well now, mister! It musta jist died b'cause you're the first buzzard to come in here."

Having been put in his place and without saying another word, the guy put his car in gear, gunned the engine and burned a little rubber driving off toward the country club. In our minds, Scotty instantly had been transformed from a teller of tall tales to our hero, a knight in shining armor.

From that day on, whatever Scotty swore to be true, we accepted without question.

Coach Korb

My brother Tom and I were dyed-in-the-wool baseball fanatics. We loved the game. Playing baseball was just about as satisfying as eating a slab of Mom's apple pie. That's an old cliché but it held true for us.

When we weren't working in the swamp or doing chores around home and the weather was decent, we played work-up ball with the neighbor kids. Frequently we talked about forming a team of our own. But we had no coach and we certainly had no equipment.

As a fifteen-year-old boy, I dreamed of participating on an organized team one day. But there were no summer baseball teams in Sherwood or Tualatin for boys our age. Tigard's team was the closest one to us. But it was some six miles away and too far to walk.

Just before the school year came to an end, Tom and I were in Sherwood with Dad when one of our high school classmates informed us that Walter Korb, a local insurance agent, wanted to form a Little League team and was looking for players. We nearly jumped out of our skins and, wasting no time, ran lickety-split to his small office.

Walter didn't know either one of us, and we knew nothing about him. But it didn't matter. We just wanted to play baseball and had high hopes that he'd accept us on his team.

From the way we burst into his office, I'm certain he had no doubts about our enthusiasm, our eagerness to play for him. After listening to his plans and what he expected of us, we assured him that we would attend all the practice sessions even if we had to walk straight from work. He had the equipment, and the high school baseball field was available to us in the late afternoons.

A week later, Tom and I were two happy youngsters, playing on a real baseball team and proudly wearing beautiful new baseball uniforms.

Walter was a World War II veteran who had been injured horribly in action. His right arm was withered and useless and hung limp at his side. We learned that he nearly lost his life during an aerial supply drop when a parachute failed to deploy and a crate of supplies struck him, ripping muscles and tendons from his arm. After a long hospitalization, he attended business school and eventually became licensed to sell insurance in Oregon.

A very capable person, Walter remodeled his office and did most of the work himself. He laid carpet over a concrete slab floor and figured ways to keep the wall paneling in place until he could nail it. But, what was most impressive about him, other than his constant smile, was his cheerful and positive attitude.

Walter's ability to hit ground balls to the infielders and fly balls to the outfielders with one arm astounded us. One of us threw pitches across the plate and he socked them, seldom failing to hit a ball to the part of the field where he intended it to go. He called out where he wanted to hit it and then he did it better than most of the seniors in high school. If he said he was going to hit a hard ground ball he did it, and if he said he was going to hit a line drive or a pop-up, he did. And, amazingly, he did it with just the one arm. The guy was marvelous.

Walter could pitch too. He had been right handed but the injury forced him to learn to throw left-handed. Perhaps he couldn't throw as well as he could have under normal conditions, but he did well enough. He wasn't one to yell, either, or carry on when we made a mistake. He was gentle, perhaps too gentle, never overly stern or scolding. Had he not sold insurance, he would have made a darned good schoolteacher.

He was indeed a wonderful coach. We won some games and we lost some games. But, most of all, the boys who grew up around Sherwood were given the opportunity to play baseball on a team with a real coach . . . and a good one at that.

Walter was an excellent example of how a person can succeed in life under adverse conditions. He never talked much about the war or how he was injured. But to us kids, he was some kind of hero. Personally, I wanted to be just like him when I grew up—he was that kind of guy.

The last time I saw Walter Korb, he was over 80 years old. And even though he'd slowed considerably, he was still involved in community activities. He hadn't coached in a long time, either, but he knew the name of every kid that played on the local teams. And it was never a good idea to get him started talking about baseball, especially if one was in a hurry to go someplace.

Bumping into Walter while walking down the streets of Sherwood, one probably wouldn't have noticed his useless arm. But one would have noticed his smile and the good-natured twinkle in his eyes.

Walter passed away some years ago. And I'll bet he's up in heaven right now and still smiling, still pitching . . . and doing it with one arm.

Fun and Games

We always thought of ourselves as a normal, run-of-the-mill family when it came to having fun. But we weren't. We were unconventional and a little crazy. While watching us play a game of softball in the pasture, and witnessing us badger each other, a friend once remarked that we were a bunch of lunatics.

We never played a game, any game, following established rules. We often made up our own set of guidelines, sometimes while the contest was in progress.

When the evenings were warm, we often played in the back yard. And Pop joined in every so often. We got a big kick out of him, especially when we played *Hide and Go Seek*. He could never understand how we were able to find him so easily. It was no problem, not even for the little kids. He always hid—at least he thought he was hidden—behind one of the oak trees. But he was easy to spot because his paunchy stomach protruded beyond the tree.

Pop's potbelly deceived people into believing that he was as slow as a turtle. But, to the contrary, he was quite agile and quick as a cat.

When Tom and I were in our early teens, we mistakenly challenged Dad to wrestle with us. We had no chance, not even if both of us took him on at the same time. And we fared no better when three tried. Dad handled all of us as easily as he did one. He had a favorite tactic. He liked to catch Tom and me in headlocks, one under each arm. Then, clasping his hands in front of him, he shrugged his shoulders, cracking our heads together. It hurt like hell. And if Dick got too close, he soon found himself caught in a vice-like grip between Dad's legs, gasping for breath.

During the winter months, our family hunkered down in the house where it was warm and played board and card games: Canasta, checkers, cribbage, Sorry, Monopoly, pinochle, rummy. You name it—we played it! But, we never once played those games according to Hoyle or any other book of rules. And the games most often turned into mini-wars, particularly when Dad played. He was exceptionally competitive. He hated to lose, even when his opponent was a small child. So we, including our mom, did everything in our power to ensure that he was a loser, even if we had to do something underhanded.

One winter, Pa couldn't win a game of checkers, Monopoly or pinochle if his life depended on it. Once he got so angry that he put his fist through the card table and another time, he kicked it, breaking the table's leg. And he even destroyed half a dozen decks of cards one winter. Our snickering and giggling just irritated him that much more and might have even pushed him over the edge on a few occasions.

We loved playing games with our dad—any game, at any time. And if we beat him, it was just that much more fun for us, especially when he erupted like a volcano.

The Beetle and The Goat

Being around my mom and dad was as much fun as visiting the zoo. Most of the time they carried on like a couple of kids instead of adults. Undeniably different, it was their carefree manner. They were unpredictable, impulsive, and a little goofy. And I loved not knowing what they might do from one moment to the next.

I gave Mom the nickname *Beetle* because it just seemed to fit her. Every morning, until she'd had a cup of coffee, hot or cold, she slowly meandered around the house without much reason or direction, kind of like a dung beetle. It was as if she were in a stupor. And there was little use in trying to converse with her either, not until she'd had her shot of caffeine. I thought about nicknaming her Zombie but that would have been pushing my luck.

Dad's nickname was *The Goat* because he used his head like a billy goat to butt his opponents when he was wrestling professionally. And he did the same to Tom and me when we wrestled with him. He was sometimes stubborn like one too.

No matter what task the old man undertook, he did it believing that he had the skill and wisdom to accomplish it correctly. But usually it was just the opposite.

Dad often prepared a delicious meal for breakfast that he called a *slumgullion*. It was cooked in a fry pan using garlic, onions, potatoes, bell peppers, mushrooms, green tomatoes, bits of bacon and topped with a couple of over easy fried eggs. I loved it. But on occasion he used wild mushrooms that he harvested from our woods. I trusted his judgment in most endeavors but not when it came to picking mushrooms or blowing up stumps.

When Pa went into the woods to pick mushrooms, he carried a small booklet that depicted the various kinds found in the Pacific Northwest that were edible. He got the book from some old crony who probably lived on the streets of Portland and who most likely didn't know a mushroom from a bale of hay. First off, the book looked as if it had been fished out of a toilet. It was faded, dirty and worn from years and years of use—or misuse. Part of the print was smudged or missing and pictures of the mushrooms were so faded and soiled that they looked identical.

Sometimes he referred to the book and sometimes not. Some mushrooms that he discarded I thought were good and some that he kept I was certain were poisonous.

After Pa cooked up his concoction using wild mushrooms, I stood back and watched him eat, waiting for him to fall over dead. But he never did. And by the time I realized the slumgullion was safe to eat, he'd devoured it, every last morsel.

Mom, trying to make cottage cheese, hung a bag of cheese curds from the clothesline to drain overnight. The next morning, she burst into the house all excited, claiming that she'd found a substitute for rubber.

When she took the bag down from the clothesline, she accidentally dropped it on the ground and it bounced right back up to her like a kid's toy ball. To prove what had happened, she dropped the bag on the kitchen floor and, sure enough, it bounced as if it were made of rubber. But, within hours, Mom's bag of synthetic rubber had degenerated into a gob of sour smelling yucky goop. Not only was the stuff unfit to use as rubber, it was also unfit to eat. It was so unpalatable that the hogs didn't want it either.

One night after everyone had gone to bed, Dad crept into the kitchen and buried his head in the refrigerator looking for food. He had no idea that Mom had followed and was sneaking up behind him. She goosed the old goat in the rear end. And instantly he struck out, demolishing the inside of our brand new fridge. Without thinking, he whirled about and head-butted Mom in the stomach, sending her sprawling across the room. Not only did he knock the wind out of her, she also suffered a broken toe when her foot caught under a piece of furniture.

Poor Mom! She gasped, wheezed and moaned most of the night. And poor Dad! He felt lower than a snake's belly.

A few days later, Tom and I helped him cut firewood for winter heat using his makeshift sawmill, a horribly dangerous contraption that frightened me to death. He used a 30-inch circular saw blade fixed on an axle mounted between two two-by-twelve boards and powered by his old farm tractor. Extremely dangerous, the blade was exposed with no safety guard. It whirred just inches from his face.

He relentlessly shoved long pieces of cordwood into the whirring saw, cutting them into foot-long lengths. Occasionally, he reached from one side of the blade to the other to catch a piece of wood before it fell to the ground. And every so often, the saw nicked the tip of his gloved fingers. I hated the entire operation, feeling dread that my dad would someday lop off a hand or even worse.

One of the pieces of wood fell. But Dad missed catching it and it struck him on the foot, mashing his toe. He crashed to the ground howling in pain. At first, I didn't want to look—I couldn't look—certain that he'd amputated a hand. But after he peeled off his shoe and I saw that he'd only crushed a toe, I felt a flood of relief.

Now that he, too, had been injured, his mood changed and he no longer felt so guilty about hurting Mom.

That night after supper, with a fire burning in the wood stove and the house warm and cozy, Mom and Dad sat on the couch holding hands like two teenagers at a movie. With smiles on their faces, they each rested a foot on a chair, each sporting a painfully injured toe.

They were as crazy as a pair of bedbugs. But they were our parents and we loved them.

Going To The Movies

Dad took us kids to see a scary movie in Newberg early one Friday evening. The show was about monsters and ghouls and vampires. As we passed the old Middleton Cemetery, we bragged that movies like the one we were about to see never frightened us. That prompted Dad to throw up a challenge, daring us to take a stroll through the spooky old cemetery on the way home. And we, like dumbbells, accepted.

The movie not only frightened the *bejeebers* out of us kids, it also scared the pants off the old man. Driving through the pitch-black night returning home, not one of us spoke a single word about stopping at the cemetery, not even Dad. When we came to it, every one of us, including Dad, was as silent as cowering sheep. He didn't stop. Staring straight ahead, the big chicken whizzed by the spooky place at the speed of sound.

All through the war, and long after its end, if Dad was home on a Friday night, we went to the movies. Most of the time, it was to Sherwood's Robin Hood Theater to see a serial movie about Zorro. It was a favorite of ours. Pop was a nut for movies too. He enjoyed them as much as we did, sometimes more.

Another thing that Dad loved as much as we kids was munching hot buttered popcorn. He never, and I mean never, passed by the theater's concession stand without buying a bag of it. Like clockwork, before going to our seats, with Dad in the lead, we all lined up at the concession stand, each of us getting a bag. And, as if rehearsed, we walked single file down the aisle, took up a complete row of seats and, in unison, sat down. One could count on this sequence of events occurring every Friday night—guaranteed. But that wasn't the half of it. The noise we made—rustling paper bags and munching popcorn—continued throughout the evening, nearly drowning out the movie's dialogue. We were as noisy as a family of raccoons raiding a dumpster.

The theater in Newberg was classy and tastefully decorated. Drapes adorned everything and, in particular, the aisle exits on the main floor and the balcony.

Watching a movie from the balcony one night, I bumped into someone at intermission who looked very familiar.

Walking downstairs to the main floor, I bought a soft drink and, upon returning to the balcony, encountered this person exiting as I was entering. I stopped, backed away and apologized. The other fellow also stopped and backed away at the same time. I stepped forward again to enter and he, too, stepped forward to exit. Then I realized who the familiar fellow was. It was *me!* The *exit* was not an exit but a mirror, the same size, height and width as the aisle exits. And it, too, was adorned with drapes. Happy was I that not a soul witnessed me dancing with my own reflection.

On our way home after watching an Abbott and Costello movie at the Robin Hood Theater, Tom and I began carrying on in the car, mimicking the two comedians. Our small captive audience seemed to be delightfully entertained, so much so that after arriving home, we continued with our tomfoolery.

We had only been in the house 15 minutes when we noticed the headlights of a car that had stopped on the railroad tracks at the entry to our driveway. Seconds later, little brother Dee burst through the front door, his mouth puckered up and bawling, *"You went home and you left me in the movie all by myself."*

Yes, indeed! Everyone had become so engrossed in our silliness that not one of us missed our little brother when we got into the car. And with so many kids, Dad simply lost count. It had happened before and it would happen again. That, too, was guaranteed.

Gettin' Bunged Up

During a weeklong period before beginning my sophomore year in high school, I got bunged up and bloodied so often that I was on the verge of needing my own private medical staff. The sight of blood bothered me somewhat and, when it was mine, that's when I got downright concerned.

My problems began when Tom smacked me in the kisser with a basketball, mashing my nose. He was a terrific baseball and football player with tremendous skills. But he was an oaf when it came to playing round ball. His two-handed set-shots at the basket were awkward and clumsy and the guy dribbled with his fists.

Playing a game of keep-away at Wager's, Tom and I against Eddie, he appeared to set himself to shoot the ball. But when Eddie darted toward him, he unexpectedly threw a six-foot bullet pass straight into my face. My nose had a well-known reputation for bleeding easily, and did it ever. It gushed out of me like water from a broken irrigation pipe. When the blood stopped flowing 20 minutes later, I no longer had a yen to play the game and wanted to go home.

It was just as well that we had stopped because Eddie had a chore to do down in the swamp, dragging their clod-busting sled over a newly plowed piece of ground. Since Eddie had to drag that thing half way to my house anyway, I figured I might as well ride on it and hopped aboard. But instead of sitting down I stood, facing to the rear. Eddie fired up the tractor and off we went, leaving a cloud of dust behind. He hadn't driven a 100 yards before stopping to open a gate. The stop was so sudden and unexpected that I lost my balance and awkwardly toppled over backward, striking the back of my head on the tractor's drawbar. The sight of seeing me stumbling off-balance and falling on my butt brought a chuckle from my buddy. Feeling pain, I clutched the back of my head as I came to a sitting position facing him. I could feel blood oozing down the back of my neck. And when I removed my blood-covered hand, Eddie's grin vanished and his face turned ashen white with concern. A sizeable gash had been opened in my scalp when I struck the drawbar. And it bled just as furiously as my nose had just a half hour earlier.

The wound on my skull hadn't had time to heal before I was at it again. A week later we went to the Galbreath farm to play a game of cross-out ball in the pasture with Erwin, the Peterson boys and the Burck's.

Pastures are noted for being littered with an assortment of unused equipment, and the Galbreath pasture was no different. An old rusted truck tire rim had lain in the same place for years and was in a perfect position to use as second base.

At bat, I hit a long ball and believed that I could stretch it into a double. As I was coming into second base, I stumbled, fell and hit the metal tire rim with my knee. The rim never moved, not one inch. But I did. In severe pain, I rolled, squirmed and wriggled around on the ground like a squashed worm, moaning and groaning. I wanted to cry but wouldn't because I was too old. My knee had been split open to the bone and my kneecap felt as if it were broken. But, very strangely, it bled little. My leg stiffened so quickly that I could barely walk. But somehow I managed to limp home.

Mom patched me up as she had been doing for 15 years, with the skill of a Florence Nightingale. With tongue in cheek, she suggested that, if I were going to continually get chopped up, I had better think about marrying someone who had access to a sizeable store of medical supplies because she was running short.

A Change In Our Lives

At supper one night, Dad surprised us kids with a surprising announcement. He'd quit his job at Albert's and had bought a tavern. For the first time in his life, he was self-employed. Mom and Dad had been discussing the possibility of going into business for themselves for some time. But still, it was quite a shock to us and it took several moments for it to sink in. And when it did, being 15 years old, I was agog with the knowledge that my parents owned their own business. I thought it a huge step up in the world. But little did I know what the consequences would be for us.

A tavern seemed to be the right choice for my dad. He knew the beer and wine industry inside and out, he was good with finances and he understood people. And Dad was just naturally a likeable person. He'd also done a bit of research too, talking to tavern owners, beer distributors and other businessmen trying to get a feel for the problems he might encounter.

When all was said and done, he knew he had to try it. But there weren't many established taverns on the market. Whenever one became available, it was sold instantly.

But Dad persisted. And one day he learned that The Echo Inn located in the tiny community of Carver east of Oregon City was about to be put on the market.

Carver wasn't big, only a couple of small stores, a service station and the tavern. Most of the residents for miles around were involved in the booming timber industry. And loggers are notorious for being a thirsty bunch of hombres.

The Echo Inn was small, run down, and had a reputation for being a rowdy dive. But the terms of the sale were good, and the price included a small house next door. The one thing that bothered Dad about it was that it was over an hour's drive from home.

Nonetheless, The Echo Inn appeared to be a good choice. And after a few visits, one with Frances and John Bohlen, Mom and Dad began negotiating with the owner. They made an offer and quite suddenly, my parents found themselves in the tavern business. And just as suddenly, Grandma found herself as the primary keeper of us kids.

Operation of the inn required nearly every minute of their time, opening it mid-morning and closing it well after midnight, seven days a week. Little time was left in their day to take the hour needed to drive home and another hour to drive back. And so, they slept in the tiny one-bedroom house next door, coming home only when it was absolutely necessary.

Poor Grandma! Suddenly faced with riding herd on six antsy kids had to be overwhelming. And what would she do if we had an emergency? We had no telephone; we'd have to use the neighbors. Our parents were aware of those problems and gave us kids stern instructions to behave ourselves and cooperate with each other.

"Your grandmother is going to need a lot of help. We're depending on you boys. So don't let us down."

Our euphoria lasted but a few days. The transition from having our Mom and Dad in the house every night to practically being parentless was a mighty tough adjustment, particularly so for Charla because of her age. We were accustomed to Dad working late and not being around . . . but not Mom. It would have been easier to cope with their absence had they been able to come home at least a few times each week. But that wasn't to happen for some time. We struggled, we cried, but in time we adjusted.

Dad hired a local maverick by the name of Johnny Vaughn as his bartender. Johnny, a rough and tumble sort, was down on his luck and desperately needed a job. Dad, being a good judge of character, couldn't have picked a better man to help him tend the bar. He and my parents developed a close, friendly, and trusting relationship. And no one could have been more faithful to our family and protective of my mom and dad than Johnny. They trusted his loyalty so much that, within a few months, both Mom and Dad were able to leave the tavern in his keeping for a couple of days at a time.

Those brief periods when our Mom and Dad came home were precious and we made the most of them. Most times, Dad came alone to buy groceries, pay bills, settle family squabbles and take us to the movies. Sometimes, he made a whirlwind trip home to leave Mom with us for a few days.

We did our best to adapt, and we survived even though it was a heart wrenching experience. And with dedication, sacrifice and an abundance of hard work, my parents changed the image and reputation of The Echo Inn. It became a respectable business and profitable.

We kids soon discovered a benefit to our parents owning the inn too. Hamburgers! The place was equipped with a small kitchen. And Mom and Dad made and sold the most delicious hamburgers in that part of the state. Not only were they tasty to us kids, they were free.

Boone's Ferry

Roy Good, the brother-in-law of my classmate, Shirley Steyaert, worked the evening shift, piloting a ferry across the Willamette River at Wilsonville. I asked him if he would allow me to ride it a few hours just for the fun of it. He welcomed my company and even offered to instruct me on the ferry's operation, if I cared to learn. I jumped at the chance. How many 15-year-old kids get a chance to pilot a ferry?

At the first good opportunity, I caught a ride to Wilsonville and met Roy. For the first hour, I remained inside the cabin out of the way because traffic was heavy and Roy was busy.

Roy wasn't the swiftest person in the world but he was a good teach-er. And I was an eager student. Within a few hours I had piloted the ferry across the river a couple of times . . . but only when it was empty. He always took control when it was time to dock and when there were cars aboard.

The crossing took maybe five to ten minutes. But sometimes we waited on one side or the other as long as 45 minutes before a car ap-peared. He told me that there were a few times that he made but two or

Boone's Ferry

three crossings during the entire night and, for the most part, his job was boring. I found out that he had a cure for his boredom—a bottle of bourbon whiskey hidden in a jacket pocket.

Just riding the ferry was fun. But the opportunity to operate it was a once-in-a-lifetime thrill.

Time passed by too quickly, though, and it was nearly midnight before I realized it. Grandma had given me strict orders to be home by midnight or shortly thereafter. But I had stayed far too long to meet her deadline. I took my departure from Roy's *cruise ship* and began a three-hour walk home, a distance of nearly ten miles.

It was pitch black and a little frightening even for a teenage boy. There weren't many homes and thus I seldom saw a light. What denizens of the dark lurked along the roadway, I didn't know. And I hoped I wouldn't find out.

Over two hours elapsed by the time I reached Tualatin. And I had another 2½ miles to go, the darkest and most desolate stretch of all. Trying to bolster my courage, I whistled tunes. But I had competition from crickets, frogs and screech owls. Their chorus made the night even spookier.

Trying to keep my mind off the unpleasantness of the moment, I tried remembering fun things that I'd done in my life: operating the ferry, playing baseball and going to the movies. But thinking of movies that I'd seen was a stupid idea. The only ones that came to mind were The Wolf Man, Jack the Ripper, Frankenstein and Dracula—just what I needed to keep me moving along at a rapid pace.

Get The Point

My very best childhood friend, Eddie Wager, punched me smack on the end of the nose. He was mad at me because I stuck him in the rump with the point of my compass.

Throughout grade school and high school, Eddie sat at the desk directly in front of me. And every so often, just to let him know that I was around, I gave him a jab in the backside with the point of my mathematics compass. And every time I jabbed him, he threatened to punch me in the snoot if I ever did it again. But he never did. In fact the only time he retaliated to any degree was when we were in the eighth grade. He stabbed me in the palm of the hand with a sharpened lead pencil. That should have taught me a lesson then and there. But, being a little dimwitted, it didn't. And I continued poking him. And he continued putting up with it.

He just wasn't the type of kid to strike back, not until one day in high school study hall early in our sophomore year. It was a beautiful sunny day but a boring one. So, I got out my trusty compass and gave my buddy a jab in the butt. He never said a word, just turned around facing me and, like a cobra striking its prey, sent a solid right-hand jab into my face. He socked me smack on the end of the old bazooka. He could have put Joe Louis on the seat of his pants with that jolt. For a split second after regaining my senses, I just sat staring at him, bewildered and stunned, not believing what he'd just done. Then the blood began to flow, gushing out of my beak like water from a Brooklyn fire hydrant on a hot mid-summer day. My buddy finally stood up to me.

At first, I was mad as the dickens at him, really miffed. But I couldn't blame him. After all, I'd been warned repeatedly for a half-dozen years.

Eddie ruined a beautiful warm sunny day but not my respect and admiration for him. Always believing that I was just a tad bit smarter than my buddy, he finally taught me a lesson. I guess one could say that it was I who finally got the point.

A Math Problem

Most of us believed that it was Charles Charles who drove Mrs. Ross, our mathematics teacher, to retire at the end of our freshman year. He was the same bully who beat up on Eddie the first week we were in high school as freshmen.

In her seventies, Mrs. Ross was a frail, petite woman and easily upset by Charles' misbehavior and disobedience. Many times, she broke her pencil, pounding it on her desk to enforce her demand that he stop being disruptive. But it did her no good. The disrespectful student never once obeyed her, and nearly drove the poor instructor to the brink of a nervous breakdown.

The school board hired Mr. George Russell, a World War II Navy veteran, to take Mrs. Ross's place. And thus he inherited the unruly, troublemaking Charles Charles.

The first day of our sophomore year, Charles predictably began stirring up trouble and causing a ruckus in class. Mr. Russell repeatedly warned him to settle down. But Charles continued to be a nuisance, testing Mr. Russell's patience. The distraught teacher finally had had enough and issued Charles an ultimatum: cease being disruptive or be ejected from the classroom. The rebellious student blurted something offensive.

As if he were shot from a cannon, Mr. Russell exploded from his chair, grabbed Charles by the scruff of the neck and seat of the pants and physically packed him from the room. He carried the kid, squirming, kicking and cursing, to the principal's office. And, like a sack of putrid garbage, tossed him on the floor.

We students were dumbstruck . . . but quite pleased to be rid of the so-called *tough*. When Mr. Russell returned to our classroom, we erupted in applause, whistles and cheers. Mr. Russell wasn't only a Navy hero; he was a hero to us too.

To our delight, we never saw Charles Charles again. He left school and never again returned. And we never missed him for one second. Good riddance to a big problem.

Sadie Hawkins' Day

Like every other boy, I participated in Sherwood High School's annual Sadie Hawkins Day race. Every year during a hilarious screaming 30-minute melee, the girls chased the boys, trying to catch a date for the Sadie Hawkins Day dance. The guys got a two-minute head start before the gals were permitted to begin their pursuit. The only rules were that the kids had to stay on the school grounds and out of the main school building.

I had no girl friend, no money and didn't care much about dancing. So I didn't want to get caught. Thus, anything wearing a skirt that got too close, I ran as if my tail was afire.

Within a few moments after the girls had been *unleashed*, I realized that Betty Lou Galbreath was after my hide. Betty Lou was at least three years older than me and not exactly a desirable person to have as a date. Through no fault of her own, she was mentally retarded, frequently smelled of urine, and was slow and simple in her speech. That was plenty of reason for me to run for my life.

Wild blackberries grew in back of the school where Homer Haines, the janitor, piled cordwood for the school furnace. I thought that by running through the thorny vines, I could escape her. But I was astonished to see Betty Lou barrel through the blackberries right behind me, hot on my heels. She didn't seem to care that the thorns tore at her legs. So, I climbed up onto one of the piles of furnace firewood that was stacked some ten feet high and perhaps 30 feet long. Betty Lou scrambled right up behind me like a cat going up and over a fence. My only chance was to simply run as if my life depended on it for the next 25 minutes and pray that I could stay ahead of her . . . and out of the clutches of any other girl who might be desperate enough to grab me.

As I ran ducking and dodging about, I noticed that at least six boys had crammed themselves into an observation box that had been constructed some 15 feet above the ground on one of the football field light poles. Hiding a ladder before the race, they used it to gain access to the box and then pulled it up behind them. They figured they were safe. But, in fact, they were dead ducks.

Within a few moments after the boys had secured themselves in their lofty perch, a half dozen girls ran down the slope from the gymnasium toward the football field. They were carrying their own ladder on their shoulders, looking as if they were part of a fire brigade.

Those boys were not only up a pole; they were up a creek, caught like rats in a trap.

I was able to remain free of Betty Lou but she caught some other unfortunate lad at the last moment. I can remember hearing the boy cry out in a sorrowful pleading voice as if he were about to be executed, *"Not me! Oh no, not me!"*

Too bad! He was in the wrong place at the right time.

Sophomore Classmates

Tom Barnett, an older fellow—he was 21—joined our sophomore class for a half-year. He'd served in the military and saw combat during World War II. And now that he was out of the service, he decided to resume his education, working toward a General Education Diploma or G. E. D.

Tom served in the Navy and being a handsome dude, was an attraction to the young ladies. One of them was my classmate Beverly Lilly. She was a cute little brunette with a very attractive smile. And she was starry-eyed over Tom. One could tell that he was attracted to her as well.

Tom didn't remain in school for long. In just four months, he received sufficient supplemental education to get his diploma and left to find employment. But he wasn't out of Beverly's life, not by a long shot. Whenever the school held a function of some kind, Tom was there—and so was she. After finishing her sophomore year, she quit school and latched onto the love of her life for keeps.

Joyce Cochran, another one of my classmates, also left school before graduating. But she left to pursue a career in modeling. She was a pretty little blond-haired girl with a quick and friendly smile too. And soon she, too, married.

Joyce and her husband were flying in a commercial airliner somewhere over the Midwest when it exploded. If I remember correctly, a young man planted an explosive device in his mother luggage so he could collect the insurance she carried on her life. Everyone on board the aircraft including Joyce, her husband and their unborn child was instantly killed. She was the first of our class to die.

Boone's Ferry

CHAPTER IX

1948

The Trombone

Shorty Holznagel, one of my high school classmates, and I were interested in the same things—mathematics, sports, music, and a certain dark-haired freshman girl. We were good friends and had become acquainted with each other before entering high school. He was one of the kids who attended St. Paul Lutheran Grade School and played on their softball team, one of Cipole Grade School's rivals. He was very musical and, not only did he sing in the school choirs, he played the trombone and the bass horn in the high school band as well.

Since I hadn't played a musical instrument in eight years, I yearned to play one again, a horn of some kind, maybe a trumpet or a trombone. I tried a clarinet but the vibration of the reed tickled my lips. I couldn't pucker well enough to make a decent noise with the trumpet and I didn't think my lips were sloppy enough to play a bass horn. So, I settled on the trombone.

With Shorty's encouragement, I asked Mr. Lindo Morandi, the school's music teacher, if he could instruct me a few minutes after school each night for a few months and perhaps loan an instrument to me. He agreed and began giving me instructions free of charge. He also allowed me to take one of the school's trombones home to practice.

But staying after school presented me with a problem. The sessions were just long enough that I could never catch the school bus forcing me to walk 2½ miles home. So I took the most direct route, the railroad tracks. It was quicker than walking on the road.

Practicing at home didn't go as well as I'd hoped. The noise I made with that thing nearly drove Granny out of her mind. And the one and only time I practiced when Dad was home, he threatened to bend it over my head. So, I followed Mr. Morandi's advice and found a place where I was certain that no one would be bothered—atop the railroad trestle crossing over Johnny Cereghino's pasture.

Walking home after school, I perched atop the trestle 35 feet above the ground like a seagull sitting atop a pier piling and practiced the scale and a few simple tunes like *Jingle Bells* for 30 minutes at a time. But, after three or four weeks, that also came to a sudden screeching halt.

Johnny Cereghino came to our house one night complaining to Grandma.

"My cows won't come to the barn to be milked, Miz Barnes. Instead, they gather down there under the trestle to listen to that grandson of yours toot on that blasted horn."

Johnny was miffed, not so much because his milk production had been interrupted, but because he had missed a few meals trying to round up his cows.

A war stopped me from playing the violin and the piano. And my nearly starting another *"war"* stopped me from playing the trombone.

Water Sports

One afternoon Grandmother and I were having a good-natured, age-old argument about men and women. We were alone in the kitchen. And for a change I wasn't in hot water, even though our raised voices might have sounded like it. She was a competitive old gal, just as competitive as the rest of us, sometimes more so, and she never, ever backed down.

We were both in a feisty mood that day, and I couldn't resist goading and prodding her with provocative remarks about women. Getting under her skin was kind of fun, kind of like poking a beehive with a stick. But you had better be ready to hightail it when the bees have had enough. It was the same with Grandma. If it meant the end of her life, she wouldn't concede a thing to me. In fact, she became so vocal in our discussion that I could no longer get a word in edgewise. Realizing that I had been completely shut out of the conversation, I had to come up with some clever scheme to end this little one-sided confab.

I had been doing the dishes and found the answer right in front of me in the dishpan. Dishwater! Without warning, I turned and flicked a spoonful of it at her.

Completely taken by surprise, Granny's mouth slammed shut making a noise much the same as when one closes the door of a car. She was caught totally off-guard and momentarily stared at me in stunned disbelief. How dare her grandson do something like that to her! She was a sight; droplets of water on her glasses and a few dribbling down her nose. I couldn't help myself and broke into belly-rolling laughter.

But Granny immediately recovered and her response was surprisingly quick. In a blink, she snatched up a glass partially filled with water and threw it on me. She got me smack in the face. My expressions must have changed as dramatically as hers had. She, too, broke into uproarious laughter.

That was the beginning of the greatest water fight in the history of Cipole. And, who knows, maybe in all of Oregon. It was quite a sight—a 66-year-old grandmother and her 16-year-old grandson each trying to drown the other and having a grand old time doing it. The water containers we used increased in volume from spoons to cups to small pots to large pots to buckets. It began in the kitchen and ended in the back yard, each of us with a garden hose. But the dousing terminated with me being the loser when my cheating grandmother crimped my hose, cutting off my water supply and forcing me to run for my life.

Absolutely soaked, we looked like two sponges. The kitchen was an indescribable disaster, a sopping mess. Everything was wet, even the ceiling dripped water. But, after we'd wiped everything down and mopped up all the water, the kitchen sparkled like never before.

Yes, my grandmother was a tough competitor, but a good sport, and I would be the last one to say that she wasn't.

Cousins Larry and Frankie

Unfortunately, my uncle Jack never matured into a reliable, trustworthy adult, not even as a sailor in the U. S. Navy, or as a police officer or parent. He always had problems and was never able to accept responsibility of any kind. Consequently his marriage to the lovely red-haired Catherine came to an end when he abandoned her and his two small boys for greener pastures.

My parents and Grandma remained close to Catherine and her sons, Larry and Frankie, providing them with as much support as possible. But Catherine felt that she needed to move back to North Carolina where she had roots and family, believing she would have a better chance to raise her boys properly. A few days before departing Oregon, she and the boys came to the farm to visit with Grandma and to bid farewell to us kids. As much as Granny disliked Jack, she loved Catherine.

After supper, we boys invited four-year-old Larry and his three-year-old brother Frankie to play outside in the yard. Grandma, with Aunt Catherine looking on, admonished us to keep strict watch over them and not let them get dirty. That was asking for the impossible. You'd think those women would have had enough sense to know that boys playing outside cannot remain clean very long.

The two little ones explored everything. And soon they became curious about two 55 gallon oil drums that Dad had intended to use as receptacles for burning trash, leaves and weeds. We told them that we held barrel-rolling contests by walking atop them and invited them to ride inside one of the barrels as we rolled it. All they need do was brace themselves as they sat inside. With a little coaxing, the kids crawled inside a barrel and pressed themselves against the inside with their feet, back and hands. Tom and I hopped atop the thing and began rolling it—faster and faster. We had rolled it perhaps, 50 or 60 feet before we lost our balance and fell off. The two little guys tumbled out of the barrel and into the dirt, momentarily dizzy and disoriented. I was completely taken by surprise when I saw their condition.

Rust that had built up inside the barrels had thoroughly coated them from head to toe, their clothing, their hands, faces and hair. They had been transformed into little red kids.

We were in a heap of trouble. A great big heap! Without a doubt, as soon as those women got a good look at those kids, they'd kill us. But before I could make any attempt to clean them up, to brush the rust off their clothing, the little squirts bolted for the house on a dead run with Tom following right behind. For the life of me, I couldn't comprehend Tom's thinking, wondering why in the world he was chasing after them. He had to know that Grandma and Aunt Catherine would turn on him like a couple of angry queen bees. Watching him disappear through the door, I knew he was nuts and had just committed suicide. For just a fleeting moment I felt sorry for him. But then I changed my mind.

"What the heck, if he gets his neck wrung, it'll serve him right for being so stupid. He should catch the blame, anyway, for all the times that I was blamed for things he did. I'll just sit this one out and let him catch heck for a change. Stupid jerk! He's gonna get massacred and it serves him right."

From within the house, I heard Aunt Catherine cry out in shocked surprise, *"Oh, my God! My babies! Just look at my babies!"*

Grandmother blurted out, *"What in tarnation did you kids do to them?"*

Instantly, they were on Tom like a dirty shirt, assailing him from all sides. It was a hornet's nest and he was getting a verbal stinging. With a smug grin on my mug and feeling a touch of euphoria because Tommy was getting his tail ripped, I stayed out of sight below an open window and listened to every scalding word.

They jumped all over the dumb sap and yelled things like, *"You know better than that . . . "* and *"Shame on you for pulling a stunt like that . . . "* and *"What did we tell you not to do?"*

Tom in his defense finally blurted out, *"I didn't do it. It was Teddy. He did it! He told them to get into the barrel. It's not my fault. I didn't do anything."*

My elation turned into panic when I heard him say that it was me that was to blame. I wanted him to keep his blasted mouth shut.

"That dirty rat! He's blaming me for getting' those kids dirty and I'm the one who's really gonna catch it."

For just a split second there was nothing but dead silence before Grandmother quite angrily resumed her tirade.

"I knew darned well that Teddy had something to do with this. Where is he? You go out there right now and tell him to get in here. I'm gonna whale the hide off his backside."

Sticking around trying to talk my way out of this predicament was out of the question. It was sure suicide. So for now, I knew I'd better hightail it for cover.

As I ran down the dirt road away from the house, I knew that, eventually, I'd find a way to get even with my tattletale brother. In the meantime, I needed a place where I felt secure. It was in the tall timber and dense underbrush of the woods. I knew it well. I spent most of my childhood there.

The DeSoto

Pa came home one night to take us to the movies and surprised us with another one of his fantastic discoveries. He had purchased a used car, an extraordinarily long sea-foam-green 1946 seven-passenger DeSoto sedan. It had been used as a taxicab in the city of San Francisco and was equipped with two jump seats in addition to regular seating. It was so roomy that our entire family, including Grandma, could ride in it comfortably.

The owner of the Robin Hood Theater in Sherwood loved to see our family coming because Dad always brought a couple of extra kids. Pa bragged that he could haul 11 screaming, wriggling kids in his car in addition to himself. That meant 12 bags of popcorn, maybe more.

With the exception of Charla and Grandma, Dad took the rest of us in his new car to the Liberty Theater in Portland. It was a misty evening so I wore my long, camel hair overcoat. I thought I was one slick looking dude.

After getting our popcorn, we entered the theater in the dark and found six seats in the same row where we could sit together. As Dad was sitting down, he caught his baggy pants on the armrest and ripped the seat of his britches open from stem to stern. He was in quite a fix. His butt was exposed. And he couldn't go to the restroom or venture into the lobby for more popcorn.

When the movie ended, we surrounded Pop and escorted him out of the building. We must have looked like bodyguards; two of us on each side of him and I close behind with my overcoat spread out like batman's cape.

On the way to the car, we passed a man who was obviously drunk. He appeared to be unconscious but, surprisingly, was standing upright. He was leaning against a light pole, stiff as a board.

Dad commented, *"There's a lot of weird things in Portland, kids, and you never know what you're gonna see."*

He was right about that. Had I lowered my overcoat, the citizens of Portland would have seen something else that was weird—my dad's flabby pink bottom.

The King of Swat

Tom and I were in the pasture with a bat and baseball practicing our bunting skills when, out of the blue, our dad showed up. He'd come home from the tavern for the day to buy groceries and spend some time with us. We were really surprised and couldn't have been happier.

Sporting a big grin on his face, he bellowed, *"Gimme the bat, boys, and stand back, way back. I'm gonna show you kids how Joe DiMaggio does it."*

Pop could hit a baseball well and hit it for some distance. But it had been some time since he'd had a bat in his hands.

I'd been pitching to Tom at the time, and not being the most accurate pitcher in the county, cautioned Dad that I was a bit wild. Paying no attention to my warnings, he insisted that I throw some fast ones to him.

My first pitch was low and inside. Concerned that he wasn't quick enough to react to a close pitch, I again cautioned him about my inaccuracy. And again he insisted, *"Don't worry about me! Just fire the damned thing in here, good and hard."*

Well, I reared back and let another one go and it, too, was inside . . . and it was mid-thigh high. Pop didn't duck away as he should have but turned right into the darned thing. And it hit him right where he shouldn't have been hit. Down he went, like he'd been pole-axed between the horns. Crawling around on the ground, he made funny gagging sounds as if he were trying to throw up. After a few moments, he quit crawling and just flopped over onto one side, curled up in the fetal position in the pasture dirt, groaning and wheezing.

Tudie squatted down beside him wanting to know if he was hurt. He managed to grunt out a tortured response, "*Get the hell away from me.*"

My poor Dad . . . ! I felt absolutely horrible and wished that I'd just lobbed a few slow ones to him. I should have known better. When I apologized to him, his response was . . . an agonized groan.

After several hours, the discomfort abated enough that he was able to crawl into the car and drive back to the tavern.

He didn't tend bar for two days because he was still hurting. He should have gone to a doctor. But he didn't want to admit to anyone, including his doctor, that one of his kids had hit him in the *tomatoes* with a baseball.

But not Mom! She couldn't keep her mouth shut and told several of their friends and regular patrons what had happened. The word spread like a wildfire.

When his so-called buddies found out that he was back on his feet and tending bar, a half-dozen of them came in just to razz him. And all of them were sporting big grins, ball caps and packing an assortment of baseball equipment, including a baseball book of rules. Not one soul had any sympathy for him.

Stopping to see his father a few weeks later, the old guy gave his son a bit of sage advice.

"*Toots! Pitsaball! Atsa no good. Next time, playa checkers. They notta kill you.*"

Puddles and The Pit

Dad had instructed Tom and me to dig a pit in the woods to bury garbage. It took us three days to dig the hole and when we finished, it looked large enough to bury a truck. But for a few days before dumping garbage in it, we used it as a fort.

It also seemed a dandy place to sleep out at night. The weather was warm. So, using fir boughs, we built a roof over it and placed a layer of sweet-smelling ferns in the bottom to make it more comfortable. Being 16, I should have outgrown the desire to *rough it* in the wild.

But I still felt an excitement camping out under the stars and being away from the house, even if it was just a few hundred yards.

Accompanied by our younger brother Dick and our faithful dog, Puddles, Tom and I ventured into the woods, leaving a perfectly good bed behind. Crawling into our subterranean pad and settling in for the night, Puddles curled up beside us to stand guard and ward off any evil denizens prowling about. Finally, late into the evening, after telling a few spooky stories, we fell asleep.

Our faithful dog, Puddles

In the wee hours of the morning, our little pooch became disturbed and excited about something. She began barking and scurrying in and out of the hole. All three of us were instantly wide-awake. Armed with rocks, we were ready to repel invaders.

Suddenly, and quite unexpectedly, one of our cows fell into the hole with us. Within a split second, the huge curious animal had destroyed the roof, our bed and the remainder of our night's rest. But never once did it step on us. With Puddles nipping at its legs, it just as quickly plowed its way out of the hole and out of the woods.

Our night of camping under a canopy of twinkling stars was ruined. And so we packed our belongings and blankets and went home, grateful for Puddles, a faithful little dog, that always kept watch over us.

MacTavish

MacTavish was one of our dogs, a loveable lazy old mutt that did little more than lie around the house, sleeping most of the time under Grandmother's bed. Just a mongrel, he looked more like a Scottish terrier than any other breed of dog, thus the Scottish name

MacTavish. I don't remember how we came by him, whether he wandered onto the farm or if a friend gave him to us. He just always seemed to be there, year after year after year. And even though he was a worthless, lazy whelp, we loved him as part of our family.

Grandma and MacTavish would have been compatible roommates had they not snored. Yes, both of them snored. And loud! The racket that came from her bedroom at night was something awful, a roaring cacophony of honking, wheezing, snarfs and snorts. Sometimes they snored so loud that they woke each other and that's when it became humorous. Grandma yelled threats and curses at poor Mac and Mac, just as irritated, growled and barked back at her.

Chasing cars, cats, chickens or kids on bikes probably never occurred to that crazy animal. But for some strange reason, he loved to chase trains. Other than attacking a soup bone, it was the only aggressive thing he ever did. Watching him barrel down the tracks after a chugging engine was not only surprising, it was entertaining as well.

One day, we were racing down Herman Road on our bikes staying abreast of the engine of a passing train, waving to the engineer and fireman as MacTavish ran on the rail bed next to it. He barked his fool head off as if trying to scare the thing and, paying no attention to what was in front of him, ran head on into a piece of timber sticking out of the ground. Knocked senseless, he tumbled end over end and nearly went under the train's wheels.

Yelling to us over the noise, the engineer asked if we would like to cure our dog of chasing trains. Naturally, we didn't want MacTavish ground up like hamburger and nodded in the affirmative. He yelled again, *"Tomorrow! Same time!"*

Now, we were really curious, wondering what the engineer intended to do to cure our loveable hound-dog of chasing trains.

The next day, we were again racing beside the train on our bikes with MacTavish pursuing the engine. The engineer signaled us to watch as our dog gradually overtook the front of the chugging monster.

Suddenly, as if a dragon were spewing scalding vapors, the engineer released a cloud of hissing hot steam, completely engulfing our canine challenger. When our poor dog emerged from the cloud of boiling spray, he ran for home at the speed of light, howling with his tail tucked between his legs.

From that day on, whenever a train rumbled past, old MacTavish wasn't to be seen . . . unless one looked under Grandmother's bed.

Giddyap Horsey

As Mom prepared to walk to Tualatin to catch a bus back to the tavern in Carver, she expressed concern about carrying a couple of bulky shopping bags. They were so cumbersome and heavy that she wasn't certain that she could manage both of them at the same time. Tom pleased his mother by offering to go with her and carry the bags.

Not until they were ready to leave, however, did she discover that he had another reason for making the offer. He wanted to ride our horse, Beauty, and planned to strap the bundles to the saddle horn. In reality, it wasn't her thoughtful son who was going to carry her belongings, but the horse.

Tommy enjoyed riding and quite often rode bareback. But seldom did he ride as far away from the property as Tualatin.

When he was mounted, he looked much like an Indian Brave because of his dark complexion and unruly black hair . . . and even more so when he was shirtless. Tommy never ever sunburned. Instead, his skin turned a deep bronze.

Mom and Tom, he astride Beauty, left before the noon hour. But walking two-plus-miles with our fidgety and sometimes ill-tempered quarter horse wasn't easy. Beauty was accustomed to running at an all-out sprint most of the time. But, unlike me, Tom was able to rein her in to a slow walk. I never could. She seldom obeyed my commands. Whenever I put my foot in the stirrup, she took off like a runaway rocket with me hanging on for dear life. And she never stopped until she was good and ready.

Arriving at the bus stop, Tom handed the bags to Mom but remained mounted to better control his nervous mount.

A train rumbling past the community on tracks across the highway barely 150 feet from the bus stop sounded its shrill whistle. It startled

Beauty — she was lightning fast

Beauty. And instantly, Tom found himself clinging to a speeding bullet, lucky that he was able to remain mounted.

After overcoming the initial shock of being astride a runaway horse, my brother became aware that the cinch had loosened and the saddle had begun to slip to one side. He grabbed her mane and, riding nearly bareback, somehow brought his runaway steed to a halt.

Mom, unaware that the train whistle had spooked Tom's horse, was perplexed and a little miffed with her son when he dashed off so unexpectedly.

"He never even said goodbye."

Bill Veedee and The Bee Tree

Warm sunlight streamed through Dad's bedroom window illuminating specks of dust floating in the still air. And just outside the window, dozens of flies did aerial combat. It was a beautiful, sleepy, peaceful morning. But it was about to change and become very, very interesting.

Dad had come home the night before, not to buy groceries or pay bills, but to rob a bee tree. And his Italian friend, Bill Veedee, was coming to help him. Neither Dad nor Bill had ever before robbed a bee tree. And live bees still inhabited the hollow of the dead tree, thousands and thousands of them.

Arising from a sound sleep, Pa sat motionless on the edge of his bed wearing nothing but a sleeveless tee shirt and under shorts. With his socks in his hand, he stared at the floor, his mouth agape, not stirring, not blinking, and barely breathing, as if he were in a trance.

As far back as I can remember he was like this for the first ten minutes every blessed morning, rain or shine. I never knew whether he was deep in thought or in a mental daze.

When he finally came to life, he took hold of the toe of each sock and beat them across the bedstead several times to knock the dust out or kill whatever might be lurking within. This, too, he did every blessed morning without fail.

Several times the previous evening, Grandma warned Dad that robbing a bee tree on a warm day was not very wise. Bees were active and aggressive then. Dad didn't want to hear any of it. He was bullheaded and believed he and Bill knew what they were doing.

Bill arrived about noontime, bearing a big grin on his flattened, dark-skinned face. With obvious sarcasm in her voice, Grandmother couldn't help but say something.

"Just in time to eat, I see."

Bill produced a couple of hats with a protective netting attached to the broad brims and some kind of bellows used to blow sulfur dust or smoke at the bees. This strange-looking gear fascinated us kids and we hoped Bill would let us wear one of the hats just to see what it was like. Grandmother was skeptical as she, too, examined the equipment, continuing to mumble and shake her head negatively.

Dad chided her.

"You wait and see, Ma. We're gonna get the honey and you're gonna eat your words."

After a quick lunch, and with us kids trailing behind, Bill and Dad sauntered into the woods to a point near the bee tree. It seemed as if they'd thought of everything. They wore gloves, loose clothing, and the broad-brimmed hats with the protective netting, appearing like creatures only found in a comic book.

Honey was oozing through cracks in the tree trunk some dozen feet above the ground. It was really ripe for the picking. They decided the best way to get at the honey was to fall the tree even though there was some chance that it could split open. If that happened, they risked losing some of the honey.

Cautiously approaching the tree, they took up their positions and began to fall it with a seven-foot crosscut saw. In just seconds, thousands of bees poured out of every nook and cranny in the tree. Stopping often, Bill used his bellows to send puffs of yellowish smoke into the swarm to drive them off. Several bees eventually landed on Dad. Not thinking of the consequences, Bill gave him a suffocating dose of smoke. Pop was caught off-guard and felt as if he were about to suffocate. Finally able to catch his breath, he scalded Bill's ears with a stream of nastiness.

With the tree finally on the ground and about a billion angry bees swarming all around them, Dad chopped an opening into the hollow log to expose the honeycombs while Bill continued to pump his putrid smoke. They had scooped out nearly enough honey to fill their washtub when some of the bees finally found a way under their protective netting. Both of them got stung. Yelping like scalded dogs, they grabbed the tub of honey and dashed toward the house.

Grandmother had anticipated that something would happen and was waiting with a garden hose to wash the remainder of the bees from their clothing. Bill had been stung two or three times on the neck and cheek and Dad once right on the end of his droopy nose. It was just a miracle that they weren't stung many more times.

Bill wrapped ice cubes in his handkerchief and placed it over the stings on his swollen neck, trying to ease the pain and reduce the swelling.

Somewhat satisfied with their success but not feeling up to having supper with us, Bill took a share of the honey and went home to lick his wounds. Everyone but Dad, who was trying to ease the pain in his snoot, got busy putting the oozing honeycombs into storage containers.

That night, while the rest of us dined on toast smothered with homemade butter and sweet honey, Dad lay on the couch holding one of his well worn stinky socks stuffed full of crushed ice against his swollen proboscis. His nose looked very much like a ripe Roma tomato. Poor Pop! He didn't feel much like eating supper and, in particular, honey.

Acting nonchalant with Grandmother, as if getting stung was nothing to be concerned about, he crowed about his victorious raid.

"I told you we'd get the honey, didn't I Ma?"

Grandma said nothing. But I'm certain she was thinking plenty.

Tudie was sitting on the couch with Dad and handed an envelope to him.

Taking it, he asked,

"What's this?"

"It's my report card, Daddy. And I got really good grades too. Look, they're all Bs."

No Camping Allowed

Since the beginning of time, pranks have been played upon poor unsuspecting souls when they've visited outhouses. And Halloween was always a favorite time of the year to pull those pranks. To me, every day of the year was Halloween. And I was a prankster. It was as simple as that.

As youngsters, we heard stories about a neighbor who had discovered their privy had been tipped over. And we heard that others had been moved to one side leaving the honey pit exposed so that some poor unsuspecting soul might step into it. There were many other pranks too, such as barring the door shut so the occupant couldn't get out. Most of the tricks were considered humorous . . . but some bordered on the sadistic.

We never targeted other people's outhouses . . . at least, I don't remember any. But the temptation was always there. We targeted ours, though. Most of the things we did to make our unsuspecting victim sit up and take notice were masterfully executed. And some things we did were quite unintentional.

Playing a trick on my brothers after they'd gotten good and comfortable and in a defenseless position tickled me pink. With their pants down and the job only partly finished, how could they give chase?

When we moved to the lower place, we toted our old privy with us. It was a little like old rickety furniture—a piece that one had grown attached to and didn't want to throw away. But, eventually, we tore it down and built a larger one—one with two holes. We believed that a *two-holer* would be a real convenience for a large family. With a two-holer, we could have company while we did our duty. And this one had a magazine rack to hold old newspapers too. Owning a modern state-of-the-art outhouse indicated that we had class.

Made of shiplap boards, the one and only defect to our privy palace was a knothole just above seat level in the back wall. Actually, the knot remained in the wall for several months before someone poked it out. Soon, it became a target for several sneaky and mischievous deeds.

Dee, Charla, Tudie, Teddy, and Tom (Dick hiding behind Tom) on the lower place

Tom was never in a hurry when he used the old sanitary shack. He camped in it for what seemed like eternities forcing the rest of us to walk cross-legged.

One day, my devious little mind working overtime, I came up with a dandy idea how to put an end to Tom's leisure time in the can . . . a spank on the bare butt with a hazelnut switch.

I cut one and fastened it to a two-by-four-bracing under the seat down in the hole. With one end of a long string tied to it, I stretched the remainder into the garden where I hid.

With the string concealed by grass and dirt and the whip bent nearly double, I waited for my victim to appear. The next one to use the place, however, wasn't Tom but my nine-year-old brother, Dee. Well, that was his misfortune. When I let loose of the string, I heard a stinging slap and a surprised yelp. Poor Dee! He squalled as if he'd been stung.

One day, brother Tom and I were busy hoeing weeds in the potato patch when we saw Grandmother enter the old palace. Tom and I said

Typical outhouse, sketch by Tom Pileggi

nothing to each other, but we knew what the other was thinking and what we were going to do next. We gave Granny a half-minute to get settled and then we bombarded the place with dirt clods aiming at the knothole. Granny squalled like a butchered calf, threatening our lives as we lit out for the woods. We had a good head start on her, at least 100 feet, and we thought we could easily outrun a 66-year-old woman. But, it wasn't so. After running as hard as we could for a couple of minutes, we stopped and found Granny right on our heels. She was barely breathing hard and she even had time to cut a switch.

After I left home, my sisters pulled a trick or two of their own. When one of my other brothers camped out in the privy too long, the girls poured water from a sprinkling can through the knothole onto his backside.

Another prank they pulled was a tad more devious. They captured honeybees and held them captive in a quart jar. When one of the guys got good and comfortable on the throne, they placed the open end of the jar over the knothole to release the nasty little insects. Just one angry bee buzzing around in the old can was enough reason to vacate it. But several caused a stampede. However, until the bees also vacated the place, no one could use it.

One of my chores was pouring lime down into the pit to keep the flies at bay and control the odor. But this one time, I'd run out of lime. And because Dad was tied up at the tavern, he wasn't home to buy more. After wondering for a time what to use in its place, I thought I'd come up with an ideal substitute. Gasoline!

"Yeah! It raises havoc with flies and we've got plenty of it. A full cup of it poured in there two or three times a week ought to do it."

Two weeks had elapsed when Dad came home to buy groceries, supplies and take care of the bills. He stayed overnight with us.

The following morning, before breakfast, he took the local newspaper in hand and went to the can, a normal routine when he was home. A few minutes passed when a resounding "ka-whump" shook the house. Out the back door we ran to see what had happened. There stood Pa just outside the outhouse with his pants down around his ankles and newspaper strewn all about him. He appeared to be smoldering, his facial hair, eyebrows and eyelashes, singed black.

Seeming to be in a daze, he murmured as he stared into space, *"What the hell happened? All I wanted to do was read the paper and . . . and . . . What the hell happened . . . ?"*

His voice trailed off into a bewildered silence.

Pop had lit a cigarette and had thrown the match down the other hole igniting the gasoline. The resultant flash explosion nearly blew him out of the place.

When we killed and cleaned a chicken, we always singed the bird over an open flame to burn off the nearly invisible, hair-like feathers. I likened Dad's backside to that of a singed chicken—fiery and blazing red. To burn his eyebrows and eyelashes, the fire had to erupt up between his legs and, although I never found out or had nerve enough to ask, he probably lost all of his lower body hair.

A large black spot was forever burned into the ceiling above the other hole. The flame had shot up, as if from a blowtorch, and burned off all the cobwebs. Caused by the disruption of exploded gasoline, the outhouse reeked horribly. It was so bad that, for over a week, I couldn't use it, preferring to go up into the woods.

Sometimes, we ran out of flour. Sometimes we ran out of salt or sugar or coffee. But never again did we run out of lime for the outhouse.

Launa

Verdi Muller and her six-year-old daughter Launa came to visit. In reality, it was a short visit for Verdi but not for Launa. She was staying.

Verdi had left Launa with us before but just a few days at a time. This time, though, she was staying for several months. Verdi, Mom, Dad and Grandma had planned this for some time. But it was a complete surprise to us kids.

Verdi had been experiencing unpleasant times and figured our family and home would provide a more suitable environment for her daughter. I wonder who fed whom that line of baloney. Nonetheless, Grandma gladly accepted the responsibility. We knew the Muller clan so well that it just seemed natural to have little Launa with us. Our house was already like a zoo, crowded with squalling kids. And

Launa

one more mouth to feed at the dinner table would hardly be noticed.

So, little Launa moved in with the other two girls. And a few days later, she enrolled in school at Cipole.

Right away, the girls whined that they needed more room and privacy. So at Grandma's request—actually, it was a stern order—Tom and I relinquished our sleeping accommodations upstairs and moved into the small bedroom downstairs.

Girls . . . they were a pain in the neck. We boys had enough trouble with Tudie and Charla. Now, with Launa on our hands, we had another feisty little twerp and tattletale to contend with. But in just a few days, we adapted to our new *sister*. And she adapted to us.

McCorkle

Alex McCorkle, a World War II combat fighter pilot, survived the war only to perish in a civilian aircraft accident in 1947. Alex and his airplane went down somewhere near Mount St. Helens. His body was never found.

Alex's mother Zelda McCorkle and my grandmother were close friends. She seldom failed to talk about her son and his exploits during their conversations. She was very proud of him. He was her only child.

Mrs. McCorkle and my grandmother were nearly the same age and possessed similar backgrounds. Both of them were pioneer-type women, hardworking and tough as leather. And both of them swore up and down that they could do anything a man could do, including work, and probably do it better. In fact, Grandmother used to say, mortifying the life out of me, *"There's nuthin' a dad-burned man can do that I can't 'cept pee on a fence post while standin'. And I think I could do that too if I had a mind to."*

After being widowed, Mrs. McCorkle lived with her older brother, Carl Theobald, on a small farm near Tualatin. Both of them referred to each other by their last names, as did nearly everyone else in the community. Theobald had suffered the loss of both legs in a haying accident. But, with the aid of crude prosthetic devices and crutches, he continued to drive a tractor and do common farm work.

Some years after Theobald died, I stayed with McCorkle for two weeks, helping her clear brush from the back part of her farm. The woman was a marvel, agile and nimble as a youngster. She regularly pushed me to the limit of my endurance when we worked. And I was sixteen. Her long red hair, usually worn in a tight bun, belied her 70 odd years. And she was a vegetarian—something that I hadn't realized until a few days before I returned home. I ate meals that were so delicious that I never once missed eating meat.

Most evenings after supper, we sat outside the house to relax or took short refreshing walks in the woods. This elderly lady was amazing. How she was able to survive so many hardships during her life and still be a happy person was beyond me. A deeply religious person, she read the Bible every night without fail just as my Grandmother did.

One sunny afternoon, we took time out to go for a stroll through the countryside to George Saum's farm, a farm of considerable size. Most of the place was overgrown by large thickets of blackberries and brush. And a decaying half-built mansion was hidden somewhere deep in the timber. Mr. Saum had been building the huge manor home, as large as a small castle, when his wife suddenly became ill and died. Heartbroken, he never completed the project. And the place went to rot, never to be occupied by anyone. People said that had he finished his home, it would have rivaled many of the estates in Europe.

We walked on through the woods discovering an abundance of beautiful wildflowers hidden among patches of sweet smelling ferns: colorful foxgloves, aromatic lady's slipper, delicate Johnny-jump-ups and the bluest violets, all growing up through a mantle of soft green moss that covered the forest floor like an endless carpet. The fir trees stood tall and straight like sentinels with their thick-needled boughs spread out, protecting nature's flowerbeds beneath. The woods were exquisitely beautiful and as magical as the woods near my home.

Nearing a farm owned by the Lee family, we encountered a barbed wire fence, preventing us from continuing our stroll. Standing next to a large fir tree, I told McCorkle that before returning to the house, I needed to go to the bathroom. She politely stepped around to the other side of the tree to give me a little privacy. But being more concerned that I was out of her sight than where I was aiming, I failed to notice the white insulators on the other side of the fence post.

"Watch out for the electric fence, Teddy."

McCorkle's warning came a split second too late. I was electrocuted for the crime of peeing on someone's electric fence and the jolt of electricity straightened me up like a broomstick. Hearing me yelp like a stung dog and realizing what I had done, McCorkle nearly split her sides with laughter.

Making certain there was nothing else that was going to nip at me, I finished my chore wishing that I didn't have to face her. What humiliation.

As we began retracing our steps back to her house, I complained about a strange sensation in my chest, a sensation that I felt was caused by the shock from the electric fence.

She just had to make a comment that caused me more embarrassment.

"You mean to tell me the shock only affected you there?"

The Hazards of Farming

We couldn't afford new farm machinery. Everything we owned was an antique. Our faded-green tractor was a homemade affair and had been assembled from an odd assortment of parts. The engine was from a 1928 Chevrolet and God only knows what make the transmission and frame were. The huge rear tires were probably from another old tractor and equipped with tire chains for gripping.

All in all, the old crate functioned well enough to do what we needed like pulling brush, working the ground and towing a trailer loaded with hay. But steering it was a bit tricky. If we turned the steering wheel to the extreme, in one direction or the other, the steering mechanism sometimes inverted itself, forcing us to steer in the reverse order. To turn right, we had to steer left and to turn left we had to steer right. It was difficult to repair, and if we couldn't fix it immediately, we just steered funny for a time.

Our plow, disc, harrow, mowing machine, and hay rake were old horse-drawn pieces of equipment that Dad or someone else had modified to be pulled by a tractor. But the controls to operate the hay rake and the mowing machine could only be manipulated from the individual pieces of equipment. Therefore one of us kids had to ride on the machine to operate it while another one of us drove the tractor.

Late in the summer, Dad took a day off from managing the tavern to help Tom, Dick and me cut what little hay we'd planted. Because the weather had been so warm, we began working early in the morning. But by ten o'clock it had already become as hot as Hades.

Haying is not a clean job and it wasn't long before we'd become covered with dirt, the inside of our noses and mouths coated with the dust we'd inhaled. To add to our misery, we had become overheated, a condition that caused us to be careless in our work and cranky with each other.

The mowing didn't go well at all. We had planted too much vetch with the oats and it had grown so thick that it clogged the mower blade, causing us all kinds of grief. So, while Dad drove the tractor and one of us rode the mower, another of us walked behind, removing the tangle whenever the equipment became fouled. And that was quite often. But clearing it usually took no time at all, not much more than a few seconds.

I was taking my turn riding the mower and Tom unclogging the blade when it became hopelessly jammed tight. Dad stopped the instant I yelled. Carelessly, I didn't bother to disengage the mowing mechanism. Tom tugged and ripped at the tightly twisted clump but couldn't tear it loose. So, never considering the danger, he stepped in front of the mower blade to get better leverage. He tore at it again.

And this time, while mumbling his displeasure, he ripped most of the clump away.

Dad seldom bothered to look back, only waited for the command to go. And this time, he did no different. Unaware where Tom had positioned himself, Pa assumed the blade had been cleared when he heard his grumbling. He released the clutch and the tractor lurched forward.

Tom was caught off guard. The mower's guide bar knocked him over on his back. And the mower blade, sawing back and forth through the guides, slid up over Tom's prone body toward his face. Struck with horror, I screamed bloody murder at Dad. Almost immediately, he stopped the tractor. But it wasn't soon enough.

Tom was pinned beneath the mower's cutting blade. And he'd suffered a horribly painful injury, blood gushing from a huge gaping wound in his forearm. He immediately went into shock and passed out. Dad quickly pulled him from beneath the mechanism and bound the wound with his handkerchief. Then, he scooped him up like a tiny child and all but ran across the hay field, carrying him to the house. And my bother was, by no means, a small boy.

Dick, who'd been tagging along behind us, flew to the house to alert Grandma that one of us was hurt.

Working with the skill of a battlefield medic, she placed a cold compress on Tom's head, cleansed the edges of the wound with peroxide, and carefully but thoroughly bandaged it.

In the meantime, Launa, Tudie and Charla scrambled upstairs. They were crying and scared to death that one of us had lost fingers or an arm or had been killed.

Dad, blaming himself for the accident, sat quietly at the kitchen table for some time. Feeling depressed and nearly in tears, he held his head in his hands. He was a strong man physically but he was a big softy at heart.

Trying to cheer him, Grandma told him that Tom was a strong, healthy kid and would be okay. Then she quipped with a little humor, *"If anything, he might get an infection from that snotty rag you wrapped around his arm. That thing's so stinkin' dirty, Elmer, ya oughta touch a match to it afore it eats a hole through yore pocket. I'll bet a hunnert dollars it'll go up in a flash."*

We were farmers and we had to accept the fact that accidents happened from time to time. Tom was a tough kid and, with the exception of a sizeable scar, he recovered from the accident. But Pa never fully forgave himself, believing that he was entirely at fault for Tom's agonizing injury. At one time, he considered selling the place to avoid any further accidents. Thankfully, he didn't. It was our home and all of us kids loved it.

The Hummingbird

The warm afternoon air was motionless. Nothing moved. And the day seemed as if it had stopped to take a rest. Tired and hot, I wanted to take a rest too. I'd been working at one of my least favorite chores, hoeing weeds from the garden.

Seeking shade, I plopped down on the ground under one of the large leafy oak trees in the back yard. Immediately, I felt welcome relief from the hot, searing sun. I leaned against the tree's rough trunk and was instantly reminded that I'd suffered a sunburned back.

I felt like going up into the cool woods and perching on a log to watch chipmunks scurry up and down trees, and to smell the green ferns and the sweet aroma of the mock orange blossoms. But there was work to be done and Granny would be a mite upset if the hoeing weren't finished by suppertime.

The soft warm dirt that covered my bare feet appeared as dry as my parched throat. I needed a drink of cold water. But I didn't feel like moving, not one inch, not for a few moments, anyway. The tomato and pepper plants also looked as if they were dying from thirst.

Finally, I found the energy to move and went for the hose. Naturally the water in it was hot from being boiled in the afternoon sun. It seemed to take forever before cold water came pouring out. I took several huge thirst-quenching swigs. And then I splashed some of the cool refreshing liquid in my face and over my head, some of it running down my blistered back. Instead of soft warm dust squirting up between my toes, it had turned into soft warm mud. Nonetheless, it was soothing and, oh, so good.

I placed my thumb over the open end of the hose to get a little stronger, forced stream of water to wash my feet when suddenly, to my astonishment, a hummingbird flew up to the stream and began to drink. It hovered no more than two feet from me. Holding the hose as still as possible, I maintained a constant even stream of water, barely breathing, not wanting to frighten the tiny bird away. It was an amazing, mesmerizing sight. I had never before been so close to one of these fragile little creatures.

It worked its way up the stream until its delicate, nearly invisible wings fluttered against my hand, feeling like gentle kisses from a warm breeze. After several seconds of flicking its long needle-like tongue into the water, it stopped drinking and rose up, hovering close, within inches of my face. It seemed to be examining me as if it were curious about its benefactor. After a few seconds it dropped down for another quick drink and then darted off.

I remained motionless, spellbound by the incident, realizing that this little bird had no fear of me. It seemed to completely trust that I wouldn't harm it. As I came back to my senses, I found that I'd nearly drowned some of my grandmother's pepper plants.

With a few well-placed squirts of water around some of the tomato plants, I was ready to turn the water off when suddenly my little hummingbird friend returned for a second drink, and also to bathe itself in the cool stream. Again I held the hose still trying to be as accommodating as possible. But this time, to my disappointment, it didn't stay as long and soon darted away.

Hoping it would return again, I remained in the same place, continuing to water the garden. To my delight it did. The tiny bird appeared a third time. But it didn't come back to drink. For a few seconds, it hovered within a few feet of my face, looking me squarely in the eyes before darting off again—this time for good.

I'd like to believe that God's little creature returned the third time just to bid farewell to me—a friend who provided it with a cold treat on a very hot summer day.

CHAPTER X

1949

The Earthquake

High school choir and the boys' glee club were two of my most enjoyable classes. I loved music and possessed a deep voice, singing back-row bass in both groups. The glee club wasn't large but, yet, we were quite good and sang in state competition.

April 13, 1949 was a peaceful and serene Wednesday. Just before the noon hour, we—the guys in my glee club and I—were rehearsing for an upcoming concert when our choir director, Lindo Morandi, announced to my classmates that I was celebrating my 17th birthday. But before anyone could congratulate me, the room began to shudder and bounce around. It was a major earthquake and shook the countryside with a vengeance. And it was the only time in my life that I sang with vibrato in my voice.

In only seconds, the violent tremor damaged our school and other structures in the area. It was a terrifying event for everyone, and especially for those individuals who had never before experienced an earthquake. And I was one of them.

The school emptied in an orderly fashion, most of the student body gathering on the football field just as we had done many times when practicing fire drills.

Several of the girls, distraught and frightened, began crying. It was quite natural to be nervous and uncertain not knowing what was happening and fearing that another quake would strike at any moment. To calm everyone, we boys began singing *Stouthearted Men*, the song we'd been practicing when the tremor hit. Within a few seconds, the entire student body had joined us. It must have been quite impressive to hear all of us singing in unison, over 100 voices. Singing bolstered our courage and re-enforced our resolve to face adversity, to stand up to disaster—even to a major earthquake.

The Best of All Gifts

Tom and I lettered in our high school's sports programs but neither of us owned a letterman's sweater. All of the other guys did. In the worst way, both of us wanted one. But they were expensive. And I had no money. But Tom did and he was about to buy one. He'd saved enough of his earnings from his past summer jobs to purchase one. But poor me! I didn't have a cent to my name.

Finding work on one of the local farms during the winter months was downright impossible. I'd talked to Mr. Johnston, Dick Walgraeve and Eddie's dad but they didn't need anyone. I even asked Alan Hanegan's dad if he needed anyone to work at his service station. But he didn't. He told me there wasn't enough to do to keep Alan busy.

Truthfully, I was easily discouraged, lacking the drive, self-assurance, and confidence to really get out and hustle, searching for work. I hated to be turned down.

The more I thought about the letterman's sweater, the farther down in the dumps I got.

A few days before Tom was to buy his, I did nothing but mope about the house, acting like a big dumb jerk. Being a big pain in everyone's butt, and in particular my grandmother's, she'd finally had enough of my broodiness and wanted to know what in blazes was wrong with me.

"For Heaven's sake, what in tarnation is ailin' you, anyhow? Ya act like the world's comin' to an end."

I whined an answer.

"I've tried finding a job to earn some money to buy a letterman's sweater. But nobody around here wants to hire me right now. Everyone else in school's got one but me and Tom. And he's getting' one tomorrow."

After listening to my sad tale, Grandma put her mending down and went into her bedroom. Returning a few moments later, she sat down at the table and laid money in front of me, the exact amount that I needed for the sweater.

"What's this for?"

"It's for yore sweater. You kin pay me back later when you git the money. I'm sick and tired of you a mopin' around here actin' like some dadburned calf that's jest been weaned off the tit."

Grandma really stumped me. She was so unpredictable. One minute she was ornery and bossy and acting as tough as nails. And the next she was almost angelic doing something thoughtful, kind and generous. After investing nearly every cent she had in building our house, I knew she had little money to spend on herself. And knowing that she'd scrimped and sacrificed all of her life, it was truly overwhelming that she was willing to share what little she had with me.

After a weak objection, I agreed to take it, vowing to pay her back as soon as I could. But, I don't really believe she ever expected me to keep my word. And I don't believe I ever did.

A few days later, two weeks before my birthday, Tom and I—two eager beavers—were on the Tualatin Valley Stage Lines bus riding into Portland to purchase our sweaters at Dehen's Clothing, a company specializing in such garments. In hours, we were proudly sporting our new red letterman's sweaters with the crimson "S" sewn on one side. The first place we visited after leaving Dehen's was our favorite Chinese restaurant on Third Street, celebrating with an order of Chinese noodles.

We were two proud and cocky kids. And rain or shine, we wore our sweaters every day, to school, to church, to the store, and to the movies. About the only place we didn't wear them was to the barn.

A few days after my 17th birthday and the big earthquake, my mother and dad came home. We were surprised and more than thrilled to see them walk in the door with beaming smiles on their faces. And they were quite happy to see us too, being very concerned about our welfare, especially after the large tremor that had rattled the Northwest.

Mom and Dad chatted with us for a few moments. And then, with big grins on their faces, they surprised the socks off me. Mom handed a birthday gift to me and both wished me a happy birthday. The gift was a beautifully wrapped jewelry case.

Opening it, I found that it contained a man's wristwatch, the most beautiful, stunning thing I'd ever seen. I could have been knocked over with a feather. It was the first watch I'd ever owned and I couldn't have been happier.

As I slipped it on my wrist, the kids gathered around me to look at it. The square case was gold and the numbers were represented by diamond and ruby chips. They were probably synthetic but they looked real. Mom had won it by playing the tavern's punchboards, hitting one of the jackpots.

Well, I'd hit a jackpot too—my mom, my dad and my grandma. What greater gift could a kid ask for on his 17th birthday, or on any birthday for that matter, than to have caring, loving parents and a soft-hearted grandmother.

The Dating Game

Asking a girl for a date was not easy for me. First of all, I was bashful and lacked confidence in myself. And second, I had no transportation of my own. And third, I was petrified that I'd be turned down.

Brother Tom, ribbing me a little, said that no girl in her right mind would go with me because I hadn't taken a bath in ten years.

Midway through my junior year, finding a little courage, I invited one of the sophomore girls to go to a school dance with me. I didn't know how to dance, though. But I was determined to struggle through the ordeal if she accepted. To my stunned surprise, she did. And she knew I had no car. And she knew I couldn't dance either.

Not the prettiest girl in school, I figured she was most likely a little desperate and accepted the first offer. But, heck, I was desperate too.

Two hours later, two excruciating hours later, we left the dance. Had I been forced to dance every number, I think I'd have died. But luckily she agreed to sit out half of them.

While walking her home, a distance of three miles, I worked up enough nerve to hug her. That was the first time I'd ever hugged a female that I wasn't related to. Since that worked so well, I thought I was ready for the next move, a kiss. But, I'd never before kissed a girl, either, not on the lips, not my mom, not my grandmother, no one. Being inexperienced and uneasy, I was afraid I'd botch it. But after three or four more pauses, I finally found enough courage to take her in my arms and plant one on her. The experience was truly quite enjoyable and much more exhilarating than I thought it would be. Each time we stopped, and we began stopping more often, I became more confident and bolder and the kisses lasted longer. The one-hour walk took well over two hours.

Stupid me, the next day I just had to brag about my date to my buddies Eddie Wager and Alan Hanegan. From then on, the two dipsticks referred to me as Romeo, Don Juan Pileggi, and the Cipole Swamp Casanova. I kind of liked the Casanova name the best.

Gaining confidence in myself, girls began to enter into my life. Among them was Linda Speight, a swell-looking little red-haired girl that I met at the Joy Theater in Tigard. I learned that Linda meant cute in Spanish and it fit her. She lived in Metzger and, although we never dated, I called her a few times from a pay phone in Sherwood.

One of Eddie's sisters gave me the name and address of another young lady. But she lived in Belfast, Ireland. Thus began my first real contact with a person living in another country. Her name was Angela Crossin. We became pen pals, writing to each other until my graduation from high school. After receiving three or four letters, she began closing them with "*Love, Angela.*" The romantic side of life was beginning to take shape, even on another continent.

Nearing the end of my junior year, I developed a romantic crush on Loyce Martinazzi, a petite girl with dark hair, soft dreamy blue eyes and ruby red lips. Her dad, Art Martinazzi, was a quiet, gentle man but his sharp features, piercing eyes, dark complexion, and his resemblance to Jack Palance frightened the soup out of me.

Loyce and I met daily at lunchtime in back of the school's stage. But we never really went out on a date. We hung around together for,

I suppose, four or five weeks before she dumped me for a senior named Ralph Shaw. He had transportation to go on a date, a pickup truck.

Poor me! The only wheels I owned were on a bicycle.

Beaver Boys' State

For years, several dozen high-school boys descended upon the campus of Oregon State College—later to be known as Oregon State University—during the summer to attend a full week of seminars and lectures on world politics, governments and economies. The event was sponsored by a non-profit organization and known as Beaver Boys' State. And those selected to attend the event were boys who had completed their junior year of high school.

Mike Wyatt and I were elected to represent Sherwood High School during the summer of 1949. Mike was a sharp kid, worldly and refined and a natural to be selected. But I'll never understand why I was chosen. Personality, intellect, leadership and grade point average were a few of the qualities used in the selection process. I was, at best, average in all of those categories.

Mike and I agreed to travel together to Corvallis. He owned a motorcycle, solving our transportation problem. But it also limited the amount of clothing and personal items we could take.

Grandma didn't like the idea of me riding on a motorcycle. She fretted and worried that I'd fall off that *carnsarned contraption*. I was somewhat concerned myself; it was my first experience riding on one.

As we packed our things into the saddlebags, she repeatedly warned Mike not to drive too fast and me to be careful. The only instructions Mike gave me were to wrap my arms around his middle, where to put my feet, and hang on tight.

As we drove down the road, I was tense and yet I felt reasonably comfortable with Mike's driving skills.

Arriving in Corvallis an hour later, we began searching for the street to the dormitory where we were to be housed and attend lectures. Mike spotted it first. And when he made a quick, unexpected left turn, I was certain that we were going to take a bad spill and stuck my foot out. When my shoe impacted the pavement, the jolt nearly unseated me and nearly caused Mike to lose control of the bike. Somehow, though, we remained upright. Only when I dismounted in the parking lot did I realize that I'd lost the heel to my left shoe.

Mike, mincing no words, told me how stupid I was and how close we came to having a wreck. From then on, I kept my feet planted and put my life in his hands.

We checked into Sackett Hall on the campus of Oregon State. About 70 other boys, most of them wearing dark colored dress slacks, white shirts, ties, sport jackets and shiny dress shoes

Teddy

also checked in. I felt out of place, like some hayseed from the sticks because I was wearing my school clothes: white corduroy pants, a tee shirt, and my letterman's sweater. Oh, and a pair of worn out oxfords, one shoe with a heel missing. It was a little embarrassing limping about from one building to another. But I had to make do since it was the only pair of shoes I had.

The facilities were first-rate, good sleeping quarters, comfortable classrooms, and good food. But I found the restrooms unpleasant. They appeared clean but they smelled mildewed and pungent.

The speakers were excellent and the topics more than a little interesting. The one that I will always remember was about the volatility of the Middle Eastern countries of Syria, Iran and Jordan. It was the first time also that I began to understand that North Africa and the Middle East were not just deserts, camels and Bedouins but a dangerous region that affected the stability and economies of the entire world.

I made many new friends and before I realized it, the week had passed and we were on our way home.

Breezing along on Mike's cycle, we were nearing Six-Corners just out of Sherwood when we drove through a swarm of honeybees. Two of them went inside Mike's leather jacket and down his back, stinging him. How he managed to stop the cycle without crashing, I'll never know. I was lucky not to get stung myself. And I can guarantee you that I kept my feet planted on the cycle until he brought it to a complete stop.

Not many days after returning home, I developed a rash, a fungus malady that athletes call *jock itch*. But being a backward, bashful, inexperienced kid, I thought I had caught a deadly venereal disease from using the communal toilets at the college. The fungus that athletes experienced had been discussed in our physical education and health classes, but I never in the world thought it could be as severe as my problem. Thus, I came to an incorrect conclusion believing that I had been infected with syphilis.

Researching our dictionary and encyclopedias convinced me even more. Mozart and others went blind, insane and died from it. There was no cure. The more I read about the disease, the more dejected, depressed and frightened I became. I had no idea how to treat it and I certainly didn't want to mention it to Grandma and cause her to worry. Soon, I had become despondent, down in the dumps and terribly withdrawn.

Grandma wondered what the devil was wrong with me. I acted differently, no longer the carefree kid that she was accustomed to putting up with. I stopped communicating, laughing and having fun. She became so concerned that when Dad eventually came home from the tavern to buy groceries and pay bills, she convinced him to take me to the doctor. By then, however, three weeks had passed and most of the symptoms had vanished. But I was certain that it was just a matter of time before I would lose my eyesight and eventually die.

Doctor Rucker examined my chest and asked if I had any pain. Of course, I told him nothing. I was too ashamed to tell anyone, even our doctor, of my diagnosis.

Football practice began a week later—just before the beginning of the school year. My heart wasn't in it. But Tom and Grandma coaxed me into going out for the team anyway.

In the shower after practice, one of the other seniors asked the coach how to treat jock itch, that he had a nasty case of it. After hearing him describe the symptoms, I realized that was what I had and nothing more.

A sudden flood of relief swept over me. I was okay and I wasn't going to die. I was ecstatic, happy as a clam that my affliction was nothing more serious.

Not many guys would be elated to discover they had a good old case of jock itch. But I was, so much so that I almost felt like bragging about it.

Pure Pain

Dean Holloman and my brother Tommy had received permission from Dean's parents to cut a few fir trees on the back of their property so the boys could make a few hard-earned dollars, selling firewood.

Working day after day for over a week, they had cut, sawed, split and stacked several cords. Nearly finished and with only a few more days of work left, both of them suffered mishaps. Tom accidentally stabbed himself and Dean's back went out.

Tom was first to be hurt, suffering a nasty puncture wound on his backside. How he was injured is still a bit of a mystery. But apparently it happened when he had a sudden and desperate urge to go to the bathroom. Scooting under a fir tree, he scraped away some dirt with his shoe and hurriedly squatted down, unintentionally sitting on a sharp stick. Anyway, that's his story.

That night, Tom lay face down on the bed feeling considerable discomfort. He asked if I would doctor his wound because he was too embarrassed to ask Grandma. Now, my brother was as hairy as an ugly ape and I wasn't any too keen about fooling with his backside. But, considering his predicament, I reluctantly obliged.

Taking a wad of cotton, I soaked it in alcohol and jabbed it in there. Poor Tom! It must have stung like old billy-hell because of the way he squirmed and writhed about and tore at the bed covers. But my method of doctoring must have been effective because he never again asked me to treat him.

Since Tom was laid up and I had nothing to do, I volunteered to cut wood for him. To be truthful, I had another reason for making the offer. I wanted to see Dean's sister, Patty. She was a cute little blond with dimpled cheeks, a girl who was in my high school class. Always too bashful to talk to her, I thought maybe I might catch a glimpse of her, if I was lucky.

The next day, I walked the two miles to Holloman's. And we went right to work. We cut and stacked wood all morning and by noontime, I was more than ready to devour a couple of sandwiches and slug down a glass of cold milk.

Dean and I had been bantering with each other all morning and, as we walked into the backyard at Dean's house, we engaged in some good-natured horseplay. Being bigger and stronger than he, I soon had him upside down, holding him by the legs. About that time, just as I'd hoped, Patty stepped outside. And did I see a lot of her. She was wearing a yellow figure-revealing swimsuit. I was so stunned when she smiled at me that I lost all thought about wrestling with Dean and loosened my grip on his legs. Unintentionally, I dropped him on his head. The result of the impact was a badly wrenched back that gave him grief for several days.

Now that both woodcutters were out of action, guess who had to finish splitting and stacking their firewood? And, would you believe it? I never caught another glimpse of Patty. And the kids never offered me one thin dime for my help. No sir! Not one thin dime.

Battling Brothers

Poor Grandma! It must have been a difficult chore riding herd on four wild boys and three whiney girls, 24 hours a day, seven days a week. Tom and I didn't help matters either. We were competitive teenagers and often at odds with each other. I'm sure we just about drove her out of her mind with some of our zany escapades, mischievousness, and constant bickering.

Since Dad was unable to come home but a couple of times a month and since I was the oldest, I thought I should assume the role as head of the household. But the rest of the kids had other thoughts about that.

Granny was pushing seventy years of age. Two people half her age would have found it difficult handling a flock of hyperactive youngsters like us. Yet, she did an exemplary job. But there were times when she was ready to give up.

Once when Pa walked in the door, after a two-week absence, he found Grandmother had packed her suitcase for the umpteenth time and was ready to walk out the door. She told him that we'd become too unruly for her to handle. And she'd had her fill of us and was running away.

After Dad had nearly gotten down on his knees and begged her to stay, she finally gave in, as she had done so many times before. Then he gave us a good ear-full and very succinctly promised that, if we didn't cooperate and behave ourselves, he'd kill us.

Dad's old Model A Ford flatbed pickup was often the cause of Tom's and my disputes. We fought over it like a pair of wildcats. Pop had warned us many times not to touch it. Nonetheless, we did. We drove the tires off that thing even though neither of us had a driver's license.

Grandma was aware that we were driving it too, and constantly worried that we'd have an accident. So she hid the key. But that didn't stop us either. We simply hot-wired the old crate.

Gone a half-hour one day, I'd driven to Sherwood to purchase school supplies from the variety store. When I returned to the pickup, I failed to notice that someone had parked directly behind me. Backing up without so much as a glance, I felt a bump and heard the shattering of glass.

I'd backed into Frank Gardinier's car and smashed out one of his headlights. And he was still sitting in the car, staring daggers at me.

Frank was our druggist, and a perpetual grouch, a person who constantly frowned. Breaking the headlight on his car just added more unpleasantness to his grumpy, dour disposition. I don't think I ever saw the man laugh, not once. The scowl on his face, when he saw his headlight splattered all over the street, could have frightened Dracula. He demanded that I give him five dollars—three for a new headlight and two for his time.

Grandma nearly had a fit when she found out that I'd crashed into someone. She warned me to tell Dad the moment he came home again, or she would.

We were always tickled to see him. But two days later when he showed up unexpectedly, I wasn't. Grandma was standing right next to me so I had to tell him that I'd had an accident with the Model A. He erupted like Mount St. Helens.

What should have been a cheerful visit turned into a dandy butt chewing. The only half-decent words he spoke for the next two hours were, *"What the hell happened?"*

Pop forked over five dollars to pay Frank but only after a lot of Italian-style arm waving and head slapping. Facing Dad wasn't easy, but facing Frank again to pay him was the worst part of the entire ordeal.

Dickie

One would think that I'd learned a lesson. But, no . . . being thickheaded, I hadn't. Just days later, Tom and I got into it again over Dad's bucket of bolts.

Dick found the ignition key and had it in his pocket. It was our chance to go for a drive. We were about to leave when Tom and his cohort, Dean Holloman, showed up at the house. They wanted the pickup and Tom demanded that I give the key to him.

Taunting him just a little, I said, *"Nope! Dick and I are takin' the pickup and goin' for a ride. You've had it every day this week, Tommy boy, and you're not gettin' it today."*

I figured we had as much right to it as he did. Besides, we had the key. But Tom didn't give up.

Trying to be intimidating, he bumped up against me, his face not more than an inch from mine, demanding that I surrender the key to him. That did it. Instantly, I was seething mad and bellowed angrily, *"Who do you think you are—the boss around here? You're not gettin' the key. You got no more right to the pickup than I have and besides, you're always drivin' it. So, Dick and I are gonna use it today. Now, get your ugly face away from me."*

I pushed him back and turned away. But he grabbed my arms and, pinning them to my sides, ordered Holloman to search my pockets. A flush of adrenaline swept through me like a tidal wave. No one was going to search my pockets, neither Tom nor Holloman, without getting into a whale of a fistfight.

Under normal circumstances, Tom could best me in most physical contests. But this wasn't one of those times.

Tom's grasp was firm but, with a struggle, I jerked free and the fight was on. We took a few swings at each other before I grabbed him by the hair and pulled his head down, locking it under one arm. With my free hand, I gave him a couple of solid wallops in the mush before Grandmother and Dick wedged us apart.

Tom lunged at me again, and again I grabbed him in a headlock. As he struggled to free himself, I challenged Holloman to come closer. In the worst way, I wanted to take a whack at him too. But, to my disappointment, he smartly kept his distance.

Grandma was afraid that I'd hurt Tom and, in desperation, hit me across the back with a broom. The blow broke the broom, broke my grip, and knocked me to the ground. Fearing that I would break Tom's fool neck, Dick tried to jump on me, hoping to keep me on the ground. But I caught him in the stomach with my foot and sent him somersaulting over my head.

Determined to thump Tom again, I scrambled to my feet. But the fight was over. Tom and Dean had disappeared, hiking down the railroad tracks toward Sherwood. My poor exasperated grandmother was crying and Dick's face was white with fright. But I felt darned good, proud of myself because I'd prevailed. And except for a sore back, I was okay. It was funny too because I wasn't mad at Tom, I wasn't mad at Grandma, I wasn't mad at anyone.

Dick and I wasted little time and, hopping in the Model A, drove away allowing Grandma to recover her wits. Other than Dee standing close by, she found herself alone, no girls or dogs, not even a cow or chicken in sight. They'd all hightailed it, frightened by the sudden outburst of violence. Grandma soon found the dogs huddled under her bed and discovered that Tudie, Charla and Launa had run into the house and had scrambled upstairs to hide under their bed.

A few days later, Tom and I got into it again over the old jalopy. He wanted the pickup and I wanted the pickup. Tom yelled at me and I yelled at him. We faced each other in the front yard, circling, preparing to have another fistfight, accusing each other of hiding the pickup so the other couldn't take it.

But then I realized something. If Tom had hidden it, he wouldn't be accusing me of hiding it and risking a busted nose. At that same instant, he must have come to the same conclusion.

It was then that we knew where it was. Little brother Dick had taken it. Like us, he didn't have a license to drive either.

Tormenting Tom

Pulling a prank on Tommy was one of my favorite pastimes. I loved annoying the hell out of him. And most of my tricks did just that. He always tried to even the score, not by pulling a retaliatory prank, but by running me down and beating the stuffing out of me. And because he was a tremendous athlete and faster afoot, I knew I had better have a huge head start before doing something to him. Otherwise, I'd suffer a severe thumping.

But it didn't always work out that way for me. Sometimes I couldn't avoid getting caught. But I made Tom pay a price. He first had to chase me down. And every time he closed in and was about to nab me, I'd suddenly dropped to the ground. Being too close, he could never stop in time and always tumbled over me. And that enraged him all the more. And before he could recover I was up and running as fast as I could, in the opposite direction.

This evasive tactic wore on both of us. But Tom, being a persistent cuss, never gave up. Finally, when I was too winded and too exhausted to run any longer, he got his revenge. Even at that, he never really hurt me. In fact, the harder he beat on me, the more I laughed at him.

Tom seldom pulled tricks on me. But one of the few he did took place during a warm, sunny, dreamy afternoon. It was a perfect day for taking a snooze. Wearing nothing more than a pair of coveralls, I took a nap lying on an old flatbed trailer, parked near the garden.

When he saw me lying on the trailer, he decided that it was time to get even with me for something that I'd done to him. He crept up on me, inserted wooden stick matches between my toes and lit them—all of them at the same time.

Suddenly wide-awake and feeling like someone had taken a blow-torch to my feet, I raced through the garden, kicking up dirt, trying to extinguish the brush fire blazing between my toes.

Now it was my turn to pound on him. But Tom, elated that he'd finally pulled a successful prank on his older brother, easily ran away from me. But his glee wasn't to last long. No sir! He had fooled around with the master prank-puller of all time. He was doomed.

Not many days later, I spotted him as he entered the outhouse. This was just the kind of opportunity that I'd been waiting for. A board at the base of the back wall near ground level was conveniently missing. I found a long stick, stuck a match on the end of it, lit the match, and shoved it through the opening upward toward Tom's exposed bottom. I heard a sizzling sound followed by a tremendous deafening bellow. Tom kicked the locked door open with such force that it ricocheted back and forth several times, making a bam-bam-bam sound. Out he came, shuffling, with his pants down around his ankles, taking small quick strides, and swinging both fists in wild arcing loops at me. His fat little cheeks flamed as red as his torched tush as he screamed, *"I'm gonna kill you, Teddy. You wait and see. You're gonna catch it good when I tell Grandma you burned me."*

Well, nothing more happened. But in the event he decided to pull the same stunt on me, I replaced the missing board, driving twice the number of nails into it to ensure it couldn't easily be removed.

Dad was home one evening and while having a congenial face-to-face chat with Tom about one of our high school football games, I saw an opportunity to do some mischief.

Everyone in the family knew that Pa was a terribly goosy fellow and his response to suddenly being pinched on the backside was unpredictable. So, nonchalantly walking up behind him, I grabbed him by the seat of the pants, snarling in his ear. His reaction was a shock to me but it was more of a shock to Tom. Dad's body tensed and he struck out like a rattlesnake, sending a straight right jab smack into the middle of Tom's forehead, knocking poor brother on the seat of his pants. Tom wasn't hurt. But he was absolutely dumbfounded by what had happened. Bewildered and wondering why Dad had busted him in the mush, he looked up, pleading for a logical answer.

"Gee whiz, Dad! What the heck did I do?"

Before either one of them could recover their senses, I made a very wise decision and hastily departed the house, heading for tall timber. Dad never caught me but Tom sure as hell did. And I paid a price—but it was worth it.

Unfortunately for Tom, we shared the same bed. All of us are creatures of habit and my brother was no different. At night when he prepared for bed, he always pulled his pants down to his ankles and then, sitting on the edge of the bed, removed his shoes, socks and finished removing his pants.

Soooooo! One night, I lifted the bottom sheet and placed half a dozen thumbtacks on the mattress.

Later in the evening, I followed little brother into the bedroom to witness his reaction to sitting on a tack. According to routine, he pulled his breeches down and plopped his bottom on the bed.

Up he jumped almost like he was climbing an invisible ladder with the sheet tacked to his behind, his teeth clamped shut and his face a brilliant red. Not waiting any longer, I barreled out of the house and into the night to save my own hide. I could hear him yelling after me, *"Yee-ow! I'm gonna get you Teddy! I'm gonna kill you!"*

As soon as he was able to disengage himself from the sheet and pull his pants on, he was in hot pursuit, chasing after me. But there was no way he could find me in the dark. He searched the shed, back yard, the outhouse, and all the while continued to bark threats. Eventually he gave up, returning to the house.

Now, I had created a problem for myself. As youngsters often do, I hadn't thought this thing out very well. And soon I realized that I had no place to sleep. I certainly couldn't go back to the house, not with Tommy ready to kill me.

Well, it was the woods again; I'd become accustomed to sleeping there.

I'd Rather Die Than Go Shopping

During my teen years, my Grandmother all but dragged me into Portland to go shopping with her. Those brief excruciating excursions were torture. And though they only occurred once or twice a year, that was often enough to give me a nervous twitch.

For the life of me, I could never understand why she did certain things that were sure to rile people.

Burrowing into beautifully displayed racks of apparel, she left clothing strewn about helter-skelter. It was like she was stirring a pot of beans. And she attacked neat rows of merchandise seemingly with a vengeance, flinging stuff about like she was cutting hay with a scythe.

Wherever she went, she left a trail of victims; wilted sales clerks that resembled ten-day-old bouquets of daisies.

With absolutely no intention of buying anything, she invariably held up a piece of merchandise and asked a poor disheveled salesperson, *"What kind of price do you have on this?"*

Regardless of the answer, with a caustic tone in her voice, she always shot back, *"Well, dearie, I kin go right across the street and get the very same thing there for a whole nickel cheaper."*

Grandma's biting remarks about prices were humiliating. I felt sorry for those poor souls called sales clerks. She treated them as if they were her prey and she was hunting instead of shopping.

But that wasn't the worst of it; paying for her purchase at the checkout counter was. It took her no less than 15 minutes to complete a transaction, no matter how small it was.

Without fail, Granny never had cash ready. Never! Only after she'd examined the sales receipt first, did she begin to dig into her purse for money. And not by any means was Granny's purse small. It resembled a miniature steamer trunk. And every compartment, pocket, and crevice in that thing was stuffed full of coupons, savings stamps, small change, rubber bands, shopping lists, pictures, clippings, and so forth.

Finding the exact amount of change was nearly impossible. But Grandma persisted. Oft times, hoping to speed things up, the cashier offered to make change. But Grandma would invariably say, "*That's okay dearie, I got it right here somewhere's. Jist keep yore shirt on a few more minutes. I'll find it.*"

She'd even dump some of the contents onto the counter. And after finding the correct amount of cash needed, she'd begin stuffing everything back, one item at a time into a specific pocket, as if it had been there in the first place.

She took her sweet time and had Granny taken notice as she departed, she'd have seen a long line of impatient, grumbling, irritated customers and poor frustrated cashiers near collapse staring daggers at her.

Mom, on the other hand, was usually fun to be with when she shopped. I say *usually* because there were a few times when her shopping didn't go as planned and gave us boys a few trying and embarrassing moments.

Mom came home from Carver one evening so that she could take Tom and me shopping in Portland. We needed to buy school clothing, in particular corduroy pants. The next morning, with brother Dee tagging along, we rode the bus from Tualatin into Portland.

The big city was a beehive of activity, the sidewalks crowded with hordes and hordes of people. I always found it fascinating, the sounds of non-stop traffic, the hustle and bustle of the crowds, the aromas of cooking food wafting onto the streets from the cafes and food vendors. And the shoeshine stands always caught my attention, amazing me how those fellows could pop and snap their shine-rags.

It was near noon when we went to the Montgomery Ward store on Vaughan Street. The store—often referred to by shoppers as Monkeys—was equipped with a very nice cafeteria. And, naturally, we three boys were hungry. We were always hungry. With trays in our hand, we found a clean, empty table among what seemed like a thousand other diners and sat down to enjoy our meals.

Presently, a waitress came to clear the table behind mother. Mom failed to notice that the woman had parked a fully loaded cart of dirty dishes right behind her. Finished with our meals, Mom pushed herself away from the table, bumped the cart and upset it. The crash of dishes hitting the floor was deafening. Just about every soul in the place leaped to their feet.

Now, my mother was not one to use profanity in public. But it just poured out of her, "*S--t, oh dear, lady! Why in God's name did you park that damned cart behind me?*"

Her voice echoed off the walls and I could feel the eyes of everyone in the near-silent cafeteria staring at us. I was so embarrassed that I just wanted to walk away as if I knew none of these people. After a short and lively conversation with the waitress, Mom clammed up, thank goodness, and led us out of there.

Ten minutes later, we were on the main floor of the building beginning our shopping spree. I was quite happy to be away from the cafeteria but, still feeling embarrassed by what had just happened and just to make certain that no one would recognize me, I removed my bright red Sherwood High School letterman sweater.

No one could say that my younger brother Dee always acted like he had a full load of bricks. Sometimes he did some really wacky things, to the embarrassment of the rest of the family.

Tom and I had found the things we wanted and had stopped in the women's foundation garment department so Mom could search for a corset for Grandmother. From behind me, I heard a funny *ploop-ploop* noise and then the booming voice of my 11-year-old brother Dee.

"Hey maw! Will these things fit your dooly-ploppers?"

I turned to see him holding, stretched out full length, a huge brassiere that looked like two hammocks sewn together. Mom, with no regret, could have easily put little brother out of his misery had she a deer rifle in her hands. Without speaking one word, her laser-beam stare was enough to inform him to put those damned things down.

Humiliated, her face blazing red, she turned to Tom and me and said, *"For Pete's sakes! Puh-leese keep an eye on that idiot brother of yours."*

Mom had arranged for Dad to pick us up at a prearranged time and location downtown to take us home.

Worn out and dragging our tails, we met him as planned. Words cannot describe how delighted my brothers and I were to see both of our parents at the same time. Too many weeks had passed since we'd been together as a family. And I looked forward to spending a delightful evening at home with them.

Working our way through a throng of shoppers to where Dad had parked the car, we paused at an intersection, waiting for a signal light to change. Mom failed to notice that Dad had lagged behind a few paces and was no longer beside her. But a complete stranger was. She reached over, took his hand and sighed, *"I just wanna get home and relax a little, Toots."*

She wasn't just shocked; she was thunderstruck when she heard,

"You know lady, you're the easiest pick up I've made in my entire life."

Her face reflected the humiliation she experienced when she realized she was holding the hand of a man that was not her husband. She jerked it away and clenched it into a tight fist. And for a fleeting moment, I thought she was going to deck the guy, as innocent as he was.

Well, my red-faced mother had done it again, not only embarrassing herself but me too. In fact, I was downright mortified. But Dad, on the other hand, thought Mom's little *faux pas* was hilariously funny. Instead of being jealous or upset, he nearly burst at the seams with laughter. Tom and Dee had seen Mom's mistake too. And they couldn't wait to tell Grandma and Dick.

To be sure, the day was memorable. It was also a day that I made a promise to myself . . . a promise to become independently wealthy before my twentieth birthday so that I wouldn't have to shop with deranged people like the ones in my family.

The Pump House Tavern

With his high-pitched vocal shriek, Eddie signaled from across the swamp that he wanted to see me. As soon as I'd finished doing my chores, I hightailed it straight to his house. Right out of the blue, he asked me how I'd like to drink a bottle of beer. The stupid grin on my face gave him the answer.

After crawling up to his lofty little bedroom above the kitchen, he told me that he'd figured a way to get into their pump house where his dad stored his beer.

Mr. Wager had built an extraordinarily large pump house with outside walls eight inches thick. The cavity in the walls was filled with loose sawdust for insulation making the inside as cool on hot summer days as our old root cellar. He used the pump house to store things that needed to be cool: potatoes, carrots, canned fruit, fresh fruit, eggs and his large stock of bottled beer. The door was solidly built—like the door on a bank vault—and it was secured with an old rusty but enormous padlock.

Eddie wanted in the worst way to sample his dad's beer and, for that matter, so did I. But, to our chagrin, his father had the one and only key and he never left it lying around.

Inside the pump house, there was a trap door to the attic and, at the end of the attic, a vent to the outside. Eddie's plan was to remove the vent screen and crawl through the opening. Then, once inside the attic, one of us could shinny down a rope through the open trap door for the beer.

His scheme worked perfectly. A few days later, we were sitting in the attic of the pump house, each of us drinking stubby bottles of beer. We named the place the Pump House Tavern and took advantage of this windfall several times each summer from the time we were 14 until we enlisted in the armed forces. But seldom did we ever drink more than one bottle apiece during each of our raids.

Disposing of the empty bottles was simple. We used the walls, dumping them and their caps into the void where the sawdust insulation had settled. It was a consummate act of petty larceny.

Eddie's dad had not the slightest idea that we had tapped his beer supply until late in the spring of 1952 when he removed the siding of the pump house to replace the sawdust with commercial insulation. To his surprise, when he tore boards loose from the outside walls, he was bombarded with dozens of empty beer bottles. At the time, Eddie was in the Air Force stationed in Alaska and I was in the Marine Corps in Korea. Frank knew who the thieves were and, as a joke—at least, I think it was a joke—sent us a bar-bill demanding payment. But yet he never figured out how we pulled it off.

Grandpa's House

If invited to Grandpa's home, who in his right mind wouldn't jump at the opportunity to go? He was a marvelous cook and always had a pot of spaghetti sitting on the stove ready to feed anyone who came to visit, invited or unexpected. I loved the way he made it, with salt pork, garlic and sweet basil, and served with plenty of homemade bread and horse beans. Not to brag, but I think he made the most delicious spaghetti dinners in all of Portland.

Dad came home from Carver one afternoon to replenish our grocery stock, pay bills and pick up the mail. But first he stopped at Grandpa's for a short visit. He learned that his father wanted me to stay with him for a week and help him with some painting. When Pa relayed the message to me, the word *"painting"* didn't register. But the words *"stay with Grandpa"* did. Naturally, I leaped at the offer. Spend an entire week with Grandpa? You bet your life.

Not until the following morning when Dad dropped me off at Grandpa's did the topic of painting come up again. What a surprise I was in for. He wanted me to paint his house. Not just part of it but the entire outside of the structure, an adventurous project that took the entire week to complete.

Moments after we arrived, Grandpa went to fetch two ladders from his junk shed, eager to put me to work. Dad, just as eager to return to The Echo Inn, backed out of the driveway too quickly and accidentally knocked over the corner post to his father's fence. Grinning sheepishly like a bad little boy when he's been caught doing mischief, he asked me not to tell his dad, that he would fix it later. After propping it up, he left . . . in a hurry.

Grandpa Pileggi — he wore formal attire every day

Grandpa brought two ladders, positioning one of them against the house. He wanted me to paint the end gables first, but it was obvious that neither ladder was long enough to reach that high. No problem for Grandpa, but a big problem for me. He fetched several shirtsleeves from his rag pile and used them to splice the ladders together, making one long but really rickety extension ladder. I didn't want to hurt his feelings but I didn't want to climb up that wobbly thing. I objected and told him why. But he wasn't at all concerned about it not being safe, and pointing up to one of the gables, urged me on.

"Atsa okay, Titty! You stronga boy! You climb!"

One can easily guess what I was thinking.

"Strong my Aunt Fannie!"

His makeshift ladder reached the gables but just barely. And when I climbed, they buckled at the splice but held together, just barely. The lower part of the ladder up to the splice was easy to ascend but the upper part above the splice was nearly straight up. With the same desperation of a rock climber who had just lost his safety rope, I hung on with one hand and splashed paint with the other, praying to God that Grandpa's makeshift ladder wouldn't collapse, killing me. By nightfall I'd only painted one of the three gables and had to face climbing that shaky thing several more times.

When darkness came, I went into the house to clean up, and was drawn to the kitchen by mouth-watering aromas. Grandpa was cooking. And it smelled so good that I could hardly wait to dig in. In addition to his fabulous spaghetti, our meal included small boiled potatoes, homemade bread, butter and horse beans.

Most Italians refer to Fava beans as horse beans because of their enormous size. They're a bush bean and bear huge bean pods. After shelling the beans, they can be cooked when green or dried and used later in soups.

After saying grace in his broken English, Grandpa dished spaghetti, potatoes and beans neatly onto his plate. And then, to my utter amazement, he mashed and mixed everything together into a thick, gooey paste. I just had to ask him why.

Someone had fed him a line of bull that pre-mixing his food would aid his stomach in the digestive process. Poor Grandpa! He was so gullible. So convinced was he it was true that, had I been a physician practicing in the field of gastroenterology, I couldn't have changed his mind in a thousand years.

After eating our supper and washing the dishes, Grandpa brought out his well-worn checkerboard, challenging me to a game. He was a master at playing checkers and seldom lost a game to anyone. Whenever he and I played, my pieces disappeared like wisps of smoke. That night, I discovered one of the reasons why they disappeared so quickly. When he removed a piece that he'd just jumped, I saw him scoop up a second checker with his little finger. I grabbed his hand asking him why he had taken two.

"Sonamungunya! She'sa sticka to my fingers."

From then on, I watched him like a hawk. But still it did little good. No matter how desperately I worked at it, I just couldn't beat him.

Grandpa told me interesting stories about his youth, the difficulties of the times, and the hardships his people had endured. Constantly working, he had little time for fun things, helping his parents support his younger brothers and sisters. He chuckled, admitting that he was forever in trouble with the local authorities, and feared he would be ordered to serve in the military, something he dreaded. He dreamed of coming to America to start a new life. And in 1902, fulfilling that dream, he left Italy.

Our conversation covered several topics and eventually we talked about sports. I expressed my delight in playing baseball on Sherwood's team. Grandpa had little use for playing games other than checkers and dominos and told me that playing baseball was a big waste of time, taking up the time when young men should be working. But he never referred to the game as baseball.

"Pitsaball! Atsa no good, Titty. You playa pitsaball, you gonna be a bigga bum."

Before retiring to bed, Grandpa read a few passages from his Bible as he did every night. I think he had been baptized a Catholic when he was a youngster living in Italy. But now he belonged to a church of a different faith.

Earlier in the year, Tom and I accompanied him to his church to attend Sunday services. We proudly wore our new letterman sweaters, sitting in the front row, invited to sit there by the minister, Brother Owens. The parishioners were all friendly people but, being Catholics, we weren't accustomed to preachers like Brother Owens. He was very animated, a bundle of energy, bounding from one side of the church to the other when he preached.

We were amazed to discover that he wore a hairpiece. When he flung his arms and bounced about, the hairpiece moved, not just a little but a lot. But without breaking stride or giving it a second thought, he shoved it back in place over and over. By the time church ended, the hairpiece had twisted around so much that instead of the center part running from front to back, it ran from one ear to the other.

Brother Owens often stopped in mid-sentence, raised his arms heavenward and cried out, *"Praise the Lord."*

The congregation immediately responded in unison, echoing Brother Owens, *"Praise the Lord."*

Then from the back of the church we could hear our grandfather's voice, *"Praisa the Lord."*

But, returning to my story about painting Grandpa's house: I finished painting the gables; they took two more days. The rest of the project was no snap either but I no longer had to mimic Spiderman hanging on the side of a building. In the meantime, several things happened to cause Grandpa to loose his temper and let fly with some Italian-style profanity.

First, he found the corner post to his fence had been broken when he bumped into it while mowing the grass. I think he knew that his oldest son was the culprit.

"Sonamungunya! Somebody, he'sa knocka my fence down. I catch, I frix 'im, good."

Later, using long-handled limb-loppers, he trimmed the small limbs of a cherry tree that hung over the electric service lines to his house. One of them didn't fall to the ground but hung up on the wires. Riled again, he let loose with more rants in Italian.

Dad arrived later in the day to pay us a visit and check on my work. Before Grandpa could ask him about the corner post being broken, Pa spotted the small tree limb hanging on the service lines and told Grandpa that he'd better hide because the electric company police would soon be after him. He believed his son's line of baloney and remained in the house out of sight until I was able to knock the limb off the wires.

The living room and Grandpa's bedroom were in the front part of the house. I didn't care to go into either one of them because they always felt eerily cold and uncomfortable to me, particularly Grandpa's bedroom. That's where Grandma Ruby died. And, for no reason that I knew of, the family seldom, if ever, used the front door. Entry was always through the back door into the kitchen. On a few occasions, we sat in the living room. But most of the time, everyone seemed to prefer to sit in the middle room where we dined.

Grandpa possessed many neat things that he'd accumulated over the years. An oval framed portrait of him hung above a curio-covered sideboard in the dining room. It was a picture that I hoped to some-day inherit. Two curios on the hutch, a beautiful pink glass ice bucket and a silver stamp box, both antiques, caught my attention every time I entered the room. Another of Grandpa's interesting possessions was a goat bell attached to the underside of his cellar door. Its high-pitched ting-a-ling sound alerted him every time one of us tried to sneak down into the cellar. None of those things was expensive or rare but, to me, they were priceless treasures simply because they belonged to him.

By the end of the week, I'd finished painting Grandpa's house, feeling fortunate that I'd survived his makeshift ladder without breaking my neck.

Dad, inspecting my work before we left to go home, asked why I had spilled so much paint on the ground. But after seeing the ladder I had to work from, he fully understood.

Grandpa paid me $10 and threw in a torn hassock and an old worn guitar minus one string as payment for my work. The best payment, though, was listening to him tell stories with his accented speech and eating his specially prepared spaghetti dinners.

Taffy's Demise

Autumn was upon us and it was time to cut firewood for the winter. Grandma gave us four boys no time to object and herded us into the woods, each one of us packing an axe or a saw or a sledgehammer, and each one of us grumbling our displeasure. Selecting a couple of sizeable fir trees, we went to work. Even though she was aging, the old gal could work ten men and a team of mules into the ground. She was as strong as an ox. And though Tom and I were growing older and stronger, we continued to have trouble keeping up with her.

The first tree that we cut didn't drop as we'd hoped and, instead, hung up in the limbs of other trees. It was obvious that it would break loose at any moment and fearing a kickback, we stepped away and waited for it to topple.

To our horror, Tom's cow, Taffy, had wandered into the woods and had walked into the area where the tree was about to fall.

All of us screamed, attempting to frighten her away. But the stubborn animal paid no heed to us. Figuring that it was now or never, I dashed toward her to grab her halter and lead her away. But the defiant Jersey tried to hook me with her horns, keeping me at bay. I could hear Grandma frantically screaming at me from the top of her lungs to get out, that the tree was beginning to twist and break loose.

By now Taffy had stopped and was standing directly under it, and in seconds it would come crashing down. Trying one last time, I grabbed a stick and whacked her as hard as I could across the rump. But she merely turned toward me, her head down as if daring me to come nearer. Hearing limbs snapping above my head, I scampered away just as the tree broke loose. It crashed, lodging between a stump and another tree, coming to rest four feet above the ground. Nonetheless, it hit Taffy in the head and flattened her.

Frantically, almost hysterically, we cut away limbs to get to where she lay. Miraculously, she was still alive but in a semi-conscious state, breathing huge irregular gulps of air. One horn was gone. And in its place, a gaping hole and a steady stream of blood oozing from it. The other horn was there but loose, barely attached. Dick and Dee ran to the house and soon returned with a sack of flour. Grandma poured some into the open wound. It eventually staunched the blood flow. But we could do nothing more than let the stricken animal lay, certain that she wasn't long for this world. Amazingly, an hour later, Taffy walked out of the woods to the barn.

She never fully recovered from the accident, though, and died three months later, her temper worse than ever.

The Awakening

I t just wasn't fair. Somewhere in the world, kids slept late on weekends ... but not us. I wished that once, just once, I could sleep in just as late as I wanted and not have to get up to do chores. And I didn't want to wait until I was an old man of 25 or 30 before I could experience that luxury either.

We didn't need an alarm clock. We had Grandma. Sometimes, I think, she stayed up all night just so she wouldn't miss the chance to yell at us in the morning, and in particular at me. Her harsh, grating voice wasn't the only disagreeable thing I experienced at first light either. Tom was the other. Unfortunately, I had to share a bed with the big hairy ape. And he wasn't exactly a pretty thing to behold first thing every morning.

One sleepy Saturday morning, before Grandma had rousted us, we woke up to the baying of hounds in Wolds' woods. It wasn't unusual to hear them except that within a few minutes they were right in front of our house. And they made a horrible racket. The dogs belonged to Chet Fischbuch. And quite often, he and some of his friends hunted fox that inhabited the wooded areas around us. I never had an occasion to see a fox myself. And I never knew whether Chet or the others ever saw one either. But from the racket the hounds made, I presumed they did.

Chet was a phenomenal marksman with a rifle and shotgun and a fair horseman. He and some of the locals even built a skeet shooting range with a sheltered dugout in the field just west of the wooded area where old Joe Miller had lived. When one heard volleys of gunfire down Herman Road, it signaled the arrival of the fall hunting season.

Later that afternoon, we heard shooting and knew that Chet and the others were at the skeet range, practicing their marksmanship. Often volunteering to work in the dugout loading the trap with clay pigeons, we boys made a beeline down there. It wasn't dangerous but it was exciting. When the shooters were ready to take a shot, they yelled, "*pull!*" That was the signal for us to trip the release mechanism that flung the clay targets into the air. We tried to trick the shooters, directing the flight of the pigeon in a direction that they least expected, to the left, right or straight ahead. Most of them were excellent shots but on occasion they missed one. And after the day's shooting ended, we boys searched the tall grass looking for the few saucer-shaped discs that were still intact, returning most of them to Chet. But we always kept a few for our own amusement.

Joe West

I was surprised to see Joe West at the range. He was one of my grade school classmates and a distant relative of Chet's. He'd moved away just before we'd graduated from the eighth grade, and I hadn't seen him but a few times since then. He'd come to practice shooting and was carrying a beautiful 12-gauge, double-barrel break-action shotgun. It had two triggers, side by side but staggered within the trigger guard so the shooter could fire one barrel at a time, that is, if he were careful.

Holding a magnificent weapon like his was like holding something that only a millionaire would own. To my surprise, Joe offered to let me shoot it. Both chambers were loaded and, when I was ready, he flicked a clay pigeon in the air by hand. It went nearly straight up. I took careful aim and squeezed the trigger. But not being familiar with the gun, I squeezed too hard and quite unintentionally fired both barrels simultaneously. I found myself pounded into the ground, sprawled out on the seat of my pants. It was a nice gun but that thing had the kick of a Missouri mule.

Thinking about Joe's shotgun that evening, I wondered if I'd ever own something as nice. I always wanted two things when I grew older: a pair of leather lace up steel-toed work boots and a 30-30 Winchester lever-action rifle.

Hitting the sack that night, my shoulder felt as if it had been struck with a two-by-four club. And my butt didn't feel much better either. I must have crushed up fifty pounds of gravel when I hit the ground. The pain in my shoulder was soon forgotten and I fell into a deep sleep.

Sometime during the night, I began to dream. And as usual, my dream was about doing something heroic and daring. This time, I fought off a giant snarling beast saving a beautiful raven-haired, fair-skinned maiden from certain death. So grateful was she that the beautiful young thing clung to me, her gentle arms wrapped around my neck holding me tight. I'd only hugged a girl a few times and even in my dreams, I was still bashful. But conjuring up some bravado, I wrapped my arms about her waist and melted in luxurious bliss, enjoying the feeling of her soft sweet breath on my cheek.

Barely audible at first, I became aware that someone was calling my name. The calls became louder and harsher. "*Teddy! Teddy! Teddy!*" I recognized the voice; it was Grandma trying to wake me.

Gradually I became conscious that it was daylight. And I also became conscious that I was embracing something hairy. It was no beauty with cherry red lips either. It was Tommy. Instantly angry, instantly feeling revulsion and disgust, and equally disappointed, I wanted to beat the living hell out of him. Just as hard as I could, I snapped him on the cheek with my fingers. As if stung by a bee, he popped straight up from a sound sleep, angry as an old boar hog, snarling at me,

"*You jerk! Why'd you hit me? What did I do?*"

"*Aw, yer nuts! I didn't touch you. It's time to get up and do the chores.*"

Let me tell you—I was grateful that Grandma had awakened me when she did. I shudder to think what might have happened had she waited another five minutes.

High School Football

Our football team suffered more humiliating defeats in one season than most teams did in ten. We were so inept at playing the game that when we scored a touchdown—the only one all season—the entire town celebrated. At least we had a perfect record for showing up at games. That should have counted for something.

We fielded about 18 kids for varsity football. That was enough for a team but not enough for a decent scrimmage.

Our equipment included the old Knute Rockne style leather helmets that a person could fold and put in their hip pocket. Every other school on our schedule used bucket helmets. And facemasks—they were unheard of in our school. And they were something I certainly could have used. While nearly every other team in the state operated from the "T" formation, we continued to operate from the old fashioned single wing. We were behind times, we were small, we were slow, and we got the hell beat out of us.

Centers in the single wing have to peek between their legs to snap the ball to the tail back. And I played the center position. After snapping the ball, I had to look up to block someone. And that's when I most often got a forearm across the snoot. My nose had been broken and mashed so many times that it kind of flip-flopped back and forth on my face and bled continuously like a dripping faucet from the first play to game's end. My poor busted beak was like a signpost. It pointed in the direction most plays were being run.

We played schools that had more boys in the freshman class than we had residents in all of Sherwood. McMinnville, for example, was one of those schools. Every fellow on the team was six feet tall and weighed 200 pounds. And there were so many players that at halftime, they were still pouring out of the dressing room. And, boy, did I ever get beat up in one of our games with them. Of course, the first injury I suffered was a smashed nose. Then I lost a tooth, got a split lip, hurt

Practice snaps, Teddy centering the football to
Peter Gale (note the old headgear)

my foot and suffered a painful hip pointer. And all of that took place in the first quarter.

The score at halftime was so ridiculous and so one-sided in favor of McMinnville that it prompted George Wolfe, one of our offensive guards, to say, "*I hope they play their girls the entire second half. They got better padding.*"

His remark tickled my funny bone, the only bone in my body that wasn't broken. But somehow I managed to grin with a split lip.

Our biggest rival was only a half dozen miles away—Tigard. Even though Tigard was a much larger school than Sherwood, the games were competitive and always nasty, rough and rugged.

Arriving at school one morning a few days before a game with them, we found that they'd paid a visit to our town during the night. The side of our school building had been covered with green paint and the word *Tigard* written on the football field. Our principal's house suffered the same fate, green paint splashed on it. Green was one of Tigard's school colors. We were outraged and planned to get revenge.

That night, at least a dozen of us visited Tigard High School. It was after dark. Some of us had brought a few buckets of red paint, one of our school colors. We proceeded to paint slogans on their bleachers and football field. And one of our gang shinnied up a drainpipe and crawled through a window into the home economics classroom. There, he found an alarm clock and, setting the alarm to go off 11½ hours later—about mid-morning—he unscrewed a vent screen and placed it inside.

The next day, all *hob* broke loose. The school boards, faculties, and student bodies of both schools met to condemn the vandals and put an end to the foolishness. It was over.

We got our butts kicked on the football field. They beat the stuffing out of us. But we might have had the last laugh. When that alarm clock went off, the students vacated the school believing it was a fire drill.

During a game at Vernonia, Red Whitehurst, one of our linemen, unintentionally caught a deflected pass. Never having the opportunity to carry the ball, he was momentarily stumped and just stood there, stock still, looking at it. Immediately, two opponents tackled him from opposite sides, hitting him at the waist. Their arms wrapped around him, they slid to the ground pulling Red's pants and hip pads down to his ankles. Red remained standing upright with nothing covering him from the waist down but a flimsy jock strap and a flaming blush on his butt, so red that it rivaled his hair. Truthfully, it was a little difficult telling just which end of Red was up.

Momentarily, everyone on the field and in the stands fell silent. You could have heard the down of a thistle touch the ground. But when everyone got over the initial shock of seeing Whitehurst's freckled pink rear end exposed to the world, the place erupted into sidesplitting, hilarious laughter.

As far as I can remember, the officials never blew a whistle to signal the play dead. But nonetheless both teams stopped action and quickly huddled around poor humiliated Red so that he could readjust his uniform. I'm certain no one in the stands caught the number on the back of his jersey because there were just too many other distractions to be seen, if you know what I mean.

To soften the blows to the head, Billy Galbreath padded his helmet with, of all things, sanitary napkins.

In a game played in Sherwood one evening, he lost his helmet when he made a tackle near the sidelines. When the dust cleared, three Kotex napkins were lying next to it. Players from both sides quickly moved away when they saw those things. Billy did too. He even tried to hide. But it was obvious the helmet was his because he was the only player not wearing one. He had no choice but to claim it. But the Kotex stayed put.

Billy was super embarrassed, to say the least. But not as much as he was the following Monday when one of his classmates asked in front of half the student body if Kotex was a brand he always used.

Then we had a game with Junction City . . . Where in the world was Junction City? None of us knew. If it was so insignificant that none of us had ever heard of the place before, we figured the town had to have a lousy football team.

After nearly two hours on the school bus, we arrived in the small farming community north of Eugene. It didn't look like much of a place causing our spirits to soar even more, figuring the game was going to be a cakewalk.

We were already on the field when our opponents came out of their dressing room. You should have seen those suckers. They looked like 300-pound apes loping onto the field, dragging their hairy arms behind them. And they wore washtubs for protective headgear. They just grinned at us during introduction as if they knew something that we didn't. The captain of their team looked like King Kong himself. Even his hair had muscles. And he was positioned on defense right over center. And the guy who played center was ME. Looking up at that massive monster was like staring up the trunk of a 500-year-old oak tree.

Well, they stomped the tar out of us. And I can assure you that there was little joy on the old school bus going home that night.

Believe me, not one of us ever forgot the town of Junction City, its football team, or its location on the map.

In another game at Sherwood, I got creamed making a tackle. During kickoffs, I usually dropped back into the center of the field as a safety, in case the rest of the team failed to tackle the ball carrier. It happened often and it happened in this game. The receiver waltzed through our tacklers like Arthur Murray on the dance floor and headed straight down the field right at me. I hadn't noticed that my brother Tom had fallen and, regaining his feet, was closing in on the ball carrier from another angle. In perfect tackling form, I dropped down low and hit the guy at the hips, connecting solidly. And just as I hit him, Tom hit him too. But my head just happened to be between the ball carrier's hip pads and Tom's shoulder pads. All three of us went down in a heap.

Nearly everyone in the place saw what had happened. Several players carried me from the field and laid me in the grass on the sidelines. I tried to regain my senses but I was still woozy when someone asked me what had happened. I really didn't know. But I blurted loudly for the entire world to hear.

"Some dumb jerk kicked me in the head."

My remark evoked a chorus of laughter from the sideline spectators because they knew the *dumb jerk* was my brother.

The Watermelon Capers

A fter playing a Friday night football game, one would think that the boys of Sherwood would enjoy spending time with their girlfriends. But, no, not us! We raided watermelon patches, instead. We were better at swiping watermelons than wooing girls or scoring touchdowns.

Two hours after losing another of our Friday night games, four of us in an old jalopy prepared to make an assault on Art Peterson's melon patch. His melons were literally ripe for the picking. Getting to them though without being detected was a bit tricky because he owned a couple of alert dogs.

We drove back and forth past his house until we were satisfied that the family had retired for the night. Stopping several hundred feet up the road, we intended to cross a wide pasture to where he'd planted his melons. The only obstacle was a barbed wire fence bordering the property.

First to crawl through it, my brother Tom discovered too late that it was electrified. When he got a jarring jolt of electricity, he yelped in surprise and tried jerking away. But his coveralls got caught on the barbed wire.

We made enough noise that Peterson's dogs heard us and began barking. And almost immediately, backyard floodlights flicked on, illuminating the countryside as if it were a San Quentin prison break. The rest of us in near panic jumped in the car and drove off leaving Tom to fend for himself.

Before Peterson could catch him, though, Tom managed to free himself and ran straight for home. I was already home when he burst through the front door. He looked like an enraged rooster. And before I could offer an excuse for leaving him, he whaled the bejeebers out of me.

One warm night after being thumped rather soundly in another game, 12 of us—two thirds of our team—raided Ray Borchers' huge watermelon patch. With several melons in our arms, we crossed stubble fields and potato patches and crept through filbert orchards, taking a shortcut into Sherwood. We made our way to the house of Homer Haines, our loveable high school janitor, intending to leave a watermelon on his back porch as a surprise gift.

Most of the kids remained hidden in the bushes in back of Homer's house while two of us crept onto the back porch. There was absolutely no light, none whatsoever, making it difficult for us to see where we were going.

None of us knew that Homer slept on his back porch during warm weather. And it was as much a surprise to me as it was to him when I bumped into his cot. Losing my balance, and my grip on the melon, I dropped it right in the middle of his stomach.

Suddenly wide-awake and wrestling with something heavy on top of him, he bellowed like a wounded buffalo. This sudden outburst in the black of night scared the soup out of us and we fled like scared rabbits, bounding into the darkness to join the rest of our gang of thieves.

Gathering together in the shadows several blocks down the road, we giggled and laughed until our sides ached, wondering what Homer thought when he discovered that he'd been attacked by a watermelon. He probably thought that he was about to be robbed.

We continued our escapade, making our way into town to Al's Corner Tavern. Through the open double doors, we were surprised to see our victim, Ray Borchers, sitting at the bar, sipping a beer and visiting with a few of his friends. He had no idea that he, too, was about to receive a gift, a gift from his own watermelon patch.

We managed to creep up to the open doors without being seen and rolled a watermelon across the oil-treated wood-plank floor toward Ray. An uproar of laughter rolled from the tavern when the patrons noticed that a watermelon had suddenly appeared from nowhere and had come to rest under Ray's stool.

Nodding at the melon and laughing uncontrollably himself, Ray was finally able to blurt out, *"Some poor sap musta had his watermelon patch raided."*

Barely able to contain our own laughter, we again scurried off into the dark, back to one of the filbert orchards to enjoy feasting on the remainder of our plunder. We had finally accomplished a successful raid and congratulated each other.

The following Monday at school, we'd gathered in the hallway to talk about the weekend when Homer, pushing his broom ahead of him, sauntered up to us with a big grin on his face. He probably sensed that we were a little uneasy as he momentarily chatted with us about trivial things. The way he acted, though, we knew that he knew we had paid him a visit.

As Homer left us to continue his work, he said, *"By the way! If you boys know anybody who lost a watermelon Friday night, tell 'em I ett all of it."*

For several days, our good buddy Homer winked and smiled as he passed us in the hallways.

Erwin Galbreath drew a map, detailing the location of a patch of watermelons growing near Cipole School. His map was a thing of beauty. Neatly drawn to scale, it included a corn patch, an acre of seed onions and a field of potatoes. But he made a colossal mistake. He failed to include a small patch of squash right next to the watermelons.

Five of us parked our car on Cipole Road and, in the dark, snuck along a dirt road toward the patch. We passed the potato patch, the seed onion patch and the cornfield arriving at what we thought was the watermelon patch. We found and picked three of the largest melons ever grown in these parts, paying little attention to their irregular shape and rough exterior. Worried that we could never get the three huge trophies and the five of us into the car, we decided to eat one on the spot. Being surprised that we had taken large, yellow, seedy squash was an understatement. But, strangling Erwin on the spot was a real possibility. And he knew it.

Some of the Japanese, who had been placed in internment camps at the beginning of World War II, returned to Oregon and resumed farming. One, who lived midway between Sherwood and Tualatin, grew nice watermelons in a patch near the highway.

Gene Gehring, Tommy Pickens, my brother Tom and I decided to try to filch a couple one night. However there was no convenient place close by where we could park a car. But we had a plan.

Gehring was to drive his old jalopy, equipped with suicide doors, back and forth on the highway while the rest of us went after the melons. After getting them, we were to hide in the ditch next to the highway and wait for Gene to stop and pick us up, that is, if no other cars were in sight.

It was pitch-black dark when we arrived at out destination. The moment we were out of the car, Gene drove away.

We found the patch. And after picking four or five nice melons, we quietly made our way back to the highway and crouched down in the ditch. Gene passed us two or three times but couldn't stop because of on-coming traffic. About the fourth pass, he signaled with his head-lights that the coast was clear. When he stopped, Pickens and my brother Tom jumped into the back seat. But, before I could climb in, another set of headlights appeared.

I retreated back to the ditch with two melons cradled in my arms. And Gene pulled away down the road. Again, he drove back and forth a couple of times before flicking his headlights to indicate that it was clear.

I popped up out of the ditch and stood on the edge of the road as Gene approached. But then a set of headlights appeared coming up behind him. Gene, also seeing the headlights in his mirror, sudden-ly accelerated. But the guys in the back seat opened the suicide door anyway. And just as I turned to jump back into the ditch, it caught me in the back knocking me head over heals. I landed in the ditch, both melons and the back of my head split wide open.

Right then and there, I came to the conclusion that swiping wa-termelons was just a tad bit more dangerous than playing football. At least, when we played football, we got to wear padding and helmets.

The Lettermen's Banquet

Every year, our Lettermen's Club celebrated with a grand banquet at the high school. We invited teachers, coaches and other important members of the community to attend. It was tradition, but not man-datory, that each of us brought an adult male as our guest. That person could be our father or someone else important in our lives.

Pa took time off from the tavern last year to be my guest. So this year, it was Tom's turn to bring him. John Bohlen would have been my choice but I'd put off asking him until it was too late. To avoid the embarrassment of admitting that I hadn't invited anyone, I conjured up a plan.

Since the banquet was a semi-formal affair, everyone wore white shirts, neckties, slacks and our letterman sweaters. Getting dressed for the big night, though, my brother and I encountered a problem. Neither Tom nor I were at all certain how to tie a necktie. We seldom wore one and always depended on Mom to tie it for us. It was evident that neither Dad nor Grandma knew. After they tried, our ties looked more like hangmen's nooses.

Searching our memories and studying a Montgomery Ward catalogue—and with a lot of coaching from both adults—we finally figured it out.

During the banquet, each letterman stood and introduced his guest to the audience. When it was our moment to be in the spotlight, Tom was first to stand. He introduced Dad, who was sitting between us, as his father and his guest. Then it was my turn. I was a little uneasy but I stood and I, too, introduced Dad as being my father and my guest. But I continued speaking, explaining that I hadn't bothered to bring another male person believing Dad would suffice since he could put away as much grub as any two normal human beings.

My witty little speech evoked uproarious laughter and applause from the crowd, but not from my daddy. He didn't stir, wince, blink or even look at me. But later, on the way home from the banquet, he had something to say, convinced that he'd raised an idiot.

The banquet meal was delicious. We feasted on roast turkey, stuffing, gravy, salads and cranberry sauce, all prepared by the home economics class under the supervision of one of my favorite teachers, Mrs. Olivia Wilkens. More turkeys were roasted than were needed. The three that remained untouched were returned to the refrigerators in the home economics room. They were saved for the teachers to dine on. Well, I didn't think that was at all fair. After all, the Lettermen's Club bought the turkeys so why shouldn't we get to eat them?

Determined that the lettermen should feast on the turkeys, and not the teachers, I devised a quick plan. When the festivities were nearing an end, I surreptitiously crept into the home economics room, took two of the birds and hid them outside in the woodpiles in back of the gymnasium.

Arriving at school the following morning, I got the shock of my life. Dogs had found and eaten our turkeys. The football field was crawling with canines, at least 50 of them, and the place was littered with turkey bones.

Several teachers had already gathered in the home-ec room. They were stumped trying to figure out how in the dickens dogs had gotten into the locked school building and into the refrigerators to take the turkeys. They never solved the mystery.

Chapter XI

1949–1950

Dressing Up and Having Fun

Tom and I were in our mid-to-upper teens and capable of going places on our own. And one of those places was Portland. A few times when the weather was decent, we dressed up in our letterman sweaters and white corduroy pants, like a couple of slick looking dudes, and caught the Tualatin Valley Stage Lines bus into the big city.

Strolling around the downtown area was a welcome change to the humdrum life on the farm. We enjoyed doing a little window shopping and taking in the sights: the lights, the hustle and bustle of shoppers, and the odors from the markets, bakeries and cafes. And we always went to a Chinese restaurant on Third Street for a real treat, a bowl of Chinese noodles. And, if we had the time and 15 cents, we went to the old Roundup Theater where we could see as many as five western movies in succession.

The theater was seldom crowded, probably because it had fallen on hard times. It seemed to me that it had become a flophouse for hobos, beggars and drunks, trying to find a comfortable place to nap. And it wasn't unusual to hear snoring while watching a film.

One afternoon, Tom and I were in the theater enjoying an old cowboy movie when some guy sat down in a seat a couple of rows in front of us. In the dark, he thought it was unoccupied. But it wasn't. Some hobo was asleep there, stretched out on three or four seats. One can only imagine the fellow's surprise when he got a sharp nip on the rump. And the melee that erupted from the incident was far more entertaining than the movie.

Tom and I yearned to see our mom and dad more often. So he and I made plans to visit them at the tavern in Carver.

Youngsters weren't forbidden inside a tavern in those days if it wasn't late at night, if food was served on the premises, and if they behaved and were accompanied by an adult. And because we were sons of the owners, it wasn't a huge problem for us.

One day, we conned one of our friends into taking us to Carver in his Model A Ford in exchange for a free hamburger. Tom and I got dressed up in our finest togs and, wearing our lettermen jackets, thought we looked like a million dollars.

Mom and Dad had no idea that we were coming; it was a huge surprise when we waltzed in. The old man, grinning from ear to ear, his buttons popping and proud as a peacock, introduced us to everyone in the place—and I mean everyone.

We spent a delightful, memorable afternoon having a great time with our parents. And we even visited with Johnny Vaughn, their trusted barkeep, and with several of the patrons. We played all comers on the shuffleboard. And you can bet that Tommy and I took advantage of the free hamburgers too . . . a couple of times.

As evening neared, Dad made arrangements with one of his friends to take us into Portland to the bus station so we could catch a bus back to Tualatin. We got home late to Grandma's consternation. But she and the others were glad to hear about our day and the fun time we'd had with our parents.

How many kids can claim they spent a serene and pleasant day in a tavern? Not many, I'd wager. But we did. It was fun dressing up and going to see our parents. And we planned to do it again soon.

Cleaning up the Neighborhood

We had a problem. Someone had been dumping trash in the woods on the other side of Herman Road. Since the end of World War II, an abandoned wagon road in the woods had become a lovers' lane. But recently, it had also become a dumpsite for trash.

It had to stop. The lovers were one thing but the trash was another. It spoiled the natural beauty of the woods, it stunk like an outhouse and it attracted flies and rodents.

I became judge and jury and was determined to punish those responsible. The perfect solution was a tire trap. Admittedly, flattening someone's tire was drastic. But I figured that those who dumped trash on or near another person's property ought to pay a penalty.

Using an eight-foot length of two-by-four board, I drove 16-penny nails through it at four-inch intervals. Next, I dug a shallow trench across the lane near where garbage had been strewn and laid the two-by-four board in it, with the nail points up. After anchoring the trap to the ground, I camouflaged it with fir needles, sticks and dried grass. Only the nail tips were visible. Then I smoothed the dust and dirt at the entrance to the lane. If anyone drove in, they'd leave tire tracks, and I'd know almost immediately that I'd caught someone.

The following Saturday morning, I found tire tracks in the dirt and knew that my scheme had worked. I'd literally nailed the guilty party. And that tickled me pink—but not for long.

Monday morning, I learned something that caused me to believe I might spend the rest of my life in prison.

One of the kids who lived on Herman Road near Tualatin told me a state police officer woke them in the middle of the night to use their telephone. His patrol car, parked in their driveway, had three flat tires, one completely flat and the other two quickly losing air. My heart sank into the pit of my stomach because I knew who had been my victim.

Worried that the cops would soon come after me, I jerked my trap out of the ground, removed all the nails and chopped the two-by-four into kindling, destroying all the evidence. Had the officer figured out where and how he got the flat tires, he probably would have concluded that someone in our family had sabotaged his car since we lived right across the tracks from the site. If he did, I didn't want anything to remain that would incriminate me.

I laid low for a long time worried that the State Police, the sheriff, and the FBI would come calling. But, thank goodness, they never did.

The Burlesque Show

Fifteen of us boys, all high school lettermen from Sherwood High School, attended a showing at the infamous Three Star Burlesque Theater in Portland one evening. Posters with the words *"Dancing Girls"* were displayed outside the theater entrance. They drew our attention. And so did the large pictures of pretty, young, shapely things clad in nothing more than a few scarves and plumes of colorful feathers. The thought of cute young females dressed in scanty costumes and dancing in a chorus line on stage brought out a prurient curiosity in me and heated the blood in my veins.

I was 17 but Tom was a sophomore and only fifteen. None of us had ever before attended a burlesque show. But, nonetheless, I thought I had some inkling of what was to come. And how do you suppose 15 kids, all of us wearing flaming red high school letterman sweaters, got into a burlesque show? It was easy, even though most of us had yet to attain the age of 18 years.

A large, portly woman who appeared to be in her sixties was selling tickets in the admissions booth. If the makeup on her face was supposed to cover her pockmarked and pasty complexion, it failed miserably. It was thicker than the paint on the side of a battleship's hull. Her hair was dyed black as squid's ink. And at least 50 pounds of cheap, gaudy jewelry adorned her flabby arms, wrists and fingers. She was in every way the exact opposite of the pretty things advertised on the placards. And that should have been a clue to what we were about to see inside.

Looking us over as we walked up to the booth, she asked with a hoarse, raspy voice, obviously that of a heavy smoker, *"Where you boys from?"*

Vernon Edwards, who looked to be in his early twenties and our leader, pointed at the red crimson "S" on his sweater and told her that we were students from Stanford. With a dubious look, she peered over the top of her glasses like an old schoolmarm, examining each one of us again. Then, shrugging her shoulders, she asked how many of us wanted to go in. Just like a bunch of dumb school kids in a classroom, we all raised a hand.

Once inside the dimly lit theater, I began to have some misgivings. Nearly every person in the place was an unkempt middle-aged male. They were rowdy and boisterous and the place was run-down, trashy, and smelled like rotten tennis shoes. Several of the derelicts stared incredulously at us. Our white corduroy pants, red sweaters and youthful appearance made us stick out like sore thumbs. One could say we were just a little bit conspicuous.

In more than one way, the place was a sewer and, very obviously, the people around us were the dregs of society. And we were about to get an education in the revolting behavior, lack of civility, and indecency of adult males.

The show began when a has-been comedian appeared on stage. His off-color, crude jokes would have made a deaf longshoreman blush. But thankfully he didn't stay long. The unruly, frenzied crowd booed him from the stage amidst shouts of obscenities and mild threats to kick his backside. They wanted to see the girls. And that they did! To the delight of the patrons-of-perversion, five women bounded onto the stage, all of them covered in feathers—feathery scarves, feathery headdresses and carrying huge multi-colored feathery fans. The audience went nuts, hooting and hollering and directing lurid invitations and indecent gestures toward them.

But something was terribly wrong. They weren't the sweet young things that were advertised on the posters outside. These women were old ladies, as old or older than my mother. For Pete's sake, a couple looked like the old gal in the ticket booth. And they certainly didn't have much in the way of talent. All they did was wriggle and jiggle and shake and prance about, stripping away flimsy things. This wasn't what I wanted to see. It was like watching my mother undress. It was horrible.

The display I was witnessing was disgusting and filled me with revulsion. I wished I hadn't taken any part in this odyssey into the so-called world of adult entertainment. Some of the younger kids in our little crowd appeared as if they'd been shot with a tranquilizer gun. They sat wide-eyed and stone-still like blocks of concrete.

After cavorting about for several minutes, the "*girls*" had nothing left but a fan. There wasn't much left to our imagination.

Suddenly, like a crazed bull, some old goat charged down the aisle toward the stage. He didn't get far, though. Three huge, burly, heavily tattooed men intercepted him and knocked his sorry butt to the floor. Then they physically carried him to an exit and literally threw him out of the building.

Slouching deep into my seat, I figured the next thing to happen would be a squad of police officers raiding the place. What a shameful mess that would be—getting tossed into jail. I could just see the headlines—Sherwood High School's entire football team arrested at a burlesque theater.

I knew one thing: this was the last time I'd ever attend one of these things. I mentally kicked myself for not spending my money on a hamburger and milkshake at a drive-in. That would certainly have been much more satisfying and a darned sight more safe. What's more, the carhops at the drive-in were more my type. They were cute—and much, much nearer my age.

The Price of a Prank

Eddie Wager had the money, Alan Hanegan had the car, and I had the ideas, a lot of them. The three of us could have done some exciting things together. But we didn't. We didn't even take part in normal high school activities such as dances and proms. Our fun time was to drive Alan's old Model A Ford Coupe through downtown Sherwood on Friday nights—only once—and then go home.

Alan and Eddie were awkwardly bashful and never dated girls until after their discharges from the Armed Forces. I dated a few times but I had no money to spend on girls let alone transportation to take them out on dates. We certainly were not considered live wires by the opposite sex. And without a doubt we were three of the most naïve and dull humans on the face of the earth.

On occasion, we tried to perk up our lives. One instance was an overnight stay at the beach in Seaside. We rented a room for $12 in a fleabag motel for one night and thought we were really big spenders. Alan and Eddie didn't want to go on the beach; they were too bashful to be seen in their swimsuits. So we spent most of the afternoon driving back and forth on the streets of Seaside looking at the girls. The most exciting thing we did that night was a peanut fight in our room.

I cooked four meals—all of them the same—runny eggs, half raw potatoes, and bacon burnt to a crisp and dripping with grease. Well, it wasn't two days in paradise. But it was okay.

When we returned home, we were happy with the knowledge that we had at least gone someplace on our own without someone else telling us what to do or how to act.

One monotonous Friday evening, Eddie, Alan and I decided to watch a Zorro movie at the theater in Sherwood. When we were ready to leave the house, grandmother pressured us into taking Tom. Now, that made four of us. And because Hanegan's Ford Coupe only had room for three in the cab, one of us had to ride in the trunk. Since Alan owned the car and drove, and Eddie had a nasty cold, it meant that it was either Tom or I who had that privilege.

The trunk, with the lid up and latched to keep it open, was reasonably safe if we were careful. It wasn't the most comfortable place to ride. But it wasn't any big deal to us; we did it all the time.

For once in our youthful lives, Tom and I compromised, agreeing that he would ride in the trunk to Sherwood and I in the trunk on the return trip home.

As soon as we entered the theater, all four of us bought popcorn. But, being a soda pop junkie, Alan also bought a coke. Unfortunately, my buddy was one of the most uncoordinated individuals I'd ever met. With too much to hang onto, he bumped his elbow when taking a seat and spilled the soda pop in his lap. As dark as it was, we could still see well enough that it appeared he'd wet his pants. How could we not laugh? Alan, grumbling and uncomfortable, his pants not only wet but sticky, threatened to make us walk home if we didn't stop giggling about his unfortunate mishap.

By the time the movie ended, it had grown dark outside and Alan's pants had dried enough that his problem wasn't noticeable. Nonetheless, to make him feel at ease, we surrounded him to prevent others from seeing his damp spot.

Eddie Wager

We were hungry and wanted hamburgers. So we agreed to go to the drive-in restaurant in Tigard, some six miles away. As the others crawled into the car, I walked around to the back, lifted the trunk lid and latched it. Alan started the engine and, as I bent over to climb in, a comb I carried in my shirt pocket dropped to the street. I shouted to Alan "*don't go.*" But he thought I was seated in the trunk and had yelled, "*let's go.*" As I bent down to pick up the comb, he drove off and left me standing there with one foot suspended in mid-air.

Quite certain that the dopes were playing a prank on me; I didn't bother to yell and waited for them to return. But when they didn't, I got miffed, certain they were hiding somewhere nearby, perhaps in an alley. Finally, I gave up waiting and walked around the block looking for them. I became more ticked off with every step. When I couldn't find them, I realized the jerks had actually gone off and left me. I thought maybe they'd done it intentionally. There was nothing else for me to do but go home, and the easiest and fastest way was to walk the railroad tracks.

In the meantime, believing that I was seated in the trunk, the three knuckleheads drove to Tigard. Arriving at the drive-in, they ordered hamburgers and milkshakes. Alan told the carhop that another person was sitting in the trunk and that he, too, would like to order something. She probably believed they were pulling her leg when she looked and didn't see anyone. Saying nothing to them, she returned to the kitchen to fill their orders.

They soon began to wonder why I was so quiet, why I hadn't come forward to talk to them.

Checking the trunk and not finding me, Eddie offered, *"He's probably gone to the restroom."*

But after a few more minutes had ticked by they knew something was wrong, very wrong.

Becoming increasingly uncomfortable, they discussed the possibility that I might have fallen out of the trunk onto the highway. After wolfing down their burgers, they returned to Sherwood, scanning the shoulders and ditches on both sides of the roadway. They looked around town and reentered the theater, asking if I'd returned. Not finding any sign of me, they re-

Alan Hanegan

traced their route back to Tigard. But they drove slower, doing a more methodical search. Still nothing. So they drove to my house hoping to find me there.

Parking on the tracks, Eddie and Alan remained in the car while Tom went to the house to see if I was home. The two cowards didn't want to face Grandma, trying to explain to her that they'd lost her grandson somewhere on the highway.

When they found that I wasn't at home, their nervousness increased unsure of what to do next. They decided to scan the highway once more between Sherwood and Tigard. Only this time one of them would stand outside the car on the running board.

Not long after they'd gone, I arrived home and sauntered wearily into the house. Grandmother told me the kids had come looking for me and had gone again to resume their search. She was quite amused when I explained to her what had happened and agreed to go along with a trick I wanted to play on them.

Walking out to the railroad tracks, I hid nearby waiting for the knot-heads to return.

It wasn't long before I spotted their headlights down the road. Alan stopped the car on the tracks as he'd done before and Tom walked to the house to determine if there was any news of my whereabouts. While they waited, I crept up behind the car and, ever so carefully, lifted the trunk lid and slid inside. Slowly lowering the lid, I kept it propped open with my foot to get some air and to prevent myself from being locked inside. Surprisingly, I could clearly hear every word Alan and Eddie were saying.

A few moments later, Tom stuck his head out of the door and yelled that I wasn't there and for them to go home and not worry, that I would eventually show up. Undoubtedly, Grandma had played her part beautifully.

They were beside themselves with concern, almost certain that I had fallen from the trunk and was hurt or possibly dead, my body lying in the ditch somewhere along the highway. Then Alan suggested something strange. He thought that perhaps I had gone to see Mary Ann Dean, a girl who lived about three miles away near John and Frances Bohlen's place. She was someone I scarcely knew. Bewildered by their thinking, I was barely able to control my giggling as they backed out of the driveway and drove toward Mary Ann's house. As they proceeded down the bumpy graveled road, talking about the incident, they continued to fret, deeply concerned about me.

Nearing Mary Ann's house, Alan told Eddie that he thought the trunk lid was ajar because it was rattling something awful. He was right about that; I was doing some things to make noise to draw their attention.

Alan stopped the car at the edge of the road and asked Eddie to re-latch the lid. When Eddie raised it to get some leverage to slam it shut, I threw my sweater into his face, growling menacingly. Eddie was so alarmed, so frightened and startled, that he jumped backwards, tumbling into the roadside ditch like some drunken sot. His girlish screech and the resultant ruckus frightened the life out of Alan. And he bolted from the car like a scared rabbit, running some distance down the road.

Crawling from the trunk, I sat on the rear bumper and visualized the hilarious sight of Eddie somersaulting and tumbling backwards.

I roared with sidesplitting laughter. I couldn't help it. I'd pulled off a fantastic prank and had scared the ever-loving pants off both of them.

Within seconds, though, I found myself sitting in the bottom of the ditch with a bloody nose. So mad were they that one of them socked me. Then the two jerks drove away and left me. For the second time that night, I was faced with taking a 2½-mile-hike home, one big price to pay for pulling a small prank.

The Mustard Incident

One day at school, I had the misfortune of incurring Venita Boutwell's wrath. I'd much rather have faced a family of snarling, ticked-off Tasmanian Devils than her. She was mad as a wet hornet and tore into me like a buzz saw ripping through a piece of stove wood.

Mrs. Boutwell was one of Sherwood High School's teachers. And I have to admit she was a good one. But she had a reputation for being an extraordinarily strict disciplinarian and a no-nonsense person.

Other than harassing the life out of my pal Eddie and playing pranks and jokes on my friends and family, being a disruptive kid or a bully was not normal for me. But one day, as I was finishing some artwork in the Home Economics room, I deviously set out to taunt the girls who sold hot dogs to the students at noontime. I guess it was a way to get their attention to notice me. And I was successful.

The room was empty when the noon bell rang. But I knew the girls would soon come for their hot dogs, buns, mustard and other supplies. As a teasing joke, and with no intent to keep it, I took the one and only container of mustard, nearly a full gallon jar of it, and hid it on a shelf in a hideaway ironing board cabinet built into the wall. But the jar was too large for the shallow cabinet and it was impossible to completely close the door. Before I could hide it elsewhere, three girls came in to fetch their supplies. Now stuck with my stupid scheme and not wanting to be discovered, the only thing I could do was lean against the cabinet door to keep the jar from toppling to the floor and try to look innocent.

Unable to find their mustard, the girls turned on me. Somehow they knew that I was responsible for it being missing. The silly grin on my face must have given me away. And, before I could speak a word, one of them ran into the hallway to find a teacher. And she found one standing just outside the door. It happened to be Mrs. Boutwell.

In an instant, the irate woman was standing right in front of me. She ordered me to step away from the cabinet and be quick about it. When I opened my mouth to ask why, she bellowed, "*NOW!*" What else could I do but obey?

The jar toppled from the shelf, burst when it struck the floor, and splattered mustard all over her legs. It was awful. She was livid, her face blazing with anger. And I was certain that my demise was imminent.

Fumbling frantically for my handkerchief, I whipped it out of my pocket intending to wipe the mustard from her legs and dress. She screamed at me to get away from her. Her next order was to get my tail downtown and buy some mustard, and to be quick about it. I beat it out of the school, yellow mustard covering my corduroy pants and shoes, and ran to the store, lucky to have enough money to purchase two small jars.

When I returned, Mrs. Boutwell was still waiting, standing knee-deep in mustard, and steaming like Grandma's teakettle. She gave me one whale of a lecture, so scathing that she could have taught Granny a few things. I offered to have her dress cleaned but she never responded, only glared daggers at me.

I'd done some stupid things but this had to be near the top of the list. The attention I got from the opposite sex wasn't what I'd hoped for. Because I'd acted like a dimwit, I was certain every girl in school believed that I was a drooling, bumbling idiot.

From that day on until I graduated, I stayed clear of the girls' hotdog stand and avoided Mrs. Boutwell as if she had leprosy. And to this day, I hate the sight of mustard.

Little Iodine

When Charla was born, my brothers and I thought she was a cute and cuddly little thing. And for a time she was. But, as she grew older, we slowly but surely changed our minds. She turned into a pest, a roguish little squirt, who was always in our hair, bugging us.

We didn't dare grab her when she'd done something irritable because of her deafening scream. And before age five, Charla could escape our clutches as easily as an elusive leprechaun. It would have been easier trying to catch a cottontail rabbit in a patch of blackberries than trying to run her down.

By the time she was two years old, Mom was already having a terrible time keeping up with her, worrying constantly that she might wander down the railroad tracks or up into the woods. But, being the intelligent and resourceful person she was, Mom solved the problem and purchased a harness, strapping it to Charla. Then she attached a dog leash to the harness and fastened the free end of the leash to a goat chain that was tied to an oak tree. Charla could no longer meander about but, like a little puppy-dog, she had the run of the back yard.

Little sister managed to do something to embarrass us more than once, and in particular, when we were in a public place.

One instance occurred the day that Mom had taken us to Portland to shop and had instructed Tom and me to keep track of her. That was a chore that neither of us found pleasant.

Sitting in a café eating our lunch, Charla whined continuously, drawing the attention of other diners to our table. During a lull in our conversation, we heard a funny string of popping sounds coming from our little sister. With a pained grin on her face, we realized she was passing gas. People sitting at tables nearest us also heard the noise and looked our way. I'd like to have ducked out of sight but Tommy was already as far

Little Iodine, Charla Marie

under the table as he could crawl. And there just wasn't enough room for me too.

When our parents purchased the tavern, Mom's absence was difficult for all of us. But it was especially so for our little sister since she was so young. And then to think how difficult it must have been for Grandma, in her advanced years, to care for an infant as active as Charla not to mention watching after the rest of us.

Finding things to keep our little sister entertained and out of trouble wasn't an easy chore. But one wintry day we hit on something that thrilled her to no end . . . and kept her out of Granny's hair for a couple of hours.

Snowing steadily for a couple of days, a thick blanket of white powder covered the earth, deep enough that we decided to hook Queenie to the clod buster sled and have some fun.

As we harnessed the old mare, Grandmother dressed Charla with bundles of clothing and slipped worn stockings over her shoes and hands for extra protection from the freezing weather. She looked like a large stuffed doll with big eager eyes.

We placed her in the middle of the sled for safety and piled on with her. Spanking our horse on the rump, we slid smoothly away, down Herman Road toward Cipole. I think old Queenie enjoyed the exercise just as much as we enjoyed the ride. Surprisingly, little sister never uttered one word. But when we returned home, the words just poured out of her. She was so excited that she could barely contain herself. And she was a very good little girl for the rest of the day.

Weeks later, Mom came home for a few days to relax, take care of family matters, visit with us and Grandma and spend part of a day shopping in Portland with Frances Bohlen.

From the moment our mother walked through the door, Charla talked non-stop. She babbled on and on about everything that had happened on the farm since Christmas, including the sled-ride in the snow. If there were any secrets that we didn't want Mom to know, Charla eventually blurted them out.

She settled down, though, and for a short time was a model child. But when Frances arrived and Charla learned that her mother was going shopping with her friend, she kicked up a ruckus. She wanted to go too. Mom attempted to explain to her little daughter that she wanted to visit in peace with Frances and do a bit of shopping. But it wasn't to be. Charla wouldn't stop whining. So, Mom gave in and agreed to take the little imp with her. Poor Frances was also hoping to spend a quiet day with Mom, catching up on all the latest gossip. But she knew there wasn't much chance of that happening, not with Charla tagging along.

We boys felt sorry for those two women and yet we were glad they were taking the little squirt off our hands.

Frances and John had been acquainted with my parents long enough to be close and intimate friends. They had been together through good times and bad times. So there were few secrets between them. Frances knew that Mom had not planned to have another baby after Tudie's birth and that Charla was an *accident.*

Because baby sister was always whining, a big pain in the butt, and because of her earsplitting screams when she wasn't getting her way, Frances sometimes referred to her as "*It*" and nicknamed her "*Little Iodine*" after a rambunctious cartoon character.

The ladies, with Charla in tow, rode the bus to town and went to Montgomery Ward to look at foundation garments. Surprisingly, Charla quieted down and became a model child for a change. But, it wasn't to last. As Frances was examining corsets and discussing the garments with a sales lady, Charla boomed out, "*You need all of those!*"

The day passed by without further incident until they returned to Tualatin on the bus. Little Iodine stood on the seat between Mom and Frances, peering curiously at the passengers behind them. Suddenly, interrupting their conversation, Charla pointed at one of the riders sitting near the rear of the bus and in a shrill voice loud enough for all to hear, bellowed.

"*Look, Mommy! There's a lady back there and she's got a dead cat around her neck.*"

Every soul on the bus turned to look at the woman, an attractive lady, who had become quite embarrassed by all of the attention. The dead cat was really a fashionable fox-fur stole.

Mom shrunk into her seat, too humiliated to face the woman and offer an apology for her little daughter's outburst. Frances, too, couldn't help but squirm feeling a little shame herself. She leaned toward Mom and, not too subtly, suggested, *"Ethel! Why don't you just drown that kid? I don't think any jury in the world would convict you."*

Overhearing Frances' comment, the faces of the passengers sitting nearest broke into huge grins and some even nodded in agreement.

Echo Inn

Taverns attract trouble like a fat wallet attracts a pickpocket. Before Mom and Dad assumed ownership of The Echo Inn, it had a reputation for being somewhat of a tough and rowdy place. Most of the tavern regulars were hearty, down-to-earth loggers who just wanted to quench their thirst and relax after a day of hard work. And some were hell-raisers, wanting to blow off steam. But then there were a few who were nothing but trouble as soon as they stepped through the door.

Dad had delivered beer to taverns for years, had even done some bartending, and he knew the problems he was facing when he bought The Echo Inn. He didn't mind people drinking a few beers and having a good time. But he disliked obnoxious drunks and boorish behavior. It wasn't long, about two days in fact, before he was tested and had to deal with a disruptive patron.

Mom had been forming hamburger patties in the kitchen. And fearing she might lose her wedding band, she removed it. When she finished with the burgers, she forgot to restore the ring to her finger and went about her business, waiting on customers.

Later in the afternoon Mom was tending bar when a tall, rangy logger entered the tavern. After consuming a couple of beers, he began to flirt with her. She assured him that his amorous advances were useless because she was a married woman. But he didn't believe her; she wasn't wearing a ring. She even told him that she had six children. But, still, that didn't stop him. And he became even more feisty and insistent.

Mom was capable of handling touchy situations herself. But Pop had had enough and, confronting the man, told him that if he couldn't behave himself, he'd have to leave. The fellow, not knowing Dad had wrestled professionally, sized him up and decided to challenge his authority. Pop rounded the end of the bar. And before the guy knew what was happening, Dad hoisted him over his head and threw the unruly fellow through the screen door as if he were tossing a javelin.

Before ending his first week in business, Dad had to physically toss out a few more boisterous and disorderly customers. Before long, the word got around that Pop was one tough hombre and it was unwise to tangle with the new owners. The reputation of the tavern began to change for the better.

The first fellow that Dad ejected returned a few days later, not to give Dad more trouble, but to apologize for his rudeness and misbehavior. Demonstrating his sincerity many times during the following weeks, he soon became a trusted and loyal friend.

The Echo Inn was one of a few small business establishments in Carver, a tiny logging community located midway between Portland and Estacada on the Clackamas River. In addition to the bar and a kitchen, the Inn was equipped with food booths, a regulation-sized shuffleboard, and a large round wooden dining table placed next to a stone fireplace. Mom and Dad's sleeping quarters was a tiny

Dad behind the bar at the Echo Inn Tavern

one-bedroom house next door. Both buildings were old and creaky structures and built above Carver Park at the top edge of a steep bank.

A bridge spanning the river at Carver connected two major highways. And the only nearby competition to the Inn was the Rock Garden tavern to the south across the river.

One dreary night, Dad was about to close when two fellows, both wearing overcoats, entered the front door. One of them approached the bar asking Dad for a pack of cigarettes while the other man, with his hands in his coat pockets, stood by the door closely watching Dad's every move. Pa had been around long enough to know that he was about to be robbed and most likely at gunpoint.

As the fellow at the bar reached into his coat pocket, Dad heard the sound of a single *"click"* behind him. Hearing it also, the two strangers looked past Dad and, seeming to stiffen, slowly removed their empty hands from their pockets. Dad's close friend and bartender, Johnny Vaughn, had positioned himself in the doorway to the kitchen with a loaded rifle cradled in his arms. He, too, sensed something unpleasant was about to happen and was prepared to shoot it out if necessary.

The man at the bar mumbled something under his breath and told Dad to forget the cigarettes. Both men quickly exited and sped away in a car. Dad called the State Police and other nightspots in the surrounding communities to alert them. And within a short time the two men were caught trying to rob another tavern.

During hot summer days, hordes of people descended on the community in search of a place to swim, picnic, fish, and relax in a cool, quiet environment. One of their targets was the park. It was a serene, treed area and an ideal place to picnic and party.

Late one evening, Dad was exhausted and not feeling well. Since business was slow, he asked Johnny to close for the night. Johnny readily agreed. And Pop was soon in bed in the little house next door. But he couldn't fall asleep. The racket from a boisterous party in the park below the tavern kept him awake. After a couple of hours, Pa gave up, crawled out of bed and returned to the tavern. Johnny asked what was wrong. And Dad told him. He also told Johnny that he could go home, that he'd close since he was up. Johnny argued but, when Dad insisted, reluctantly obliged.

Twenty minutes after his barkeep left, an explosion rattled the windows. Dad wondered what the heck had happened.

A few minutes later, his trusted friend returned and, looking solemn, announced that the party in the park had broken up. Then Johnny's face broke into a wide toothy grin. He revealed to Dad that he'd thrown a stick of dynamite into the park from the bridge. And the partygoers took flight like a band of pigeons.

Johnny's confession worried the life out of Dad. Fearing the law would take his bartender away, he instructed his loyal friend to never speak of the incident again. He didn't. And nothing ever came of it.

We children yearned to see our Mom and Dad. So, whenever we had the opportunity to go to The Echo Inn, we jumped at it. In fact, Tom rode his bicycle to Carver on at least three occasions. It was a distance of well over 40 miles in one direction. And most of it was on narrow, winding, unsafe roads.

There was another enticing reason for us going to the tavern too—free, mouth-watering, scrumptious hamburgers. My parents made the best hamburgers in the country, probably because they toasted the mayonnaise-coated buns.

Tom and I, playing summer baseball for the Lion's Club in Tualatin, pressured our parents to allow us to bring a few of our team members to the tavern for free hamburgers. Reluctantly, the old man gave in. After an afternoon game in Oregon City, eight of us, with ravenous appetites, crammed into one car and went to the inn.

Like the Italian that he was, Pop was beside himself and flung his hands in the air and slapped the top of his head, whining, *"For Pete's sake, Ted! You said a few of your teammates, not the entire team. I'm gonna go broke feedin' this bunch."*

For some time I'd planned to pull a slick prank on Tommy and now was the time to put my plan in action. While he and the others were conversing with Mom at the big dining table in the rear of the tavern, I made my way into the kitchen. Johnny had just finished making burgers for us. But before delivering them to our table, I put some tiny, but very hot, red peppers into one of the sandwiches. Gleefully chuckling, I asked Johnny to please make certain that my unsuspecting brother got the *treated* sandwich.

Returning to the table, I was barely able to control myself. I kept visualizing Tom's reaction when he discovered that he was eating fire.

Johnny placed a burger in front of each of us and stood back. Hungry as a bunch of hound-dogs, we dove in, eagerly devouring our food. I watched Tom's face closely for the first signs of panic. But, suddenly, it was my mouth that began to sizzle, like I'd bitten the hot end of a blowtorch. I twisted around and saw Johnny standing in the kitchen door, arms folded, watching me, and grinning from ear to ear. My friend, the turncoat, had turned the tables on me and I had become the victim of my own underhanded shenanigans.

One brutally warm Saturday afternoon, the inn was swamped with a relentless surge of hungry people. And nearly all of them ordered hamburgers. Shorthanded and on the verge of being overwhelmed, Dad, Mom and Johnny handled everything themselves. Mom was in the kitchen slapping burgers together. And Dad and Johnny took turns running the bar, taking orders, and fetching supplies.

Mom was near collapse, partly from the rush of orders and partly from the stifling heat of the stove and the exceptionally warm day. But she endured and kept flinging burgers and buns on the grill. Dad tested her Indian temperament many times by yelling at her, through the service port, to fill the orders quicker.

Late in the afternoon, Dad, his face aflame with embarrassment and frustration, burst into the kitchen with several partially eaten hamburgers and bellowed, *"What the hell's the matter with you, Ethel? There's no meat in these things."*

Unbelievably, Mom had flung four or five sandwiches together, forgetting to put meat patties in them. She shot back at him nearly deafening the old man and every other soul in the place, *"If you want meat in these damned things, Elmer, you make 'em yourself."*

Dad, for some silly reason, dumped the remnants of the meatless sandwiches on Mom's sizzling grill. And that did it! She was no longer a calm, serene little Indian gal but a savage on the warpath.

Scooping up a partially thawed 20 pound loaf of hamburger meat, she mashed it over the old man's head. Then she stomped out of the place, leaving him bewildered and stunned and raw hamburger strewn about on the kitchen floor.

Quick thinking on his part, though, bailed him out of trouble as far as the tavern was concerned. He enlisted the aid of two loggers, who were just sitting around guzzling beer, to take orders, clean up and fetch supplies while he flipped the burgers and Johnny tended the bar.

In the meantime, Mom, frustrated and angry, took a quick shower, changed clothes, packed a bag, and hiked down the road toward Portland. Four hours later, after a hitched ride, two bus rides and a three-mile walk, she arrived home to the surprise of us children. She was still angry, but not so much at Dad as she was at herself for leaving him in such a mess.

A few days later, a florist delivered a bouquet of flowers to her, a reconciling gift from her husband.

The next morning, Mom, looking as cute as a new bride, walked back to Tualatin, caught a bus into Portland and then one to Carver. Four days later, however, they had another spat. And this time it was Dad who ran off in a huff.

We were happy to see our parents no matter why they came home. But, Grandmother, on the other hand, had become a little miffed by their childishness.

"Good grief! Sometimes yore parents are worse than you dadburned kids. Somebody oughta spank their danged rumps good."

Johnny's younger brother Red, a tall strapping, handsome kid, but a hotheaded hellion, barged into the bar one night looking like he'd run his face into a meat grinder. He'd obviously been in a fight. Everyone in the bar gathered around as he explained what had happened.

Returning from Portland, he became angered when a car overtook and passed him in an unsafe manner. Determined to teach the other driver a lesson, he overtook the car and forced it to stop. Both drivers exited their vehicles in a snit. Red, seeing the other fellow was smaller in stature, didn't wait for an explanation and took a swing at him. He missed with his punch but the other guy didn't, jolting Red with a sharp jab in the face. Again Red swung and again he got a fist in the face. Over and over, Red swung furiously at the other guy. And over and over, the other guy pummeled Red in the face with precise accuracy.

Never once landing a blow, cut and bleeding, Red backed away, his hands raised conceding defeat. The other driver wasn't even breathing hard and in an almost apologetic voice, informed Red, *"Hey, fella! You didn't give me a chance to warn ya. I'm a professional boxer."*

Cliff Chitman, a stubby middle-aged man with thick glasses, owned and managed the service station across the highway from The Echo Inn. He loved fishing and he liked Dad. And Dad liked him. But Cliff was the town gossip and a scheming prankster. As far as scheming was concerned, however, he was about to meet his match in my father. And then some!

During a conversation about handguns and bragging that he was a good shot, Cliff challenged Dad to a shooting match. Dad owned an old chrome-plated .32 revolver that was a piece of junk and a danger to shoot.

Betting two dollars on their marksmanship, they met in back of Cliff's station to shoot through a sizeable knothole in a solid board fence. Pa fired five shots at the knothole without touching wood. Cliff, striking wood every time, couldn't match Dad's amazing accuracy. Nearly speechless, he asked Dad if he could examine his pistol. The chrome was peeling and the weapon rattled when shaken.

Returning it to Dad, he commented in disbelief,

"How can you shoot that danged thing, Elmer? It's an antique. It's just a wonder it didn't blow up in yer hand."

"It ain't the gun, Cliff. It's the man."

Dad's haughty reply chafed Cliff somewhat but, reluctantly, he paid the two-dollar bet. The word soon spread around the community that not only was Dad as strong as an ox and able to whip most men in the county, he could shoot like Billy The Kid as well.

Dad had a secret, though. His gun had been loaded with blank ammunition. Cliff never knew. But he wasn't about to allow my dad to best him without paying a price. And, gleefully, he knew what he had in store for his friend.

Cliff sold fireworks to the public when it was still legal to do so. And he always had some left over. This year was no different. And he was going to use a few large firecrackers to torment Dad.

Three mornings in succession, Cliff detonated a large firecracker under Dad's bedroom window, waking him from his sleep. On the fourth morning, Pa was ready for him.

Cliff snuck under his window and was about to light an M-80 fire-cracker when he heard a voice, *"You're gonna die, Chitman."*

Cliff looked up only to stare into the barrel of Pa's .32 caliber re-volver. Jumping up, he ran back across the highway toward his station. And Dad began banging away with his gun. Of course, he didn't fire at Cliff; he discharged it into the air. But certain that Dad was shooting at him, he yelled and screamed, *"Don't hit the gas pumps! Don't hit the gas pumps!"*

The gun was again loaded with blanks—and again Cliff didn't know it.

Dad thought he'd had the last laugh. But he didn't. He was careless and left a couple of the blank rounds on a nightstand in his bedroom. Mom, believing they were empty casings, eventually discarded them into a wastebasket. And not long after, my father's conspiring ways were revealed to the world.

Mom and Dad had given us boys a Morse code set for Christ-mas when we were younger. Two thin wires connected two battery-powered send-and-receive units to each other. A switch on each unit permitted the operators to choose the kind of signal they wanted to receive: click, buzz, or flashing light. But with the volume and light turned off, one could still feel a signal being transmitted by placing a finger on the switch.

When we'd outgrown the toy, it was stored away in a closet and was soon forgotten. Dad remembered it, however, and took it to the tavern. He intended to use it, sending signals to Johnny when they played cards with their friends.

During chilly winter nights after closing, Dad and Johnny invited a few of their logger friends to play pinochle at the big table in the rear of the tavern. With a cozy fire burning in the stone fireplace, they often played into the wee hours of the morning, sipping beers that the losers had purchased. And Dad and Johnny seldom lost.

One morning before opening, Mom gathered all the wastebaskets from the house and the tavern and dumped the contents, most of it paper, into the fireplace. The two blank pistol rounds were among the trash.

That night after locking up, Pa started a fire in the fireplace before he and Johnny sat down to play cards with two of their friends. A few moments later, both rounds exploded in quick succession, sending sparks and cinders flying across the room. The four men quite natural-ly believed someone was shooting up the place. And in their panicked haste to take cover, upset the dining room table.

Recovering from the shock, they soon realized they weren't about to be murdered. The two card-playing loggers realized something else too. They'd spotted the wiring and strange electrical gadgets taped to the underside of the table. And that's when they knew they were going to get free beer for a very, very long time.

Cipole Characters

Every community has its share of memorable characters. And Cipole was no different. This story is about three of those people—Clarkie Johnston, Herman Schmidt and Erwin Galbreath. They lived at the edge of the Cipole Swamp and they were friends. But they were as dif-ferent as apples and oranges and nuts—especially the nuts.

Clarkie Johnston and my brother Dick were the same age and in the same grade in school. He was a blond-haired, oval-faced, gangly kid who never acted like the sharpest tack in the drawer. But he, in fact, was just the opposite. He was just as intelligent as the others in the community. But it was his manner and slow speech that gave people the impression that he was just a tad bit slow on the draw. When Clar-kie spoke, people usually fell asleep before he finished a sentence.

Clarkie might have been a little mischievous at times. But I can't recall a single incident when he was. He was never overbearing, always gentle, courteous and well mannered, particularly so with women and older people. Every blessed time he greeted my mom, he'd say, *"Howdy Miz Pileggi. Yore the purtiest woman Ah've seen all day."*

Now, when you speak that sentence, slow it down to one half of your normal speaking speed and you've imitated Clarkie to a "T."

Herman Schmidt, a crusty old German immigrant, lived in a shack across the highway from where Clarkie lived. No one

Clarkie Johnston holding a weaner pig

knew his exact age but he had to be in his seventies at the time. A bachelor, he had little income, if any. He more or less lived off the land: wild blackberries, fish from the river and nearby creeks, dandelion greens, a few egg-laying chickens and the generosity of his neighbors.

Herman loved fishing even though he probably never possessed a fishing license in his life. He caught crappie by the buckets. So everyone referred to the old guy as Crappie Schmidt.

Naturally, he spoke with a deep guttural German accent. It was difficult to understand him. And when he spoke, he sprayed saliva. If a person didn't relish being showered with spit, he or she stood some distance from him. And to the horror of some, concentrating on Herman's every word, they soon discovered his speech was liberally laced with crude language.

Erwin Galbreath was the third in the trio of memorable characters. His mother was Mary Galbreath, a tiny, white-haired widow of Italian heritage. She had several children, four of them boys. And though this story is not about her, she was a memorable character in her own right.

A kind lady, she treated every child as if he or she were her own. But we learned early in our young lives that it was best to leave her alone during radio broadcasts of the Portland Lucky Beavers baseball games. She loved the Lucky Beavers and was beyond being an avid, loyal fan; she was a fanatic. Not a flood, a tornado nor an earthquake could have prevented her from listening to Rollie Truitt, the voice of the Lucky Beavers, as he broadcast the games on the radio. When her team scored a run or made a spectacular play, she cheered, danced and shouted with glee. But, if the game wasn't going well, one had better duck out of the way because it wasn't uncommon for her to hit the radio with a broom or throw a shoe at it.

Erwin was Mary's youngest child. Half the time, he was a fun kid to have around. And the other half, he was still a nice kid but a pesky pain in the neck. Like Clarkie, he too was about the same age and in the same grade as my brother Dick. His older brothers, Joe, Bud and Bill, ran the family farm. But Erwin—he just ran—usually from one of his older brothers who wanted to kill him for one reason or another.

Erwin had a habit of making a funny sound, kind of like snorting, when he talked. And when he ran, he sounded just like a horse. He could proudly squirt spit for a distance of 15 feet through a sizeable gap between his two front teeth. And his feet were not proportionate to his build. One would think their large size would make it awkward for him to run. But, to the contrary, he could run with considerable speed, particularly when he was in trouble and needed to vacate the premises. And that was fairly often.

One warm summer day, Herman, Clarkie and Erwin with my brothers Dick and Dee went fishing for crawdads in a pool at the foot of a waterfall in a remote area of Yamhill County. Now, Dick and Dee were memorable characters themselves. But that's a different story. The boys took potato chips and soda pop for snacks and a cook pot and seasoning to cook their catch.

Using a rope, the kids lowered Herman down a steep bank to the edge of the pool. And in short order, the old fellow had filled the pot with water and had built a fire to heat it. He was ready to cook a mess of crawdads.

The kids discarded their clothing and went skinny-dipping in the pool. They caught the crawdads by hand, gobs of them. And soon, Herman's cook pot was filled. Then the horseplay began.

The kids paired up—Clarkie and Dick versus Dee and Erwin. They had a dandy water fight. But Clarkie and Dick claimed Erwin cheated. He didn't splash water on them with his hands; he spit it at them through the gap in his front teeth.

Presently Clarkie had had enough and crawled atop a rock in the middle of the pool. He stood there with his eyes closed enjoying the warmth of the sun on his bleached, naked body. In the meantime, Dee, Erwin and Dick continued paddling around in the water just having fun, waiting for Herman to call them to feast on their catch.

Dee spotted a sizeable mature crawfish at the base of the rock where Clarkie was perched. With the precision of a mongoose attacking a snake, he caught it. Glancing up at Clarkie, he spied a certain male appendage and immediately a wicked thought popped into my little brother's head. Holding the crawdad up, the critter snapped onto poor unsuspecting Clarkie with a vengeance. Suddenly feeling a horrible pain where he had never felt this kind of pain before, he looked down at the crawdad that had clamped onto him and cried out in his normal slow manner, *"Ah damn, that smarts!"*

Clarkie swatted the crawdad and sent it skittering across the pond like a flat rock. But the pincer, broken off, still hung onto him with a firm excruciating grip. After a few agonizing seconds, he managed to pry it loose and, with a mild curse, threw it into the water. Not only was he hurting, he was also bleeding.

By this time, Dee had become so weak from hysterical laughter that he was barely able to keep his head above the surface of the water. Having swallowed some and choking, he was finally able to blurt out, *"You can kill me if you want to, Clarkie. But, I just had to do it."*

Clarkie in his slow, droning manner replied.

"Aw, that's okay Dee. Ah wuz never gonna use that thing fer much anyway."

The Looney Clan

If anyone called you loony, a word that means you're crazy, wouldn't you be tempted to punch that person in the nose? Well, we had friends that we called Looney and they didn't punch us in the nose. It was their real name, just spelled a bit differently. And by no means were any of them off their corks.

The name Looney is Irish. Actually, it was O'Looney. But when some of the clan migrated from Ireland, the letter "O" was dropped.

George and Mildred Looney were both west coast natives. They lived near Sherwood in an old house near the railroad trestle at the upper end of the big swamp not far from the Steyaerts. They, too, had several children.

Sometime near the end of the war, the family moved to a place near Roamers' Rest and Jurgens' Park at the junction of Highway 99W and Tualatin Road.

George was an industrious fellow and always looking for a way to make extra money. One day he placed a table at the edge of the highway and put his wife Mildred to work selling fruits and vegetables to the motoring public. Over the following four years, their small business expanded from a simple table to a covered stand to a full service grocery.

Their only daughter, Georgia, was in the same grade as my sister Tudie. She was a temperamental, loquacious little girl who didn't like to wear dresses, hair ribbons or shoes. Simply stated, she was a tomboy.

When she was five, her mother dolled her up preparing to take her to Sherwood. Georgia threw a fit. As soon as her mother's back was turned, she snuck out of the house into the back yard and stood under a dripping bag of cheese curds hanging from a clothesline. She'd turned her beautifully combed hair, dainty dress, and black shiny shoes into a gooey mess.

When Georgia was a youngster, she suffered from frequent nosebleeds. One day while in school, her nose began to drip blood. And it seemed as if it would never stop. Naturally, her teacher was concerned and tried to get Georgia to sit still and hold her head back. But Georgia, being a bouncy little girl, refused to remain seated.

Tudie could stand it no longer and blurted out that she knew a sure-fire remedy to stop nosebleeds. It was the one that Grandma had told her; stick a knife in the ground. Of course it was a superstition thing and the teacher scoffed at such a notion. But Georgia, easily swayed, wanted to try it. Putting up a fuss, the teacher finally gave in and gave Tudie permission to poke a knife into the ground.

Sister hurried downstairs to the school kitchen, got a table knife, went to the playground in back of the school, and drove it into the dirt. And sure enough, Georgia's nosebleed stopped—eventually. And from that day on, she was sold on Tudie's method for stopping nosebleeds, swearing it worked.

George Looney, Georgia's dad was a Jack-of-all-trades. He worked on his uncle's farm, worked as a carpenter, worked in the logging industry and, at one time, drove a team of horses building roads on the coast. He even managed a restaurant in Portland. But he never thought of himself as being a common laborer. He considered himself as being a shrewd, tough businessman.

One day while helping his wife manage the fruit stand, a customer approached him carrying a box of apples, asking the price.

Rubbing his chin, he said, *"That'll be two dollars, please."*

Then looking up and spotting the fellow's shiny black Cadillac, added, *"and 25 cents."*

Tablers

Dad's great uncle Steve Tabler passed away on Friday, March 31, 1950 at the age of 61. Born in Oregon's Malheur County, he was raised in the community of Westfall under extremely difficult conditions.

Steve's father died when he was four years old. And not many years later, his mother, suffering from mental problems, was committed to the mental hospital in Salem where she died. He was forced to work as a youngster to help support his brothers and sisters and had little opportunity to attend schools. Even with all the adversity he endured in

Dad's uncle, Stephen Edward Tabler

his early youth, he matured into a wise, thoughtful person.

I had a great admiration for Uncle Steve. And the one trait that I liked most about him was that he was a fun-loving rascal, a person who took life as it came and made the most of it.

Not long after the funeral, Dad took us to visit Uncle Steve's widow, Aunt Catherine, and her family. It didn't seem right that he wasn't there. The atmosphere and conversation were subdued and lacked the excitement that it so often had when he was involved. So, while our parents visited with Aunt Catherine inside the house, we younger people went outside to give them privacy.

Uncle Steve, Aunt Catherine and their five children, Catherine Margaret, Helen Rebecca (Becky), Benjamin Edward (Eddie), Annabelle May (Annie) and Betty Jane lived for years in an old two-story house on Edison Street in the St. John's District of Portland. The property, sloping gently to the west, overlooked the shipping lanes in the Willamette River.

When we visited, I enjoyed being outside and watching river traffic come and go. Had I lived there, I'd have spent considerable time perched in their cherry tree watching the cargo ships and barges plow back and forth through the water and dreaming of far-off places.

Uncle Steve had been employed by the city of Portland for years as a bulldozer operator working in a landfill. Being a youngster, I envied him. Every farm boy that I knew dreamed of operating a bulldozer at one time or another. It had to be the ultimate in fun things to do.

And in a landfill, too! What could a person break in a landfill if one made a mistake?

Annie, a nice-looking blond, was my age. I had a horrible crush on her and even went to the trouble to determine if it was legal to marry one's distant cousin. Eddie and the older girls weren't much older than I. Yet they were more mature and always well mannered. Eventually, Eddie entered the Navy as an officer and a gentleman and married an admiral's daughter.

Uncle Steve was an avid outdoorsman and could catch fish when others couldn't. And I was

Benjamin Edward "Eddie" Tabler

certain he could spot a deer in the dark and could hear a jackrabbit's heartbeat. Who knows—had he been born a hundred years earlier, he might have become a famous frontiersman.

All things must come to an end, even the life of a good person like Uncle Ed. But good memories linger, sometimes forever.

Baseball Games Remembered

As a teenager, I lived and breathed the game of baseball. It was my favorite participation sport, and I was reasonably good as a player, but not as skilled as I'd have liked.

In my mind, first base was by far the best of all positions to play. But I wasn't the ideal person to play it. Coaches favored someone rangy, taller than average, and preferably left-handed. But I had none of those attributes. I overcame many of those obstacles, though, playing the position with all the heart and zeal of an eager youngster. My quickness and ability to leap made up for my lack of height. Plus I was decent at fielding the position and a pretty fair hitter too. But unfortunately I was as slow as a pregnant pig on the base paths. And I had a weak throwing-arm, lucky to sling the ball across the diamond without it bouncing forty-five times.

My first base mitt was made in Brockton, Massachusetts. It was the only one of its kind. I'd never seen another one like it. And I can't remember how I came by it. It was extraordinarily long, black, and the pocket was secured with straps instead of leather laces. Someone gave it to me. And when I left school, I handed it over to another kid who was as eager to play first base as I'd been.

When I played high school and summer league ball, two officials worked the games. But there were times when only one umpire was

Sherwood's Baseball Team, Tom standing second from left and Ted to his left, smiling

available. When that occurred, the fellow most often stood behind the pitcher instead of behind the catcher to call balls and strikes.

Playing for the Tualatin Lion's Club, Tom and I had played in a game in Oregon City when neither official appeared. So, the coaches agreed to let one of the local fathers, a teacher in the high school, umpire the game. He had no mask or padding and elected to call the game standing behind the pitcher. His selection to officiate was our misfortune.

The game was one of two that we played in Oregon City. And Dad had taken a few hours off at the tavern to come and watch Tom and me. He sat in the stands directly behind home plate.

In most cases, leadoff hitters are selected because of their ability to get on base and for their blazing speed on the base paths. Our coach had selected me to be the leadoff hitter—a mysterious decision indeed knowing how slow I was. Stepping to bat, I heard a familiar voice behind me shouting, *"Show 'em how to hit the ball DiMaggio."*

It was the old man and his remark annoyed me, feeling it was bad luck. But, to my delight, I smacked the first pitch, a slow roller down the third base line and lit out for first base. I was quite certain that I had an easy hit because the third baseman was playing too deep at his position. I heard the pop of the ball in the first baseman's mitt after I'd crossed the bag. But the homegrown umpire bellowed, *"Yer out!"*

I couldn't believe the call and no one else on our team could either. Amid shouts of protests from my teammates, I heard someone yell from the stands, *"Hey! You blind or sumthin'?"*

Of course, it was the old man.

A few innings later and at bat again, I hit the ball solidly and again I beat the throw to the bag by a good stride. But the umpire, never moving from the mound, called me out again. And again amidst a chorus of boos from my teammates I heard Dad yell, *"Hey! You blind or sumthin'?"*

It might have been different had the plays been close but they weren't. It was quite obvious that the umpire was prejudiced and giving the edge to his kid's team.

The third time at bat, I sliced the ball between first and second base and, as I ran down the base path, I could see the second baseman going for it. He got it and made a slow looping throw to first but far too late to put me out. But, unbelievably, I was called out for the third time. My dad cried out again, *"Hey! You blind or sumthin'?"*

I ran straight at the umpire, who was still standing on the pitcher's mound, to vent my frustration and to argue the call. I could only think of one thing to say and echoed my dad's remarks, screaming at the guy, *"Hey! You blind or sumthin'?"*

Well, the old man got away with it but I sure as hell didn't. And I'll bet you know where I spent the rest of the game? Yep! Sitting next to my pop in the stands, yelling at the so-called umpire, *"Hey! You blind or sumthin'?"*

Another memorable game was played under the lights at Tigard High School. Tigard's pitcher, Toby Lewis, a nice guy whom I respected very much, was left-handed and threw horribly wicked curve balls.

While I was batting, one of his pitches got away from him and came in on me, nailing me behind the left ear as I ducked away. The last thing I heard was the umpire calling out *"strike one."* He believed the ball had struck my bat when it bounced off my skull. I went down in a heap, sprawling out on home plate as if I'd been shot. A few moments later, when I regained consciousness, Doctor Rucker was peering into my eyes while a crowd of concerned players, including Lewis, huddled around me. Not thinking clearly, I told the good doctor that I had been hit in the back of the head, not in the eyeballs.

Woozy and light-headed, but okay, I remained in the game, and went to first base.

For some reason, I thought the coach had given me the steal sign and on the very next pitch, I was off and running for second base. I felt like I was moving in slow motion, kind of floating, figuring the catcher would easily throw me out before I could reach the bag. But he didn't. I beat the throw. And that became the one and only base that I ever stole. And I did it when I was half goofy.

Believe it or not, we won most of our games. But, one game, an American Legion game that we lost by a couple of runs was played at Hillsboro against a tough bunch of hombres. They wanted to do mayhem to me because of a stunt I pulled. It was a day game and, again, there was only one official umpiring the game. But this fellow was a regular certified umpire, one who took his position behind the plate. And, I must admit, he did a credible job.

I noticed that when the bases were empty and the batter had hit a ground ball, he routinely followed the batter down the base path, watching his feet and the feet of the first baseman while listening for the pop of the ball in the first baseman's mitt to determine if the batter was safe or out.

We were on defense in the field when one of our opponents smashed a hard ground ball to Glenn Huitt playing at shortstop. Glenn muffed the grounder and failed to get off a throw to me. I could clearly hear the batter and the umpire running down the base path sounding like two buffalo heading for a watering hole. Just before the batter reached the bag, I stretched out as if Glenn had thrown the ball me and smacked my mitt with my bare hand. Hearing the sharp whacking sound, the umpire shouted, *"Yer out!"*

Everyone, the teams and the fans, were dumbstruck by the call—but only momentarily. Our opponents erupted, exploding off their bench like a riotous mob and zeroed in on the poor victimized umpire . . . and me.

After realizing what I'd done, he changed the call and warned me not to try tricking him again, a word of caution that I took seriously. The members of the other team also had a few choice words for me. But they were words that I had no intention of taking seriously. Since we weren't winning the game, I rather enjoyed getting under their skin and riling them.

One high school team that we beat with regularity boasted that they had the fastest high school athlete in the state. His name was Jack, he was extremely fast, and no one on our team could come close to matching his blazing speed. Playing center field, he was able to catch everything hit in his direction. And he was a terror on the base paths. He had a reputation. But it wasn't for his speed; it was for his big mouth. The guy was an arrogant braggart.

During a game in Sherwood, Jack strutted up to the plate as the leadoff hitter. With a smug grin on his face, he pointed his bat directly at our pitcher, an obvious challenge. Our pitcher, Chuck Tykeson, was only a sophomore but he wasn't the least bit intimidated by the big bag of wind standing before him. His first two pitches, though, were to the outside and both were called balls.

Jack demonstrated the kind of egotist that he was. He laid his bat on home plate and, with hands on his hips, announced to the umpire that he had come to play baseball, not watch two kids play catch with each other. Nothing on earth could have riled us any more than his arrogance.

Chuck's next three pitches were the meanest curve balls I'd ever seen him throw. And all three sliced over the heart of the plate. Jack appeared stunned, so much so that he swung desperately and awkwardly at each one of them. He missed so horribly that he looked like a helpless six-year-old kid at bat.

Striking out, he angrily slammed his bat to the ground and walked back to the bench, to sit and glare at Chuck.

It was the beginning of a war, a war that we won. And Jack never got on base and never got to show off his blazing speed.

Gassed

Dad's favorite food was anything set on the table in front of him. He could make rib-eye steaks, pork roasts, chicken and dumplings, and even fried liver disappear in the blink of an eye. About the only type of pie he couldn't tolerate was mincemeat, and that was only because he once ate a slice that contained a hair. It made Pa gag, and when Pa gagged, it wasn't at all "*purty.*"

From that time on, my Pappy refused to eat mincemeat pie, regardless of who made it.

Pa was fond of soups and stews too. And in particular, he loved eating good homemade chili with beans. If there was a café in Portland that specialized in making homemade chili with beans, he knew of its location.

One Saturday, Dad took us kids to the zoo in Portland, an excursion we hadn't taken for some time. But we paid dearly because Pa had recently visited one of those restaurants that made exceptionally good chili.

Once in the car, we were trapped. From the time we left home until we arrived at our destination, his stomach growled, churned and rumbled as if it were mixing cement. As soon as he parked, Tom and I leaped from the car, inhaling huge gulps of clean fresh air. My nostrils felt as if they'd been seared by a blowtorch.

Tom and I went off on our own and hadn't seen any of the family for an hour, not until we happened upon Dad peering through an extraordinarily high wire fence looking at a herd of camels. We'd just begun chatting with him when, quite by accident I'm sure, he let loose a voluminous amount of stomach gas. It was a dad-gummed eruption, a real ripsnorter, kind of like a volcano clearing its throat before the big blast. People who were also looking at the camels and standing nearby quickly moved away from us.

Tom and I didn't hesitate one moment either. We wheeled about and took off at a fast pace, our faces blushing red, nearly the color of our crimson letterman sweaters. He yelled at us to wait. But we pretended not to hear him, and just kept walking as fast as we could.

We loved our dad. We loved him dearly. But not when he'd been eating chili with beans.

Teddy and Tommy

Melvina

It happened to me just as it happens to most guys. A girl! Her name was Melvina... and she was a heartthrob. She was lovely, tall, slender and shapely. And she made me feel like mush.

Until midway through my senior year, I'd had only three dates while in high school. And those were with girls that I had to meet at school functions. Until I became interested in Melvina, I did nothing more than flirt with a few members of the opposite sex. She said yes to both questions when I asked her to go to a school dance and be my steady girlfriend.

Asking a girl to be a steady girlfriend required certain commitments from a guy, one being that he gives his letterman's sweater to her. And so I did. Not only did I give her my sweater but, within a few days, I had also given her my beautiful wristwatch, both treasured gifts from my parents and my grandmother.

Shorty Holznagel began dating my old flame, Loyce Martinazzi. I could only conclude that she had dropped Ralph Shaw as her boyfriend for Shorty because Shorty owned a nice car and Ralph was still driving his old rattletrap pickup truck. She was working her way up from bicycles to pickups to cars. In jest, I suggested to Shorty that, if he wanted to keep Loyce as a girlfriend, he'd better keep her away from airports and yacht clubs.

We double-dated one Saturday evening, taking our girls to an accordion recital in Hillsboro. The girls were stunning, so captivating that Shorty, paying more attention to Loyce than to his driving, got a citation from a city policeman for running through a red light. Shorty was not a boorish, vulgar person. He was quite the opposite, but when he heard the siren behind us, he blurted some rather foul words, very out of character for him. It was the first time that he'd had an encounter with the law and it bothered him that his clean driving record had become tarnished.

After the concert, we stopped at a drive-in to buy Cokes and hamburgers. While sitting in the car, we spotted two police patrol cars parked nearby with lights turned off. The girls thought my comment was humorous when I warned Shorty that they were watching and waiting for him to make a mistake. But not Shorty! It made him edgy.

A half-hour later, driving out of town, hearing another siren behind him, he whipped his car to the side of the road, moaning, *"No, no, not again!"*

But, it wasn't a policeman. It was I in the back seat pulling a prank on my already nervous classmate. It evoked giggles from the girls but growls from my jumpy buddy. Other than the traffic infraction, it was a wonderful evening. But, it was the last time that Melvina and I dated each other.

Just before the end of the school year and my graduation, we broke up for some mutual reason. Perhaps it was for the best. We were alike, both of us exceptionally moody individuals. As for the letterman's sweater and my wristwatch, as far as I know, she still has them. I never had the guts to ask her to return them.

That experience alone should have cured me of doing stupid things like giving away my possessions to a girl who had captured my heart. But, regrettably, it didn't.

Graduation and Memories

Because of circumstances beyond their control, my mom and dad never had the opportunity to attend high school. However, they made certain that I did. They sacrificed their time, money and sometimes their sanity so that I could get a good education.

I loved school. And I developed a good rapport with my teachers and got along well with my new classmates. So my parents never really had to worry that I'd drop out of high school as a few of my friends had.

A few of the classes were easy, music and art for example. Maybe it was because I had natural talents along those lines. The one class that I disliked most was mechanics. It wasn't the fault of the instructor, Earl Knight, though. He was a peach of a fellow. It was because I disliked working around machinery, particularly anything covered with grease.

The subjects in which I excelled were mathematics: trigonometry, calculus, algebra and geometry. They seemed to come naturally to me.

My instructor was George Russell, a terrific person and a fine teacher. I had the utmost respect for him. And not surprising, he was a World War II Navy veteran. To me, the man was a real honest-to-goodness hero. And not only did we learn mathematics, we also heard some great true-to-life war stories.

My geometry class was small, only four students: Henry Rupprecht, Shorty Holznagel, Rudy Bohm and me. As a rule, chewing gum was forbidden in class. But because we were so few, Mr. Russell permitted it. Every day throughout each week of the semester one of us, including Mr. Russell, brought a five-stick packet of gum to class, one stick of gum for each of us.

Mister Russell once challenged me to find an easy way to trisect an angle. For years, I tried but never succeeded. And after graduating from high school, I continued corresponding with him, even from Korea when I was in the service.

Another teacher who had a big impact on my life was Jean Foster. She taught English and literature. They certainly weren't my best

Sherwood High School stage play "The Late Christopher Bean" Teddy did the stage decoration

subjects but, because she was a better than average instructor, she made the classes interesting and I did well.

With Miss Foster's encouragement, I wrote several fictional short stories for extra credit. The ones she considered to be excellent were titled, "*The Obsession, Whispers, The Old Tree, Satan's Path*" and, the longest and most difficult, "*Old Methuselah, A Girl's Dog.*"

During our junior year, my class had to study Shakespeare's Hamlet. I didn't mind studying it but I disliked standing before my class and reciting passages from the work. It didn't seem manly for a teen-aged guy to say words like *thee* and *thou* and *begone with ye*. It was embarrassing. And I didn't like it.

So, I made a proposition to Miss Foster. In lieu of reciting Hamlet before the class, I offered to write and produce a 30-minute stage play. She agreed but warned me that if I didn't do the rest of the work well or if the play was not successful, she might have to flunk me. That suited me fine; I was confident that I could do it.

So, I wrote the play. It was a comedy that I called "*Christmas Wings.*" My classmates helped me present it during the school lunch hour. It was so successful that not only did the student body roll with laughter, so did our principal Karl Kahle which surprised me because he was not easily amused.

I got my passing grade and I got out of reciting Hamlet, thanks in part to some nifty classmates who were not only great friends but real goofy hams on stage.

And I also continued corresponding with Miss Faster too until she passed away many, many years later. She was a fine friend.

High school had been a fantastic experience, a time of growing and maturing. But it was time to gradate.

Thrilled to have successfully arrived at this milestone in my life, I was also sad knowing that my years in high school had come to an end. I was also saddened, knowing that several of my classmates would be moving on and that we would never be together again. We enjoyed each other's companionship, just as if we were one large family. And that included our teachers. Now, the family was breaking up.

If the law had permitted, I'd have remained in school a couple more years. But the inevitable happened. The big night came, the 19th of May, and I graduated.

After the ceremonies had come to an end, all of us gathered in the home economics room to bid each other good luck and to say goodbye.

The room was filled with emotion, laughter and smiles, mixed with occasional sobbing, as we embraced each other, boys and girls alike. It was truly a beautiful evening, especially so because some of the girls kissed me. After Donna Erickson did, I wanted to begin the evening all over again. She had the sweetest personality, was one of the most naturally beautiful girls on the face of the earth, and could make granite crumble with her smile.

The teachers gave us a half hour to get through the emotional stuff before they came in to wish us luck. The first words out of Mrs. Wilkins mouth was to ask if Ted had been near the refrigerators, evoking a roar of laughter from the rest. I guess I had developed a slight reputation for being a chowhound.

Yes, it was a wonderful, happy evening, and yet melancholic. None of us wanted it to end. But unfortunately, like all good things, it had to.

Not A Care In The World

Now that I'd graduated from high school, I wanted to do nothing more than kick back and live a life of quiet leisure for a few months. My plans were simple: sleep late in the morning and bask in warm sunlight while sacked out in the backyard hammock in the afternoon.

But Dad had other thoughts. He wanted me to begin looking for work immediately. And he was adamant about it.

"I know what'll happen if you lay around for a month or two. It'll turn into seven or eight months or maybe a year. No, you're going to look for work now. No ifs, ands or buts about it. Try layin' around on your own hook and see how long it lasts."

Pa pushed me hard. I didn't want to be at loggerheads with him. So, grudgingly, I began searching for a job. But nothing was available in Sherwood or Tualatin, and the farmers around us didn't need my help.

The best chance I had of finding employment was in Portland. But the problem was getting there. I had no car and no driver's license. If I wanted to go to Portland, I had to take the bus from Tualatin. But that meant nearly a three-mile walk from home to Tualatin and nearly three miles back every day. Besides, I had no money for bus fare.

Other than driving a homemade tractor and throwing dirt clods, I had no specific skills to lean on. Dad often told me that he hoped I would become an electrical engineer some day. What the hell an electrical engineer did, I had no idea. And I doubt that he did either. But it sounded good to him. About the only job I could think of that I might be qualified for was driving a truck like dad. But there again was the rub . . . no driver's license.

During a two-week period, I managed to get into Portland three or four times. But, lacking motivation, I submitted perhaps a half-dozen applications for employment. But nothing came of them. It was disheartening.

Easily discouraged I slacked off and went back to the hammock. Pa was tied up at the tavern and seldom able to check up on me to determine if I was doing as he ordered. And, if I stayed clear of Grandma, she left me alone.

In the meantime, my bother Tommy wasted no time working on a new project. He was always dreaming up some cockeyed thing to build. And, surprisingly, most of his contrivances really worked.

He was in and out of the shed every day. So I just figured he was building another boat or plane. But I was dead wrong.

One afternoon I was asleep in the hammock when my brother set off an explosion. It shook me awake real quick.

The blast reminded me of Dad when he was blowing stumps. And for just a fleeting second, I thought he'd come home, found me sleeping, and blew his top. Grandma was in the house and thought I'd blown up the outhouse with gasoline again. Naturally, the first thing out of her mouth when she opened the back door to investigate was, *"Teddy! What in blue blazes did you do now?"*

I was really taken aback when I asked Tom what he'd done to cause an explosion. He told me that he'd built a cannon using a blasting wedge.

Blasting wedges filled with explosive powder were used to split logs when a regular wedge was impractical. And, unless a person knew how to use one properly, it posed some real dangers.

When Tom was satisfied that he'd thought out every minute detail and that the thing would work, he packed his makeshift artillery piece into the nearby woods and armed it, filling it with powder, nuts and bolts. Then, placing one end of it securely against a stump, he aimed the lethal end at a nearby target placed against a tree. He inserted the wick, lit it and stepped behind another tree for safety—and a good thing he did. The resultant explosion shook the woods, destroyed the stump and blew the hell out of the target and the tree behind it. The power of the blast frightened Tom so much that he nearly wet his pants. And it scared me out of a half-year's growth.

Tom never again duplicated the experiment and instead, stuck to making safer contraptions like planes, boats and canoes.

As for me . . . I wasted no time crawling back into the hammock. And immediately I dozed off, dreaming about beautiful maidens and thrilling adventures.

But my bubble was about to burst . . . or should I say, blow up . . . and not with Tommy's help either.

Chapter XII

1950–1951

Another War

Mondays through Thursdays, normally slack periods of time at the tavern, were days when Mom or Dad or both of them came home to catch up on family events and maybe take us shopping or to a movie.

It was one of those days in late June when Dad walked in the door. We were astonished to see him because he'd been home just a few days earlier.

First off, he found me dozing on the couch like a lazy sheep dog. No excuses, no explanations were good enough when he asked why I wasn't out searching for work. I was trapped. And Grandma stood right there to make certain that I told him the absolute truth, that I had put forth little effort.

That evening after supper, Dad remained at the table working his way through a mountain of bills. But a news bulletin on the radio diverted his attention away from his paperwork. North Korean armies had invaded the country of South Korea. And small units of our military were right in the thick of the battle. Perplexed and troubled by these reports, Dad finally asked, *"Where in the hell is South Korea?"*

None of us looked up. None of us knew anything about the country except that it was somewhere on the other side of the world. We weren't concerned and just shrugged our shoulders.

But Dad, remembering the events that led up to World War II, was alarmed and feared that something horrendous was building, something dangerous that could very well involve his oldest sons. And he was correct.

In what seemed like a few hours, all hell had broken loose in the Far East. And our country had become involved in another all-out gut-wrenching war.

For several days, our beleaguered armed forces fought valiantly. But the situation had become grim and desperate. The casualty lists grew and our military units continued to give up ground as the fighting intensified by the hour.

A dreadful feeling began to build in the pit of my stomach. I was 18 and old enough to fight in a war. And I was old enough to be drafted into the Army. Both were very strong possibilities.

There was hope, though. Help was on the way. In just weeks, the nightly newscasts began to report that more men, Army and Marine reservists, were being called to active duty and would soon join in the fighting. And several nations of the United Nations had also become involved and were sending reinforced military units.

In the meantime, Eddie and Alan were experiencing the same feelings of dread as me. And every time we got together, the conflict was the main topic of our conversations. We were absolutely convinced that if the fighting continued for any length of time, we'd be drafted into the Army.

Eddie and Alan didn't want to go to war. And neither did I. So, we decided that we'd enlist ... but only in the Air Force ... and only if we felt the dreaded draft was closing in on us. For the time being, though, we elected to sit back and wait.

The Driving Test

John and Frances Bohlen treated us kids as if we were their own. They even allowed us to fish and swim in the Tualatin River from their dock. The only thing they asked of us was that we let one of them know when we were going down there.

One day, Mr. Bohlen hired me to clear a patch of weeds near his house, offering to pay me ten dollars when the job was finished. It wasn't a huge patch and I would have gladly done it for five.

I couldn't wait to get started. The ground was hard as a rock though, causing me to believe that I'd be working at it for a couple of days. But I worked diligently and finished before I thought I would. I did a good job too. Mr. Bohlen was more than satisfied and gave me a friendly pat on the back when he paid me.

The next time Dad came home, before he asked if I'd been looking for work, I told him about the small job that Mr. Bohlen had given me, and the amount of money I'd earned. He was pleased. But he was also puzzled. His friend owned a small farm tractor for such jobs. So, why didn't he use it? He could have done the job in a half hour and it wouldn't have cost any more than a few pennies for fuel. His only conclusion was that John knew that I needed the money and had given the job to me out of the goodness of his heart.

None of what Dad had considered occurred to me. But I knew that he was right on target. Mr. Bohlen was, indeed, a good friend.

Tom and I had been itching to get our driver's licenses for some time. And since I ad a few dollars in my pocket, I was ready. But we had one whale of a problem. We had no car in which to take the driving test. Dad's car wasn't available because he was seldom home during the hours the Hillsboro Motor Vehicle Office was open. But we had us a plan. We took advantage of the Bohlen family's generosity and sweet-talked their daughter, Mary Jo, into letting us take the driving test in her car, a beautiful shiny black 1947 Ford Convertible.

The day was sunny and warm when Mary Jo arrived at our house. To our joy she had lowered the convertible top. On our way to Hillsboro, she pulled off the highway onto a remote gravel road and allowed us to drive a couple of miles to familiarize ourselves with her car. That was a mistake. In only a few seconds, a thick layer of dust covered us and blanketed the inside of the car.

In Hillsboro, Mary Jo waited patiently as Tom and I first took the written test.

I had diligently studied the driver's manual and was reasonably confident that I'd passed. Tom, on the other hand, had scarcely looked at the cover of the manual, let alone read the contents inside. I figured that he'd be lucky if he spelled his name correctly. But when we received our test results, I was disappointed, getting a score of 85 percent. And to make it worse for me, that dumb Tom aced it, not answering one single question wrong. I couldn't understand it. I began to think that maybe it paid to be like him—lucky and simple minded.

I was first to take the driving test. When the examiner saw the condition of Mary Jo's car, he rolled his eyes probably wondering why we allowed the inside of it to become so dirty. Before climbing in, he whipped his handkerchief back and forth across the seat, cleaning a spot where he could sit.

I adjusted the mirror as the examiner gave me some advice and then we drove away. During the next 15 minutes, the examiner told me three or four times that I was doing exceptionally well. Returning to the Motor Vehicles office, the last exercise I had to complete was parking. I had never before parked a car and informed the examiner of that fact. He told me how it should be done. Following his instructions, I parked perfectly on my first attempt. The examiner again complimented me about how well I'd driven. I was elated and quite relieved when he gave me a score of 98.

Now it was Tom's turn to be tested, and it was a good thing that I had taken the test first and that the examiner had a strong heart.

Mary Jo and I watched my brother as he confidently crawled behind the wheel. The examiner momentarily conversed with him, as he had with me, giving him some advice. And then, gesturing toward the roadway, he said, *"Drive down the street one block and then make a left turn toward the highway."*

Tom nodded that he understood and started the car. And suddenly, the shiny black convertible rocketed forward as if it were jet-assisted. The examiner's head snapped back, his hair standing straight out like the tail of a racehorse at full gallop. A split second later and a block up the street, Tom made the left turn as if on two wheels and disappeared from our sight, leaving only a trail of swirling dust behind.

Mary Jo gulped, gurgling something incoherent. I couldn't hear but I was certain it was something only spewed out of the mouths of rowdy longshoremen and surly loggers. I was stunned too by the way Tom bolted away, as if his butt were on fire.

"Man! I just hope he comes back without smashing her car to pieces and killing that poor guy."

Fifteen minutes later, Tom returned driving much slower than when he left and, as slick as a whistle, performed the parking routine flawlessly.

The examiner looked as if he'd been wind-tunnel-tested at Lockheed Aircraft. Tom had explained to him that he was unfamiliar with the car and the reason why he'd zipped away so quickly. With a trembling voice, the examiner told my maniacal brother that he was going to give him a passing grade only because he didn't want to risk life and limb riding with him again.

We got our licenses and went home as happy as two baby chicks in an incubator. And I'd bet my last dollar that the Bohlen family prayed to God that we'd never again ask them for a favor.

What's My Name?

Job-hunting was frustrating. I encountered one disappointment after another, one obstacle after another and one surprise after another. Frankly, I didn't know how to go about searching for employment. For one thing, I figured that filling out an application was all there was to it. I never once thought about returning to ask if I was being considered. And another thing: I needed a social security card. Without it, I couldn't go to work even if I found a job.

So, I got a social security card and put it in my wallet with my new driver's license. But without a car or a job, they were nothing more than two worthless pieces of paper.

The Korean War and the military draft were always in the back of my mind. I couldn't see any sense in wasting time looking for work if I was about to be drafted. And that was a definite possibility.

Tom and I accompanied Dad to a livestock auction on the east side of Portland one afternoon. I think he wanted to buy some weaner pigs. I wanted to put my new driver's license to use and had been building up the courage to ask Pa if I could borrow his car. I knew I didn't have a snowball's chance in hell that he'd loan it to me. But being naïve and simple of mind, I thought I'd try.

Dad was sitting between us when, during a lull in the auctioning, I popped the question.

"Dad, can I borrow the car for a couple of hours tonight?"

Overhearing me, Tom's mouth dropped open. Then I saw a grin break out on his dumb face as if he knew I was about to be verbally creamed. His smug reaction irritated me. But, like it or not, he was right on the money. Pa never even looked at me when he gave his answer.

"When you get off your dead butt and get a job, you can buy your own car. And you can drive it any time you want. But you're not gettin' mine. You might wreck it. And I can't afford the insurance."

Returning to Carver the next morning, Dad detoured into Portland and dropped me off downtown so I could look for employment. During the next four or five hours, I filled out just two applications. But neither looked promising even though one employer asked if I had a birth certificate to prove my age. Another surprise and another roadblock! Of course, I didn't have one. I'd never needed one before.

A few days later, with Mom's help, I submitted a request to the State of Oregon for a copy of my birth certificate. When it came in the mail, I was in for a shock.

The name recorded on the certificate was Vito Paxton Pileggi and not Theodore Vito Pileggi as I'd expected and as had been printed on all of my other identification. I was stumped.

Where the hell did the name Paxton come from? I always thought my middle name was Vito and my first name was Theodore.

Since Mom and Dad weren't home, Grandma gave me the answers. And some of them were real stunners.

Theodore was a baptismal name given to me weeks after my birth. Vito, of course, was from Dad's side of the family. So, one would believe that Paxton came from Mom's side. Well, it did—in a way. It was the middle name of Grandma's old boy friend, John Paxton Spaulding. I'd never heard of the guy before. I never knew that Granny had a boyfriend either. Of course when I asked her about him, she told me to mind my own business. If I was named after the guy, I figured it WAS my business. Another thing that shocked me was Mom's first name. It was recorded as Thelma, not Ethel. Ethel was her second name. And Dad's first name was Vito. Elmer was his middle name.

Wondering if there was something else that I hadn't been told, I immediately checked the date of Mom and Dad's wedding and the date of my birth.

Double Trouble

My two sisters were as different as night and day. Tudie played with dolls, wore ruffled dresses and enjoyed music while Charla was perfectly at ease wearing a pair of boy's shoes, chasing grasshoppers and packing a baseball glove.

Tudie was nine when, for the first time in her young life, she baked cookies, about 24 harder-than-a-rock imitation hockey pucks. Fresh out of the oven, they were thick and pasty. But after the things had cooled, they set up like concrete. We boys tried to down a few when they were warm but they tasted like chalk.

The so-called cookies were still sitting on the kitchen table the following morning when Tom, Dick and I went to the barn to milk. After finishing our chores and returning to the house, we ran into trouble. At the same moment that we entered the back door, Tudie burst into the house through the front door, bawling and carrying on as if her world had come to an end. Immediately, Grandmother assailed us concluding that we had done something to our sister and demanded that we confess.

Tudie in her 'Alice Blue Gown.'
She sang at several local schools.

Charla

I never knew why that whenever one of the girls was distressed about something, without question, Grandma figured it was one of us boys who had something to do with it. It was an automatic death sentence, especially for me, tried and found guilty every time—and without a jury.

This time, though, our brother Dee was the culprit. He was the one who had upset little Sis.

She saw him scoop up a handful of her baked bombs and take them outside. She presumed that he was going to eat them. But how could he? Those things couldn't be broken even when struck with a hammer. Instead, she caught him throwing them, skipping them across mud puddles like flat rocks.

Charla was a cute little squirt but she could make a lot of racket for a five-year-old girl. She possessed the vocal strength and lung capacity of a 40-year-old opera diva. If she didn't get her way, everyone else paid a price—a loss of hearing. She was very competitive but she was a pest, a pain in the butt to us boys. We considered her too small to play football or baseball with us. But she was amazingly athletic and could fling a baseball as far as most boys twice her age. And she hit targets with uncanny accuracy. If we didn't cave in to her whining and squalling, she'd simply steal our ball and run like the dickens. And, believe me, catching Halley's comet with a butterfly net would have been easier than catching her.

Riding herd on six unruly grandchildren and Launa—not to mention our neighbor's son Butchie Reichel because he was always there too—often put Grandma in a surly mood.

One day, Charla's incessant whining and bickering nearly drove the old girl out of her mind. Exasperated, she issued a stern and final warning to her disobedient granddaughter, *"If you do that once more, little girl, I'm gonna tan yore onery little hide."*

But Charla, being the brazen thing that she was, continued to be disobedient. Grandma had had enough and went outside to cut a hazelnut switch. Now, Grandmother often threatened us with a whipping when we'd misbehaved but seldom carried through with it. But, impish Charla was certain that she was in for it and bolted the doors, locking Grandma out. Poor Grandma was fit to be tied and, circling the house like a condor over a lamb's carcass, threatened to whale the hide off her granddaughter.

Even at five years of age, Charla knew that she'd committed an unforgivable act and that she couldn't keep her grandmother locked out

Charla at the beach, five years old

*Charla Marie "Little Iodine" and
Verna Theresa "Tudie"*

forever. After several minutes she unlocked the doors and then scrambled up the crawl ladder to the bedrooms upstairs to avoid punishment. She knew that Grandmother couldn't follow. But even then she wasn't certain and crawled out a window onto the porch roof. She jumped to the ground and spent the balance of the day at Butchie Reichel's house delaying the inevitable, a well-deserved spanking.

A few days later, Dick, driving the tractor from the barn to the house with Charla riding on the fender, hit a chuckhole and bounced her off onto the ground. Landing nearly headfirst on the hard roadway, she immediately began screaming and wailing and carrying on. The sudden, ear-splitting outbursts that came from her cavernous mouth were so loud that it frightened the life out of me. Not realizing that she had suffered a fractured collarbone, we tried to quiet her, promising her everything under the sun if she would just shut up. I wanted to preserve my hearing and, in addition to that, we knew that if Grandma heard her, she'd assume that we'd done something horrible to our sister and jump all over us.

But how could Grandmother not hear her screeching? She was waiting in the doorway when we arrived at the house. Just as I'd expected, she asked me what in blazes I'd done to my little sister. Charla, still squalling, pointed at Dick and yammered that he'd thrown her from the tractor. It took several minutes and an act of congress to convince Granny that it was an accident.

Charla quieted down to an occasional whimper. But over the next two days, she continued to complain that her shoulder hurt.

Somehow we got in touch with Dad at the tavern. That afternoon, he came home and took Charla to a doctor in Portland. The doctor informed us that little sister had indeed broken her collarbone. His final instructions to Dad, after treating his squirming little patient, were to keep her quiet.

"Do not allow her to become too active. Give the fracture time to heal."

How could Dad prevent her from being too active? How could anyone? The very next day she was outside flinging rocks at a squirrel. Nonetheless the break healed but keeping her quiet was a flipping impossibility.

Every Thursday, a hefty fellow visited the local farms driving a black delivery van, selling bread, eggs, and a variety of other foodstuffs. We called him the *bread man*. Mom happened to be home from Carver one day when he paid us a visit. The girls shouted his arrival at the top of their lungs so that he, Mom and everyone else within earshot could hear.

"Hey Mom! Its time to get bread."

Mom was mortified by the way that sounded. And, had she been able to catch her impudent offspring, I'm certain that we'd have had to visit our mother in prison for the remainder of her life.

Dee, too, was victimized by our sisters, but seldom caught on to their diabolical schemes until it was too late.

When he was in the fourth grade, he came home from school one afternoon nearly in tears, his face aflame with anger. Pouting, he told Mom

Tudie and Dee

that someone had written a nasty word on the wall in the girls' rest-room and printed his name beneath it. The girls reported it to their teacher, and she in turn collared Dee, asking if he knew anything about it.

Of course, the teacher knew that Dee was innocent because, first of all, he couldn't spell worth a hoot, and secondly, he'd never have left his name.

The identity of the person who wrote the vulgarity was never dis-covered. But years later, his sister Tudie confessed that it was she who wrote his name below it. By then though, Dee was far too late to get any revenge. One reason was that her husband was one tough hombre and very protective of his wife.

At the movies one night, Dee noticed Charla, Tudie and Launa chewing gum and asked if they had more. Tudie whispered that she had just one piece left and had already unwrapped it, intending to chew it herself. Nonetheless, she gave it to him and he popped what he thought was a piece of bubble gum into his mouth. But, it wasn't bubble gum. It was a gob of pre-chewed gum peeled from beneath one of the theater seats.

When Tom and I moved our bed downstairs, the three girls took over our space. The upstairs had never been finished and the floor, made of shiplap boards, contained a few knotholes. When the girls cleaned, they were too lazy to take up the sweepings of dust and lint and merely funneled the debris down the knotholes. And quite soon, the cavity between the living room ceiling and the upstairs bedroom floor had been filled with trash.

One hot, sultry afternoon, Clarkie Johnston, Tom, Dick and I were in the living room, chatting with each other. Grandmother, sit-ting nearby in her rocking chair, was contentedly reading a newspaper, paying little attention to us. And the girls, lying on the floor upstairs in their little bedroom, were reading as well.

Because of the poor lighting, they lit a candle and stuck it in one of the knotholes in the floor. But, the knothole was too large and the candle slipped through into the dead space igniting the accumulation of lint. In a panic, Launa grabbed a lard can they used as a nighttime commode, gave it to Tudie and she poured its contents into the knot-hole, trying to extinguish the flames.

Hearing the commotion upstairs, we looked up and noticed a wet spot forming on the ceiling directly above Grandmother. She stopped rocking, and with a puzzled, questioning look, focused in on us boys as yellow droplets began patting one corner of her newspaper.

In his slow drawl, Clarkie droned, *"Ah think ya got a leak in yer roof, Miz Barnes."*

Well, she certainly couldn't blame this one on me. No sirree, Bob! I was innocent. I had witnesses.

Fighting Fires

After doing our evening chores, all of us kids cut across the pasture with a gallon of fresh milk for our newest neighbors, Charlie and Bunny Dukes. They'd moved into a tiny house next to the tracks just east of us that had been unoccupied for some time. They were nice folks and invited us in for a cup of hot cocoa. Presently, Tudie, Launa and Charla, burst into their kitchen babbling about seeing millions of fireflies hovering above our house. Fireflies? We had seen glowworms. But none of us had ever seen fireflies around Cipole.

Stepping outside, we were stunned by the horrific sight of flames and sparks shooting 30 feet into the night sky from our chimney. We raced home to warn Grandma that she was in danger. But when we bolted into the house, we found her adding more pieces of pitch-soaked firewood to the heating stove. The metal stovepipe between the stove and the concrete block chimney was scorching red.

Grandma didn't think it was all that warm. But the house was like an inferno, as hot as the pits of hell. Grabbing what we considered valuable, we camped outside in the cool night air with garden hoses at the ready and waited until the fire had died down and the house cooled. After it was safe, we reentered the house. But we continued to keep a wary eye on the chimney and frequently examined the roof upstairs, hoping not to find anything aflame.

Fire was a constant concern to us. Had any major structure on our farm caught fire it would surely have burned to the ground before we could have summoned help. The best fire department in the area by far, was the volunteer fire department in Tualatin. The chief was Bill Barngrover, legendary for his two-fisted drinking and his firefighting skills.

A fire, probably set by transients one hot summer day, engulfed a sizeable portion of the dense woods across the railroad tracks from our house. The blaze was small, very small, compared to most forest fires. But it was still deadly. Within an hour after being discovered, a warm choking smoke had enveloped our farm. Volunteer firemen from the Tualatin Fire Department arrived, driving a couple of fire trucks and a tanker unit. And following right on their heels, armed with shovels, saws and axes, were two carloads of our neighbors. Eager to pitch in myself, I grabbed a spade from the barn and joined a fire line of sweating, grunting men furiously chopping brush and shoveling dirt to hold back the flames.

I soon found out what it was like to fight a fire. It was horribly hot, grueling and fatiguing. Firefighting was not a glamorous and thrilling adventure. And whoever started that rumor had never fought one before.

I was awestruck watching one fireman as he expertly peeled the burning bark from tree trunks with a powerful concentrated stream of water. His tactic kept the fire in the underbrush and prevented it from climbing into the treetops.

Late in the afternoon, most of the blaze had been extinguished. And we all began to relax. Taking advantage of a lull in the action, one of the Cereghino boys hopped in his car and made a run to Tualatin. He soon returned with several cases of beer. The weary farmers set up a temporary camp and while watching for any sudden flare-ups, celebrated by quenching their thirst with a few cold ones.

When half of Sherwood's old town burned to the ground, the only fire department to successfully respond to the call was the Tualatin volunteers. Sherwood's one and only fire truck, a relic and destined to become an antique within a decade, wouldn't start. While the Sherwood volunteers towed their truck through the back streets unsuccessfully trying to start the engine, the Tualatin firemen fought the fire.

Al's Corner Tavern was one of the structures to burn. And during the process of trying to save the old building, several kegs of beer were rolled to the back of the property. When no one was paying attention, a few of our high school boys salvaged a keg, loaded it into a vehicle, and secreted it under the bridge in Rock Creek at the head of the big swamp. But the keg rolled into the deep murky water and sank out of sight, never to be seen again.

One of these days I'm going on a treasure hunt.

Pushing Granny's Buttons

Grandma, cleaning and rearranging things around the house, had been on the prod all morning. She grumbled about one thing or another and had run Tom and me out of the house several times. She even ran poor MacTavish out of her bedroom, swatting the poor unfortunate pooch on the backside with a broom. She was in a snit, so it was very wise to stay clear of her. And I did—most of the time.

Sauntering leisurely into the living room, my mind a 1,000 miles away pondering the Korean War and my fate, I was quickly brought back to reality when I heard the sound of a pop in Grandma's room. Something flashed across the floor past me and bounded off the wall. At first, in my stupor, I thought it was a mouse. But after recovering my senses, I saw that it was a tennis ball, of all things.

I slid the curtain open to Granny's room to find her standing by her bed staring directly at me. She held a child's baseball bat in one hand and a broom in the other. She'd found the bat and tennis ball under her bed. Fumbling about with too many things in her hands, she dropped the ball and, when it bounced, angrily swung at it with the bat. And by golly, she accidentally hit it, sending a Yogi-Berra-type line drive under the doorway curtain into the living room.

I knew that had I smacked that thing inside the house, she'd have come after me with a delivery van loaded with freshly cut hazelnut switches.

Maybe I had a bit of a wry smirk on my face, I don't know, but I had to ask, *"Did you hit that tennis ball, Grandma?"*

She grumbled, *"Mind yer own durned business."*

Pushing her buttons a little more, I prodded, *"If I'd have done that in the house, you know you'd be after me with a stick."*

It was obvious that her impudent grandson had gotten under her skin because her face flamed red with irritation.

"I've a good mind to take a stick to you anyways, so you'd better watch yer Ps and Qs, young man. Now git outta here. Ain't you got chores or somethin' to do outside?"

Here I was 18 years old and 187 pounds and she an elderly woman. But I knew when I was overmatched. So, I vamoosed out of there. After all, she was still armed with a baseball bat.

Benny's Well

B enny Blaser was nearly a legend before reaching the age of eighteen. It wasn't because he'd done something brilliant or heroic. It was because of the wild daredevil escapades he performed with his motorcycle.

In mid December every year, the townspeople erected a large Christmas tree in the center of the main intersection in Sherwood. It didn't pose a problem for motorists; they had no trouble going around it. And the tree wasn't an obstacle for Benny either. It was a target.

On a cold blustery afternoon, Benny calmly rode his motorcycle into the intersection, grabbed one of the limbs, and rode around in circles, spinning the tree around with him as if he were on a merry-go-round. The city fathers were not at all happy. And he stayed clear of town for several weeks.

Benny wasn't really a bad kid ... just a bit of a hell-raiser. And I liked him. One could say that he was a loner, quiet, almost shy. He wasn't overly fond of going to high school and dropped out at an early age, staying home to work on the family farm.

My friend mentioned one day that he was going to re-line a well with three-foot concrete sleeve tiles. And he needed help. Since I'd worked with tiles in a couple of our wells, I offered to give him a hand. But I had an ulterior motive for doing so. Benny had five sisters. And though I had never seen any of them because they attended an all-girls' parochial school in Portland, I'd heard they were gorgeous. And I wanted to see for myself.

The well was located in the bottom of a small canyon not far from the house. To get supplies to it, we used a small John Deere crawler, a tracked vehicle used on many of the farms in the community. The dirt road down to the well was steep and bordered by several acres of black-cap cane berries on one side and a dense wood with thickets of dense underbrush and wild blackberry vines on the other.

Benny and I worked nonstop for three straight hours. He stayed up top and hoisted buckets of debris to the surface while I worked down inside the well, removing old crumbling brick.

At noon, we rode the crawler up the hill to the house for lunch. His mother, Matilda, had prepared sandwiches for us. But I was more eager to see Benny's sisters than eat. I was disappointed though. I saw not a trace of one, not even a picture.

After lunch, we loaded three two-by-twelve ten-foot-long planks on the crawler's fender and, with me at the controls and Benny sitting on the boards, began our return trip down the hill. Approaching the steepest part of the road, I threw the crawler out of gear to coast. It picked up speed rapidly, so quickly that Benny shouted a warning that I had better stop before I lost all control. I jumped on the brakes as hard as I could. The tracks nearly locked, bringing the tractor to a sudden skidding stop. But Benny and the planks didn't stop. They took flight, leaving the crawler's fender like a toboggan going off the end of a ski ramp.

When the forward ends of the planks touched ground and bit into the dirt, they upended, propelling Benny end over end into the brush. In an instant he was gone out of sight, burrowing a tunnel through the thickets into the woods. I'll never forget his desperate scream. It sounded like the shriek of a person falling over a cliff and hurtling to their doom. When I got to him, I couldn't find any broken bones but he was nicked, cut, scratched, torn, gouged and bleeding, appearing as if he'd been in a fight with a litter of angry feral cats.

Hauling Benny's carcass to the house, Matilda treated wounds on his arms, hands, neck and head with blotches of Mercurochrome and patches of gauze and tape. He looked like an overused practice dummy from a first-aid class. He told me that he'd taken a few spills riding his bike but none could compare with being slung through a half acre of brambles.

"Ma's told me a lotta times that I'm gonna kill myself someday 'cause I ride my bike too dad-gummed fast. But you! You danged near killed me drivin' a crawler that won't do 12 miles an hour on flat ground."

When we returned to work, I reluctantly went back into the well. I say reluctantly because Benny stayed atop, threatening to get even with me by sealing the well shut with me in it.

Two days later, we finished our work. Benny was happy and re-lieved—happy that the well had been properly re-lined and relieved that I hadn't asked to drive the crawler again. I was somewhat disap-pointed, though. Oh, I didn't mind helping him. But I would have enjoyed the work much more had I gotten to see at least one of his adorable sisters.

The Ranch Hand

Dad wasn't able to exert much pressure on me to find a job since he was busy operating the tavern. So, he took matters into his own hands and made some inquiries. And by golly he found someone will-ing to hire me.

The fellow's name was Lester Horrigan, the owner of a ranch near Gateway north of Maupin in Central Oregon. He was looking for a couple of strong lads to help him put up hay for the winter. The pay: $3.00 a day plus room and board. And the job started in ten days and would last approximately three weeks.

When Pa sprang this little surprise on me, I could hardly believe my ears. The thought of working on a ranch was in no way appealing to me. But, I didn't have much choice. At least doing something—even ranch work for a few weeks—was sure to satisfy him for the time being. And, if I were lucky, I might make enough money to buy a car.

I knew that John Garfield was looking for a job too. And when I asked him if he'd like to go with me, he jumped at the chance. He was a big ox of a kid and super strong. The only physical problem he had was his eyes; he needed super thick glasses to see. But, otherwise, he was in perfect health and perfect for the job. He was easy to get along with too, a great sense of humor and a toothy grin. And John owned a 1933 Plymouth Coupe providing us with the transportation that we needed.

With three dollars in our pockets, we left Sherwood at dusk, driving through Portland, taking the old Columbia River Gorge highway east. By taking turns driving and sleeping, we intended to arrive at six o'clock the following morning, in time to begin work.

John grew sleepy and, somewhere east of Portland, pulled off the highway into the driveway of an old abandoned service station to let me drive. We switched places, John in the passenger side and me behind the wheel. Making himself comfortable, he placed his jacket under his head, laid back and closed his eyes to take a nap.

A grassy ditch lay between the old station and the highway. But in the dark it appeared to be level ground. So I drove across it to get back onto the pavement. One could only imagine my surprise when the car suddenly plopped down and stopped, lying atilt on its right side.

John's eyes popped wide open. He looked through the right side window and saw nothing but grass three inches from his face. Then, he turned toward me with a puzzled look on his face.

"What happened?"

What could I say?

"We're in a ditch."

There was just enough light to see his face change color. The big guy suddenly erupted, screeching at me with a high-pitched voice in the range of an alto with flabby thighs.

"Can't you drive over 50 feet without crashin' my damned car, for Pete's sake?"

I crawled out as my fuming friend pulled himself behind the steering wheel. With all my might, I pushed, heaved and shoved upward on the right side of the old jalopy as John gunned the engine and spun the tires. And, by golly, he drove it out of there as slick as a whistle.

Clumps of dirt and a few blades of grass had stuck to the right side door handle and fenders. But, luckily, the car hadn't suffered any damage.

I knew the answer I was going to get but yet I asked,

"Don't you want me to drive?"

"Are you crazy? You're not touchin' my car again."

Later in the evening, John pulled off the highway and we slept for a couple of hours.

Arriving about nine in the morning, three hours later than planned, we ran into a hornet's nest. Mr. Horrigan was upset with us because we were late. He claimed that our tardiness had already caused him to lose a half-day's work. We found out right away that our new boss had a nasty, unpleasant temper.

The ranch, over 1,500 acres of it, was located in the most miserable part of the state, nothing but dry desert country. The nights were as cold as the Arctic and the days as hot as Hades. Added to that discomfort, there were snakes—plenty of them—and they were the kind that rattled.

Mr. Horrigan took us to the bunkhouse and introduced us to a scrawny middle-aged cowboy named Chuck. He was a regular hand who worked on the ranch during the summers. Chuck was no ordinary cowboy. He had but one arm, the other one gone above the elbow.

After stowing our gear, we hopped into the back of Mr. Horrigan's pickup truck and went to work in the hay fields.

Acres of hay had been cut and raked into windrows for quick drying. For the remainder of the day, we pitched hay, first onto a wagon and then into a barn. It was hot, dusty, tiring work. But both of us were quite strong and capable, having done this sort of work before.

We marveled at how well Chuck could handle a pitchfork with one arm. He stuck the end of the handle under the armpit of his severed arm and using it as a fulcrum, easily tossed hay up onto the wagon. And though he protected his armpit with a heavy folded cloth, John and I both surmised that it was likely as calloused as his one hand.

Mr. Horrigan's wife came promptly at lunchtime with sandwiches and hot coffee. Not getting the opportunity to eat breakfast, John and

I were starving. We unwrapped our sandwiches and discovered they were made of fried liver with a trace of mayonnaise, sparse and unappetizing. John's eyes looked like little glassy beads as he peered in disbelief at me through his quarter-inch-thick lenses. I personally liked liver. But this stuff was cold, dry and as tough as a shoe tongue. Fifteen minutes later, with a bad taste in our mouths, we were back at it, pitching hay.

Mr. Horrigan left us for 20 minute periods two or three times to fetch his pickup because we had worked our way across the field, leaving it some distance behind. His absence was a relief; he wasn't carping at us.

We worked until sunset and sunset comes late in July. So did dinner. John and I were ready to drop in our tracks and planned to go to bed right after supper. We were starving when we sat down at the kitchen table in Mr. Horrigan's house. But our appetites were not at all satisfied. Dinner was nearly the same as lunch—more fried liver. But this time it was hot.

After supper, Chuck, John and I retired to the bunkhouse. It was a small building and not much more than a dilapidated shack. A pump and water trough were close to the front door and a wash pan and an obviously used towel hung on nails on the outside wall of the shack. The outhouse was in back. Chuck told us if we wanted hot water to wash and brush our teeth, we'd have to make a fire in a little stove that sat in the middle of the room and heat it ourselves. But John and I were too worn out and wasted no time crawling into our beds, beds that were nothing more than hard cots.

After the lantern had been extinguished, I could see stars through the roof where shingles were missing.

"Room and board included—what a joke! The hop yards were better than this place."

Chuck said little while we worked in the field. But, brother, in the bunkhouse, he turned out to be quite a talker. He chattered on and on about everything under the sun as John and I tried to go to sleep.

First off, he told us that Mr. Horrigan was a real slave driver and a hard man. I had already figured that out by myself. He also warned us that sometimes snakes were found in the hay. He had nearly become the victim of snakebite on several occasions. I hated snakes and knowing they could be in the hay made me apprehensive about working here. Then Chuck told us that he'd lost his arm while attempting to break a horse. It turned on him and stomped his arm so badly that it had to be amputated.

I don't know when John fell asleep. But I drifted off during one of Chuck's many stories—a story about coyotes or some kind of wild animal.

The next day, we were up before daylight. The place had turned ice cold during the night. After washing the drowsiness out of our eyes and brushing our teeth with frigid water from the well, we went to the ranch house for breakfast. Mrs. Horrigan served us hot coffee, cold toast and more liver.

John and I climbed into the back of the rancher's pickup for the ride out into the hayfields, both of us shivering from the cold temperature. But we knew that we'd be warm soon enough.

Both of us were dying to ask Chuck a question. And we'd soon get our answer.

The first time Mr. Horrigan left us to fetch his pickup, we asked our workmate, *"How come we get nothing but liver for our meals?"*

Chuck's response was surprising.

"A truck haulin' meat turned over on a curve up the road from here a few days back. The ranchers hereabouts salvaged most of it and hauled it home. They do it all the time 'cause the stuff spoils real quick in this here heat."

Being curious, we continued to ask, *"Wasn't he able to get any steaks or roasts?"*

Chuck only shrugged his shoulders, probably as mystified as we were.

Throughout the remainder of the week, we pitched hay, sweated in the heat, shivered in the night and ate liver for most of our meals.

On Sunday, John and I suggested to Chuck that we go to Madras to see a movie and get a hamburger. He seldom left the ranch and thought that a swell idea.

We left early only to find the movie was one that all three of us had seen and none of us liked. So, we continued driving farther south to the small city of Bend. The movie in Bend was fine but the 170-mile round-trip drive wasn't worth it.

We arrived back at the ranch in the early hours of the following morning a few hours before breakfast—and probably more liver.

To our surprise, however, we drank coffee, ate toast and feasted on beef stew. No liver! We found out after lunch—which was also stew— that a vegetable truck had turned over somewhere up the road.

A few days later Mr. Horrigan surprised me when he told me to fetch the pickup. It wasn't far away, perhaps a quarter of a mile.

Thinking more about the heat than where I was walking, I accidentally stepped into a thistle. My first thought was that a snake had bitten me and, hoping it wasn't true, I sat down for a few seconds to examine my leg.

The field was rough and uneven. So I took my time and slowly drove the pickup back to where they were working. As I exited the truck, Mr. Horrigan angrily barked at me, *"The next time I tell you to do something, Mister, I want you to get the rag out."*

His tirade was a shock to me and I thought to myself, *"What's wrong with this guy? I'm trying to be careful and not wreck his darned pickup and he gives me hell. He's nuthin' but a slave driver and I don't have to take this abuse from him, not for three lousy dollars a day and liver sandwiches."*

Later in the afternoon, the temperature probably 100 degrees, Mr. Horrigan ordered John to get the pickup. John dropped his pitchfork and sprinted across the field.

Minutes later, Mr. Horrigan stopped working, his mouth agape as he stared in astonishment in the direction where his pickup had been parked. I looked up to see it bouncing wildly off the ground and coming straight at us at a high rate of speed, leaving a cloud of dust behind. Burlap sacks, pieces of lumber and pitchforks flew helter-skelter from the vehicle's bed as it bounded over the rough terrain.

John brought the pickup to an abrupt, skidding halt, stopping only feet from the hay wagon. He jumped from the cab and exclaimed in his high-pitched voice, *"When you tell me to do somethin' boss, I get the rag out."*

Horrigan was so dumbfounded, so flabbergasted that I think he swallowed his chew of tobacco.

John told me later that the accelerator had gotten stuck and that he was afraid to stop and fix it for fear it would give Mr. Horrigan an excuse to yell at him too.

That night, I quit and John drove me back home. I had $27.00 in my pocket for nine days of hard work.

Maybe, I thought, I'd better join the Air Force now and not wait. At least in the service no one would yell at me and I'd get good hot meals and a nice warm bed to sleep in. Brother! Little did I know!

Dad and Mom's Surprise

John wasted no time driving me home after I abruptly quit working for Mr. Horrigan. When we pulled across the tracks toward the house, I spotted Dad's DeSoto parked in the driveway. My heart sank because I knew he'd be unhappy when I told him that I'd quit Horrigan.

Walking in the front door, I was surprised and very pleased to see not just Dad but Mom too. And everyone was grinning. The kids and Grandma just learned that Mom and Dad had sold the tavern. And in a couple of days, they'd be moving back home . . . to stay.

I was elated. In fact, I was more than that. I was euphoric. After three long years, we were going to be a complete family again. And Grandma was just as happy as we kids. She could relax for a change and let someone else ride herd on us hell raisers.

Pa had a new job too. The moment that he and Mom had made the decision to sell the tavern, he called a couple of wine and beer distributors to determine if any sales jobs were available. Lemma Distributing, knowing his reputation, hired him immediately. Their plant was located in Linnton north of the St. Johns' bridge on the west side of town. He was going to work an eight-to-five job, Monday through Friday. That suited us just fine. Our dad would be home with us in the evenings and on weekends. And that meant we'd live normal lives again . . . and maybe go to the movies once in a while.

The day suddenly turned into a festive rollicking occasion. And Dad wasn't the least bit angry with me either, not after I'd explained to him how abysmal the conditions were working for Mr. Horrigan. But he gave me a warning. Now that he was home again, he expected me to go to Portland with him to look for work—words that I expected but didn't particularly want to hear.

Kenny and Dee

Kenny Cereghino and my 11-year-old brother Dee had become good pals just like Eddie, Alan and me. And they had also begun to copy some of our antics. Most people thought they were still delightful, innocent young boys. But they weren't. They were fast developing into conniving twerps and youthful tricksters.

One clear but cold night, they rigged a prank to pull on any unsuspecting motorist who happened to be driving down Cipole Road. The spot they picked for their bit of shenanigans was between Kenny's house and the school near where Eddie and I crashed my bike.

Stretching a strand of white packaging string across the road, windshield high, they tied one end of it to a power pole and the other end to the branch of a bush. In the dark, the driver couldn't see the string until the last second. And when he or she did, it would appear as large as a 1/4 inch steel cable. How they thought this one up was anyone's guess.

They just wanted to surprise someone and never once gave thought that their prank could cause an accident.

The two scamps crouched down in the roadside ditch out of sight and, as they patiently waited for their innocent victim to appear, conjured up another scheme. They worked out a plan to swipe a chicken and have a cookout in Wold's abandoned cabin in the woods near the Cipole rail siding.

They were giggling and having a good time when headlights appeared up the road from the direction of Highway 99. As it drew nearer and nearer, the kids scrunched down, inhaled and held their

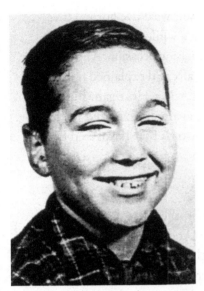

Dee, dreaming about another chicken cookout

breaths. Only a few feet from the string, the driver spotted it and crammed on the brakes. The car nearly went into the ditch as it skidded sideways in the gravel. And that scared them. They didn't expect that kind of reaction or result.

The driver bolted from his car, bellowing obscenities, and ran back to where he'd hit the string. Dee was stunned. He recognized the fellow's voice. It was Dad.

Pa barked threats, certain the miscreant was still lurking nearby and watching. Dee and Kenny dared not move. They knew full well that, had he caught them, he'd have blistered both of their butts without a moment's hesitation. Only after he drove away did the two youngsters breathe deeply again. And they vowed to each other to never pull that stunt again.

At breakfast the following morning, all of us including Dee listened intently as Dad recounted the upsetting event that took place the night before. He said that had he caught the person who pulled the prank, he'd have beaten the hell out of him. Dee never said a word. But I did.

Grinning like the idiot I am, I just had to draw attention to myself and asked, *"Did ya make a mess on the car seat, Dad?"*

Pa wasn't the least bit amused by my question. And firing back, he asked if I'd found a job. Stupid me! Eighteen years old and I still didn't have enough sense to keep my big yap shut.

Kenny's dad and his uncle had purchased Wold's woods next to our property as an investment. A shack, back in the woods some distance from the road where the Wold family had once lived, was still standing . . . but barely. With the exception of an old rusted wood-burning cook stove, there was nothing inside but a few apple boxes, a couple of burlap sacks and dozens of newspapers. The shack had become a perfect haven for hobos to take refuge and for kids to have chicken cookouts.

The plan to have their cookout was still in the works. But they had been pushing their luck for some time. Grandma and Kenny's parents knew that the kids had been swiping chickens and had nearly caught them a few times.

The little snips agreed that they needed to find a new source of poultry, one that had yet to be tapped. So, they invited soon-to-turn-eight Butchie Reichel to join them . . . but on the condition that he furnish the chicken. Well, Butchie, not being the smartest kid in the community, probably didn't realize that he would be taking all the risks. But eager to finally participate in one of their famous cookouts, he agreed.

He caught one of his dad's White Leghorns and, stuffing the frantically flopping hen into a burlap bag, lit out for the woods. And soon the trio were cooking chicken in a fry pan on a real stove.

Butchie was hooked on this cookout thing. And slowly but surely, throughout the remainder of the summer, his dad's small flock of chickens dwindled. A pile of white feathers in back of the shack, that looked more like a heap of snow, was clear evidence that the three youthful chicken thieves were eating very well.

Dad

One Friday evening, Dee and Kenny walked the tracks to Sherwood to see a movie at the Robin Hood Theater. Dee surprised Kenny, producing a bottle of wine. The little sneak had filched it from the trunk of Dad's car, one of several sample bottles that Pa carried on his route. Being immature kids and inexperienced drinkers, they swigged huge gulps of the stomach-warming liquid. By the time they reached the edge of town, they'd guzzled two thirds of the wine and had become woozy and out of sorts. Hesitant to take the bottle inside the theater, they stashed it in back of the Catholic Church, planning to drink the remainder on the walk home.

If they thought they'd enjoy the film once inside the warm theater building, they were sadly mistaken. They fell asleep.

The moment the movie ended, the two youthful sots, reeling and unsteady on their feet, retraced their steps along the railroad tracks to where they'd left their stash. They quickly finished it off and immediately paid the consequences. Before they'd reached the trestle, both had become wretchedly sick to their stomachs and began vomiting. Kenny felt as if he were going to die and could only remember crawling along the rails, praying a train would come along to end his misery.

When Dad came home the following evening, he lit on me with both feet and wanted to know if I'd taken a bottle of wine from his car. I was completely defenseless. He demanded answers that I couldn't give.

"Why blame me for taking your wine, Pa? I don't even like the junk. Maybe it was Dick or Tom."

Dad knew they had no chance to pilfer it, and he never once suspected my innocent little brother Dee, believing he would never do such a thing. So, in his mind, that only left one person to blame. Poor convenient me!

Mister Hibbard

It would have been understandable had Dewey Hibbard turned his car around and driven away at breakneck speed to summon the police. When he first drove up to our house, he must have thought he was about to witness a crime, most likely murder. But he had visited our home before and it quickly occurred to him that what he was observing was nothing more than good-natured horseplay.

Tom and I were Indian wrestling in the back yard, three of the boys, Dee, Clarkie and Kenny, had tied Tudie to a tree to keep her from pestering them, and Mom was chasing Dad around the yard with a towel, trying to snap him on the backside.

Mr. Hibbard was Dad's insurance agent. He'd been a friend of our family since my parents married. Yet, in all that time, he never fully grasped the fact that we weren't normal, ordinary human beings. We were a bag of assorted nuts and loved to play. We never hurt each other—nothing permanent that is—we just had fun.

Mom and Dad were talking to Mr. Hibbard by the time Tom and I had run around to the front of the house to see who had come to visit. After chatting for a moment and exchanging pleasantries, my folks invited him in for a cup of coffee. We hadn't taken but a few steps toward the house when the front door swung open and our dog, MacTavish, burst through it as if it were running for its life. Well, the poor pooch was. Grandma had kicked the mutt outside,

Charla, Butchie, and Launa, astride our workhorse, Queenie

assisting it along with some threatening language and a swat on the backside with a broom.

Unaware that company had come to visit, Granny was surprised when she saw Mr. Hibbard and, grinning sheepishly, quickly returned to her bedroom to finish cleaning. That was one of the few times in my life that I ever saw Grandma blush with embarrassment.

Sitting at the kitchen table with Mom and Dad and us kids huddled around, Mr. Hibbard inquired, "*Other than moving back home from the tavern, has anything exciting been happening in your life Elmer?*"

Pa, grinning, just shrugged his shoulders!

"*Naw! Nuthin' ever happens here.*"

After twenty minutes of casual conversation, Mr. Hibbard got around to the reason for his surprise visit. He wanted to bring Dad up to date on his insurance policy and determine if he needed or wanted additional coverage.

"*You're probably due to upgrade your coverage, Elmer. But when I first pulled up to the house and saw Ethel chasing you, I wondered if my company should take on the added risk.*"

Not only was Mr. Hibbard an excellent insurance agent, he was a gentleman and a wonderful and loyal friend. He treated us kids just as a kind caring uncle would treat his nephews and nieces.

During the hard times after the depression, he paid Dad's insurance premiums when Pop was short of money. Throughout the years, all of us addressed him as "*Mr. Hibbard*" although he'd given Dad permission many times to call him "*Dewey.*" We admired Mr. Hibbard and we had the deepest respect for the man.

Preparing to leave, he took the time to bid goodbye and good health to each one of us kids. Tickling Charla under the chin, he asked if she'd been an obedient little girl. She just smiled and nodded in the affirmative. Then, looking at Launa, he recognized that she wasn't a member of our family and, being a bit puzzled, commented, "*You've got a nice family, Elmer. But I thought you had two girls of your own.*"

Before Dad could determine who was missing, my grinning brother Dee piped up with an explanation, "*Oh, we do! My sister Tudie's still outside but she couldn't come in 'cause we got her tied to a tree.*"

The Stray Cat

No matter how intelligent, how worldly I thought my mother was, in many ways she was as innocent and naïve as a two-year-old child. With no intention and with little difficulty, she sometimes got into trouble in some unique ways. And the one person whom she relied on most to bail her out of a sticky predicament was Dad.

A seemingly harmless incident occurred late in the fall when she believed she was saving a homeless animal.

After our parents moved back home, we began going to the movies regularly again. Dad purchased another car, one that was newer and more useful in his new job. It wasn't as roomy as the DeSoto. But it was quite adequate for hauling all of us.

Near the theater on cold nights, we often spied a beautiful black cat lying atop the hood of a recently driven car to keep warm. A few times, we found it curled up on ours. It appeared to have no home. Mom wanted to take it home but Dad quickly voiced an objection. He didn't want to tend to any more animals. As it was, he figured there were already too many cats, too many dogs, and too many kids. There were

Mama and Ted

just too many of everything. And he didn't feel the need to burden himself with more.

One night as we left the theater, Dad remained inside, pausing for a few moments to buy another bag of buttered popcorn for the road. And the cat was there perched on top of a car parked right behind ours. Mom seized the opportunity and told the girls to catch it and hide it in the car but not to tell the old man. They didn't hesitate and did as mother had instructed, keeping it out of sight in the back seat of the car.

Pop nearly had kittens, himself, when he saw the purring, black feline lying contentedly in Mom's lap later that night. Well, so be it. What could he do now? So, the cat became a part of the family—at least for a week.

The following Friday evening, our family went again to the movie in Sherwood. Getting our bags of popcorn, we took up a row of seats and enjoyed the first movie of a double feature. At the intermission, Mom went to the restroom and was late returning to her seat but just in time to catch the beginning of the second feature. After the movie, we went home. It seemed like an uneventful evening—that is until we got inside the house. Mom appeared flustered; her face flushed as if she were fighting the flu. It was evident that she was upset about something. Then she sprang some news on us.

When she had gone to the restroom, she saw a poster in the lobby, a poster offering a $30 reward to anyone who found and returned the *theater owner's* black cat. Pop couldn't believe his ears. None of us could.

"You mean to tell me, Ethel, that you stole somebody's cat? For Pete's sake! There's thousands of stray cats prowlin' the countryside and you gotta go and steal somebody's pet."

Mom didn't respond to Pop's ranting; only set her jaw as she always did when she felt put upon. Had she been able to drive to Sherwood herself, she would have returned the cat without telling anyone, especially Dad. Then brother Dick's two questions riled her even more when he asked, tongue in cheek, if she could be considered a *cat burglar* and if she could be arrested for *catnapping*. We thought it amusing, but not our dear, red-faced mommy.

Now for a little quiz. Do you know who had to return the cat to the theater owner and explain to him how he came by it? Of course, it was Dad, the very person who wanted nothing to do with it in the first place.

A Little Dab'll Do Ya

Preparing for school most mornings had always been a hectic ordeal in our house, particularly so because we had no indoor toilet facilities. The house was like a zoo, everybody yelling, everyone scrambling. Mom was always in a tizzy, like a chicken with its head cut off, trying to ensure that all of us kids would get off to school on time. Why, one morning, she pushed poor Dee out the door before he'd put his shoes

Launa, Charla, Dee, and Tudie, on my old bicycle

on . . . and it was snowing. And, when I was going to high school, I don't know how many times she yelled at me.

"If you don't get your tail out to the road right now, yore gonna miss the school bus."

"But, Maw, it's Saturday."

Even after I left home to be on my own, Mom continued to try to organize the disorganized. One morning, she got into it with Charla because she hadn't brushed her teeth. Little sister always tried to avoid that little chore, whining one excuse after another. But Mom, obstinate as a mule, grabbed her equally stubborn daughter by the coat sleeve and pulling her into the kitchen, shoved her up to the sink, growling an order,

"Brush yer damned teeth."

"But Maw, I ain't got time."

"Do it now, young lady, or I'll make you wish you had."

"But Maw!"

"You heard me."

"But Maw, there's no toothpaste."

"Don't 'But Maw, me.' Brush your teeth and be quick about it."

"But Maw, there's really no toothpaste. How can I?"

Grabbing a tube of paste, Mom flung it on the counter next to the sink, bellowing,

"Now brush!"

"But Maw!"

"I said brush."

"But Maw, this is a tube of Brylcreem, not tooth paste."

"I don't care if it's axle grease. BRUSH!"

Monkeys

Most mornings, Dad usually dropped me off in the center of town so I could look for work, Grudgingly, I walked block after block and visited one business office after another, filling out dozens of applications. But I had not one ounce of luck whatsoever.

One stop that I remember vividly was at the office of Portland Bag and Burlap. The office manager asked what experience I had to qualify working for them when I asked for an application. She must have thought I was some kind of dolt when I answered, "*Oh, we work with bags all the time on the farm.*"

The incredulous look on her face quickly informed me that I had no chance of getting a job there. Nonetheless, she handed an application to me, a form that merely required my name, address and a few spaces to write what I considered qualifications for a job as a common laborer. When I returned the completed form, she put it in a file cabinet that contained other forms appearing to be identical to mine—at least 10,000 of them. And she filed mine behind the last one in the drawer.

No matter where I went, the results were the same: employers weren't interested; they weren't hiring at the present time; I was too young; I only had a high school education; I was eligible for the draft; I had no qualifications and so on and so on. But I was persistent only because Dad was persistent, always questioning me about where I'd gone and if I was aggressive in my search, and so on and so on.

But Lady Luck finally smiled on me. I struck employment pay dirt. Near the end of August 1950, I secured a job working in the floor-covering department at Monkeys, the Montgomery Ward store on Vaughan Street in northwest Portland. It was a temporary position, terminating after Christmas. But it was a start. And the pay was an astounding $1.16 an hour.

The location was ideal too because Dad could provide my transportation. He drove by the store every day going to and coming from his job in Linnton.

The heavy and bulky flooring materials were not stored on the bottom floor as one would have expected but on the very top floor of the eight-story building. Every morning, just for the exercise, I ran up the eight flights of stairs to work.

Several people worked in floor covering, and every one of them was a different sort of character. One fellow sang opera as he worked. He sang very well but he also sang very loud. And that was irritable to the other employees. The department manager gave him a job way back in a corner of the building just to keep everyone else from quitting. But he could still be heard. Every morning before reaching the sixth floor,

I could hear the guy's voice echoing down the stairwell, crooning away as happy as a lark.

Augie Sinsick, a happy-go-lucky fellow of Polish decent, was my immediate boss. Louis was the custodian. Gloria, a shapely blonde, was the secretary, and a 25-year-old man named Charles was the warehouseman. Other than the floor manager, these were the workers that I had the most contact with.

Louis was an elderly colored fellow who had seen a lot of life and was quite the philosopher. He smoked a mixture of Rum-and-Maple and Sir Walter Raleigh tobacco in an ancient beat-up pipe. The aroma was wonderful and so appealing to me that I bought a pipe myself. And I smoked the same mixture. But unfortunately—or fortunately—the tobacco gave me a bite on the tip of my tongue. So I gave it up preferring to smell the aroma from Louis's pipe rather than from my own.

Gloria was an attractive woman in her late twenties. Fortunately for us guys, she wore dresses that were just a smidge too tight across her nicely proportioned posterior. She frequently appeared on the floor with batches of unfilled orders. And when she did, work came to an absolute standstill. Augie seldom missed a chance to tell her a joke because he loved the reaction it got from her. We all did. She giggled and she giggled easily. And, to our delight, when she giggled, she jiggled and she jiggled all over.

Charles, a verbose freewheeling character, was a bulky-looking fellow with bushy, unkempt red hair. He usually went unshaven for several days at a time. And his long-sleeved shirts were never fully tucked in. By no means, was he neat and tidy. He was a constant griper and carped incessantly about not having enough spending money. Frequently during coffee breaks, he searched the want ads for a second job. One day he announced to us that he'd found one—hauling flowers in a hearse on Saturdays to funeral homes and cemeteries.

Two weeks went by when, on a Monday morning, Charles came to work and told us about an incident that had occurred the previous Saturday that nearly scared him to death.

After loading an empty hearse with flowers, he drove up Burnside Avenue. As he reached up to adjust the rear-view mirror, he was horrified to see the reflection of a hand reaching toward him from the rear of the hearse. Charles slammed on the brakes and quickly exited, the motor still running. He stood for some time staring at it from across the street, trying to determine if someone or something were inside. But he didn't have the courage to go near it. Telephoning his employer, he told them with a quivering voice to get someone else to drive their haunted hearse, that he was quitting.

What Charles had seen wasn't a ghost. It was the reflection of his own hand in a window that separated the driver's compartment from the back of the hearse. But that didn't matter to Charles. He vowed never again to ride in another one, not even for his own funeral.

My job was wrapping cuts of linoleum and vinyl flooring with heavy paper, preparing them for shipment to customers. One of the heaviest pieces I had to lift weighed 226 pounds. The rolls were bulky, heavy and difficult to handle. But there was a trick to lifting them. I rolled the product onto the toes of my shoes, an old pair that were two sizes too large, enabling me to insert my fingers under the roll to grasp and lift it onto the wrapping table.

Augie filled most of the customer orders from stock stored on the floor. It seemed easy but it wasn't. Some of the vinyl looked the same, but the color and thickness varied by the smallest degree. The correct roll of product had to be found, moved to the cutting area and each piece cut to specification. Unlike the rolls of linoleum, the vinyl stock contained a continuous sheet of tissue paper. After rolling out a piece of vinyl, the tissue was discarded into a trashcan.

Augie wanted me to learn how to read and fill orders as well as pre- pare the material for shipment to customers. He gave me an order for a 12-foot length of six-foot wide vinyl. Augie watched closely as I searched the storage bay for the correct product and, using an overhead crane, moved the sizeable roll to the cutting area. I measured 12 feet of it and cut. I gathered the tissue paper and, as I grabbed the metal trash can lid, I got a nasty surprise—a zap of static electricity. Augie went ballistic with laughter. I found out the hard way that my foreman was a prankster, a practical joker as well as a teller of tall tales . . . just my kind of guy.

Not many days later, we received a huge order for 60 feet of vinyl. Augie rolled out the required amount of the material and cut. Just as he finished wadding up the enormous amount of charged tissue paper, Gloria walked onto the floor with a batch of orders. Of course, all of us had stopped working to ogle her. As she passed Augie, who was still on his knees, he pointed his forefinger at her very active backside and unleashed a major thunderbolt of blue static electricity, zapping her on the right cheek of her buttocks. Screaming like a banshee from hell, she launched herself through the storage bay at the speed of a spit-wad shot from a rubber band. Unfilled orders went flying helter-skelter and slowly floated down from the upper reaches of the building like giant confetti.

Gloria was damned angry with Augie, and Augie—well, he regretted what he'd done, not realizing that the static shock would be so strong. They were good friends but for several days after pulling his little stunt, she avoided him and his electric finger, as if he had the plague.

Being a curious kid, but having no guts to ask, I wondered if Gloria's wiggly backside had been scorched, maybe just a little.

My workmates were a crazy cast of characters . . . and there were few dull moments. Take it from me; the monkeys in the zoo were not nearly as entertaining as the *monkeys* at Montgomery Ward.

Rejection and Dejection

Not long after I went to work at Montgomery Ward, the war in South Korea turned in our favor. Our armies, re-enforced and re-supplied, had recouped and forcefully drove the North Korean forces back into their own country. The situation looked so positive that Eddie, Alan and I were certain this war would soon be over . . . and we wouldn't have to enlist in the Air Force after all. But our Euphoria didn't last long.

Late in the fall, the Chinese entered the war, joining forces with the North Koreans. Tens of thousands of them poured in from the north. And suddenly our armies were overwhelmed and on the defensive again.

My two friends and I knew what was in store for us—the dreaded draft. It was like a terrible nightmare, like a punch in the abdomen when we least expected it.

We had heard that once a person had received a draft notice, the recipient had no choice but to go into the Army. Whether it was true or not, we didn't know. But we didn't want to take the chance and decided to join the Air Force . . . immediately.

I told my parents what I planned to do, and they seemed to have no problem with my decision. I told my boss at Montgomery Ward that I was quitting to enlist in the military and they, too, had no problem with my decision. In fact, they wished me the best of luck. And so, the table was set.

In mid-December, a few days after my last day at work, Eddie, Alan and I drove into Portland to the Air Force recruiting office to enlist. We were nervous but excited.

Three hours later, Eddie and Alan were in the Air Force. But not me! They turned me down, not because I wasn't in good health, but because I was five pounds over their weight limit. It was ridiculous. I couldn't believe it. I was an athlete and much more fit than Alan. He was shorter than me and had a potbelly. Yet, they accepted him, but wouldn't take me.

Eddie and Alan's departure for boot camp was scheduled for late January. They were going and I was not. And our dream of staying together was shattered. But the recruiters gave me some hope. If I lost the weight before the end of January, I could still go with them.

Mom put me on a starvation diet. But it did no good. By the end of the first week, instead of losing weight, I had somehow gained a pound. I kept trying but I felt as if I were starving to death. And to make my predicament worse, the Christmas holidays were fast approaching. How the heck was I supposed to lose weight with all the food Mom planned to serve?

Suffering long enough, I finally gave it up, realizing that my two best friends were leaving without me. It was a hard pill to swallow.

Down in the dumps, feeling sorry for myself, and worrying about being drafted, I did nothing but lie around the house for several days.

But Pop would have none of that nonsense and soon was on my back again pushing me to go back to work.

I didn't want to go through the ordeal of searching for work anymore. And I didn't want to be at odds with my Dad either. I just wanted to be left alone for a while to think this thing out and make my own decisions.

The Challenge

My mood worsened during the weeks following my attempt to join the Air Force. No longer happy and carefree, I became surly, short-tempered, and argumentative. I snapped at everyone in the house including my mother. I bickered constantly with Tom. I rebelled against Grandma's advice and counsel. And I was constantly angry with the little kids for getting in my hair. But most of all, I ducked Dad. I avoided him like the plague because I didn't want to hear him carp at me any longer about finding work.

I was absolutely certain that I'd be drafted and it could happen any moment, I felt helpless. Over and over, I asked myself, "*What should I do? What should I do?*"

I was in a quandary; I didn't have an answer. And it seemed that not one soul understood my predicament. Everyone and everything seemed to be working against me.

The last Saturday in December was a nasty day: cold, blustery and rainy. And it was soon to become even worse. Dad hadn't said a word to me about finding work all week most likely because it was the Christmas holidays. But I knew he was building up a head of steam and was about to unload on me.

In a lousy mood, I had been a real jerk all morning, bitchy and grouchy with everyone. When Mom called us to eat lunch, Dad caught me before I could get to the kitchen. Point blank, he asked me why I had been treating everyone so rotten and why I hadn't done anything constructive to find a job since quitting Montgomery Ward.

At age 18 and a half-inch taller than Pa, I suppose I felt ready to challenge his authority. Our voices grew louder and louder as we stood face to face, toe to toe, in the middle of the living room. Within seconds, we were at each other's throat. Our conversation erupted into an ugly war of words and our faces flushed with anger. My attitude was horrible and my smart, sassy remarks riled Dad even more. Finally, having enough of me, he barked, *"For two cents, Ted, I'd knock you on yer ass."*

Coincidentally having some small change, I jammed a hand into my pocket, pulled out a few pennies, and defiantly shot back, *"Well, Pa, if you think you're big enough, go ahead."*

That was definitely a stupid mistake. My remark and gesture put him on the spot. And the next thing I knew, he put me on the spot—right on the seat of my pants, sprawled out on the living room floor like a sack of spuds.

Daddy

Leaping to my feet, I beat a hasty retreat out the door and ran for the woods, wanting to cry, not because Dad hurt me physically but because he actually struck me. But what else could he have done? I had shown utter contempt and disrespect for him, challenged his authority, and dared him to do something he probably didn't want to do. No man worth his salt could have let that go.

Once in the woods, I crawled into a thicket among a patch of dead ferns and fallen leaves and sat on the wet mossy ground, pouting like a little boy who hadn't gotten his way. I didn't know what to do with my life, which way to turn. I knew I hadn't given Dad a fair chance. I hadn't once told him of my worry about the draft and how the thought of going to war scared the hell out of me. It wasn't his fault. It might not have changed anything but at least he would have understood had

I opened up to him. The blame really belonged on the North Koreans for starting this mess.

I had been deep in thought for close to an hour, soaked to the skin from a heavy mist, when I saw movement. It was Dad walking up the wagon road toward my hiding place. He was carrying the .22 caliber rifle. For just an instant, I thought he was coming to shoot me. But then I saw Dee following close behind and realized they were merely going to do a little target practicing. Worried that he might shoot into the brush, I walked out to the road in front of them.

Dad asked if he'd hurt me. Shaking my head no, I apologized. He did too. And then he smiled. At that instant, I knew it was all right between us, at least for the moment. But something had to change. I knew that too. And it had to be me. I needed to be responsible. I needed to do something positive with my life.

For some reason I felt calm, my mind clear and I knew then what I was going to do.

"Tomorrow! Yes, tomorrow! But today, I only want to be happy and contented and at peace with my dad."

An Ending, A Beginning

The holidays ended smoothly but my *Life of Riley* didn't. It ended with a thump. I'd come to realize that life wasn't always a bed of roses as I'd wished. Dad, Mom and Grandma had faced hardships and roadblocks. Now it was my turn. It was my time to be an adult, to make decisions for myself, whether I wanted to or not. And so I did. I made a monumental decision, one that changed my life forever, one that ended my selfish, childish, immature ways, one that proved that I could stand on my own two feet.

There were no jobs available and I had no money for college. That was a fact. So, the only logical choice left was to enlist in a branch of the armed forces. And even that was limited. The Air Force didn't want me. That was another fact. I wanted no part of the Army. And I could never tolerate the Navy or Coast Guard because of my queasy landlubber stomach. So, what was left? Every door seemed closed to me with one exception. The Marines!

Without mentioning my intentions to anyone in the family, I accompanied Dad into Portland to look for work, as I'd done so many times in the past weeks. The weather was miserable, cold and wet when he dropped me in the center of town. I plodded around in the dampness for several minutes before I mustered enough courage to walk into the Marine Corps recruiting office and asked to enlist. Within a few hours, I had completed all the required paper work and had been accepted. I only needed to return with my birth certificate to prove my age.

To say that I was a little nervous would have been a colossal understatement. My guts churned and I was truly apprehensive about fighting in a war, especially with the Marines. They were always in the thick of it. But I felt they were the best choice and that I'd made the right decision. Most certainly, my mom and dad never in the world thought that I would join any branch of the armed forces other than the Air Force. Even if I were drafted, they were certain there would be little chance that I would see combat. My enlistment was going to be a tremendous shock to them.

On the way home that evening, I told Dad that I'd joined the Marine Corp. He didn't expect me to make that kind of announcement. His face seemed to drain of color and he shuddered as if a chill had penetrated to his very soul.

"I wanted you to get a job, Ted, not go to war."

Surprisingly, each member of the family reacted differently. Mom was quiet and said very little. But I knew she was feeling deep concern. Grandmother wrung her hands and cried. And the kids grinned, marveling that their big brother was going to fight in a war.

I tried to reassure everyone that I would be okay. But I was frightened and never once mentioned the uncertainty that I felt and the feeling of foreboding that was gnawing at me.

It was done. And on Wednesday, the 7th day of February 1951, I was sworn into the United States Marine Corps. It was a date that I will never forget. I left home immediately with orders to report to the Marine Corps Recruit Depot in San Diego, California for basic training. Unsure of my fate, I wondered if I'd ever see my family again.

Six months later and on the other side of the world far from home, I found myself packing a Browning Automatic-Rifle and in the middle of a nasty shooting war. It was far, far worse than I'd ever imagined. The constant threat of raking machinegun fire, frequent artillery barrages, booby-traps, snipers and ambushes wore on me mentally. And though I was among dozens of Marines, there were many moments when I felt absolutely alone and totally helpless.

But leafing through photographs of my family during lulls in the fighting helped me cope. I could envision Granny with a fly swatter in her hand; Mom and Dad chasing each other; the little kids playing in the back yard; Dick repairing the tractor; and Tom bellowing threats that he was going to tell Grandma on me when I'd done something irritable to him. They were a crazy lot . . . a cast of zany characters. And reminiscing about them brought a smile to my face and made me feel warm inside and lifted my spirits. It probably never entered my mind as a youngster that I loved each and every one of them—but I knew it then. And God, did I miss them.

End

Jim Muller, Ted, and Dad, six weeks before Ted left for Korea

Alan, Ted, and Eddie, on boot camp leave, in front of Eddie's house

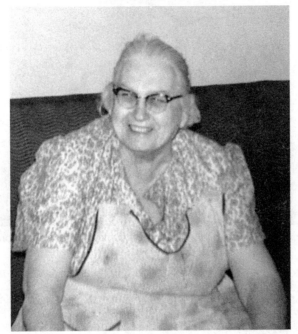

My Grandma

LIST OF PHOTOS AND ART

The author and his siblings; Ted, Tom, Dee, and Dick in back,
Charla and Tudie in front

ABOUT THE AUTHOR

My mother wanted to write a book about us but, unfortunately, she never got to it. Had she though, she'd have chosen the title, *My Six Gray Heirs*, one "gray heir" for each child. It crossed my mind to use her title but that would have been a little like stealing from her, wouldn't it—as if I'd never stolen anything from her before, like a piece of her fried chicken. But because my brothers and sisters constantly threatened to tattle on me when I did mischief, I chose to call my story, *I'm Gonna Tell Grandma!* Those words still ring in my ears.

This collection of events took place during my youth, most of them being the same stories that my mother likely would have written. Only, she would have put a slightly different slant on them.

The oldest of six children, I was raised in rural Oregon on a small farm and attended schools near Sherwood. Other than five and a half years in the Marine Corps, one year of that in Korea, I've lived all of my life in Oregon, and was employed by the Oregon State Police, retiring at the rank of lieutenant.

Throughout the years I've been an active singer and board member with Festival Chorale Oregon and have coordinated performance tours for the Chorale throughout mainland Europe and Carnegie Hall in New York.

Currently, I live in Stayton, Oregon, was married and have five children: Stephen, Thomas, Angela, Richard, and Joseph.